THE CONCEPT OF IRONY

Søren Kierkegaard

THE CONCEPT
OF IRONY

WITH CONSTANT REFERENCE
TO SOCRATES

Translated with an Introduction
and Notes by
LEE M. CAPEL

INDIANA UNIVERSITY PRESS

BLOOMINGTON & LONDON

Contents

Historical Introduction

Kierkegaard, like most other modern authors, had very definite ideas about reading and writing books. But in his case such reflections on the activity of a writer go beyond the usual statement of literary credo, the interpretative hint, and the interested *nota bene* to tabulators of style. In addition, we find a constantly developing theory of communication extraordinarily aware of the reader and of a confrontation with him. For Kierkegaard writes about substantive issues in such a way as to activate his reader, and to undertake to understand him is to accept the risk of interpreting him. There have been some who look back wistfully at this early essay as an interpreter's paradise because the problem of the pseudonyms does not arise. Such a view presumably sees no problem in a work issued under Kierkegaard's own name. In turning to the essay on irony, however, such a reader may be surprised to find that Kierkegaard writing about substantive issues in his own name is as elusive and problematical as ever he was in any of his pseudonymous works. He was a writer with a natural predilection for such ingredients as ambiguity, irony, humour, satire, and polemic, so much so that this same tendency was formalized through the usage of pseudonyms, masks, concealment and postures into a theory of indirect communication which, together with his edifying or direct communications, culminated in the developing construct that he called his 'authorship'. There is, therefore, an initial continuity (at the very least, of techniques) between the academic essay on irony and the pseudonymous works.

That there is also a continuity of ideas was articulated by Georg Brandes, with whom the serious study of Kierkegaard began in 1877, when he called attention to the importance of the essay on irony by maintaining that it was 'the true point of departure for Kierkegaard's authorship'.[1] Historically, the work has nevertheless most often been dismissed by other interpreters as a youthful effort without real significance for understanding Kierkegaard. The grounds most frequently put forward in support of neglecting the essay are two. First, even a cursory glance at the work discloses so much Hegelianism in its terminology, perspectives, and the specifics of its representation of Socrates and the German romantics as to convince many that the indebtedness was so great as to preclude any originality on Kierkegaard's part.[2] Secondly, Kierkegaard himself, in *The Point of View for My Activity as an Author*, did not include the essay on irony in his 'authorship', and refers to it ambiguously in his pseudonymous works[3] and disparagingly in his late Journal.[4]

A greater appreciation for the complexities of Kierkegaard's out-put and the seriousness of his career, together with a growing awareness of his self-consciousness as a writer, have wholly reversed this earlier negative evaluation of the essay and made a return to the insight of Brandes possible. Today, it is generally conceded by interpreters that the essay on irony is itself an ironic work. Accordingly, the questions inevitably arise as to *why* and *how* it is ironic, questions which, as they have never been adequately dealt with, I shall attempt to answer in this historical introduction. The first task will be to establish a concrete context indispensable for identifying the author's intention controlling the work's composition, in short, the literary situation to which the essay as an instance of ironic communication relates, and apart from which its levels of meaning hover as indeterminate possibilities. I shall begin with a sketch of the occasion for the essay, its intended readers, and its initial reception.

1. The year 1840-41 was as productive and stormy as any Kierkegaard lived through. After ten years at the University of Copenhagen he finally completed the examination in theology on the 3rd July 1840 with the grade of *laudabilis*. Within two weeks he left Copenhagen on a three-week pilgrimage to Jutland to visit his father's birthplace. Returning around the middle of August, he resumed reading and writing with a view to submitting an academic dissertation as soon as possible. On September 8th he proposed to Regine Olsen and was accepted two days later. On November 17th he enrolled in the Royal Pastoral Seminary for practical training in homiletics, and preached his first sermon in January as part of this training. Ostensibly, Kierkegaard had decided to marry and settle down to a career as a parson or perhaps wait for an appointment in the university. This is the interval during which he finished his academic dissertation, *The Concept of Irony, With Constant Reference to Socrates*. The work was submitted in fulfilment of the requirements for the degree of Master of Arts on the 3rd June 1841. The previous day Kierkegaard addressed a formal petition to the king, requesting permission to submit a dissertation written in his mother tongue, a formality then required of all academic dissertations not written in Latin. The work was formally accepted on the 16th July 1841 under the signature of F. C. Sibbern, dean of the faculty of philosophy, and the oral defence took place on September 29th. In spite of the fact that academic procedure required the oral defence to be conducted in Latin, the contemporary newspaper accounts report that the occasion had attracted 'an unusually large audience'.[5] The oral defence lasted over seven hours. Besides his two official opponents, F. C. Sibbern and P. O. Brønsted, seven others came forward to dispute with Kierkegaard about his essay, including two leading Danish Hegelians: J. L. Heiberg, who in 1824 had introduced Hegel's philosophy into Denmark,[6] and A. F. Beck, whose review[7] of the book in a local newspaper some months later drew an ironic response from Kierkegaard.[8] Conspicuously absent on the occasion of Kierkegaard's public defence of his essay on irony was Hans Lasson Martensen. A few days after the oral defence the final rupture with Regine Olsen was complete, and on October 25th Kierkegaard left Copenhagen on the first of his three flights to Berlin. The rest of the well-known narrative need not concern us further.

Fortunately, the journal of the faculty of philosophy during these years survives, and, due to the researches of Carl Weltzer,[9] it is possible to determine from Sibbern's official entries how this essay was received and regarded by the six professors who read and approved it. Sibbern, the first reader, recommends the work to his colleagues with the following comment:

> As regards the content of the work, the first and longest part . . . views Socrates as the chief representative for that species of irony related to the subsequent development of scepticism in Greece, and which, by opposing itself to the Sophists, appears to have been a natural transition to a more profound kind of philosophizing. (16th June 1841)

He has serious reservations, however, regarding certain literary excrescences in the manuscript that reflect 'an inferior style', and recommends that these be removed in the final revision. After noting such objectionable passages in the text, he sends the essay to J. N. Madvig, the university's influential philologist. From Madvig's response we learn that Kierkegaard had already shown him portions of the manuscript, most likely the earlier sections in which the argument depends most heavily on the Greek texts. While Madvig has no doubts about the value and intellectual content of the essay, he does complain that the composition exhibits considerable looseness and even suffers from a lack of systematic arrangement in the development of its concepts, notably at the transition from Part One to Part Two. The work displays, he feels, a self-indulgent hankering after the piquant and witty, and not infrequently becomes simply vulgar and void of good taste. While voting in the affirmative, he reacts as follows:

> One might be tempted to make it a condition for the work's acceptance that the worst of these excrescences be eliminated, were it not for the fact that such negotiations [with the candidate] would be difficult and tiresome. Due to the author's individuality and partiality for these ingredients, to express a wish in this matter would be in vain. (20th June 1841)

Sibbern next sends the manuscript to the two professors of Greek, F. C. Petersen and P. O. Brønsted. The first votes for its acceptance on the condition that the candidate furnish Latin theses to be used in the oral defence, that these theses as far as possible embody the essential moments of the work, and that they be submitted for approval prior to publication. Petersen confirms Madvig's opinion that while the work would gain much by a thorough revision, 'This could not be achieved inasmuch as the author, in light of his personality, neither can nor will undertake such changes.' (4th July 1841) At the least he urges that the passages marked by his colleagues as revealing an excess of sarcasm and mockery be eliminated as unsuitable in an academic essay. His colleague P. O. Brønsted replies, however, that if scholarship speaks well for the content, the candidate himself must assume responsibility for any deficiency in expression and style.

> One had better be reconciled to the fact that it is the faculty's concern merely to approve the candidate's knowledge and scholarship and not try to bring about better taste in one who, in light of his knowledge, ought to know better. (7th July 1841)

Sibbern next sends the essay to the Rector of the university, H. C. Ørsted, who is officially involved in such matters. He replies in an undated letter as follows:

> Thanks dear friend and colleague for letting me have Kierkegaard's essay for examination. The brief period of time, together with other matters, have limited me to the most cursory examination. Although I clearly see expressions of considerable intellectual force in this work, I cannot deny that it makes an overwhelmingly unpleasant impression upon me, particularly by two things I abhor: prolixity and artificiality.
>
> Although I have no doubts that this essay deserves to be accepted more than many another, and that the examination of it by additional readers will not change the already established verdict, still, with respect to its form it seems necessary that either Martensen . . . or Nielsen . . . also read and vote on it.

Martensen had just laid down his post as *Docent* in Moral Philosophy in order to accept an appointment as Professor of Speculative Theology, while Rasmus Nielsen had newly been appointed Professor of Philosophy as the long postponed replacement for Paul Martin Møller.[10] To a contemporary reader like Ørsted, writes Weltzer, the matter of Kierkegaard's stylistic excesses could be judged most satisfactorily by Martersen, since, among other things, his name, together with that of J. L. Heiberg, appears significantly in the last section of the essay. Due to Kierkegaard's attack on Nielsen for accepting his appointment without being prepared to fill it, an attack made to Sibbern personally and known to Nielsen, the latter understandably excused himself from voting on Kierkegaard's essay. Accordingly, the final reader of Kierkegaard's essay on irony, and the only one who might have explored its philosophic contents further or perhaps thrown some light on its more obscure references, was H. L. Martensen. But Martensen did not volunteer any interpretation of such passages nor offer any additional explanation of the work—and this in spite of the fact that he, too, had previous acquaintance with at least one section of the essay. His rather terse reply[11] was as follows:

Inasmuch as Professor Sibbern has requested me to submit my vote in this matter, I hereby declare myself to be in agreement with the judgment already expressed and vote for the acceptance of the essay.   (12th July 1841)

In evaluating this material, Weltzer observes that in the opinion of his professors Kierkegaard was obviously something of a problem: brilliant, elusive, sophistic, incorrigible, but apparently able to hold his own [*en Karl for sin Hat*]. The content of the essay was adjudged substantial enough to outweigh the unanimous objections by the faculty as to its form and style. The latter was ascribed to the author's 'individuality' and 'must remain his own affair'. Unfortunately, the original manuscript does not survive, hence it is only possible to surmise which passages were so uniformly objectionable to the faculty. It is most probable that Kierkegaard did not accommodate himself to the wishes of the faculty in the matter of the requested changes. This judgment is reinforced by the fate of the fifteen theses submitted for use at the oral defence. Brønsted objected to the first and fifteenth theses, the first because of the 'delicate subject matter' and the fifteenth because it would be difficult to dispute about in Latin. He also requested that the ninth thesis eliminate the words *substantialitas*, *realitas*, and *idealitas*. Petersen, on the other hand, approved of the ninth thesis as it was, but wanted the thirteenth changed. In the end every thesis had been challenged by at least one of the readers. Yet it is clear from the specific changes requested in each case that Kierkegaard did not alter a single one. To function as his official advocate in defending the theses Kierkegaard had chosen his elder brother, Peter, who was himself notorious for his Latin disputations. It remains to be noted that the oral defence open to the public was a mere formality, the acceptance or rejection of a dissertation depending entirely on the vote of its academic readers. Such are the facts surrounding the occasion, the readers, and the initial reception of the essay on irony.

2. At this juncture it may seem to the modern reader that the attitude of the young Kierkegaard in this affair is innocent enough and not unfamiliar in the case of aspiring candidate-authors heavily laden with literary pretensions. That something of the kind is clearly the case may be seen from the only surviving Journal entry expressing Kierkegaard's own evaluation of his essay at this time *vis-à-vis* its academic readers.

I have laboured on this essay with fear and trembling so that my dialectic would not consume too much. Some will criticize the freedom of style, and *some half-learned Hegelian robber* will say that the subjective aspect is too prominent. In the first place, *I must ask him not to plague me with still another recipe of this new wisdom* which I already regard as outdated, and, in the second place, ask him not to make such great demands on me: *as if the Idea's own movements should come to expression in me.* . . . Finally, I shall say that one cannot write about a negative concept except in this way, and *instead of giving constant assurances that doubt has been overcome, that irony has been vanquished, for once to allow it to speak.* As for the rest, I may occasionally have been too verbose, but when Hegel with his authority says that *Geist* is the best epitomist, *then modestly and without any demands let me be judged—but by boys I will not be judged.*

And should this seem to some like madness, then I will answer with Socrates (*Phædrus* 244 A): 'For if it were a simple fact that insanity is an evil, the saying would be true; but in reality the greatest of blessings come to us through madness, when it is sent as a gift of the Gods.' And should there happen to be, particularly in the first part of the essay, various things which one is otherwise unaccustomed to meet with in academic dissertations, then the reader will have to forgive me my gladness, and that I sometimes sing as I work in order to lighten my task.   (*Papirer, III B* 2)

The italics in the above passage are mine, and are intended to underscore a dimension of personal satire directed particularly against H. L. Martensen. It seems to me that the conclusion to be drawn from Kierkegaard's recalcitrant attitude toward his academic readers, together with the dimension of personal satire overflowing from the essay into the above entry, is that the essay on irony is indeed a consciously ironic work, that it is a polemical rejoinder intended mainly for local consumption but having conceptual application as well to the larger intellectual issues of the day. There is in the above entry, for example, the consummate fusion of intellectual issues and personal allusions characteristic of the style of the essay on irony. As he required literary types to embody and give presence to philosophic standpoints or stages of intellectual and psychological development, so his discussion of concepts and cognitive issues was not without concrete reference to living personalities in his immediate milieu. Intellectually, one would like to know what Kierkegaard in the above entry understands by his dialectic, by a negative concept, by the juxtaposition of doubt and irony together with the possibility of overcoming them, by the style which allows irony to speak, by the appeal to the authority of Hegel against his academic readers, by the denial of a pervasive subjectivism while admitting the presence of a lyricism which sings throughout in a most unacademic fashion, and by the obscure reference to a divine madness akin to that defended by the Platonic Socrates. Inasmuch as Kierkegaard only writes about what he has appropriated (this is the limit beyond which his expression may not go), so the clarification of some of these problems may be illuminated by inquiring initially into how this personal satire directed at H. L. Martensen came about, for, together with a similar satire directed at J. L. Heiberg, it is a recognizable feature of Kierkegaard's style here, and relevant to the entire format of the essay. In this connection recent Danish Kierkegaard studies[12] furnish expanding documentation that the pseudonymous works assume the shape of polemical answers to philosophic and literary problems under discussion in the intellectual circle of his immediate environment, that the principal targets of this polemic were Hegel and Goethe, but that such polemic extends even to personal satires upon local personalities construed as spokesmen for these opposed standpoints. That Kierkegaard was fully conscious of this dimension goes hand in hand with his insistence that in his pseudonymous works, at least, he has resorted to the use and invention of literary devices for distancing and detaching his own personality from his literary productions and hence from his readers. That Kierkegaard was a master of irony will scarcely be denied by anyone. In trying to understand the essay on irony, therefore, all factors of the communication-situation are relevant.

3. As it is the nature of such personal satire to be a literary function of genuine philosophic disagreement, so an inquiry into its origin constitutes itself as an investigation into the genesis of the philosophic standpoint of its author. This can appropriately take the form of a brief historical sketch of Kierkegaard's development during his crucial first period

(1830-41), the formative decade of his student years at the University of Copenhagen. This was an extremely impressionable period, characteristically lived at maximum intensity, during which he went through an eclectic development, drawing sustenance from such diverse intellectual phenomena as rationalism, scepticism, romanticism, Hegelianism, neo-Hellenism, and punctuated by a rash of literary projects. The latter, as recorded in his Journal, provide an obvious and convenient vehicle for plotting and assessing his reaction to the wealth of impressions feeding this rapid metamorphosis. Here it is worth noting that the Journal itself begins under the grateful impetus of conversations with Martensen whom he secured as his private tutor in 1834. Kierkegaard's Journal begins:

> To see one light clearly always requires another. For if we imagine ourselves in total darkness and presented with a single point of light, we would be unable to determine what we were looking at because it is impossible to determine spatial relations in the dark. Only by being provided with a second light would we be able to determine the position of the one in relation to the other.
>
> *(Papirer, I A 1)*

The thread of continuity running through his earliest insights is from the theme of predestination to reflections contrasting the opaqueness of sublime nature with the transparency of works of art. Evidence of a classical education is everywhere apparent in his preoccupation with delineating certain literary types, the organic unity of universal and particular, the Idea embodied in concrete personality. The earliest of these is a sketch for a Promethean 'master-thief', but soon his reflections cluster around the characters of Don Juan and Faust; later, Ahasuerus, the Wandering Jew, is added to this germinal constellation.

At the beginning of 1835, Kierkegaard, as a twenty-two-year-old student, had abandoned the academic study of theology with biting refutations of the leading orientations available to him at the University, and had embarked upon a self-conscious search for his own philosophic standpoint. The central document signifying the beginning of his quest for intellectual integrity is the remarkable Gillileie Journal, particularly the June and August letters to a distant relative, the botanist P. W. Lund. The first begins by recalling how some years previously Kierkegaard had been fascinated by Lund's account of his scientific observations of the primitive Brazilian landscape and of the paradisiacal impression it had made on the botanist. He then identifies such feelings and impressions as his own, though his activity lies 'in a wholly different sphere'. In a series of compressed similes the June letter goes on to equate one's life and work with the growth and fruit of a plant, together with the need to have one's roots in soil properly one's own. In the matter of a vocation there are some happy natures with an inner categorical imperative who from the first are inclined in a definite direction. There are others with an external categorical imperative who are so wholly guided by their environment that the question of a destination never arises.

How few belong to the first class, and to the second I have no wish to belong. Far more numerous than the first are *those who are forced to test in life what this Hegelian dialectic really means.* It is quite in order for wine to ferment before it becomes clear; but this condition is often unpleasant in its particular moments, though, considered in its totality, it has of course its satisfactions, insofar as within the *universal doubt* it has its relative results. In particular, *it has great significance for a person who, by means of it, has arrived at clarity concerning his determination or vocation,* not merely for the sake of the subsequent repose in opposition to the foregoing storm: but because such a one then possesses life in quite a different sense than before. *It is this Faustian element which in part makes itself felt in every intellectual development,* and this is why it has always seemed to me that *one ought to allow the Idea of Faust world historical significance.* As our forefathers had a goddess of longing, so *Faust, I hold, stands for us as the personified doubt.* But more than this he is not—and *it is surely a sin against the Idea when*

Goethe allows Faust to repent, and similarly with Merimée's
Don Juan. (*Papirer, I A 72*)

What is so striking about this passage is not the juxtaposition
of Hegel and Goethe. Such a cultural alignment had already
been 'authoritatively' articulated in Denmark two years
earlier by J. L. Heiberg in his essay 'On the Significance of
Philosophy for the Present Age.'[13] What is genuinely significant about this passage is *the frank espousal of the Hegelian
negative way with the Idea of Faust as Kierkegaard's very own*, the
conscious echoes from Hegel's *Phenomenology* conjoined to an
original conception of the Faust legend necessitating the total
rejection of Goethe's *Faust II*.

These letters, which appear to have been written to parallel
the student scene in Goethe's *Faust I*,[14] go on to apply this
'universal doubt' to various hypothetical vocations as Kierkegaard runs through the various faculties and careers open to
him: physical science, theology, jurisprudence, and even a
career as an actor are conjured forth, and all are rejected as
mere tangential possibilities, yet not before a perpendicular
refraction has been drawn to illumine the central theme of
this document. The apparent envy of Lund with his vast
Brazilian horizon circumscribing his manifold observations of
external nature is an obvious literary foil employed gratefully
by the young Kierkegaard in order to affirm himself as a sufficient field of observation and endeavour.

How fortunate are you, who in Brazil have found an
enormous field for your observations, where each step
affords new discoveries, and where the shouts of the rest of
the republic of letters do not disturb your calm. For it
seems to me that the learned theological world is like being
on *Strandvej* on a Sunday afternoon when Deer Park is
open. They storm past one another, yell and shriek,
laugh and poke fun at each other, drive their horses to
death, overturn and run over each other. And when
they finally arrive dusty and breathless at the park below
the summit [*Bakken*]—they stare at each other and turn
homewards. As for their return journey, it would be as

juvenile of me to hurry them along as it was childish of
Achilles' mother to try to conceal him so as to avoid a
quick but honourable death. —Live well!

So ends the first part of this document. Its leading idea, however, is the recognition that his proper vocation is the Socratic
way of self-knowledge, the need for 'a truth which is truth for
me, the Idea for which I am willing to live and die', the search
for 'the Idea which is the discovery of myself', of that 'individuality' with 'its own style' which he likens to 'the worship
of the unknown god'. He still acknowledges 'a cognitive
imperative', to be sure, but one that is 'organically assimilated
within myself', as a 'postulate' wherein he lives and whereby
it ceases to be a postulate and becomes a proof.

> It is this inward life of man, this inward deed, this human
> aspect relating to the deity which everything turns on, and
> not a multitude of particular knowledge. For the latter
> will surely follow, and will then not appear as accidental
> aggregates or a sequence of particularities side by side
> without coherence, without a point of heat wherein all
> radii are gathered.

If in the June letter Kierkegaard wants to *know* what he himself should do, in the August letter he wants to *act*. The second
part of this document therefore ends by answering the first
with lyrical resolution:

> The lot is cast—I cross over the Rubicon . . . I will hasten
> forward on the way I have found, and call to whomever
> I meet: Do not look back like Lot's wife. Remember
> only that it is an ascent [*Bakke*] we are endeavouring to
> make.

The centre of gravity of the Gillileie Journal is the implicit
acknowledgement by the young Kierkegaard of an identity
problem that consumes him, together with the resolute
decision of a questing spirit to resolve himself wherever the
journey may lead. The resolution to such a problem he here
christens 'an organic view of life' [*Livsanskuelse*].

It is only after the Gillileie document that the Journal begins to speak of 'my enterprise' [*mit Forehavende*],[15] and certain related themes recur with a frequency indicating the presence of a problem requiring solution. Characteristically, this material finds expression in his first sustained literary project: the Idea of Faust. It is the fate of this Faust project to contribute the intellectual ferment propelling the young Kierkegaard towards his first sundering experience of total crisis. Here again I am indebted to recent Danish Kierkegaard studies for the clarification of this material, in this case the excellent monograph by the late Professor Carl Roos, *Kierkegaard og Goethe*, Copenhagen, 1955, pp. 56-157.[16] The serious study and reflection on the Idea of Faust occupies Kierkegaard's attention for two years (1835-7), develops in conscious opposition to Goethe's *Faust II*, and ends in total failure with an explosion in December 1837. Early in 1838 he writes a sardonic comedy simultaneously parodying Goethe's *Faust* and the Hegelian philosophy and its enthusiasts, wherein caricatures of Heiberg and Martensen are conspicuous. Kierkegaard's lifelong opposition to and polemic against Hegel and Goethe (which even accelerated his need to appropriate from both of them: I must understand in order to refute), together with the pervasive dimension of personal satire directed at their Danish disciples, date and derive from this critical experience.[17]

His concern is first with Goethe's *Faust*. With Stieglitz as his guide, he copies out a bibliography of 107 items, and reads Schubarth's lectures on Goethe's *Faust* (1830) followed by Koberstein (1823). He argues with Schubarth's interpretation of Mephistopheles as 'irony brought to consciousness', and calls Goethe's vaunted invention 'a dumb devil', rejecting completely the optimistic view of evil. For Kierkegaard an 'irreligious' irony lames the individual. In connection with Koberstein's version of the legend originating, as Roos relates, in a *songfest* between the Christian poet Wolfram and the magician Klinsor, aligned with the evil, and Koberstein's claim that the great cleft in man between spirit and nature is represented by two individuals in the legend but

20

within a single individual by Goethe, Kierkegaard becomes involved in reflections which culminate when his 'three great Ideas' (Don Juan, Faust, and Ahasuerus) are consolidated into a single mediated type: Faust, who assimilates all three Ideas of sensuality, doubt, and despair within himself. Goethe's *Faust II* is everywhere rejected because it is not true to the Idea: the doubt unto despair. Without the true enthusiasm for knowledge, which must be characteristic of Faust, the seductive element is wholly lacking. Faust may not end either in suicide or apotheosis, for Faust is an Idea and must pass over into another consistent with its dialectical dénouement. The medieval character of the material, the dogmatic presuppositions of the Idea, dictate that the forms of worldliness 'outside Christianity' must move from sensuality through doubt and on to despair. But a Faust who repents, who breaks with the Idea and reconciles himself with the world, no longer tempts the imagination. Hence Goethe's *Faust II*, when he finally does make his choice, makes the wrong one: Faust chooses the world instead of God.

The course of the Faust theme moves from Goethe to the folk story, the Faust of legend, which confirms for Kierkegaard his rejection of the former. He underscores the lines about 'the anxiety of conscience' which even the devil was unable to suppress in Faust, and deems it appropriate to say that the Idea of Faust 'was in the beginning' and eternal, even now, even in him. Every age has its Faust, to be sure, though such a Faust may all too easily degenerate into a mere portrait of that age. A Faust who repents is not a portrait of Faust, but, as Roos writes, a self-portrait of the 18th century: 'The century of civic virtue, quite banally practical action as a citizen of society, an unproblematical reconciliation of life with knowledge.' Kierkegaard rants on about this unfaustian Faust which is everywhere among his contemporaries whom he calls 'the confirmed consumers'. Nor is there anything Faustian in the busy scholars, among whom are some of the most gifted persons of the age. Another group, 'the younger generation', does indeed have something Faustian, yet oddly enough attaches itself to Goethe's *Faust* who has nothing of the seductive element that Don Juan possesses at various moments.

This leads to a conception of 'the contemporary Faust' which, unlike Goethe's 18th century Faust, is like the Faust of legend, and which Kierkegaard identifies as himself. For the moderns 'the true Faustian element only appears when energy is in one way or another lamed. The laming factor derives from a consciousness that as all knowing is only fragmentary, so every view [*Anskuelse*], even the greatest, is also fragmentary. The modern Faust is impressed by the insurmountable knowledge of the age, he is tempted by it, but lamed at the very moment he is impressed, for he knows that even this in all its vastness is nothing in comparison with what he desires: the Absolute.'[18]   Hence the modern Faust is isolated, a fantast, subject to the stormy passions. 'Finally, the real test for the modern Faust is the confrontation with his own caricature: the inescapable Wagner. The image of him fills Kierkegaard with the despairing wish "to withdraw himself from everything, to forget, if possible, that he has ever known anything, to herd cows, or perhaps transport himself over into another world"—to commit suicide.' These statements about the modern Faust's Wagner, writes Roos, and the wish they evoke to want to forget and to disappear, lead directly over to the mysterious entry of the 2nd December 1837.

(1) I will no longer speak with the world. I will seek to forget that I have ever done so. I have read of a man who kept to his bed for fifty years without speaking to a single human being. I will do likewise, and (like Queen Gudrin after having been out and quarrelled with Odin) go to bed after having quarrelled with the world. Or else I will seek to move to a place where no one knows or understands my language, nor I theirs, where I can stand like Kasper Hauser—without really knowing how it has all come about—in the middle of Nürnburg Street.

(2) The misfortune is that no sooner has one discussed something than he is the thing himself. I communicated to you the other day *an Idea for a Faust*—now I feel *it was*

myself I described. I have barely read or thought of a disease before I have it myself.

Each time I wish to say something there is another who says it at the very same moment. It is as though *I thought double*, and my other self continually stole a march on me; or while I am standing and speaking everyone thinks it is another, so I can rightly ask the question which the bookseller Soldin put to his wife: Rebecca, is that I who am talking? I will flee out of the world (not to a cloister —I have strength in me yet) in order to find myself (every other driveller says the same), no, in order to forget myself. Nor shall I go where some jabbering brook plods across a field. I don't know if this verse is by some poet, but I could wish *an inflexible irony* would compel some sentimental poet to write it, yet *in such a way that he himself all the while read something else*. Or Echo, yes Echo, thou great master of irony! You who parody in yourself the highest and deepest on earth: the Word which created the world, since you merely give the contour not the fullness. Yes Echo, *avenge* all the sentimental twaddle that conceals itself in wood and meadow, in church and theatre, and which now and then detaches itself and drowns out everything for me. When in the woods I don't hear the trees conversing of old legends. No, *to me* they whisper all the drivel they have so long been witness to, and ask me in God's name to cut them down so as to be set free from all the nonsense of these nature enthusiasts. Oh, if all these drivel-heads sat on one throat, I would know with Caligula what I had to do. I see you are already afraid I might end on the scaffold. No, you see, there is where the drivel-head (I mean that which comprises all the particulars) would have me; yet you forget that it does no harm in the world. Yes, Echo, you whom I once heard chastize a nature lover when he exclaimed: 'Hear yonder, the lonesome flute tones of a lovelorn nightingale' [*Nattergal*]—and you answered: 'Mad' [*gal*]. Yes, *avenge, avenge yourself—you are the man*!

No, I will not leave the world—I will enter a *madhouse*,

23

and I shall see if *the depths of insanity* will not disclose to me the secret of life. Oh, fool, that I have not done so long ago, long ago understood what it means when the Indians honour the insane and go out of the way for them. Yes, to the madhouse—don't you think I can come in there?

(3) It is fortunate that *language has a number of expressions for nonsense and drivel.* Otherwise I would have become mad, for what else does it prove except all that one said was nonsense. Oh, how fortunate that language is so developed in this respect: that way one may yet hope occasionally to hear *reasonable discourse.*

(4) It is called a tragedy when the hero risks his life for an Idea—madness! (I praise the Christians who called the day on which the martyrs died their birthday, for thus they curse the happy idea one usually has.) No, it is a misunderstanding. I grieve when a child is born, and wish: God grant it may at least never grow up to be confirmed! I weep when I read or see *Erasmus Montanus*; he is right and succumbs to the *masses*. Ay, there's the rub! When every confirmed consumer is qualified to vote, when the majority decides an issue—doesn't one then succumb to the masses, to the meat-heads? So it was with the *Titans*, didn't they, too, succumb to the masses? And yet—and this is the only comfort remaining!—didn't they now and then frighten the hottentots who trot over them by drawing in a deep breath and expelling *a glowing sigh of fire*, not in order to complain—no, all condolence refused—but in order to terrify.

I will — — No, I will nothing at all. Amen!

(5) And when one meets *an Idea* that sprang fresh and living from the brow of an individual, meets it at twentieth hand and more—*how much truth is still remaining*? At most one can say with the proverb: It always tastes of crow, said the old crone, as she brewed a soup with a twig on which a crow had sat. (*Papirer, I A 333*)

Roos writes of these passages as follows (p. 107 ff.):

I shall attempt to find the thread through these fragments. The speaker (either Kierkegaard personally or an
imagined person, a 'pseudonym') feels himself (1) misunderstood and will give up the world. He has again
experienced the vexation that another has said what he
thinks before he himself was able to say it (2). Thus some
one else has developed *an Idea for a Faust* identical with the
one he was working on. The thought of two people saying
the same thing gives rise to the idea of *an echo*, which
indeed repeats but does not reproduce fully. He is reminded of how often echo, no matter where he goes—be
it in nature or among men—has depressed him with its
emptiness, but also amused him by *parodying*. He has
heard it render false emotion ridiculous, a thing doubly
amusing because the person who called forth the parody
did not understand it. He 'constantly read something
else', was an offer for an *'inflexible irony'*. This idea gives
rise to a new idea (3): he will reverse the echo, he will use
this 'great master of irony' to take revenge upon those
who before vexed him. How? Naturally, he who was
misunderstood when he spoke seriousness and reason will
resort to that language which is understood: the language
of the madhouse. The world is a madhouse, if he embraces
its language his words will have weight. The language of
the madhouse, nonsense, drivel, is richly varied, so much
so that it even admits of being employed as 'reasonable
discourse'.

There follow the references to the 'tragic', the 'majority', and
the 'Titans' (4).

For (5) that which the masses have profaned: the Idea,
fresh and living when it sprang from the brow of its
originator; what still remains when one meets it again
thoroughly banalized after its passage through vulgarity?
Nothing!

Roos remarks that the grim humour of the passage, immediately associated with the problem of Faust, seems surprising. Hence he asks if anything had occurred, subjectively and objectively, to account for this turn of events. He points to a note in the spring of 1837 taking account of a brief review of 'a little play by Johannes M. [Martensen] on Lenau's *Faust*'. Obviously, Kierkegaard had not read it yet, for he thinks it is a play, and remarks about the conclusion as described in the review. The work he is referring to is a very slight book by H. L. Martensen, written in German while in Vienna during his two-year travelling fellowship, and published in Stuttgart in the autumn of 1836. Roos then picks up another undated passage where the reaction is quite different.

> Oh, how miserable am I not—Martensen has written an essay on Lenau's *Faust*! (*Papirer, II A 597*)

Roos cites another from the same section of the Journal as the first reference to Lenau's *Faust*.

> Precisely! It fares with me and all I touch like the verse in *Des Knaben Wunderhorn*.
> > *Ein Jäger stiess wohl in sein Horn,*
> > > *wohl in sein Horn,*
> > *Und alles, was er bliest, das war*
> > > *verlorn.* (*Papirer, II A 51*).

These passages derive from sections of the Journal replete with such fragments containing involved but consistent references to Martensen and the collapse of Kierkegaard's Faust project. Roos shows that the second reference to Martensen's essay, with its powerful negative reaction, is due to the fact that Martensen, after arriving back in Copenhagen, rewrote the German piece in Danish, furnishing it with a long conceptual introduction setting forth the Idea of Faust in its full significance for the present age as the doubt unto despair,[19] rejecting Goethe's *Faust II* on identical grounds, and generally reduplicating Kierkegaard's conception of Faust in all its essential features.[20] It was published in Heiberg's journal *Perseus* as 'Reflections on the Idea of Faust. With Reference to Lenau's *Faust*', in June 1837. Kierkegaard comes to feel he has met his Wagner and identifies the more readily with his own Faust. He enrolls in Martensen's lectures on 'Speculative Dogmatics' in the autumn, and when Martensen includes in his fifth lecture (November 29th) a sketch of the modern Faust, Kierkegaard is hearing himself described and parodied from the lectern: the confrontation with his own Wagner was complete.

Roos next analyzes the draft for a satirical, quasi-Aristophanic comedy entitled 'The Conflict Between the Old and the New Soap Cellar',[21] which he convincingly interprets as a Faust parody, and argues that it is the initial literary expression of his use of echo as the master of irony. Needless to say, the ironic satire upon both Martensen and Heiberg is withering! Such is Professor Roos' illuminating account of the fate of Kierkegaard's Faust project, and the situation within which his personal satire against Martensen and Heiberg originated.

That there were, at this point, compulsive overtones on Kierkegaard's part in this relationship is too obvious to bear comment. But there were also intellectual issues to be discussed, and for this he must needs become fully conscious of himself. If almost four years of self-scrutiny and discipline were to elapse before he achieved the kind of emancipation which triggered the remarkable productivity that ensued, still, he could already announce in September 1838 in his first substantial publication, *From the Papers of One Still Living*, that he was in possession of the philosophic goal posited for himself in the Gillileie Journal: an organic *Livsanskuelse*. In the course of a brilliant critique of Hans Christian Andersen as a novelist, the presence of an integral view of life animates throughout this highly tooled prose. A couple of quotations will have to suffice:

> A view of life is more than a sum of sentences or a summary of theses held fast in their abstract neutrality, more even than experience, which as such is always atomistic. A view of life is the transubstantiation of experience, an inviolable certainty in self wrested from all empiricism.   (*XIII, 73*)

Such a view of life is not mere knowledge by description any more than it is mere knowledge by acquaintance. It is a new third kind of awareness, far older than either, a mode of self-vindicating knowledge insofar as it *becomes* at every moment what it *is*, is ever *struggling* though forever *victorious*. Kierkegaard regards it as the rarest of intellectual goods: a golden equilibrium between the self and its world. To have such a view of life is therefore to be possessed by a species of

> resignation that is not the consequence of external pressure . . . but developed from an internal elasticity, from that gladness which has triumphed over the world. (*XIII, 63*)

More explicit is the following passage:

> If we next inquire how such a view of life comes about, then I shall answer that for the person who does not allow his life altogether to slip away from him, but endeavours as much as possible to lead its particular expressions back into himself once more, there must of necessity occur that moment wherein a novel light breaks forth upon life without in any way requiring one to have understood every possible particular, yet for whose successive understanding he now has the key—there must occur, I say, a moment when, as Daub observes, life is understood backwards through the Idea. (*XIII, 74*)

Before the year was out Kierkegaard was already at work on the earliest sections of the essay on irony. It remains to be seen whether this work, too, is not another enactment of sense in nonsense, the consummate fusion of seriousness and jest, the *magnum opus* of echo, the great master of irony.

4. The transition from the Idea of doubt to the concept of irony is not so discordant as may appear at first glance. For a doubt that despairs of communication there is only the role of repressed silence—to accompany the angry Myrmidon sitting idly by his hollow ships watching his men take to sport —or the desperate search for concealment, for masks and other voices with which to speak out of hiding as it were, the impulse to play with language, consciously structuring it into a fabric vibrant with meanings, to make his peace with the fickle echo that formerly mocked his own fullness. The rebound takes place conceptually almost at once, for immediately after the Journal entry '*Ein Jäger stiess wohl*', and a scarcely veiled blast at Martensen, comes the following reconstruction (the conversation with Paul Møller about Socrates having occurred in July).

> Faust must be paralleled with Socrates. As the latter designates the severance of the individual from the state, so the former, after the abrogation of the Church, designates the individual severed from its guidance and abandoned to himself—and here his relation to the Reformation is denoted, and the latter parodied by unilaterally emphasizing the negative aspect.   (*Papirer, II A 53*)

The serious study of the figure of Socrates now commences, who, as something of a new type, wholly displaces Faust as the major paradigm for Kierkegaard's intellectual relationship to humanism and the world—though one may expect to find this initial Socratic portrait not without daemonic moments resembling its romantic predecessor. At the same time the Journal gradually swells with parodic passages practising the exhibiting dimension of dialectical structure so characteristic of Hegel and his school. That these passages showing the homologous relation between form and content also entail an irony over himself is evident from the melancholy tone pervading most of them, while their essentially parodic function may foreshadow his subsequent usage of the Hegelian dialectic insofar as Kierkegaard held that every development ends with its own parody. The following may serve as examples.

> I, too, have united the tragic and the comic: I utter witticisms, people laugh—I weep.   (*Papirer, II A 132*)
> Situation: someone is writing a novel in which one of the characters goes mad. During the composition he himself becomes mad, and finishes it in the first person.
>   (*Papirer, II A 634*)

There remains the problem of what format this ironic

response should take. Quite obviously, he needs the freedom and security of his mother tongue for such an undertaking, but this is complicated by the fact that an academic essay had to be in Latin—at that time permission to write in Danish had only been granted once before, and that as recently as the preceding year (1836). The continuity between his studies in romantic literature and philosophy and an academic essay is apparent in the following reflections on this obstacle.

> To write about romantic material in Latin in an adequate mood is as unreasonable as to require that one describe a circle with squares. The hyperboles of the humorous life-paradoxes surpass every schema, burst every strait jacket—like pouring new wine into old leather flasks. And should Latin finally seek to master it by a forced marriage to the youthful lover, then the toothless old biddy unable to articulate her speech had better excuse him if he seeks his satisfaction elsewhere. (*Papirer, II A 111*)

Within two months he proposes a possible theme.

> Now I know an appropriate theme for a dissertation: on the concept of satire among the ancients—the internal relationship between the various Roman satirists.
> (*Papirer, II A 166*)

While Kierkegaard is teaching Latin at this time and the idea might easily have suggested itself, the fact remains that these passages were written after the appearance of Martensen's Danish essay on Faust and are inseparable from the larger context. There is the possibility, as I believe, that the proposal indicates a reading of Hegel's lectures on aesthetics has begun, for the significance of Roman satire in Hegel's evolution of the Ideal through its three types or stages is to be a moment of transition, the severance of form and meaning, of external and internal, of phenomenon and essence signifying the final dissolution of the classical type in the interest of an incipient subjectivity—an obvious parallel to Kierkegaard's interpretation of Socratic irony.[22] Satire, rejected as the subject matter of the essay, is nevertheless assimilated into its substance, and insofar as the essay remains true to its initial conception it belongs to the *genre* of satire under the species of parody, the model for which was the Hegelian system, perspectives, and terminology as appropriated by his contemporaries. What Kierkegaard submitted in the form of a master's essay was also literature of a recognizable art form.

If one inquires into the integrity of the work, how this satire is effected, he will discover that Kierkegaard subscribed to Hegel's theory of 'substantial form', and that, over against the romantics, he committed himself to a content-aesthetic. As applied to a classical work of art, this theory holds that the content has its own immanent form (as the Idea is absolutely dialectical, so each of its moments comes with its own inherent structure already posited by its locus in the Idea), which, when expressed in an adequate medium, is consonant with the external shape of the work, so that ideal significance coalesces with external expression in such a way that matter and manner, meaning and style, the *what* and the *how* constitute one organic whole. As art demands unity, so there is a reduplication of structure between internal and external form, a harmony between essence and phenomenon. At either extreme from the classical type, however, this harmonious unity of internal and external is severed, leaving essence incommensurable with phenomenon: the antecedent type is termed 'symbolic' and culminates in the classical, the subsequent type 'romantic' and ends with 'the death of art'. Kierkegaard's innovation consists in transferring Hegel's prescriptions for classical art to a romantic subject matter. It is to the content of irony that we must look not only to identify its proper medium, but to discern the conceptual structure reduplicating itself ironically in the external expression of the work.

While verbal irony may or may not express an ironic world view, as irony 'writ small' it nevertheless affords the opportunity of comprehending certain pervasive characteristics of all forms of irony. For Kierkegaard the basic feature of even the simplest instance of irony, the ironic figure of speech, is to say the opposite of what is meant: the essence (meaning) is not the phenomenon (word), the external not the internal. The ironic figure of speech cancels itself, however, for the speaker presupposes that his listener understands him, and hence through the negation of the immediate expression *the essence remains identical with the phenomenon*. Ironic communication is deliberately contingent, therefore, and the incommensurability posited in its structure enables the speaker to detach himself from the linguistic expression and distance himself from the listener. In this way he is said to emancipate himself in the interest of negative freedom, a subjectivity coupled with isolation. Communication has now become precarious, indirect, at once exclusive and selective, for the ironist does not wish to be universally understood. Accordingly, if the basic communication-situation has five components: a speaker, a medium, an expression, a context, and a respondent, still, the *what* of ironic discourse remains a nothingness. For this to be present, as possibility, we require a further condition, viz., the Platonic assumption that every man has the truth in himself. For such a possibility to become actual, however, we require yet a final condition, viz., the operation of a Socratic agency, the maieutic artist, whereby the listener is activated to make the same movement of reflection, whereby he ventures to engage his own subjectivity. The *what* may not be asserted from without but only enacted from within, for with finite man the word must come after the deed and that is its truth. Here it may be seen that the art of indirect discourse, as conceived by Kierkegaard, aspires to nothing so much as to create something out of nothing. To comprehend this much of the ideal significance of irony is to grasp its meaning as *contradiction* (ambiguity), its structure as *dialectical*, its medium the *language of reflection*, its style *antithetical*, and its aim *self-discovery*.

Irony, for Kierkegaard, is obviously not so much a matter of words, nor even of characters or situations, as a total perspective, and its most precise designation is the Hegelian formulation: 'infinite absolute negativity', the nadir of contradiction, a dialectical moment of the Idea. To give this abstraction some substance (while confining myself to a single line of descent), it may be said that the concept is not without a history. It was already implicit in the expansive vision of a reality pregnant with teeming relativities and clamorous contradictions grasped as 'the characteristic' in a work of art by the æstheticians of Storm and Stress, nurtured and cultivated through the æsthetics of German classicism until becoming buoyant and boisterous as romantic irony, then given definition and vocation by Hegel as ambiguity was wrought into a dialectic of opposites whose turning point became the negation of negation, the moment of transition, the place of crisis, the liberal energy of the 19th century concentrated into a dialectical weapon of massive potential heralding the violence of revolution and the imperative of social change. This 'infinite absolute negativity', as the way of modernity, was read back into antiquity by Kierkegaard and identified with Socratic irony: the method of questioning in order to *humiliate*, and answering in order to *infuriate*, a process culminating in the shock of intellectual awakening at once the spin of reversal and the spark of recognition, the overmastering *repulse* from which one is thrust backward from the blinding heat of infinite striving into the shaded chiaroscuro of patient endeavour, the vertigo between pride and humility, the movement of inward transformation which Kierkegaard ultimately terms 'mastered irony' and asks that it be applied to the individual in the interests of a whole personality and an authentic existence.

If we conjoin the meaning of irony with its structure, we have to do with a dialectic of opposites. As its medium is the language of reflection, so the unity appropriate to an ironic communication is posited only in reflection: it *is* and it *is not*. It is for it exists for thought; it is not for it is invisible to immediate observation. The point I am making is that whereas Hegel develops his positive concepts beyond the sphere of reflection to the speculative *unity* of opposites, Kierkegaard resolutely sustains the negative concept in the sphere of reflection as the ironic unity of *opposites*. The first is apparent and direct, the second transparent and indirect; the one is the word ('lines void of thought, and sonorous trifles'), the other silence ('speak out that I may see you'). Hegel, of course, was aware of this dialectical overlap, which Kierkegaard has here exploited, when he wrote: 'The logic of mere understanding is involved in speculative logic, and can at will be elicited from it by the simple process of omitting the dialectical and "reasonable" element.' (*The Logic of Hegel*, Wallace, p. 152). Here we have arrived at *a point of coincidence* from which a perspective may be had into the polemical strategy of the whole essay. For the 'unity of opposites' may signify equally well either the Hegelian dialectic in the sphere of reflection, the dual categories of essence, or the Protean variability, the vibration between opposites characteristic of romantic irony. Here Hegel and the German romantics once more confront each other and resume their obstreperous quarrel over the Kantian limits to the understanding, and their respective claims of an indulgence for Reason or Intuition. The essay does have its own dialectic, as Bohlin suspected, with Hegelianism and romanticism made to negate each other reciprocally. But such reciprocal negation is also determination, and so it seems necessary to say that Kierkegaard speaks for neither while endeavouring to master both. Was it Kierkegaard's intention to insinuate a third alternative between Hegel and the romantics?

It would appear that this correlation of opposites within the sphere of reflection is hyperbolically 'fastened together at the top' like pleasure and pain, like movement and repose, classicism and romanticism, identity and contradiction, and it is Kierkegaard's curious fusion of the two which makes the total structure and design of the essay an ironic whole—a singular jest. Hegel's prescriptions for a classical work of art, the fact that his theory of 'substantial form' entails something like an isomorphism between inner and outer form, are applied to the romantic subject matter *par excellence*, namely, irony. The result is that although the conceptual significance of irony posits a formal *opposition* (the external is not the internal, the internal not the external—the essence is not the phenomenon, the phenomenon not the essence), and though this immanent form reduplicates itself in the medium of the work imparting to the linguistic expression its own shape (the pervasive Hegelianism of the essay conceals a discreet parody on Hegel, not to mention the Danish Hegelians); still, there remains an *identity* between the internal and the external though the formal assertion of the first be contradiction and the material enactment in the second contradictory, remains an organic unity between essence and phenomenon though the implicit structure of the first be incommensurability and the explicit representation of the second exhibit itself as incommensurable. The classical harmony between the internal and the external, as formulated by Hegel, is here superimposed upon a romantic content whose inner and outer form is identical: contradiction. *Both* as essence *and* as phenomenon the internal is not the external, the external not the internal. The apparent similarity between Kierkegaard and Hegel is posited in real dissimilarity. Kierkegaard's philosophic essay on irony is also a literary satire.

Other points of coincidence between Kierkegaard and Hegel will yield a similar result. The ultimate significance assigned to irony, to take but another, discloses the vast disparity between their respective interpretations of the scope and value of subjectivity. For Hegel, irony is treated as a single moment in the development of the subjective or moral aspect of the ethical concept, all morality being regarded as the negation or further elaboration of a natural concrete ethic induced by the advent of reflection, a development wherein subjectivity ultimately seeks to isolate itself and hence degenerates into what Hegel terms 'the moral forms of evil' with irony (romantic) assigned its place as the final phase in such an aberration, *the furthest reach of subjectivity*. While Kierkegaard ultimately consents to Hegel's decisive rejection of this form of irony, he is nevertheless pained in doing so. Such an irony concerns his own past experience, and signifies his honest philosophic gropings no less than his familiarity with the psychology of the intellectual dissipate. Understandably, he is constrained to make it count for something. Accordingly, Kierkegaard regards irony as *the mere beginning of subjectivity*, and assigns to it the value of marking the birth of the personal life. But first he is concerned to give this reflective phenomenon an organic life of its own, and to induce irony to manifest itself and speak out as the live option he knew it to be. Hegel's single negative moment becomes for Kierkegaard a negative concept, a structured whole of experience in the medium of reflection which cannot be disposed of by a dialectical sleight of hand within the system but only experientially outlived in 'the dialectic of life' as it is inherently self-consuming. With only a semblance of fidelity to Hegel's dialectic, inasmuch as the definitions of the successive phases of the concept admit of dialectical formulae to combine in a quasi Hegelian 'deduction', Kierkegaard plots three points which describe not a circle but a past, a life, a whole: the beginning, middle, and end of the career of irony—its inception in the figure of Socrates, its illusory zenith in the romantics, and the point at which irony enigmatically disappears, experientially metamorphosed through resignation into self-mastery. The essential thing to notice, therefore, is how irony is overcome and what is able to overcome it: for Hegel the concrete universal, for Kierkegaard the concrete individual. This much of his clarified experience Kierkegaard is concerned to communicate in the essay on irony, and this note of tempered humanism abides as the authentic seriousness of the work—the true point of departure for his subsequent 'authorship'.

To say that the essay on irony is itself an ironic work, even a satiric parody, need not in any way militate against its also being the vehicle for serious meaning and the repository of philosophic value. Indeed, its essential jest is its existential pathos. The work also contains his own personal views, sometimes alluded to only obscurely, sometimes set forth as ringing affirmations. Between the work's conception and consummation lies much experience: what he called 'the great earthquake', his religious conversion, the death of his father, a solid book of criticism, a penetrating study of Plato and Hegel and much else besides, the discipline of an academic degree, a disillusioned engagement, but most important the mastering of the irony he writes about. Compelled to study Hegel in order to maintain himself, he came to the conclusion that there was much more to it than his contemporaries perceived, and for this he chided them:

> For with the word 'Hegelian' I must *either* associate the idea of a man who with seriousness and energy has comprehended the world-view of this philosophy, has appropriated it and found repose in it, and now with a certain true pride said of himself: I, too, have had the honour of serving under Hegel . . . in which case . . . I would be reluctant to use so significant a predicate of myself, although I am conscious of having tried to make myself familiar with Hegel's philosophy; *or* by the word 'Hegelian' I understand a person who, superficially moved by this thinking, now deceived himself about a result he did not possess.[23]   (*Papirer, III B 1,* p. 108)

It was under the tutelage of the Platonic Socrates, however, that the hollow echo of parody acquired the serious dimension of the maiuetic method holding fast to the object while trying to extricate oneself in order to deflect the subject back into himself. Kierkegaard studied Plato and the result was a theory of indirect communication, a literary device for simulating the experience of a Socratic conversation. In its didactic function irony becomes in the hands of Kierkegaard an instrument for disabusing his readers of what is not personally appropriated, of stripping away what is not permeated with consciousness and enjoyed. It is not the truth but surely the way, albeit the negative way, whereby illusion and imaginary results forsake him. The bantering with his contemporaries is therefore profoundly serious and aims at returning them to truth and actuality. What Kierkegaard with his fondness for the biblical phrase maintained of the novel is no less true of the essay on irony.

> The essential thing is the resulting totality given through the discrete manifold of representation, for even here it is the case that what is sown in corruption is raised in incorruption.   (*Papirer, II A 312*)

The work modestly announces itself in the motto as a voyage

he is about to make, and we may add, that he has made. And if in such a quest Arion had his dolphin, while such as Kierkegaard have their genius, many others capsize and would surely drown if no earthly miracle be found. In the absence of all these the reader has the reports of those who have successfully navigated the Scylla and Charybdis of reflection, and one such report is the essay on irony.

5. The present translation is based on the second edition of Kierkegaard's collected works (*Samlede Værker*, vol. XIII, pp. 101-428). This text is the same as the original edition except for the removal of obvious typographical errors. Unlike the later works, no draft of the essay survives. A few notes and references of uneven import have been brought together by the editors of the second edition of Kierkegaard's collected papers (*Papirer, III B 2-30*; *IV A 198-212*) as directly pertaining to the essay, and amount to some thirteen pages. Most of this material derives from marginal notes in two extant copies of the first edition from Kierkegaard's library. In addition, many entries in the first three volumes of the collected papers concerning irony, humour, dialectic, speculation, language, communication, classicism, romanticism, Socrates, Christianity, etc., must be regarded as relevant background material for the composition of the essay. The use of this extensive material to illuminate various points in a frequently difficult text, however, is complicated by the problem of an obvious development in Kierkegaard's aesthetic, philosophic, and theological views during the decade he was a student; a development brought to fruition in the present work. I have included relevant portions of this material in the translator's notes when a connection seemed clear to me. Somewhat more helpful in the work of translation have been the German translations of H. H. Schaeder, W. Kütemeyer, and especially E. Hirsch.

Although the work originally carried the usual Latin formulæ and theses to be used in the oral defence, Kierkegaard also issued the book to the general public. For this purpose he removed the Latin material from the volume and added to the title page a motto from Plato. The present volume conforms to the latter format, and so the Latin material together with an English translation has been accorded a place in the Appendix at the end of the volume. The correct title of the essay is *On the Concept of Irony, With Constant Reference to Socrates*. I have felt, along with others, that the 'On' was merely a concession to the Latin *De* common to academic dissertations, and have eliminated it from the English title as redundant. As for the practical features of punctuation, every instance of parenthesis (except for an occasional source) is that of Kierkegaard, while my own difficulties have been confined to the use of square brackets. In the present essay Kierkegaard occasionally uses an isolated dash, as does Hegel, for some sort of visual indication of subordination, i.e., a statement to be elucidated often ends with an isolated dash, while the related parts of the discussion are each preceded by an isolated dash. As I have found them useful, and since one easily becomes accustomed to them, I have retained them for whatever visual subordination they may indicate to the reader. Kierkegaard's own extensive notes are indicated by asterisks in the text and printed at the bottom of the page on which they occur, while the notes of the translator are numbered in the text and printed at the back of the volume. I have observed that to break up some of Kierkegaard's long antithetical periods occasionally obscures rather than clarifies the meaning. I have therefore retained a few of them without, I hope, compromising my intention to produce as clear and accurate a translation as I am able. All problems of terminology have been dealt with in the Glossary at the end of the volume. It goes without saying that the price one pays for consistency in dealing with key philosophic terms, the principle behind any useful glossary, will be an occasional awkward phrase at the least.

As for the numerous Plato quotations, I have in the main used the revised Jowett translation (4th edition), but occasionally those in the Loeb Classical Library and The Library of Liberal Arts. The extensive Hegel quotations both in the text and in the notes are based on the standard English translations of Hegel. I would here gratefully acknowledge permission to quote from the following: The Clarendon Press, Oxford

(*The Dialogues of Plato*, *The Logic of Hegel*, Hegel's *Philosophy of Right*); Harvard University Press (Aristophanes' *Clouds*, Xenophon's *Apology*, *Memorabilia*, Plato's *Phaedo*, *Republic*—the occasional lines from other classical authors are all rendered in the Loeb translations); The Bobbs-Merrill Co. (Plato's *Apology*); The Humanities Press and Routledge & Kegan Paul (*Hegel's Lectures on the History of Philosophy*); George Allen & Unwin (Hegel's *Phenomenology of Mind*, *The Science of Logic*); G. Bell & Sons (Hegel's *The Philosophy of Fine Art*); Macmillan and Co., Ltd. (Kant's *Critique of Pure Reason*); A. G. & G. M. Drachmann, Copenhagen (A. C. Drachmann's notes to 2nd edition of *Samlede Værker*, vol. xiii); Emanuel Hirsch and Eugen Diederichs Verlag, Düsseldorf-Köln (E. Hirsch's notes in the German edition of *Irony*); Peter P. Rohde, Copenhagen (notes to 3rd Danish edition of *Irony*); Niels Thulstrup, Copenhagen (notes and quotations from an article published in Switzerland); Billeskov Jansen, Copenhagen (notes from his selected Kierkegaard edition); Fru Kamma Brun Roos, Copenhagen (Carl Roos' *Kierkegaard og Goethe*).

I wish to express my sincere thanks to Howard A. Johnson and Niels Thulstrup, both of whom have been extraordinarily generous with their time and knowledge in discussing the many linguistic problems in what has been for me a difficult text. I would long ago have abandoned the translation but for their assistance and encouragement. I am further indebted to Hr. Thulstrup for some appreciation of the problems of historical research in dealing with a work by Kierkegaard. I wish also to thank Professor Paul O. Kristeller of Columbia University for correcting my first draft translations of the frequent German and infrequent Latin quotations. While these three scholars have saved me from many a slip, I must naturally assume responsibility for whatever errors and defects remain in the present translation. I wish also to thank Professor James Gutmann for encouraging me to undertake the present translation, and express to him my sincere appreciation for his interest, his understanding and example over the course of several years. Finally, I wish to acknowledge my indebtedness to Professor Robert D. Cumming for much insight and assistance, and in the present connection for introducing me to Kierkegaard and to the ironic structure of the essay on irony.

It remains to acknowledge gratefully the material assistance of a Fulbright Grant, and to thank Mrs Karin Fennow, and her associates, of the U.S. Educational Foundation for every help and consideration while studying Kierkegaard in Denmark.

L. M. C.

Salt Lake City
December 1964

THE

CONCEPT OF IRONY

with Constant Reference
to Socrates

By

S. A. KIERKEGAARD

The problem to be solved is anything but easy. Why
yes, I said, but the fact is that when a man is out of his
depth, whether he has fallen into a little swimming-bath
or into mid ocean, he has to swim all the same. Very
true. And must not we swim and try to reach the shore,
while hoping that Arion's dolphin or some other
miraculous help may save us?   *Republic* 453 D

COPENHAGEN
1841

PART ONE

THE STANDPOINT OF SOCRATES
CONCEIVED AS IRONY

Introduction

If there is anything for which one must praise modern philosophic endeavour with its splendid progress, its grand appearance and manner,[1] it is certainly for the genial[2] strength with which it grasps and holds fast to the phenomenon. Now if it is fitting for the latter, which as such is always *fœminini generis*,[3] to surrender itself to the stronger because of its feminine nature, then one may fairly demand of the philosophical knight the courteous demeanour, the deep enthusiasm, instead of which one too often hears the jangling of spurs and the master's voice.[4] The observer should be an eroticist, no feature, no moment should be indifferent to him; on the other hand, he should also feel his own preponderance, but only use it to assist the phenomenon to its complete manifestation. Even though the observer brings the concept with him, therefore, it is essential that the phenomenon remain inviolate and that the concept be seen coming into existence [*tilblivende*][5] through the phenomenon.[6]

Before proceeding to the discussion of the concept of irony, therefore, it will be necessary for me to secure a dependable and authentic conception of the historical-actual, phenomenological existence of Socrates with reference to the question of its possible relation to the transfigured[7] conception which has fallen to his lot at the hands of an enthusiastic or envious age.[8] This is absolutely necessary because it is in Socrates that the concept of irony has its inception in the world.[9] Concepts, like individuals, have their histories and are just as incapable of withstanding the ravages of time as are individuals. But in and through all this they retain a kind of homesickness for the scenes of their childhood. As philosophy cannot be indifferent to the subsequent history of this concept, so neither can it content itself with the history of its origin, though it be ever so complete and interesting a history as such. Philosophy always requires something more, requires the eternal, the true, in contrast to which even the fullest existence as such is but a happy moment. Philosophy relates to history as a confessor to the penitent, and, like a confessor, it ought to have a supple and searching ear for the penitent's secrets; but after having listened to a full account of his confession, it must then be able to make this appear to the penitent as an 'other'.[10] And as the penitent individual is able to rattle off the fateful events of his life chronologically, even recite them entertainingly, but cannot himself see through them, so history is able to proclaim with loud pathos the rich full life of the race, but must leave its explanation to the elder (philosophy).* History can then experience the pleasant surprise that while at first it would almost disown its philosophic counterpart, it afterwards identifies itself with this conception of philosophy to such a degree that, finally, it would regard this as the essential truth, the other as mere appearance.

Hence there are these two moments which both ought to receive satisfaction and which constitute the proper issue [Mellemværende][11] between history and philosophy: the phenomenon, on the one hand, must receive its due,† and philosophy is not to distress or intimidate it with its own superiority; philosophy, on the other hand, must not allow itself to be

* Perhaps someone will take me to task for designating philosophy the elder. I still maintain, however, that the eternal is older than the temporal, and though philosophy in many respects comes after history, still, it takes such an imposing stride at the very first moment[12] that it immediately overtakes the temporal, regards itself as the eternal *prius*,[13] and, coming to itself in an ever deeper awareness of itself, recollects itself ever further back in time into eternity, recollects this not as in a dream, but more and more as awake, not as the past, for it recollects the past as a present.[14]

† In its truth, philosophy relates to history as eternal life to the temporal according to the Christian view; in its untruth, as eternal life to the temporal according to the Greek and the ancient view generally. Eternal life, according to the latter conception, began when one drank of Lethe in order to forget the past;[15] according to the former conception, however, eternal life is accompanied by a consciousness of every hasty word uttered, a consciousness piercing even to the dividing asunder of the joints and marrow.[16]

deceived by the charm of the particular nor distracted by its abundance.[17] The same is true of the concept of irony, for philosophy must not become infatuated with one particular aspect of the concept's phenomenological existence, and above all not with its mere appearance, but see the truth of the concept in and with the phenomenological.

Everyone knows that tradition has linked the word 'irony' to the existence of Socrates, but it does not follow from this that everyone knows what irony is. Furthermore, if one were to acquire an idea of what was characteristic of Socrates through an intimate acquaintance with his life and career, one would still not have a complete concept of irony. We say this in no wise as if we nourished the lack of confidence in historical existence that would make becoming [*Vordelse*] identical with a falling away from the Idea, since it is more like the unfolding of the Idea. This, as we have said, is far from our intention; on the other hand, neither can one suppose that a particular moment of existence as such should be the absolutely adequate medium of the Idea. It has been correctly observed of nature that it is incapable of maintaining the concept,[18] partly because each particular phenomenon contains only a moment, and partly because the whole sum of natural existence is still always an imperfect medium producing not satisfaction but longing.[19] Something comparable may rightly be said of history, for each particular fact, though evolving, is only a moment; and the whole sum of historical existence is still not the absolutely adequate medium of the Idea, since it is the temporality and fragmentariness of the Idea (as nature is its extension) which longs for what issues from consciousness as a repulse which looks backward, face over against face.[20]

So much for the difficulty that remains for every philosophical conception of history and the caution which ought to attend this pursuit. Special circumstances may present new difficulties, however, and such is particularly the case in the present investigation. What Socrates valued so highly, namely, to stand still and come to himself,[21] i.e. silence, this is what his whole life is in relation to world history. He has left nothing from which a later age can judge him. Indeed, were I to imagine myself his contemporary, he would still always be difficult to apprehend. He belonged to that species of human beings with whom one is not content to remain with the external as such. The external always suggested an 'other', an opposite. He was not like a philosopher lecturing upon his views, wherein the very lecture itself constitutes the presence of the Idea;[22] on the contrary, what Socrates said meant something 'other'. The outer and the inner did not form a harmonious unity,[23] for the outer was in opposition to the inner, and only through this refracted angle[24] is he to be apprehended. Forming a conception of Socrates, therefore, is quite another matter than forming a conception of most other men. Here lies the necessity of the fact that Socrates can only be apprehended through an integral calculation.[25] But as there are now thousands of years between him and us, and since not even his contemporaries could grasp him in his immediacy, so it is easy to see how doubly difficult it is for us to reconstruct his existence, for we must endeavour to apprehend through a new integral calculation this already complicated conception. If we next say that the substantial aspect of Socrates' existence was irony (this is indeed a contradiction,[26] but also meant as one), and, if we postulate further, that irony is a negative concept,[27] then one easily sees how difficult it becomes to secure an image of him, yes, that it seems impossible, or at least as baffling as trying to depict an elf wearing a hat that makes him invisible.[28]

CHAPTER I

The conception made possible

We pass now to a survey of the conceptions of Socrates left by his immediate contemporaries. In this regard there are three to be considered: Xenophon, Plato, and Aristophanes. However, I cannot fully share the view of Baur* that Xenophon, next to Plato, deserves most attention. Xenophon was content to remain with Socrates' immediacy, and in many ways, therefore, has certainly misunderstood him.† By contrast, Plato and Aristophanes have made their way through the hard exterior to a conception of Socrates' infinity, an infinity which was incommensurable with the manifold events of his life. Hence one may say of Socrates that just as he journeyed through life constantly between caricature and ideal, so he continues to wander between them after his death. Baur correctly observes of the relationship between Xenophon and Plato (p. 123): 'There immediately appears a difference between these two which in many ways may be likened to the well-known relationship between the Synoptic Gospels and

* Baur, F. C., *Das Christliche des Platonismus oder Sokrates und Christus*, Tübingen, 1837.[1]

† I shall quote the example of the youth who ate only meat (*Mem.* III, 14, 2).[2] Now one of two alternatives must be the case here: either it is one of those infinitely deep ironies which encompass the most trivial things with profound seriousness, and in this way mock everything most profoundly; or else it is nonsense, one of Socrates' weak moments when an ironic nemesis allowed him to lapse into the category of the infinitely trivial (more of this later).[3] But neither of these alternatives is the case with Xenophon. Here it ends with the youth by no means becoming so melancholy that he gave up eating meat altogether: 'The young man, guessing that these remarks of Socrates applied to him, did not stop eating his meat,' but by becoming so morally bettered that he ate bread too: 'but took some bread with it'(4).

the Gospel of John. For as the Synoptic Gospels chiefly describe the external aspect of the phenomenal appearance of Christ, the aspect connected with the Jewish Messianic Idea, whereas the Gospel of John focuses mainly upon his higher nature and the immediate presence of the divine; so the Platonic Socrates has a much higher ideal significance than the Xenophontic with whom we essentially find ourselves always on the level of the conditions of immediate practical life.' This observation of Baur is not only striking but quite appropriate if one bears in mind that there always remains the difference between Xenophon's conception of Socrates and the Synoptic Gospels, namely, that the latter merely reproduced the immediate, true image of Christ's immediate existence (which, be it noted, did not mean anything 'other'* than it was), and, insofar as Matthew seems to have an apologetic purpose, this was the matter of justifying the life of Christ in conformity with the Messianic Idea; whereas Xenophon is concerned with a man whose immediate existence means something 'other' than appears at first glance, and, insofar as he conducts a defence for Socrates, merely does so in the form of a plea addressed to a rational and highly esteemed age. On the other hand, the observation concerning the relationship of Plato to

* Christ says: 'I am the way, the truth, and the life';[4] and as for the conception of the apostles, this was tangible and not just a clever artifice: 'that which we have heard, which we have seen with our eyes, which we have looked upon, and our hands have handled,' I John 1 : 1. Consequently, Christ also says[5] that kings and rulers have longed to see him. Socrates, by contrast, was invisible to his age, as remarked above: he was invisible to the eye and only visible to the ear (*loquere ut videam te*),[6] his existence was apparent not transparent. So much for the existence of Christ. As for his discourse, one could always take him at his word, for his words were life and spirit. Socrates, on the other hand, was only to be misunderstood through his words, for he was animated only by a negativity. I could wish—were this wish not already outside the limits of the present essay—that it were possible for me to go into the relationship between Socrates and Christ about which Baur, in the above-mentioned work, has said so much that is noteworthy. I say this notwithstanding the fact that there still always remains for me a modest, little, asthmatic doubt, namely, that the similarity consists in dissimilarity,[7] and that there is only an analogy because there is an opposition.

John is also correct if one maintains that John found and immediately saw in Christ all that he, by imposing silence upon himself, has depicted with complete objectivity, for his eyes were open to the immediate divinity in Christ; whereas Plato creates his Socrates through a poetic activity, since Socrates in his immediate existence was wholly negative.

But first an account of each.

XENOPHON

We must first bear in mind that Xenophon had a purpose (and this is already a defect or troublesome superfluity*), namely, to show what a monstrous injustice it was of the Athenians to condemn Socrates to death. Xenophon has been so successful at this, moreover, that one more readily believes his purpose was to prove it was an absurdity or mistake. Indeed, he defends Socrates in a manner whereby he is rendered not only innocent but utterly harmless. Thus one falls into the deepest wonder as to what kind of demon must have bewitched the Athenians to such an extent that they were able to see more in Socrates than in any other good-natured, garrulous, and ludicrous old geezer who does neither good nor evil, who opposes no one, and who is so amiably disposed toward the whole world if it would only listen to his chatter. And what pre-established harmony in folly, what higher unity in madness could be imagined than that Plato and the Athenians should join hands in killing and immortalizing such a proper old Philistine? This would surely be an irony upon the world without parallel. As in a dispute it occasionally happens that when the crux of the argument is brought to a head and begins to be interesting, some well-meaning third party takes it upon himself to reconcile the

* Xenophon has so distrusted Socrates and the truth generally that he has not dared to let him stand on his own two feet. Hence Xenophon is always ready to exclaim how unfair, how unjust it was of the Athenians, and how completely otherwise it all seemed to him.

warring powers and leads the whole affair back to a triviality, just so much Plato and the Athenians have felt out of sorts with Xenophon's irenic interpolation. In fact, Xenophon, by cutting away all that was dangerous in Socrates, has finally reduced him to utter absurdity—compensation, no doubt, for his having done this so often to others.

What makes it still more difficult to get a clear idea of the personality of Socrates from Xenophon's account is the total neglect of the situation. The basis upon which the individual conversation turns is as invisible and trivial as a straight line, as monotonous as the monochromatic ground upon which children and Nürnbergians ordinarily compose their paintings. Yet the situation was of the utmost importance with reference to the personality of Socrates, a personality which must have allowed itself to be felt as a mysterious presence in, and mystical hovering over, the vari-coloured manifold of the exuberant life of Athens, a personality which must have allowed itself to be explained through a duplicity of existence like a flying-fish in relation to both fish and bird. This emphasis on the situation was particularly important in order to show that what was central for Socrates was not a fixed point but an *ubique et nusquam*.[1] It was needed in order to point up the Socratic sensibility which under the subtlest and weakest contact immediately discerned the presence of the Idea, immediately felt the electricity pervading the whole of existence. It was needed in order to illustrate the true Socratic method, which found no phenomenon too insignificant to function as a point of departure for working itself up into the sphere of thought. This Socratic possibility of beginning wherever he might find himself—although when actualized in life it would as often as not go unnoticed by the multitude, for whom it always remained a mystery how they had come to discuss this or that subject, since their investigations most often began and ended at a stagnated* horse pond; this steady Socratic perspective for which no object was so compact that he could not

---

* With Socrates nothing was static in this way, and what we read in the Gospel[2] concerning the pool of Bethesda may here be applied to his view of knowledge, namely, that it was only healing when moving.

instantly see the Idea* in it—and this not hesitatingly but with immediate certainty, yet also having a practised eye for the apparent abbreviations of perspective and so did not draw the object to him surreptitiously, but simply retained the same ultimate prospect while it emerged step by step for the listener and onlooker; this Socratic parsimony which formed such a biting opposition to the empty noise and undigested fodder of the Sophists—all this is what one must wish that Xenophon had let us feel in Socrates. And what a life would thereby have been depicted when in the midst of the busy labour of the artisans, the braying of the pack animals, one had seen the divine web which Socrates worked into the very fibre of existence. When in the midst of the tumultuous clamour of the market place one had heard the divine harmony reverberating throughout existence [*Tilværelse*], since each particular thing was for Socrates an imagistic and not infelicitous designation of the Idea. What an interesting conflict between the earthly life's most mundane forms of expression and Socrates, who, so it

* Since I here conceive the Socratic view of the relation between Idea and phenomenon positively, and by this cause the attentive reader to find me guilty of a contradiction with reference to my subsequent conception of this relation for Socrates, I shall here interpose a few remarks by way of explanation. In the first place, it is grounded in the Socratic polemic against the Sophists, for as the latter were unable to come to terms with actuality, their speculation became so elevated and their eloquence so inflated that, finally, they were unable to say anything at all for sheer Ideas. In opposition to this, Socrates dwelt constantly upon the most mundane conditions of life, on food and drink, on cobblers, tanners, herdsmen, and pack animals. By forcing the Sophists down into this sphere, he compelled them to acknowledge their own affectation. In the second place, existence itself was for Socrates only an image, not a moment in the Idea. While this shows that his Idea was abstract, it is confirmed still more by the fact that he provided no qualitative determinations regarding the relation of the phenomenon to the Idea. One thing was as good as another, because everything was an image and only an image—just as it must also be regarded as a sign that one has the Idea only in its abstraction when one finds God as perceptibly present in a piece of straw as in world history, since it essentially means that he is nowhere really present. And lastly, the Idea possessed by Socrates was always the dialectical idea, the logical idea. But more of this later.

seems, said the very same things. Nor is this significance of the situation lacking in Plato, except that it is purely poetical; yet in this way it clearly indicates not only its own validity, but its absence in Xenophon as well.

As Xenophon lacks on the one hand an eye for the situation, so on the other he lacks an ear for repartee. Not as if the questions Socrates asks and the answers he gives were not correct; on the contrary, they are all too correct, too tenacious, too boring.* The Socratic rejoinder was not the immediate unity of what was said, it was not a flow but a constant ebb; and what one misses in Xenophon is an ear for the infinitely reverberating, backward echo of the reply in personality (for otherwise a reply merely transmits thought forward in sound).[3] The more Socrates undermined existence, the deeper and more necessarily must each particular utterance gravitate towards that ironical totality which, as a spiritual state, was infinitely bottomless, invisible, and indivisible. But Xenophon has no intimation of this secret. Allow me to illustrate my meaning with an image. There is an engraving that portrays the grave of Napoleon. Two large trees overshadow the grave. There is nothing else to be seen in the picture, and the immediate spectator will see no more. Between these two trees, however, is an empty space, and as the eye traces out its contour Napoleon himself suddenly appears out of the nothingness, and now it is impossible to make him disappear. The eye that has once seen him now always sees him with anxious necessity. It is the same with Socrates' replies. As one sees the trees, so one hears his discourse; as the trees are trees, so his words mean exactly what they sound like. There is not a single syllable to give any hint of another interpretation, just as there is not a single brush stroke to suggest Napoleon. Yet it is this empty space, this nothingness, that conceals what is

---

* Were Xenophon's conception of Socrates correct, then I should have thought that in sophisticated and fickle Athens one would sooner have had Socrates out of the way because he bored them than because they feared him; and one will have to admit that having bored them was just as valid a reason for executing him as was the celebrated justice of Aristeides a valid reason for the Athenians to ostracize him.[4]

most important. As in nature we find examples of places so curiously situated that those who stand nearest the speaker cannot hear him, but only those who stand at a fixed point often at a great distance; so also with Socrates' replies when one recalls that in this case to hear is identical with understanding, not to hear with misunderstanding. It is these two basic defects that I must urge against Xenophon, yet the situation and the reply are the complex forming the ganglia and cerebral systems of personality.

We pass to a collection of observations which Xenophon attributes to Socrates. These observations are usually so shallow and stunted that it is not difficult for the eye to become sluggish and overlook the whole lot. Only seldom do his observations elevate themselves to a poetic or philosophic thought, and in spite of the nice language the discussion is quite in the same taste with either the coarseness of our own *Folkeblad*,[5] or with the heavenly cry à la Per Degn*[6] of a

* Only seldom does one hear amidst this degenerate prose a remark still having anything of its lofty origin remaining, yet always with a disturbing admixture. For Xenophon's sake I shall cite as an example *Mem.* I, I, 8. Socrates is speaking of the things human wisdom is able to accomplish, and adds: 'but the deepest secrets in these matters the gods reserved to themselves. . . . You may plant a field well; but you know not who shall gather the fruits.' The Socratic dimension in this is the relation of opposition suggested between the feverish activity of man and that which is actually accomplished within the limits defining the sphere of human activity. The Socratic approach is first to portray the area inaccessible to human ken (§6: 'but if the consequences could not be foreseen, he sent them to the oracle to inquire whether the thing ought to be done'); and afterwards to indicate those things which mankind is still able to accomplish. But when the mind has come to rest in this security, then suddenly to stir it up again by showing that not even here is mankind able to accomplish anything— by thawing the ice as it were with which they are frozen and held fast as on solid ground, and causing them to be driven once more before the stream. But in order to do this we must not be without irony, for this is what wrests from them their former security. Yet this is exactly what is missing in Xenophon. This consideration began with the words: 'but the deepest secrets' (naturally, the Socratic approach would have been: now only one small mystery remains, etc.). On the other hand, neither can we do without the possibility, the disposition, and the threat of a dogmatic

nature-admiring seminarian functioning as parish clerk. Although these Socratic observations preserved by Xenophon often appear to be mere step-children, we shall nevertheless endeavour to pursue the possible family resemblance.

We hope the reader will agree with us in holding that the

---

view which must have been characteristic of Socrates. In order to establish the remark that in finite matters the gods have reserved to themselves the most important secrets, Socrates shows that no man knows his future fate, and hence that this ignorance is a crag upon which every clever assurance may be stranded. It was more to be expected that Socrates, precisely when he appeared to render men self-efficacious, would have emphasized the fact that they were not at all collaborators[7] with the deity, that all their feverish activity was a nothingness or a prior dispensation, so that though they dug with heavy tools instead of their hands, and ploughed furrows a fathom deep, they would still not find the earth fertile were the deity not willing. This ignorance of man's ultimate fate here emphasized by Socrates as our common lot was surely never unknown to men; but this total barrenness, which in the sphere of action is the proper analogy to total ignorance in the sphere of knowledge, was always in need of a Socratic enjoinder.—It might be objected that in the very passage under discussion there is mention of another arrangement, of a hidden possibility in the secret councils of the gods to the effect that the opposition is between what can never be the object of any reckoning, and that which at first glance seems to admit of certain calculation. But surely everyone will admit that irony is lacking here in every case. Moreover, if things were ordained as just described, it would afford a much more Socratic insight into the nature and essence of man were Socrates to bring mankind into collision not with chance but with necessity. For it was indeed possible that hailstones might beat down the farmer's crops, but that there should be no germinating force in the ground were the deity not willing, and this in spite of every human operation, is yet a much deeper negation. The one is a conception of possibility as possibility, the other an attempt to exhibit actuality as hypothetical possibility.—I shall cite another example where Socrates, still according to the conception of Xenophon, seems to come closest to irony, the well-known conversation with Critias and Charmides (*Mem.* i, 2). But here Socrates moves more in the domain of the Sophists: 'Am I to give no answer, then, if a young man asks me something that I know?—for instance, "Where does Charicles live?" or "Where is Critias?" ' (§36). Accordingly, this is only ironic to the degree to which a Sophist may approach, but still qualitatively different from irony. But more of this later. Curiously enough, empirical determination is the polygon, intuition[8] the circle, and that there remains to all eternity a qualitative difference between them.[9] With Xenophon the gallivanting conscious-ness traipses forever about in the polygon, no doubt often deceiving itself. When a long stretch opens before it, such a consciousness believes itself to possess true infinity,[10] and hence, like an insect crawling along a polygon, takes a tumble, since what appeared to be infinity was only an angle.

The useful, according to Xenophon, is one of the points of departure for the Socratic teaching. But the useful is simply the polygon corresponding to the inner infinity of the good: departing from and returning to itself, not towards any of its moments indifferently but moving in them all, wholly in them all and wholly in each one. The useful has an infinite dialectic, but also an infinitely bad dialectic. The useful is the external dialectic of the good, its negation, yet when torn loose as such becomes a kingdom of shadows where nothing endures but all things formless and shapeless condense and diffuse according to the inconstant and superficial gaze of the observer, where each particular existence is merely an infinitely divisible fraction of existence in an eternal calculation. (The useful mediates all things, even the useless, for as nothing is absolutely useful, so neither can something be absolutely useless, since absolute usefulness is but a fleeting moment in the unstable flux of life.)

This general view of the useful is found developed in the conversation with Aristippus (*Mem.* III, 8). In Plato, Socrates is continually drawing an affair out of the accidental con-cretion in which it is regarded by his associates, and leading it toward the abstract, whereas in Xenophon's account it is Socrates who demolishes the obviously feeble attempt of

---

Charicles is here actually more witty than Socrates, at least his notorious reply far outbids Socrates: 'Take care, lest you, too, cause the cattle to decrease.'[11]—I have discussed these two examples rather extensively in order to show that even where Xenophon comes closest to a conception of Socrates he still captures nothing of the *bifrons* in him, but merely some-thing which is neither the one or the other.

Aristippus to approach the Idea. It is not necessary to develop this conversation any further, for the initial attitude of Socrates shows at once the skilled fencer and the rules governing the whole inquiry. In answer to Aristippus' question whether he knows anything good, wherein the discursive *raisonnement* is suggested from the first, Socrates replies (§3): 'Are you asking me whether I know of anything good for a fever?' The whole conversation proceeds in the same manner with an immobility that does not even attempt to avoid the apparent paradox in (§6): ' "Is a dung basket beautiful then?" "Of course, and a golden shield is ugly, if the one is well made for its special work and the other badly." '

Although I have merely cited this conversation as an example and must essentially rely on the impression of the whole constituting its vitality, still, since it was also intended as a typical example, I shall mention a difficulty relating to the manner in which Xenophon introduces this conversation. He gives us to understand that it was a captious question of Aristippus designed to embarrass Socrates by the infinite dialectic residing in the good conceived as the useful. He implies that Socrates saw through this stratagem. Hence it is conceivable that the whole conversation was preserved by Xenophon as an example of Socrates' mental gymnastics. It might seem, perhaps, that there yet slumbered an irony in the entire behaviour of Socrates, that by venturing into Aristippus' proposed trap with feigned gullibility he thereby demolished his wily design, and forced Aristippus to argue against his will for what he had supposed Socrates would have advanced. But certainly everyone who knows Xenophon will find this highly improbable, and to contribute to this reassurance Xenophon has also provided a wholly different reason why Socrates behaved in this manner, namely, 'in order to benefit his companions.' Hence one clearly sees that according to the conception of Xenophon Socrates is dead serious in calling the inquiry's enthusiastic infinity back to the bad infinity surrounding the empirical.

Here the commensurable is altogether Socrates' proper playground, and his business in large part is to encompass the whole of human thought and action with an insurmountable wall, excluding all traffic with the world of Ideas. Neither must the study of the sciences overstep this cordon of health (*Mem.* IV, 7).[12] A person should learn only so much geometry* as suffices to keep an eye on whether his property is being correctly surveyed; the further study of astronomy is dismissed, and he advises against the speculations of Anaxagoras. In short, every science is reduced *zum Gebrauch für Jedermann*.[13]

The same attitude repeats itself in every sphere. His observations on nature are through and through factory work, finite teleology in a multiplicity of patterns. —His conception of friendship may not be accused of enthusiasm, for surely he means that no horse† or ass can be worth as much as one friend; but naturally it does not follow from this that several horses and several asses cannot be worth as much as one friend. And this is the same Socrates of whom Plato, in order to characterize his whole inward infinity in relation to his friends, uses so sensuously spiritual an expression as: 'to love young boys according to the love of wisdom' (παιδεραστεῖν μετὰ φιλοσοφίας).[14] And Socrates himself says in the *Symposium* that the only thing he really knows anything about is 'matters of love' (ἐρωτικά). But when in Xenophon (*Mem.* III, 11) we hear Socrates conversing with the ambiguous lady Theodoté, where he boasts of the love potions he possesses for attracting young men to him, we become as disgusted with him as with an old coquette who still believes herself able to charm. Yes, we are more disgusted here because we cannot

* One should compare this with the value which Socrates, in *Republic* VII, places upon geometry and its significance in leading thought away from becoming [*Vordelse*] towards being: 'Then if geometry compels us to view being, it is beneficial; but if becoming, it is not beneficial' (526 E). Cf. Ast's edition of Plato, vol 4, p. 404.[15] But becoming (γένεσις) is manifestly the empirical manifold, and immediately afterward[16] he speaks of astronomy in the same way, and holds that these sciences serve to awaken and purify a faculty of the soul more precious than ten thousand eyes. He therefore censures astronomers as well as musicians for not going beyond the empirical sciences of motion and harmony.

† *Mem.* II, 4; I, 3, 14.

even conceive of the possibility that this Socrates could ever have managed it.[17] —We find the same finite sobriety in relation to the many kinds of pleasure in life; whereas Plato so splendidly attributes to Socrates a kind of divine healthiness rendering him incapable of excess, and instead of depriving bestows upon him the fullest measure of enjoyment.* When in the *Symposium* Alcibiades informs us that he has never seen Socrates intoxicated, the inference is that it was impossible for Socrates to get drunk, just as in this dialogue we see him drink all the others under the table.[18] Xenophon would undoubtedly have explained this away by saying that Socrates never went beyond an experientially proven recipe for *quantum satis*.[19] Hence it is not the beautiful, harmonious unity of a natural determination and freedom which Xenophon describes in Socrates by the term prudence ($\sigma\omega\phi\rho\sigma\sigma\acute{\upsilon}\nu\eta$), but an ugly composition of cynicism and Philistinism. —His conception of death is equally impoverished, equally small of heart. This appears in Xenophon where Socrates rejoices, now that he shall die, because he will be free from the burdens and infirmities of old age (*Mem.* IV, 8, 8). Admittedly, there are more poetic features to be found in his *Apology* (§3),[20] where Socrates suggests that he had prepared himself for his defence throughout his whole life. But to this it must be added that Socrates, after declaring his intention not to defend himself, is not even then viewed by Xenophon in extraordinary dimensions (as the divine silence of Christ, for example, in the presence of his accusers), but merely as guided—inexplicably, perhaps, to Socrates—by his daimon's solicitude for his posthumous reputation. When Xenophon next informs us (*Mem.* I, 2, 24) that Alcibiades was a very proper person so long as he associated with Socrates and only afterwards became dissipated, we marvel more that he remained so long in Socrates' company than that he afterwards became dissipated. For after leaving such an intellectual Christiansfeldt,[21] a refor-

---

* *Symposium* 220 A: 'Yet at a festival he had no equal in his power of enjoyment; though not willing to drink, he could if compelled beat us all at that,—wonderful to relate! no human being had ever seen Socrates drunk.'

matory of such constricting mediocrity, he must have been fairly consumed with pleasure indeed. In the Xenophontic conception of Socrates, therefore, we have the parodying shadow corresponding to the Idea in its manifold appearance. Instead of the good we have the useful; for the beautiful, the serviceable; for the true, the established [*Bestaaende*]; for the sympathetic, the lucrative; and for harmonious unity, sobriety.

Finally, as regards irony,* we find not the slightest trace of it in Xenophon's Socrates. In its place appears the sophistic. But sophistry is the perpetual life-and-death struggle of knowledge with the phenomenon in the service of egotism, a struggle which can never be brought to a decisive victory because the phenomenon arises again as fast as it falls; and as only that knowledge can triumph, which, like a saving angel, drives out the phenomenon of death and translates it into life,† so sophistry finally sees itself overrun by the infinite hosts of phenomena. The Chladni figure[22] corresponding to this monstrous polygon, the hushed inward infinity of life corresponding throughout all eternity to this noise and clamour, is either the system, or irony as 'infinite absolute negativity'[23], naturally with this difference: the system is infinitely eloquent, irony infinitely silent. Thus even here we see that Xenophon has quite consistently arrived at the reflected image of the Platonic conception.

There is a substantial number of sophisms in the *Memorabilia*,‡ but they not only lack bite (for example the short sentences in *Mem.* III, 13), they lack the infinite elasticity of irony, the

* The ironic dimension to be found in Xenophon is not the hovering of irony happily reposing in itself, but an instrument of good breeding: now encouraging those from whom Socrates really expects something (*Mem.* III, 5, 24), now simply chastizing (*Mem.* III, 6).

† Courage is involved in all knowing, and only the man who has the courage to offer his life shall save it. Everyone else is like Orpheus who wished to descend into the underworld to bring back his wife, but the gods showed him only a phantom[24] of her because they esteemed him to be a sentimental zither player without the courage to offer his life for love.

‡ A whole web of such sophisms is to be found in *Mem.* IV, 2, especially §22.

secret trap door* through which one is suddenly hurled down-ward, not like the schoolmaster in *The Elfs*[25] who falls a thousand fathoms, but into the infinite nothingness of irony. His sophisms, on the other hand, are equally distant from ever approximating an intuitive view. I shall cite as an example the conversation with Hippias (*Mem.* IV, 4). Here, too, it is apparent how Socrates only pursues a question to a certain point, without allowing it to answer itself in an intuitive view.[26] After justice has been determined as identical with the lawful, and after all doubt concerning the lawful (with reference to the fact that laws change, cf. §14) appears to have been pacified by observing what men everywhere have recognized as lawful (the law of God), Xenophon is left holding particular examples in which the very consistency of vice is most obvious. Similarly with the example cited in §24 concerning ingratitude, wherein the thought must have been connected with the pre-established harmony pervading existence, the observation clings to the mere externality that the ingrate loses friends, etc., and never swings itself up into that more perfect order of things where there is no change or shadow of variation,[27] where vengeance is exacted without being diverted by the finite. For so long as we content ourselves with watching the external, it is possible to believe that the ingrate, for example, will never be over-taken by a limping justice.

I am now finished with my conception of Socrates such as it appears from Xenophon's peepshow. In conclusion, I would only ask the reader, insofar as he has been bored, not to place the blame on me alone.

---

* A tolerable exception is *Mem.* IV, 4, 6: ' "Still the same old senti-ments, Socrates, that I heard from you so long ago?" "Yes, Hippias," he replied, "always the same, and—what is more astonishing—on the same topics too! You are so learned that I dare say you never say the same thing on the same subjects." ' It is well known, however, that the same question by Polus[28] and the same answer by Socrates appear in the *Gorgias*,[29] and it cannot be denied that the phrase added by Xenophon, 'are so learned', does not render the irony more profound but only more playful.

PLATO

Throughout the foregoing the reader has undoubtedly stolen many a glance at the world which will now be the object of investigation. This we do not deny. It has its cause, however, partly in the eye itself, which after staring so long at one colour involuntarily develops its contrary; partly in my own somewhat youthful, perhaps, infatuation with Plato; and partly in Xenophon himself, who would have been an unpleasant companion were it not for those fissures in his account which Plato fits and fills so naturally that one is compelled to see Plato in Xenophon *eminus et quasi per transennas*.[1] In truth, this longing was in my soul, and it most assuredly did not diminish during my study of Xenophon. Dear reader![2] allow me but one sentence, one innocent parenthesis in order to express my gratitude for the solace I found in reading Plato. For where is one to find solace if not in that infinite calm wherein the Idea, during the stillness of the night, silently, gracefully, yet so mightily unfolds itself in the rhythm of the dialogue as if nothing else in the world existed, where each measured step is repeated slowly, solemnly, because the Ideas know, as it were, that there is time and playground enough for them all; and when should one have need of repose if not in our time when Ideas precipitate each other with insane haste, when they merely suggest their existence [*Tilværelse*] deep down in the soul by a bubble on the surface of the deep, when Ideas never blossom but are consumed as tender shoots, when they barely poke their heads into existence [*Tilværelse*] and immediately die of sorrow, like the child Abraham a Sancta Clara[3] tells about, who, at the very instant it was born, was filled with so much anxiety for the world that it fled back into its mother's womb.[4]

Introductory remarks

As a system has the apparent possibility of allowing every moment to become a point of departure, though this possibility never becomes actual because each moment is essentially determined from within, borne and sustained by the system's own conscience;* so actually every view, and especially a religious view, has a definite external point of departure, a positive, which exhibits itself as the higher causality in relation to the particular, as the *Ursprüngliche* in relation to the derivative. The individual ever aspires from the report and through the report to pass back to that contemplative repose which only personality can give, to that trustful surrender which is the mysterious reciprocity of personality and sympathy.[5] It must be borne in mind, however, that such a primitive personality, its *status absolutus*[6] in contrast to the *status constructus* of the species, is only given and can only be given once. On the other hand, one must not overlook the fact that the analogy corresponding to this, history's repeated approach[7] to this infinite leap, also has its truth. Now it was such a personality as this, such an immediate vehicle of the divine that Plato perceived in Socrates. Such an original personality's effect on and relation to the species fulfils itself partly through a dispensation of life and spirit (as when Christ breathed on the disciples[8] and said: receive the Holy Ghost), and partly through an emancipation of the latent powers of the individual (as when Christ said to the man afflicted with palsy:[9] stand up and walk); or to be more precise, it fulfils itself through both at the same time. The analogy corresponding to this also may be twofold: either positive, i.e. fructifying, or negative, i.e. assisting the individual paralyzed and weakened in himself to regain his original resiliency, protectively and attentively allowing the individual thus strengthened to come to himself.†

*Every particular moment has a different meaning within the system than it has outside the system; it has, so to speak, *aliud in lingua promptum, aliud pectore clausum.*[10]

† It will not be denied that this relationship to personality is also a state of love, that it even calls to mind that species of love which Plato everywhere attributes to Socrates: 'pederasty'—naturally with reference to the initial awakening of youth from the slumber of childhood and the coming to self that ensues—and that it provides a not unfortunate hint of that partiality with which Socrates apprehended and even delighted in the little shortcomings of his disciples. Hence we read in the *Symposium* 181 D:

For the secondary individual the relationship to such a personality in both analogies is not merely impelling but dating;[11] indeed, it becomes for such an individual an inexplicable fountainhead to an everlasting life.[12] We might say: either it is the word that creates the individual, or he is begotten and engendered by silence. The reason I have adduced these two analogies is at this moment, perhaps, not clear to the reader, but I hope it will subsequently become so. That Plato has seen the unity of these two moments in Socrates, or rather, illustrated their unity in Socrates, cannot be denied. But it is no less obvious that there is another conception which has seen in the fact that Socrates' mother, Phaenarete, was a midwife,[13] a definitive image of his activity as a deliverer, that is, another conception which has emphasized the second side of the analogy.[14]

But what is the relationship between the Platonic Socrates and the actual Socrates? This is a question which cannot be dismissed. Socrates completely pervades the fruitful domain of the Platonic philosophy, in fact, he is omnipresent in Plato. How much this grateful disciple believed he was indebted to Socrates, or rather, how much this infatuated youth in his enthusiasm actually wanted to be beholden to Socrates—since nothing was dear to Plato if it did not come from Socrates, or unless Socrates was at least a partner and collaborator in these cognitive love secrets, for when one is of a like mind there arises a self-expression not constricted by the limit of the 'other' but expanded until it attains supernatural dimension in the conception of the 'other', since thought only understands itself, only loves itself when assimilated into the essence of the 'other', and for beings so harmoniously disposed towards each other it is not only irrelevant but impossible to decide what belongs to each, since the one constantly has nothing because he possesses everything in the 'other'—all this will not be pursued any further here. As Socrates so beautifully binds

'For they love not boys, but intelligent beings whose reason is beginning to be developed, much about the time at which their beards begin to grow.'

mankind firmly to the divine by showing that all knowledge is recollection,[15] so Plato feels himself indissolubly fused with Socrates in a unity of spirit so that all knowledge is for him compresent with Socrates. It is obvious that the need of Plato to hear his own commitments on the lips of Socrates must have become even greater after Socrates' death, that he had to return transfigured from the grave for an even more intimate association with Plato, and that the confusion between mine and thine must now have become greater. For no matter how much he humbled himself, or how unworthy he regarded himself to add anything to the image of Socrates, it was nevertheless impossible for Plato not to confuse the poetic image with historical actuality. —After this general consideration it seems appropriate to recall the fact that even in antiquity men were aware of this problem concerning the relation between the actual and the poetic Socrates in Plato's representation. The division of the dialogues reported by Diogenes Laertius[16] into two groups, narrative and dramatic, represents one mode of solution. The narrative dialogues, therefore, should be those most concerned with the historical conception of Socrates. To this group belong the *Symposium* and the *Phædo*, and according to the sound observation of Baur in the above-mentioned work[17] even their external form suggests their significance in this regard. He writes (p. 122): 'In the first species of dialogues, the narrative ones, the true dialogue furnishes only a narrative, as in the *Symposium* Plato places the entire story in the mouth of Apollodorus, while in the *Phædo* he has Phaedo relate to Echecrates and others what Socrates had said to his friends during his last days and all that had transpired. Thus by their external form they seem to suggest that they possess a more historical character.'

It is impossible for me to decide, however, whether the historical element in their form relates merely to the scenic apparatus, and the opposition to the dramatic dialogues lies in the fact that the dramatic element in these (what Baur calls: *die äussere Handlung*) is Plato's free creation, or whether the opposition lies in the fact that the essential content of the narrative dialogues is Socrates' own thoughts, while in the dramatic dialogues it is the views of Plato transferred to Socrates.[18] Once again I must both subscribe to and inscribe the sound observation of Baur: 'Although Plato gave these dialogues precisely this form with regard to this historical basis, still, nothing may be concluded from this as to the historical character of the whole.' With this we approach the important problem of what in the Platonic philosophy belongs to Socrates and what to Plato, a question which we can scarcely refuse however distressing it may be to separate two so intimately united. Here I must complain that Baur has left me in the lurch, for after having shown how Plato necessarily subscribed partly to folk-consciousness (this is the significance of the mythical for Baur), partly to the personality of Socrates as the positive point of departure, he then ends the whole discussion with the observation that the essential significance of Socrates was method.* As method in Plato is still not seen in its absolutely necessary relation to the Idea, the question inevitably arises: how did Socrates relate to the method of Plato?

Hence it is essential to say something about method in Plato. Surely everyone feels that the dialogue did not become the dominant form in Plato merely by accident, surely this must have a reason. Here it will not be possible to investigate the relation between a dichotomy as found in Plato, and a trichotomy as required by the more modern and in a strict sense speculative development.[19] (I shall say something about this when I discuss the relation between the dialectical and mythical elements[20]—a dichotomy in Plato's earlier dialogues.) Although I indicated the necessity of a dichotomy for Hellenism, and in this way acknowledged its relative validity, I shall nevertheless not have time to exhibit its relation to the absolute method. The dialogue tempered and disciplined by Socrates is an attempt to allow thought to appear in all its objectivity, to be sure, but the unity of successive conception and intuition, which only the dialectical trilogy makes possible, is naturally lacking.[21] The method properly consists in simplifying the multitudinous combinations of life by reducing them to an

* As it would be too lengthy to quote Baur, I shall refer the reader to the section beginning on p. 90 and ask him to read pp. 90, 91, and 98.

always more and more abstract abbreviation. As Socrates begins most of his investigations not at the centre but at the periphery, at the variegated manifold of life so infinitely entangled in itself; so, assuredly, a high degree of art is required to develop not only the dialogue, but also the abstract complexities of life together with the complications of the Sophists as well. The art we are here describing is the famous Socratic art of asking questions,* or, to recall the necessity of dialogue for the Platonic philosophy, the art of conversing. It is in this connection that Socrates so often and with so much irony lectures the Sophists[22] for understanding how to discourse but not how to converse. What he desires to censure by contrasting discoursing with conversing is the egotistical quality in eloquence that longs for what must be called abstract beauty, *versus inopes rerum nugaeque canorae*,[23] and which sees in the expression itself, torn loose from its relation to an Idea, an object for pious veneration. In conversation, on the other hand, the speaker is compelled to hold fast to the object,† that

* The opposite of this is the alleged Sophistic art of answering questions. Hence they are always greedy to have someone ask them questions so their wisdom can gush forth, and they 'can set all sails before a sweeping wind and fly out upon the ocean of truth where one loses all sight of land'.[24] As an example I might cite the beginning of the *Gorgias* where both Gorgias and especially Polus are as excited as cows that have not been milked on time.

† Cf. *Symposium* 201 c: 'I cannot refute you, Socrates, said Agathon:— Let us assume that what you say is true. Say rather, beloved Agathon, that you cannot refute the truth; for Socrates is easily refuted.' Cf. *Protagoras* 331 c: 'But what matter? if you please I please; and let us assume, if you will, that justice is holy, and that holiness is just. Pardon me, I replied; I do not want this "if you wish" or "if you will" sort of conclusion to be proven, but I want you and me to be proven: I mean to say that the conclusion will be best proven if there be no "if".' *Protagoras* 334 c: 'When he had given this answer, the company cheered him. And I said: Protagoras, I have a wretched memory, and when any one makes a long speech to me I never remember what he is talking about. As when, if I had been deaf, and you were going to converse with me, you would have had to raise your voice; so now, having such a bad memory, I will ask you to cut your answers shorter, if you would take me with you.' Cf. *Gorgias* 454 c: 'Yet I would not have you wonder if by-and-by I am found

is, if the conversation is not to become the same as singing an eccentric antiphony where everyone sings his part without heed to the other, and which has only the show of conversation so long as they refrain from talking all at once. This concentricity of the conversation is expressed even more distinctly inasmuch as the conversation is conceived under the form of question and answer.[25] Hence we must inquire further into what it means to ask questions.

---

repeating a seemingly plain question; for I ask not in order to confute you, but as I was saying that the argument may proceed consecutively, and that we may not get the habit of anticipating and suspecting the meaning of one another's words; I would have you develop your own views in your own way, whatever may be your hypothesis.'—Accordingly, there is this tenacity in maintaining and pursuing the object which permits nothing to distract it. Cf. *Gorgias* 473 D: 'There again, noble Polus, you are raising hobgoblins instead of refuting me; just now you were calling witnesses against me.' And a little later on Socrates says: 'Do you laugh, Polus? Well, this is a new kind of refutation,—when anyone says anything, instead of refuting him to laugh at him.'—No attention is paid, therefore, to whether several are of the same opinion or not, but only to whose opinion is correct. Polus appeals to the fact that the present company agrees with him and challenges Socrates to ask them. *Gorgias* 474 A: 'O Polus, I am not a public man, and only last year, when my tribe were serving as Prytanes, and it became my duty as their president to take the votes, there was a laugh at me, because I was unable to take them. And as I failed then, you must not ask me to count the suffrages of the company now; . . . for I shall produce one witness only of the truth of my words, and he is the person with whom I am arguing; his suffrage I know how to take; but with the many I have nothing to do, and do not even address myself to them.'—(In opposition to this Socratic seriousness, which binds itself to its object as vigilantly and attentively as a warden to his prisoner, we find him one single time pursuing the slight internal quarrels and reconciliations of the conversation, together with the erotic element entailed in this. And for this Phaedrus reproaches him. *Symposium* 194 D: 'Here Phaedrus interrupted them, saying: Do not answer him, my dear Agathon; for if he can only get a partner with whom he can talk, especially a good-looking one, he will no longer care about the completion of our plan.'—Now the conversation of lovers is usually the direct opposite of an actual conversation about something, for it is as edifying to the lovers as it is nonsense to a third party). Hence in the *Phaedrus* Socrates advises in Eulenspiegelian

To ask a question signifies in part the relation of the individual to the object, in part the relation of the individual to another individual. —In the first case, an attempt is made to emancipate the phenomenon from every finite relation to the subject. When I ask a question I know nothing and dispose myself receptively toward the object. In this sense the Socratic questioning bears a distant yet unambiguous analogy to the negative[26] in Hegel, except that with Hegel the negative is a necessary moment within thought itself, an internal determination, whereas with Plato the negative is exhibited outside the object in the individual asking the question. With Hegel it is not necessary to question thought from without, for it questions and answers itself in itself. With Plato, on the other hand, thought answers only insofar as it is questioned, but whether or not it is questioned is accidental, and how it is questioned no less accidental. But while the form of questioning should emancipate thought from every merely subjective determination, in another sense it is wholly dominated by the subjective so long as the person asking the question is regarded as only accidentally related to what he examines. If, on the other hand, to ask a question is regarded as entailing a necessary relation to an object, then to question becomes identical with answering. As Lessing[27] has so wittily distinguished between replying to a question and answering one, so there is a similar difference underlying the proposed distinction between questioning and examining. The true relationship is of course that between examining and answering.* There is, to be sure, something subjective still always remaining, but if it be borne in mind that the reason the individual asks this or

---

fashion (237 c): 'All good counsel begins in the same way; a man should know what he is advising about, or his counsel will all come to nought'—which comes to pretty much the same thing as when Eulenspiegel gave the tailors the important bit of advice that they ought to tie a knot in the thread so as not to lose the first stitch.[28]

* The identity between them is appropriately expressed in German, where the word for drawing someone out is *aushorchen*.

that question is not due to his arbitrariness* but to the object, to the necessary relationship that functions as a copula in joining them together, then this too will disappear. —In the second case, the object is what is at issue [*Mellemværende*] between the questioner and answerer, and the development of thought actualizes itself in an alternating (*alterno pede*) gait,[29] a hobbling from side to side. Naturally, this is a species of dialectical movement, but as the moment of unity is lacking, since every answer contains the possibility of a new question, so it is not the true dialectical evolution. This significance of questioning and answering is identical with the significance of the dialogue, which in turn is symbolic of the Hellenic conception of the relation between man and the deity. Although this relationship has reciprocity, it contains no moment of unity (neither the immediate or the higher).[30] Moreover, the true moment of duality is essentially lacking, since the relationship exhausts itself in mere reciprocity: like a *pronomen reciprocum*[31] it has no nominative but only the *casus obliqui*,[32] and that only in the dual and plural forms. —If this discussion has proceeded correctly, it will be seen that the purpose of asking a question may be twofold. One may ask a question for the purpose of obtaining an answer containing the desired content, so that the more one questions, the deeper and more meaningful becomes the answer; or one may ask a question, not in the interest of obtaining an answer, but to suck out the apparent content with a question and leave only an emptiness remaining. The first method naturally presupposes a content, the second an emptiness; the first is the speculative, the second the ironic. Now it was the latter method which was especially practised by Socrates. When the Sophists had beclouded themselves and an auspicious company in the fog of their own eloquence,† it was a pleasure for Socrates—always in the most

* As a divining rod mysteriously corresponds to water concealed beneath the surface of the ground, and divines only when water is there.

† Cf. *Gorgias* 461 E: *Soc.* I beg of you, Polus,[33] 'that you spare us the lengthy speeches which you indulged in at first. *Pol.* What! do you mean that I may not use as many words as I please? *Soc.* Only to think, my friend, that having come on a visit to Athens, which is the most free-

polite and modest way imaginable—to introduce a slight bit of a draught* that quickly dispelled all these poetic vapours. These two methods have a close similarity to each other, especially for an observation which considers only the moment. Indeed, this similarity becomes even more pronounced in light of the fact that this Socratic questioning was essentially directed against the knowing subject, and attempted to show that from first to last they knew nothing at all. Every philosophy which begins with a presupposition naturally ends with the same presupposition. As the philosophy of Socrates began with the presupposition that he knew nothing, so it ended with mankind in general knowing nothing. The Platonic philosophy, on the other hand, began with the immediate unity of thought and being and persisted in this. The same tendency that asserted itself in Idealism as reflection on reflection also made itself felt in the questioning of Socrates. To question, i.e. the abstract relationship between the subjective and objective, became at last his chief concern. I shall endeavour to elucidate what I have in mind by examining more fully a statement of Socrates in Plato's *Apology*. In general, the entire *Apology* is admirably suited for obtaining a clear concept of this ironic

---

spoken state in Hellas, you when you got there, and you alone, should be deprived of the power of speech.'

* Cf. *Protagoras* 328 E and 329 B: 'Yet I have one very small difficulty which I am sure that Protagoras will easily explain . . .' But it is precisely this 'very small difficulty' on which everything depends.—Or, to take another example from the *Apology* 17 A: 'I do not know what impression my accusers have made upon you, Athenians. But I do know that they nearly made me forget who I was, so persuasive were they.' And again in the *Symposium* against Agathon (198 B): 'Why, my dear friend, said Socrates, must not I or any one be in a strait who has to speak after he has heard such a rich and varied discourse? It culminated in the beautiful diction and style of the concluding words—who could listen to them without amazement? . . . (198 D): For in my simplicity I imagined that the substance of praise should be truth. . . . Whereas I now see that the intention was to attribute to Eros every species of greatness and glory, whether belonging to him or not, without regard to truth or falsehood.' Cf. *Protagoras* 339 E and 340 A.

activity of Socrates.* In connection with Meletus' first accusation that he was a blasphemer, Socrates discusses the celebrated pronouncement of the Delphic oracle which had affirmed him to be the wisest of men. He relates how this saying at first puzzled him, and how in order to ascertain whether the oracle had spoken truly he inquired of one of the most celebrated wise men. Although this man was a statesman, Socrates soon discovered that he was ignorant. He next inquired of one of the poets, but when he requested a more complete explanation of his own poems he discovered the man knew nothing about them. (Here he points out that the poem must be regarded as due to a divine inspiration, of which the poet understands as little as do prophets and diviners of the beautiful things they talk about.) Finally, he inquired of the artisans and found that while they definitely knew something, they were afflicted with the delusion that they knew other things as well, and hence were subject to the same condition as the others. In short, Socrates relates how he has traversed the entire kingdom of intelligence and discovered the whole realm to be bounded by an Oceanus[34] of illusory knowledge. We see how thoroughly he has conceived his task, how he has conducted experiments with every intelligent power. He finds this confirmed by the fact that his three accusers represent the three great powers whose advancement in personality he has exposed as nothingness. Meletus appears on behalf of the poets, Anytus on behalf of the statesmen and artisans, and Lycon for the orators. Indeed, he conceives[35] it as his divine call, his mission, to go about among countrymen and strangers,

* The whole *Apology* when taken in its entirety is clearly an ironic work, since the several accusations reduce themselves to nothingness—not in the usual sense, but a nothingness which Socrates gives out as the content of his life, and which in turn is irony. The same may be seen from his proposal[36] that he be maintained in the prytaneum, or be fined, but most of all from the fact that the dialogue actually contains no defence at all. Instead, he uses the occasion to get the best of his accusers, and to have himself a friendly chat[37] with his judges. Consistent with this is the well-known story[38] of how he received a defence oration written for him by Lysias, but declared he felt no occasion to use it, although it was unquestionably a fine speech.

and when he hears that someone is wise and it turns out that he is not wise, then to come to the aid of the god and prove that he is not wise.* This is the reason he has had no time† to accomplish anything of importance either in public or private affairs, but on account of this service to the god he is destitute in every way. Socrates, to return to the passage under discussion, mentions how pleasant it will be after death to associate with the great men who have lived before him and shared a similar fate, and then adds: 'And, above all, I could spend my time in examining those who are there, as I examine men here, and in finding out which of them is wise, and which

---

* He includes everyone in this labour of refutation, especially his countrymen: 'This I shall do to everyone whom I meet, young and old, citizen or stranger, but especially to citizens, since they are more closely related to me. This, you must recognize, the god has commanded me to do.' Cf. *Apology* 30 A. He relates that many have attached themselves to him, since it is not uninteresting to see people who imagine they know something become convinced that they know nothing. 'And, as I have said, the god has commanded me to examine men, in oracles and in dreams and in every way in which the divine will was ever declared to man.' Cf. *Apology* 33 C.

† By contrast, let me ask the reader to recall Xenophon's account, where Socrates is fairly consumed by his efforts to bring up his disciples to be good citizens. In the *Apology* of Plato, however, Socrates stresses the significance of being a private person, a fact thoroughly harmonious with Socrates' otherwise negative relation to life. Now to be a private person in Hellas meant something quite different from what it means to live as an ordinary person nowadays. In Hellenism every particular individual had his life bounded and borne by the life of the state in a far deeper sense than in our time. Thus Callicles (in the *Gorgias*) censures Socrates for continuing to devote himself to philosophy, for Callicles holds that philosophizing is like stammering, i.e., a thing forgivable only in children, whereas an adult who persists in philosophizing ought to be punished. 'For, as I was saying, such a one, even though he have good natural parts, becomes effeminate. He flies from the busy centre and the market place, in which, as the poet says, men become distinguished; he creeps into a corner for the rest of his life, and talks in a whisper with three or four admiring youths, but never speaks out like a freeman in a satisfactory manner.' Cf. 485 D. —I scarcely need remind the attentive reader how much this lecture of Callicles resembles the scientific moderation endorsed by the Xenophontic Socrates.

of them thinks himself wise when he is not wise' (41 B). Here we come to a point that is decisive. One cannot deny that Socrates becomes almost ludicrous with this zeal for spying on men, a zeal which allows him no peace even after death. And who can refrain from smiling when he visualizes those sombre shades of the underworld with Socrates in their midst indefatigably engaged in examining them and showing them that they know nothing. It might seem, however, that Socrates meant that some of them were wise, perhaps, for he says he will discover which of them is wise and which of them thinks he is wise but is not. However, one must bear in mind that this wisdom is neither more nor less than the above-mentioned ignorance,* and also that he says he will examine them there the same as here, which seems to suggest that the great men there will presumably fare no better under this *tentamen rigorosum*[39] than did the great men here in life. Here we have irony in all its divine infinity, which allows nothing to endure [*bestaae*]. Socrates, like Samson,[40] seizes the columns bearing the edifice of knowledge and plunges everything down into the nothingness of ignorance. That this is authentically Socratic will certainly be admitted by all—Platonic, on the other hand, it will never be. I have, therefore, arrived at one of those duplicities in Plato indicating precisely the course I shall follow in order to discover the purely Socratic.

The above-mentioned distinction between questioning in order to discover content and questioning in order to disappoint and humiliate, also exhibits itself in a more determinate form as the relationship between the abstract and the mythical in Plato's dialogues.

In order to elucidate this further, I shall examine in some detail a few of the dialogues in order to show how the abstract

---

* Insofar as there might still be some question of a knowledge of something other than this ignorance, a faint trace or fleeting hint of a positive knowledge, then Socrates himself says in the *Symposium* 175 E: 'My own wisdom is of a very mean and questionable sort, no better than a dream,'—and in the *Apology* interprets the pronouncement of the Delphic oracle as: 'Human wisdom is worth little or nothing.' Cf. *Apology* 23 A.

may culminate in irony, and how the mythical may betoken a more fulsome speculation.

The Abstract in the early Platonic Dialogues culminates in Irony

Symposium

The *Symposium* and *Phædo* afford turning points in the conception of Socrates, since, as is so often remarked, the one depicts the philosopher in life, the other in death. In the *Symposium* are also the two genres of representation described above, the dialectical and mythical. The mythical begins when Socrates steps aside and introduces the Mantineian seer Diotima[1] in the role of speaker. Socrates, to be sure, remarks[2] at the end that he was convinced by her tale and is now seeking to persuade others, in other words, he makes us uncertain whether this tale, though acquired at second hand, is not really his own. Yet no conclusion may be drawn from this concerning the historical relation of the mythical to Socrates. There is another way in which this dialogue attempts to realize full knowledge, namely, the abstractedly conceived Eros is finally illustrated in the person of Socrates by the discourse[3] of the drunken Alcibiades, but naturally this discourse can provide us with no further enlightenment concerning the question of the Socratic dialectic. We shall now examine more closely the dialectical development in this dialogue. Everyone who has read the dialogue with but slight attention will certainly agree with our previous remark that the method consists in 'simplifying the multitudinous combinations of life by reducing them to an always more and more abstract abbreviation.'[4] The final representation of the nature of Eros can hardly be said to inhale what the preceding discussion exhaled; instead, the reflection elevates itself always higher and higher above the atmospheric air in a continuous ascent, until breathing almost ceases in the pure ether of the abstract. The preceding discourses are not to be viewed as moments in the final conception, but as an earthly ballast from which thought must become increasingly free. Although the various discourses do not have a necessary relation to the final discourse, they do have a mutual relation to each other, inasmuch as they are discourses about love deriving from the heterogeneous viewpoints given in life, viewpoints from which the speakers, like allies, everywhere encompass the domain constituting the proper essence of love. According to the Socratic conception, however, the essence of love as abstract shows itself to be as invisible as a mathematical point, without this point in turn reflecting the various relative and distorted conceptions. All these discourses are therefore like sections in a telescope with the one account terminating ingeniously in the next, all the while bubbling forth so lyrically that it is like drinking wine in artistically cut crystals, since it is not merely the sparkling wine that is so intoxicating but also the infinite refraction, the pool of light that presents itself when looking down into them. Although the relationship between the dialectical and the mythical is not so strongly pronounced in the *Symposium* as in the *Phædo*, for example, and hence is less serviceable to my undertaking in this respect, it nevertheless has the advantage of clearly throwing into relief what Socrates himself says and what he has heard from Diotima.

Phædrus begins. He portrays the eternal in Eros. Eros triumphs over time as characterized by the fact that he has no parents. He triumphs—with the help of that rapturous blush of modesty—not merely over man and his pettiness, but over death as well, and so brings back his beloved from the underworld, being rewarded by the gods who are themselves deeply moved by all this. Pausanias focuses his gaze on the dual nature in Eros, yet not so that this duality is apprehended in a negative unity as in Diotima's account, where Eros is a son of Poros and Penia. The one love is the motherless daughter of Uranus, the heavenly; the other love is much younger, has as its basis the difference between the sexes, and is the common. He then discusses the significance of that species of heavenly pederasty which loves the spiritual in man and is not degraded or debased by the sexual. As it happens that Aristophanes has got the hiccoughs, he declares that the physician Eryxi-

machus must either cure him or speak in his place. Eryximachus begins. He returns to the point made by Pausanias,
with which he also agrees, but grasps the duality present in
love from quite a different aspect. Whereas Pausanias got no
further than two species of love whose disparity he attempted
to describe, Eryximachus apprehends the matter as two factors
present in every moment of love, and goes on to exemplify
this especially in nature considered from the standpoint of
medical science. Thus love is the unity in hostile elements,
and as Asclepius understood how to infuse love into the most
contrary elements (warm and cold, bitter and sweet, dry and
wet), so he became the founder of the medical art. The same
repeats itself throughout all nature, for even seasons and
climates, etc., depend on these manifestations of love. The
same is true of sacrifices and whatever pertains to divination,
for this constitutes the art of communion between gods and
men. His whole discourse resembles a kind of phantasy on
physics.* After Aristophanes had got rid of his hiccoughs
(in this connection he suggests quite a different relation of
opposition than previously described by the physician, for he
is relieved of his hiccoughs through sneezing), he takes his turn
and establishes the opposition present in love more deeply than
any of the preceding speakers, illustrating it through the opposition between the sexes and the corresponding halving of mankind by the gods. Indeed, he even suggests there is a possibility
that the gods might have it in their heads to slice up men still
further should they not be content to be what they are: the

* There is still some confusion in the discourse of Eryximachus. He
overlooks, on the one hand, the necessity of an immediate moment of
unity, the bonds of unity encompassing the duplicity, and this in spite of
the fact that he cites[5] the words of Heraclitus: like the strings of a lyre or
bow, whatever is at war with itself is at peace with itself. On the other
hand, the divided Eros still exists for him exactly as it did for Pausanias,
as something external, an external division, and not as the reflex of a
duplicity residing in love and proceeding necessarily from love. Hence
love is now the relation of opposites itself, now a kind of personal relation
to opposites, now a vacuous *prius*[6] outside the relation of opposition, now
something over against the opposites. In short, his account is a mixture
of traditional elements and nature poetry.[7]

half part of a human being, 'for like bisected flatfish, we have become two out of one.'⁸ He next gives his wit free reign to portray the original indifference between the sexes together with the condition of mankind in this state, and also when, with deep irony, he apprehends the negative in love, the longing for union. And throughout this Aristophanic interpretation one involuntarily comes to think of the gods who, presumably, have had priceless fun watching these half men, in endless confusion among themselves, seeking to become whole human beings. After Aristophanes the tragedian Agathon speaks. His discourse is more ordered. He calls attention to the fact that the others have not been praising the god so much as they have been congratulating mankind made happy by the goods the god bestows, while the nature of him who bestows these goods has not yet been mentioned. Agathon will therefore show what the god himself is, and what are the goods he bestows upon others. The whole discourse is an ode to Eros. He is the youngest of the gods (for he is ever young and in the company of youth); he is the most delicate of the gods (for he dwells in the tenderest place: in the hearts and souls of gods and men, and departs from every insensitive nature); his complexion is the fairest of all (for he dwells constantly among flowers); etc., etc. He has granted to mankind the mastery of every art and craft, and only those inspired by Eros shall have fame.

As it would lead us too far afield to enter into a more exhaustive investigation of the relation between these various discourses, I shall now turn to the last speaker, namely, Socrates. In his simplicity he had imagined that one ought to set forth the truth about any object one would praise. So much was essential, but then one ought to select those things which were most beautiful and set them forth in the best manner: 'Whereas I now see that in order to pay a goodly tribute of praise to anything, you must attribute to it every species of greatness and glory without regard to truth or falsehood—that doesn't matter. It looks as if the original proposal was not that each of us should really praise Eros, but only that we should appear to praise him' (198 D). As usual Socrates now goes to work with his questions. He begins with one of those authentic, Socratic, blood-sucking questions: whether Eros according to its nature is the love of something or of nothing. Inasmuch as love desires that which is its object, surely it cannot possess it but must be in need of it. This must be so even when such a need is apprehended as identical with a desire for continued possession in the future, for one still desires what one does not have when one desires to keep in the future what one already has. Thus love is the lack of and desire for what one has not. Moreover, as love is the love of the beautiful, so Eros must lack beauty and does not possess it. And as the good is also the beautiful, Eros lacks the good as well. The same applies to all Ideas. Hence we see how Socrates gets at the nut not by peeling off the shell but by hollowing out the kernel. This concludes the discourse of Socrates, for the subsequent account is merely a report. Should the reader not yet have seen what I wish him to see, I hope that he and I will both succeed if he continues to lend me his attention.

Socrates introduced his discourse with a little irony, but this, if I may say so, was merely an ironic figure of speech; and if he were distinguished merely for the dexterity with which he spoke ironically, just as some can speak jargon,[9] then he would surely not deserve to be called an ironist. The preceding speakers had said a great deal about love, much of which was certainly irrelevant; yet the assumption remained that there was still much to be said about love. Socrates now proceeds to tell them. Look here, love is desire, love is the absence of something, etc. But desire, the absence of something, etc., is nothingness. Here we see his method. Love is emancipated more and more from the accidental concretion in which it appeared in the preceding discourses and reduced to its most abstract determination. It exhibits itself not as the love of this or that, for this or that, but as the love of something which it has not, i.e., as desire, longing. In a certain sense this is quite true, yet love is also the infinite love. When we say that God is love, we mean that he is the infinitely self-communicating. When we speak of abiding in love, we are speaking of participation in a fullness. This is the substantial aspect in love. Desire, longing, on the other hand, is the negative aspect of love, that is to say, the immanent negativity. Desire, want, longing, etc., represent the infinite subjectivizing of love[10]—to use an Hegelian expression suggesting what must be borne in mind. This determination is also the most abstract, or, more correctly, it is the abstract itself, not in the ontological sense but in the sense of lacking content.[11] One may either conceive the abstract as constitutive of everything, pursue it in its own silent movements and allow it to determine itself toward the concrete and unfold itself in this; or one may proceed from the concrete and, with the abstract in mind, locate it in and out of the concrete. But neither of these alternatives is the case with Socrates. It is not back to the categories that he recalls the affair. His abstract is a designation utterly void of content. He proceeds from the concrete and arrives at the most abstract, and where the inquiry should begin, there he stops. The result arrived at is actually the indeterminate determination of pure being: *love is*; for to add: it is *longing, desire*, is no determination at all but merely a relation to something not given. Similarly, one may trace knowledge back to a wholly negative concept by determining it as appropriation, acquisition, for manifestly this is the only relation of knowledge to the known, though it is also possession. Thus as the abstract in the ontological sense has its validity in speculation, so the abstract as the negative has its truth in irony.

Here again we are confronted with a duplicity in Plato: the dialectical development is pursued until it disappears in the purely abstract, whereupon a new genre of discussion begins which will yield up the Idea. As the Idea does not have a necessary relation to the dialectical, however, it seems improbable that the whole evolution belongs to one only. But neither can we arbitrarily attribute one genre to one of them, the other genre to the other, so long as each merely receives something. Socrates and Plato must each have had a view which, however different they may have been, must have had essential points of coincidence. These are the ironical (for the dialectical as such is not constitutive of any view having an essential relation to personality), and the speculative. How far the discussion set forth by Socrates as deriving from Diotima advances the matter, and what significance should be attributed to the dichotomy: love and the beautiful (wherein the negative moment is placed outside and the positive moment is an apathetic and indolent quietism, whereas a trichotomy would at once see them in and with each other, and hence avoiding what happens to Diotima for whom the beautiful once more becomes the beautiful in itself, a pure abstraction, as will subsequently appear)—all this will be treated more fully when I discuss the mythical element in the dialogues.

In the foregoing I alluded to the familiar observation that the *Symposium* attempts to complement the deficiency of the dialectical conception by rendering love intelligible in the person of Socrates, so that the eulogies on love end in a eulogy on Socrates. Although illustration of the Idea through a personality is only a moment in the Idea itself, still, it does have significance as such in the development. The dialectical movement in Plato, no matter how ingeniously it develops, remains foreign to the Idea itself because it is not the Idea's own dialectic. Accordingly, while the rest of the speakers grope for the Idea as if they were playing blind man's buff, the drunken Alcibiades grasps it with immediate certainty. Moreover, the fact that Alcibiades is intoxicated seems to suggest that it was only in a state of intensified immediacy that he felt secure in this love affair, an affair which, when sober, must have occasioned all the anxious though sweet insecurity of uncertainty. If we direct our attention to the nature of the love affair that has arisen between Socrates and Alcibiades, then we must agree with Alcibiades when he relates how Socrates has spurned his love, and adds: 'And he has ill-treated not only me, but Charmides the son of Glaucon, and Euthydemus the son of Diocles, and many others in the same way—beginning as their lover, the deceiver has ended by becoming the beloved' (222 B). Alcibiades is thus unable to tear himself away. He binds himself to Socrates with complete passion: When I hear his voice 'my heart leaps within me more than that of any Corybantian reveller,[12] and my eyes rain tears when I hear him speak' (215 E). It is impossible for other speakers to affect him in this way, and he feels with resentment his grovelling condition, indeed, life seems unbearable in this state. He flees from him as from the voice of the sirens, and stops his ears[13] so as not to become captivated and grow old sitting at his feet. Indeed, he often wishes Socrates were dead, yet he knows that if this happened his pain would be even greater. He is like one bitten by a serpent, yet bitten by something even more painful and in the most painful place: in the heart and soul. Naturally it goes without saying that the love affair existing between Socrates and Alcibiades was intellectual. But if we ask what was there in Socrates that made such a relationship not only possible but necessary (for Alcibiades is correct when he says that he is not the only one bound to Socrates in this way, but almost everyone who associated with him), then I have nothing to reply except that it was Socrates' irony. If their love had consisted of a profitable exchange of ideas, or a rich outpouring on the one side and a grateful reception on the other, then surely they would have had the third [*Tredie*] in which they loved one another, namely, in the Idea. Such a relationship would never have given rise to this kind of passionate turmoil. But as it pertains to the essence of irony never to unmask itself, and since it is equally essential for irony to change masks in Protean fashion,[14] it follows that it must necessarily cause the infatuated youth much pain.* As there is something forbidding about irony, so also it has some extraordinarily seductive and enchanting moments. The disguise and mysteriousness which it entails, the telegraphic communication which it initiates, inasmuch as the ironist must always be understood at a distance, the infinite sympathy it assumes, the elusive and ineffable moment of understanding immediately displaced by the anxiety of misunderstanding—all this captivates with indissoluble bonds. Should the individual feel himself emancipated and enlarged

* The ironist raises the individual out of immediate existence, and this is his emancipating function; but thereafter he lets him hover like the coffin of Mohammed, which, according to legend, is suspended between two magnets—attraction and repulsion.

under the first moment of contact with the ironist, inasmuch as the ironist opens himself to this individual, at the next moment he has fallen into his power. This is probably what Alcibiades means when he relates how they have been deceived by Socrates, that instead of the lover he has become the beloved. Furthermore, as it pertains to the essence of the ironist never to express the Idea as such, but merely to hint at it elusively, to take with one hand what is given with the other, to possess the Idea as his personal property, so naturally the relationship becomes even more exciting. In this way the disease develops within the individual in complete silence, a disease as ironic as any consumption, for it causes the individual to feel best when his dissolution is nearest. The ironist is a vampire who has sucked the blood out of her lover and fanned him with coolness, lulled him to sleep and tormented him with turbulent dreams.

Now it might be asked: what is the point of this discussion? I shall answer that it serves a double purpose. First, it shows that even in Alcibiades' conception of Socrates irony was the essential feature; and secondly, it suggests that the love affair which has come about between Socrates and Alcibiades, together with the information we derive from it concerning the essence of love, are both negative. —In considering the first point we must bear in mind that some have attempted to prove the necessity of much positive content in Socrates by appealing to the enthusiasm with which Alcibiades discusses his relationship to him.* It seems important in this connection to investigate more fully the nature of such an enthusiasm. This enthusiasm seems to be a parallel in the sphere of emotion to what La Rochefoucauld calls *la fièvre de la raison*[15] in the sphere of the understanding. If it were possible for something else to have provoked this enthusiasm in Alcibiades (that it could have been induced by irony has been shown in the foregoing), then it would surely have been suggested in Alcibiades'

---

* By way of anticipation, I shall inform the reader that the same problem recurs in another form when I discuss how far it is necessary to presuppose a positive content in Socrates in order to account for the fact that so many philosophic schools derived from him.

eulogy of Socrates. Let us see. Alcibiades emphasizes the Silenus-like character of Socrates: 'Socrates says that he is ignorant in all things and knows nothing. Is not this appearance like a Silenus? to be sure it is; for with this he has merely clad himself externally like a carved image of the Silenus. But when he is opened, what a fullness of wisdom, dear brothers in drink! do you imagine you would see in him . . . He conceals himself from mankind and always has his fun with them; but when he became serious and opened within, I do not know if anyone has seen the divine images in his soul. I have once seen them, and they appeared so divine, golden, and in every way so beautiful and wondrous, that I decided at once to do whatever Socrates commanded' (216 D, E). In this connection the following should be noted. On the one hand, it is not easy to get an idea of what Alcibiades really means, and to this extent not altogether unfair to suppose that neither has Alcibiades wholly understood his characterization of Socrates. On the other hand, Alcibiades suggests that it was an extremely rare occasion when Socrates opened himself in this manner. And pursuing his description further we see that he uses the expression: 'I have once seen them'. Alcibiades has seen these divine images. Now if one thinks of anything in this connection, one must surely think of the presence of divine personality sustaining the irony. Yet this is to say no more about Socrates than can be said of him as an ironist. Such moments of transfiguration prove at most the presence of a divine fullness obscurely (κατὰ κρύψιν[16]), so that one still may not say it was a positive content inspiring this enthusiasm. Next, if we recall that Socrates' essential element was discourse, conversation, then it seems to be with a kind of emphasis that Alcibiades uses the expression 'to see', as it is also a little strange to hear him say: 'For although I forgot to mention this to you before, his discourses are like the images of Silenus which open' (221 D). This would also seem to suggest that Alcibiades was essentially in love with Socrates' personality: an harmonious natural determination consummating itself in a negative relating of the self to the Idea and an omphalopsychic staring into himself. To be sure, Alcibiades says that when one had seen these discourses opened, they were then the most understandable, the most divine, that they abounded in the fairest images of virtue and had the widest comprehension. But if this had been prominent or even readily apparent in the discourse of Socrates, then the source of all the passionate turmoil, the demonic, in his love becomes inexplicable, since one would sooner have expected that the companionship of Socrates would have served to develop in Alcibiades the incorruptible essence of a more serene spirit. Hence we see that the whole matter ends with Socrates once more employing his irony to bob Alcibiades out upon the billowing deep, for in spite of his exhilaration, his enthusiasm, and his many words, Alcibiades is no closer in his relation to Socrates than he ever was. Indeed, Alcibiades must resign himself to the fact that just as he 'crept under Socrates' cloak with sensual desire[17] and with both arms embraced this divine and truly wonderful man, and lay there all night with Socrates in his arms; but was then spurned, derided, and ridiculed in spite of his beauty, and arose from the couch with Socrates as though he had slept beside a father or elder brother,' so here he finds himself again thrust away by Socrates with the remark that he, Alcibiades, had made his whole speech out of eagerness for Agathon: 'For the whole speech is an attempt to separate Agathon and me, since you think I ought to love no one but you, while Agathon ought not to be loved by anyone but you' (222 D). —Secondly, the information obtained from this discussion of the essence of love as embodied in Socrates should convince us that theory and practice were in complete accord. The love here described is that of irony, but irony is the negative in love, the incitement of love; it is in the sphere of intelligence what bantering and lovers' quarrels are in the sphere of the lesser love. That there is in the ironist, to recall it once more, an *Urgrund*, a hard currency, is indisputable; yet the coin he mints does not itself bear the real value but is a nothingness like paper money; and yet all the ironist's transactions with the world are carried on with this kind of currency. The abundance in him is a natural determination;[18] it is not in him immediately as such, nor is it acquired through reflection. As a high degree of health is entailed in being sick, yet one does not perceive health in any positive content but in the vitality constantly nourishing the disease, so it is with the ironist and the positive fullness in him. It does not unfold itself in a fullness of beauty. Indeed, the ironist even attempts to conceal his lifeline with the atmospheric air which nourishes him.

Before leaving the *Symposium*, however, there is one thing more I wish to say. Baur[19] makes the attractive observation that the *Symposium* ends with Agathon and Aristophanes (the discursive moments) finally becoming intoxicated, while Socrates alone remains sober as the unity of the comic and the tragic. He also calls to mind the analogy which Strauss has drawn, to my mind not a very attractive one, between this conclusion of the *Symposium* and the transfiguration of Christ on the mountain. Insofar as there can be any question of Socrates furnishing the unity of the comic and the tragic, manifestly, this can only be insofar as irony itself is this unity. If one will imagine that Socrates, after all the others had become intoxicated, had subsided into himself as was his wont, then he might by this vacant staring, to which he so often surrendered,[20] provide a plastic image of the abstract unity of the comic and tragic here under discussion. To stare may signify either a contemplative absorption (this most likely would be the Platonic), or to stare signifies what we say: to think about nothing so that 'nothingness' almost becomes visible. Such a higher unity Socrates might possibly provide, but this unity is the abstract and negative unity in nothingness.

Protagoras

I shall next discuss the *Protagoras* in a similar fashion and attempt to show how the entire dialectical movement so prominent in this dialogue ends completely negatively. Before proceeding with this, however, a general observation concerning Plato's dialogues must here find a place, and the correct place I do believe, since the *Protagoras* is the first dialogue to afford such an occasion. If one feels inclined to divide the Platonic dialogues into groups, I believe one is correct in following the distinction made by Schleiermacher[1] between those dialogues in which the dialogical is the essential moment, with an indefatigable irony sometimes resolving and sometimes fettering the dispute and the disputants; and the constructive dialogues which are distinguished by an objective and systematic presentation. Among the latter are the *Republic*, *Timæus*, and *Critias*, and both tradition as well as their own inward character assign them to the last phase of the Platonic development. In these dialogues the form of the question is essentially a vanquished moment with the answerer performing more like a notary public or alderman with his 'yes' and 'amen'. In short, they no longer converse. Accordingly, the irony has also partially disappeared. But if we recall how necessary it was for Socrates to converse, that he constantly offers but one choice: whether he should ask and the other answer, or whether the other should ask and he answer,* then we shall here see an essential difference between Plato and Socrates, regardless

---

* In this connection it should be remarked that by much practice it has become so necessary for Socrates to ask questions that even when he allows Protagoras the same privilege it usually does not last more than two or three exchanges before Socrates employs the interrogative form in his answer, and proceeds once more to ask questions. He insists that the form of the question be properly observed, and that there be no mixture of the oratorical mode of questioning. Thus in the *Gorgias* (466 A-C): '*Pol.* And are the good rhetoricians meanly regarded in states, under the idea that they are flatterers? *Soc.* Is that a question or the beginning of a speech? . . . *Pol.* What! are they not like tyrants? They kill and despoil and exile any one whom they please. *Soc.* By the dog, Polus, I cannot make out at each deliverance of yours, whether you are giving an opinion of your own, or asking a question of me.' —Towards the end of the *Gorgias*[2] where Socrates, after having silenced the Sophists, continues the investigation alone, he does so still in the form of a conversation with himself. In the *Crito* where the laws and the state are personified as discoursing, they say: 'Do not be surprised, Socrates, at our questions;[3] you are in the habit of asking and answering questions' (50 C). And in the *Apology* Socrates conducts his defence in the form of question and answer, even calling attention to this fact (27 A): 'And do you, Meletus, answer; and you, gentlemen, as I asked you in the beginning, please bear in mind not to make a disturbance if I conduct my argument in my accustomed manner.'

of whether Plato consciously apprehended this or merely reproduced it with immediate fidelity. The constructive dialogues will therefore concern me very little, since they contribute nothing to the conception of the personality of Socrates, either as it was in actuality or as imagined by Plato. Surely everyone who knows anything of these dialogues will feel that the personality of the speaker relates so externally to the object that the name 'Socrates' has almost become a *nomen appellativum*[4] merely designating the speaker or lecturer. To this must be added that when the umbilical cord joining the discourse to the speaker is severed, the fact that the dialogical form continues to be employed appears wholly accidental. It is most surprising that Plato, after frowning upon the poetic representation in contrast to the simple narrative in the *Republic*,[5] has not permitted the form of the dialogue to give way to a more rigorous and systematic form.

A great many of these early dialogues end without a result, or as Schleiermacher says, all the dialogues before the *Republic* which treat one or another virtue fail to discover the correct solution. He writes: 'Thus the *Protagoras* considers the question of the unity and teachability of virtue without resolving the concept, while in the *Laches* the discussion is about courage, and in the *Charmides* about prudence. Indeed, as the opposition between friend and enemy also forms a significant moment in the question of justice, we must here also think of the *Lysis*.'[6] The fact that they end without a result admits of being determined still further, namely, that they end with a negative result. The *Protagoras* will serve as an example of this, and also the first book of the *Republic*, which, according to Schleiermacher,[7] likewise ends without a result. All this is of the utmost importance for this investigation, for if there is any possibility of discovering the Socratic in Plato, it must be within the earlier dialogues.

As regards the purpose of the *Protagoras*, whether it is to make a tentative effort towards a definitive solution of those problems contained in the dialogue (the unity of virtue, and the possibility that virtue can be taught), or whether, as Schleiermacher supposes,[8] the purpose resides not in any particular point but is incommensurable with those issues raised in the dialogue, so that, hovering above the whole throughout the successive disappearance of each particular point, the purpose first consummates itself in the emergence of a purified and regenerate illustration of the Socratic method—all this I shall not attempt to decide. Instead, I shall content myself with the observation that I can generally agree with Schleiermacher if the reader will bear in mind that according to my view the method does not consist of a dialectic in the form of the question as such, but in a dialectic proceeding from and returning to irony, a dialectic born of irony. Towards the end of the dialogue, therefore, both Socrates and the Sophist find themselves *vis-à-vis au rien*[9]—as the French only say of one. They stand facing each other like the two bald men who, after a lengthy quarrel, finally found a comb. The main thing for me in this dialogue is naturally its thoroughly ironic design. The fact that it arrives at no decisive solution to the problems it proposes would certainly confirm what Schleiermacher says, namely, that the dialogue ends without a result. But there would certainly be nothing ironic in this, for the fact that the inquiry was broken off at this point might be connected with a mere accident of which it is possible to imagine a whole infinity, or it might be connected with a deep longing to be free from its previously unfruitful labour as after a completed birth. In other words, the dialogue might be conscious of itself as one moment in a much larger investigation. The dialogue in this way would certainly have ended without a result, but this 'without a result' is in no wise identical with a negative result. A negative result always presupposes there is a result,[10] and a negative result in its purest and most undiluted form can only be provided by irony. Whereas even scepticism always posits something, irony, like the old witch, constantly makes the tantalizing attempt first to devour everything in sight, then to devour itself too, or, as in the case of the old witch, her own stomach.

This dialogue is therefore fully conscious of this lack of result. Indeed, it enjoys the whole magic of annihilation with a kind of relish, and gloats not merely over the annihilation of the Sophist. Socrates himself says: 'The result of our discussion appears to me to be singular. For if the argument had a human voice, that voice would be heard laughing at us and saying: "Protagoras and Socrates, you are strange beings" ' (361 A). After the two antagonists, since Protagoras has abandoned his ostentatious discourse, have tried their hand at every kind of wrestler's hold, inasmuch as Socrates first asks and Protagoras answers, then Protagoras asks and Socrates answers, and finally Socrates asks and Protagoras answers, so that, to use as pictorial expression as possible, they have tested each other's salt repeatedly, there occurs the strangest phenomenon, namely, Socrates defends what he had intended to refute, and Protagoras attacks what he had intended to defend. The entire dialogue reminds one of the well-known dispute[11] involving a Catholic and Protestant, which ended with each convincing the other, so that the Catholic became Protestant and the Protestant Catholic*—except that in this case the ludicrous is also assimilated into the ironic consciousness. —One objection might possibly be made which I should now like to consider, and this so much the more since only an attentive reader could make it. It might seem as if it were Plato who applied this ironic lever, and with good-natured playfulness bounced not only Protagoras but also Socrates high into the air. But however amusing it might be to see Socrates in such a mêlée, I must nevertheless refuse such an interpretation on his behalf. It is Socrates who makes the above remark, and surely every sympathetic reader will not fail to

---

* This anecdote yields the other form of an ironic negative result, for here the irony lies in the fact that one arrives at an actual result, but this actual result is wholly personal and as such indifferent to the Idea.[12] Accordingly, it might be conjectured that the neophyte Catholic will in turn have the same converting effect upon the neophyte Protestant as the latter previously had upon him, and so forth. Hence one sees in this the possibility of an infinite dispute in which the disputants are at every moment convinced without either of them at any moment ever having a conviction. Only this correspondence between them remains: at the moment A is Catholic, B becomes Protestant, and at the moment B becomes Catholic, A becomes Protestant. This, of course, is due to the fact that while both constantly change habit, neither of them ever changes *habitus*.[13]

visualize the play of ironic seriousness reflected so ambiguously and discordantly in that ironic smile[14] accompanying his ironic surprise over the fact that the whole contest had acquired this outcome, the amazement with which he watches Protagoras discover what he necessarily knew he must discover, since he himself had hidden it.

So much for the over-all design or form of this dialogue. If we next direct our attention to the content, that is to say, to those problems inserted into this dialogue like *meta*[15] on a race-track, inasmuch as they provide fixed points around which the contestants speed, pressing ever closer and closer to them as they race always faster and faster past one another, then I believe one will find in the whole a similar negative irony.

This is especially the case with the first problem: whether virtue is one. Socrates raises the question whether justice, prudence, piety, etc., are parts of virtue or merely names for one and the same thing. Furthermore, whether they are parts in the same way as the mouth, nose, eyes, and ears are parts of the face, or whether they are like the parts of gold, which differ from each other in nothing internally, nor from the whole, except with regard to largeness and smallness. Without involving myself any further in a detailed discussion of the many sophistries advanced by both sides, I shall only say that Socrates' argumentation essentially aims at reducing the relative dissimilarity among the various virtues in order to preserve the unity of virtue; whereas Protagoras constantly focuses on the qualitative dissimilarity but lacks the bond of unity able to embrace and integrate this rich manifold. The Idea of mediation, therefore, never becomes clear to him, and he stumbles in its twilight when, in order to vindicate the unity, he clings fast to the subjectivized Idea of mediation depending upon the identity of the similar and the dissimilar. In a certain respect, he says, everything resembles everything else. Even white resembles black in a certain way, hardness resembles softness, and similarly with whatever things appear to be most opposed to each other. According to the Socratic conception, on the other hand, the unity of virtue* is like a

* Since it is well known that *opposita juxta se posita magis illucescunt,*[16] I

94

tyrant who lacks the courage to rule over the actual world, and so first massacres all his subjects in order to rule with perfect security over a silent realm of shades. If holiness is not justice, argues Socrates, then to be holy is the same as to be not-just, i.e. unjust, i.e. ungodly. Here the sophistry in Socrates' argumentation is apparent to all. But what I must call particular attention to is the fact that this unity of virtue becomes so abstract, so egotistically terminated in itself, that it becomes the very crag upon which all the individual virtues are stranded and torn asunder like heavily laden vessels. Virtue traverses its own determinations like a whisper, a shiver, without ever becoming audible much less articulate in any one of them. It is like imagining an infinitely long row of soldiers, wherein each soldier forgets the password the very instant he whispers it in the ear of his neighbour. As the password would properly never exist [være til], so neither would this unity of virtue. In the first place, it is obvious that the determination of virtue as one, in the Socratic sense, is essentially no determination at all, since it is the weakest and least animated expression of its existence [Tilværelse] possible. By way of further explanation, I shall merely call to mind the penetrating judgment of Schleiermacher in his dogmatics[17] concerning the significance of the divine attribute of unity. In the second place, it is a negative determination, for the unity

---

shall here mention the positive conception of the unity of virtue that must be regarded as Platonic, and which is certainly not the fruit of the species of dialectical development suggested above, but belongs instead to quite a different order of things. Cf. *Republic* 445 c: 'I said, the argument seems to have reached a height from which, as from some tower of speculation, a man may look down and see that virtue is one, but that the forms of vice are innumerable. . . .' Manifestly, the positive unity of virtue is here the rich, full content of a happy life, while its opposition is the unhappy sundering and multiple divisiveness of the bad, its many-tongued self-contradiction. Cf. *Republic* 444 E: 'Then virtue is the health and beauty and well-being of the soul, and vice the disease and weakness and deformity of the same? True.' The positive is here the vegetative content of health. Of course, both these determinations are readily seen to be immediate, since they lack the dialectic of temptation.

here established is as anti-social as possible. The irony lies in the fact that Socrates tricks Protagoras out of every concrete virtue: by reducing each virtue to unity, he completely dissolves it; while the sophistry lies in the power through which he is able to accomplish this. Hence we have at once an irony borne by a sophistic dialectic, and a sophistic dialectic reposing in irony.

The second thesis concerns whether virtue can be taught, as Protagoras claims, or cannot be taught, as maintained by Socrates. Naturally, the former insists too much upon the discrete moment, for he allows one virtue to develop wholly at the expense of another, all the while permitting virtue as unity to be present in the individual and thereby crowning one still in the race. Socrates, on the other hand, affirms the unity to such a degree that although in possession of an enormous capital, he is nevertheless bankrupt since he is unable to bring it to fruition. The Socratic thesis that virtue cannot be taught seems to contain a high degree of positivity, inasmuch as it reduces virtue either to a natural determination or to something fatalistic. But virtue apprehended as immediate harmony, as well as in its fatalistic dispersion (διασπορά), is in another sense a completely negative determination. By contrast, the thesis that virtue can be taught must be understood in one of two ways: either it signifies an original void in man gradually supplemented through teaching, and which is a contradiction since something absolutely foreign to man can never be assimilated; or it is the expression of an inward determination of virtue developing gradually under a succession of teaching, and hence presupposing its presence originally. The error of the Sophist is in seeking to arrogate something to man; the Socratic, on the other hand, in denying in every sense that virtue can be taught. Hence it is obvious that this Socratic conception is negative: it negates life, development, in short, history in its most universal and widest sense. The Sophist negates original history, Socrates subsequent history. —If we next inquire to what more universal consideration this Socratic view must be referred, in what totality it reposes, then it obviously has the significance attributed to recollection. Recollection is retrograde development, however, and hence the reflected image of development in the strict sense. In the thesis that virtue cannot be taught, therefore, we have not merely a negative determination but an ironic negative determination moving wholly in the opposite direction. It is so far removed from the thesis that virtue can be taught, and lies instead so deeply buried in the individual that one might fear it were forgotten. The Platonic approach would be to reinforce existence with the edifying thought that mankind is not driven into the world empty-handed, through recollection to come to oneself in an awareness of the abundance of the human endowment. The Socratic approach, on the other hand, is to get the whole of actuality disaffirmed, and then refer mankind to a recollection that recedes further and further toward a past itself receding as far back in time as the origin of that noble family which no one can remember. Socrates, to be sure, does not remain with this thesis, but we shall next see that what he offers in its place is no less ironic. That virtue can or cannot be taught I have thus far conceived in the sense of having experience. I have understood it according to that school of experience in which virtue is taught. We observed that while the Sophist continually sent mankind to school by maintaining, or more correctly, by relaxing and loosening at every moment the dissolute in experience, so that mankind, like the dumb Gottlieb,[18] never learned anything from experience; Socrates, on the other hand, made virtue so prudish and narrow that for this reason it never became experience. But Socrates makes a more profound attempt to show that virtue is one, that is, he seeks to discover the 'other' in which all the virtues love one another, as it were, and this then becomes knowledge. This thought, however, is never pursued to the depths of sorrowless Pelagianism so characteristic of Hellenism, where sin becomes ignorance, misunderstanding, delusion, and where the moment of volition, namely, pride and defiance, is ignored. In order to gain a foothold, Socrates argues *e concessis*[19] by positing the good as the pleasurable, and the knowledge he thereby vindicates becomes the art of measurement, a delicate rationale in the sphere of enjoyment. But

97

such a knowledge essentially cancels itself, since it always pre-supposes itself. Whereas the previously mentioned irony in the entire dialogue exhibited itself in the fact that Socrates, who declared virtue could not be taught, nevertheless reduces it to knowledge and thereby proves the opposite, and con-versely with Protagoras; so now irony is apparent in the fact that Socrates advances a knowledge which ultimately cancels itself, since the infinite calculations pertaining to the state of enjoyment hinder and stifle enjoyment itself. Thus the good is the pleasurable, the pleasurable depends upon enjoyment, enjoyment upon knowledge, and knowledge upon an infinite comparing and rejecting; that is to say: the negative lies in the always necessarily and inherently fatal dissatisfaction of an infinite empiricism, the irony in the '*bon appetit!*',[20] so to speak, which Socrates wishes Protagoras. In a certain sense Socrates has therefore returned to his first thesis that virtue cannot be taught, since the infinite sum of experience is like a series of plain, mute, alphabetic characters: the longer it grows, the less it admits of being articulated. The first potency of irony lies in formulating a theory of knowledge which annihilates itself; the second potency of irony lies in the fact that Socrates pretends he has come to defend Protagoras' thesis acciden-tally, although by this very defence he destroys it. For it is wholly unreasonable to suppose that the Platonic Socrates should have advanced the thesis that the good is the pleasur-able, and evil the painful, for any other reason than to refute it.

Phædo

I shall now discuss the *Phædo*, a dialogue in which the mythical is more prominent, just as the dialectical was found unabated in the *Protagoras*. This dialogue contains the proofs for the immortality of the soul, and in this connection I shall include an observation of Baur (p. 112): 'This belief (in the continuance of the soul after death) is based upon the proofs which Plato has Socrates advance; but these proofs them-selves, when we examine them more closely, refer us to something else bearing the most immediate relation to the person of Socrates.'

Before investigating the nature of these proofs, however, I shall submit my own small contribution towards answering the question of the relationship between the *Symposium* and the *Phædo*. It is well known that Schleiermacher,[1] and after him Heise[2] here in Denmark, have placed these two dialogues in the most intimate connection, since they suppose that these dialogues encompass the whole of the Socratic existence both as it was in the world and beyond the world. In their arrangement of these two dialogues within the cycle of Platonic works, they have supposed them to provide the positive element to the *Sophist* and *Statesman* (since according to their view these last-named dialogues did not achieve their intention of exhibiting the nature and essence of the philosopher), which must especially be the case with the Sophist's relation to these dialogues, since the Sophist must be the negation of the philosopher. The matter is quite different with Ast.* In *Platons Leben und Schriften* he classes the *Phædo* with the first group of Platonic dialogues, the so-called Socratic dialogues, of which he counts four: *Protagoras*, *Phædrus*, *Gorgias*, and *Phædo* (cf. p. 53). He writes of the relation between these four dialogues (p. 157): 'If the *Protagoras* and *Phædrus* incline toward comedy because of the predominance of mimicry and irony, then the *Phædo* is decidedly tragic and its character sublime and pathetic.' Furthermore, he claims that Schleiermacher has wholly misunderstood the spirit of this Platonic composition by aligning it with the *Symposium* (pp. 157, 158): 'In the *Symposium* the Hellenic sage is represented as a thoroughgoing eroticist, while in the *Phædo* the serene, translucent sky of Hellenism disappears and the Greek Socrates is idealized into an Indian Brahmin living only in longing for reunification with God, and whose philosophy is therefore a meditation upon death. . . . The mind flees from sensuality that troubles

---

* Stallbaum[3] also disapproves of this arrangement and holds that the *Phædo* must be grouped with the *Phædrus*, *Gorgias*, and *Statesman*; however, he does not pursue this any further but refers the reader to Ast. Cf. *praefatio ad Phædonem*, p. 19.

and agitates the spirit, and pines for release from the fetters of the body imprisoning it.' —It is obvious that upon first consideration there is a considerable difference between the *Phædo* and the *Symposium*; on the other hand, one cannot deny that Ast completely isolates the *Phædo*. His attempt to relate it to the *Phædrus*, *Protagoras*, and *Gorgias*, by characterizing it as tragic wherein the pathetic predominates, does not actually harmonize with what he himself says about the dark, oriental mysticism that forms such an opposition to the bright, translucent sky of Hellenism arching over the *Symposium*. For the fact that the *Phædo* is tragic is no reason for the Greek sky not to shine as beautifully, as serenely, as cloudlessly as ever, since it had already been witness to many a tragedy without becoming either overcast and cloudy, or without its atmosphere becoming heavy and oppressive like that of the Orientals. But if it is not Greek in this way, then one seeks in vain to incorporate it into Plato, much less rank it with other dialogues. As for the conception of Schleiermacher, however, it cannot be denied that the view of life presented in the *Symposium* and the view of death set forth in the *Phædo* do not completely harmonize. This may be seen from the fact that the *Phædo* makes death the point of departure for a view of life, whereas the *Symposium* sets forth a view of life in which death is not assimilated as a moment. These two conceptions may scarcely be regarded as so favourably disposed towards each other as to be able to accommodate one another without the assistance of a third conception. This third conception must be either a speculative consideration capable of overcoming death, or it is irony—the irony which in the *Symposium* made love the substantial element in life, but then took it back again with the other hand by conceiving love negatively as longing—the irony which here in the *Phædo* conceives life retrogressively, seeking at every moment to return to the obscurity from which the soul issued, or more correctly, to a formless infinite transparency. Death, to be sure, is conceived wholly negatively in the *Phædo*. Naturally, death is and remains a negative moment, but as soon as it is apprehended merely as a moment, then the positive within it, the liberating metamorphosis[4], triumphantly seeks to survive the negative. When I now declare myself for irony (in spite of such passages as : 'I reckon, said Socrates, that no one who heard me now, not even if he were one of my old enemies, the comic poets, could accuse me of idle talking about matters in which I have no concern'),[5] it might at first glance seem to some to be most unreasonable, but after closer inspection it will, perhaps, appear quite acceptable. The speculative unity cannot be present in a way that is invisible and imperceptible, but the ironic unity can.

When I say that irony is an essential element in the *Phædo*, naturally I do not mean the ironic ornamentation found here and there in this dialogue. However significant such passages might be, and however much they are expanded through deeper consideration, they furnish at most but a hint of the ultimate view pervading the whole dialogue. Let me cite a few examples. 'Still I suspect that you and Simmias would be glad to probe the argument further. Like children, you are haunted with a fear that when the soul leaves the body the wind may really blow her away and scatter her; especially if a man should happen to die in a great storm and not when the weather is calm' (77 D). Subsequently, Socrates reproaches Crito for asking in what fashion he wished to be buried, and adds that Crito apparently believes that everything he has just said, how he will pass on to the rewards of the just 'whatever they might be,' is only said in order to reassure his disciples and himself (115 E): 'And therefore I want you to be surety for me to him now, as at the trial he was surety to the judges for me: but let the promise be of another sort; for he was surety for me to the judges that I would remain, and you must be my surety to him that I shall not remain, but go away and depart.' Although such ironic utterances admit of being easily conjoined with the presumed seriousness and deep emotion so pervasive in this dialogue, still, one would surely not want to deny that such utterances are much more effective when one perceives in them the quiet, secretive growth of irony.

The first piece of evidence I shall submit in order to support my position is an argument that the spirit of this dialogue is not oriental but authentically Greek. According to the idea of oriental mysticism which I am able to gather, the dying away here in question consists in a relaxation of the soul's muscle power, of the tension that is consciousness, consists in a dissolution and a melancholy absorbing languor, in a soaking whereby one becomes not softer but heavier, whereby one is not volatilized but chaotically compounded so as to move unsteadily as in a fog. Well might the Oriental wish to be free of the body and feel it as something oppressive, yet this is not in order to become more free but more bound, as if instead of locomotion he preferred the vegetative still life of a plant. It is to prefer the hazy, drowsy yawn of an opiate to the expanse of thought, to prefer the *dolce far niente* of an illusory pause in some undertaking to the energy of action.[6] But the sky of Hellas is soaring and vaulted, not low-pitched and oppressive; it does not sink downward in despair but ascends higher and higher. Its atmosphere is clear and transparent, not vaporous and dense. The longings which concern us here, therefore, are directed towards becoming lighter and lighter, towards becoming concentrated in an ever more volatile sublimation, and not towards evaporating in a feeble lethargy. Consciousness will not be macerated in vapid determinations but more and more intensified. The Oriental endeavours therefore to go back behind consciousness, the Greek to go beyond the succession of consciousness. This utter abstractness which it seeks, however, becomes at last the most abstract, the most volatile, in short, nothingness. Here we arrive at the point of coincidence between these two conceptions, a coincidence deriving either from subjective mysticism or from irony. Surely everyone who has read this dialogue will acknowledge that existence in the *Phædo*, since it results from continually dying, is conceived wholly abstractedly. However, it will not be out of place to substantiate this point a little further. This may be accomplished in two ways: first, by showing how Socrates conceives the nature of the soul, since the correct conception of the soul must properly contain in itself, must be impregnated by, the correct proof for its immortality; and secondly, by carefully analysing the various statements to be found concerning the soul's future *how*. In this second investigation I shall make subsidiary reference to the *Apology*, which, as a historical document, will be able to guide us on our way.

I shall begin by remarking that in view of the importance which such a question as the immortality of the soul must always have, it is highly significant that this question is treated by Platonism in connection with the death of Socrates. It is to the first inquiry that I now turn, that is, to the question: how does Socrates conceive the essence of the soul? since this leads us into a closer discussion of his proposed proofs for its immortality.*

* I shall here touch briefly upon two other proofs more indirectly contained in the *Phædo*. The first occurs at the beginning of the dialogue where Socrates counsels against suicide[7] and recalls the words of the mystery that we human beings are on duty, and one must not release himself or run away. If this consideration had been allowed to come to itself and reflect upon its rich content, if it had been expanded into a representation of man as collaborators with the deity,[8] together with real existence apart from God, as this implies, then there would be contained in this consideration, though in a form more popular and edifying than convincing, a view which in the rebirth of thought would emerge with speculative character. But this does not occur. To Cebes' typically Greek remark that if one actually believed this, he ought then to cling to life and not wish to die as do the philosophers according to Socrates, but cling on to life so as not to slip away from the jurisdiction of the gods, Socrates answers, somewhat darkly, that he, too, would be reluctant to die if he did not hope to come to other gods who are also good. Here an abyss is consolidated between this life and another, for in connection with death there always remains an ambiguous relation to the gods of this life, since death is always a withdrawal from their power. Only when one comes to know that it is the same God who has led one by the hand through life and who at the moment of death releases one, as it were, so as to open his embrace and receive the soul filled with longing,[9] only then does this proof attain a fully developed form as a representation. —The second indirect proof is wholly personal. The gladness, the cheerfulness, the openness with which Socrates goes forward to meet his death, the indifference with which he almost overlooks it, naturally has something which is highly inspiring for these contemporary witnesses, as well as for all those through the centuries, who, by their help, have become witnesses to this event.[10] He sends Xantippe away[11] in order not to hear any weeping and complaining. He jests[12] about how soon the pleasant follows upon the painful: 'Just as it seems in

As an introduction to the essential argumentation, Socrates first elucidates how this relates to the philosopher's wish to die. If death is the separation of the soul and the body, as admittedly it is, and if essential knowledge depends upon an abstraction from lower sensation, since through sensible observation one never confronts that which constitutes a thing's essence according to which it is what it is, such as size, health, strength, etc. (cf. 65 D); then it clearly follows that philosophers should seek to have as little to do with the body as possible (cf. 66 D, E). Indeed, they should seek to become purified and set free by death from the contamination of the body in order to consummate what they have been attempting to do here in life (cf. 66 A), namely, to pursue the pure essence of things through pure thought. Obviously, the soul is here conceived just as abstractly as the pure essence of things forming the object of its search. Though the philosopher with much exertion seeks to frighten this pure essence of things from behind all its hiding places, there still remains a serious doubt whether there will ever appear anything other than the purely abstract (health, size, etc.), which, in its opposition to the concrete, is nothingness. Accordingly, in order to become wholly congruent with its object, the soul in its cognitive

---

my case, after pain was in my leg on account of the fetter, pleasure appears to have come following after.' It strikes him as comical that the pleasant and the unpleasant are conjoined at the top, and muses that this is a task for Aesop: 'And I cannot help thinking that if Aesop had remembered them, he would have made a fable about the god trying to reconcile their strife, and how, when he could not, he fastened their heads together.' He takes up the cup of poison[13] with composure, with the same zest for life with which he would have raised the foaming goblet at a symposium. He asks the jailer: 'What do you say about making a libation out of this cup to any god? May I or not?' Now all this is very good. But if in the midst of this one remembers that he did not know how the future would be constituted, nor even if there would be a future; when in the midst of this poetry we hear the prosaic calculation that, still, it can never do one any harm to suppose that there is another life, another fullness to be announced in its own time—then one sees that the persuasive force of this argument is rather limited.

activity must become nothingness to the same extent.[14] Indeed, the soul must so far strive to become increasingly lighter and lighter that it is only those souls which have cultivated too much intercourse with the body that will be weighted down and drawn back to a visible scene, flitting about tombstones and graves like shadowy apparitions (cf. 81 c). It is as phantoms that these souls must appear to us—souls which have not obtained complete release, but, still having part in the visible, are themselves visible. To conceive of ghosts as an imperfect existence would not be objectionable in the least, but when one posits the 'formless' as the ideal, it is easy to see how negatively everything is conceived and how the soul comes to be [*bliver til*] a nothingness. Hence if one agrees with Socrates in propounding the dilemma (cf. 68 B) that one of two things must be supposed: either we never have knowledge or else it is only possible beyond the grave, then one must also be rather critical of the Socratic solution. I have lingered somewhat longer over these preliminary considerations because they give us to understand what may be expected from the entire discussion that follows. To set forth the individual arguments and examine each one would be too lengthy, and I refer those readers who prefer not to pursue these arguments in their genesis [*Tilblivelse*] out of the conversation, but to see them as far as possible in a wholly systematic form, to the discussions of Baur and Ast.

It seems more important, however, to observe that the individual arguments advanced do not always harmonize with each other. When one relates the argument derived from the consideration that opposites arise from opposites, and that between the members of such an opposition there are two movements: the transition of the first into the second and the return of the second into the first;[15] when one relates this to the argument deriving from a consideration of the pre-existence of the soul as this manifests itself in the nature and essence of recollection, and attempts in this way to establish a continuity;[16] then to the best of my understanding the concept of the soul's pre-existence either excludes the idea of its coming into being [*Tilblivelse*], or, if one wishes to maintain pre-existence in harmony with an intuition of becoming [*Vordelse*], one must suppose that Socrates has proved the resurrection of the body.[17] But this completely contradicts his other theory. An inconsistency always remains between these two arguments which cannot be removed by the uncertainty concerning what death is, as found in the first, nor by the unwarranted assumption, to which Baur rightly objects (cf. *op. cit.*, p. 114), that death is not the cessation of life but merely a different species of existence. One will certainly agree with Baur when he rejects the force of these arguments and maintains that they are merely an analytical exposition of the concept soul, and hence that immortality only follows from them insofar as it is already presupposed in the concept. Nevertheless, one must not overlook the fact that the recalcitrancy which the soul here acquires, as is elsewhere the case with the good, the beautiful, etc., is not present here as a point of departure but as a result, that it is precisely because observation seeks to grasp the essence of the soul that it exhibits itself as impenetrable, and not because of an impenetrability of the soul that one enters into the manifold of arguments. What I must again emphasize is that this is a negative result, the other a positive presupposition.

If we turn next to what the nature of the soul must be, what specific existence it must have, insofar as the answer to these questions may be had from the argument for its immortality as derived from the nature and essence of recollection, then we arrive once more at the most abstract determinations. When one is sensibly affected, these sense impressions give rise to certain general representations, e.g., equality (cf. 74 A ff.), the in-and-for-itself beautiful, good, just, holy, etc., and in general to everything 'which we describe in our questions as well as in our answers as that which is.' (Cf. 75 D.) These general representations are not acquired through an atomistic observation of experience, nor by the usurpations of induction; on the contrary, they always presuppose themselves. 'Either we all have this knowledge at birth, and continue to know through life; or, after birth, those who are said to learn only recollect, and learning is simply recollection.' (Cf. 76 A.) The speculatively unexplicated (insofar as everything speculative is paradoxical at first glance) synthesis of the temporal and the eternal is here pacified poetically and religiously. What we meet with here is not the eternal self-positing of self-consciousness that allows the universal to close tightly and firmly around the particular, viz. the individual; on the contrary, the universal flutters loosely about the particular. The salient point in the argumentation is essentially this: just as Ideas exist prior to sensible things, so the soul exists prior to the body. This sounds perfectly acceptable in and for itself, but so long as it remains unexplicated how and in what sense Ideas exist prior to things, it is clear that this 'just as', the point upon which everything turns, remains an abstract equal sign between two unknown quantities. If one thinks to obtain further enlightenment by a closer examination of the given quantities on one side of the equal sign—and this belief is already strengthened by the thought that this concerns the in-and-for-itself good, beautiful, just, and holy—this confidence is again stifled when we consider that it is the pre-existence of the Idea of equality, etc., upon which the pre-existence of the soul depends. For if the pre-existence of the soul fares no better than do such universal representations, it is easy to see that it disappears the same as they do in this infinite abstraction. The transition from this point, either in the form of a triumphant speculation or a loss of faith, to a positive conception can certainly be formed, but this never happens; and what the reader must assimilate in himself as an eternal *in Mente*[18] with even the least calculation throughout this inquiry is that this point is not the nothingness from which one begins, but the nothingness which one arrives at through the perplexities of deliberation. One may go further. Assuming that a representation could be attached to this existence of Ideas apart from every concretion, one would still have to ask how this would relate to the pre-existent soul. In terrestrial life the activity of the soul was to convey the particular back to the general, but the concrete relationship between particular and universal given in and through individuality is manifestly out of the question. The connection between these two powers realized by the soul was not permanent but wholly transitory. To this extent the soul in its previous existence must have been completely volatilized in the world of Ideas, and in this connection it is happily expressed by Plato[19] that in its transition to sensible life the soul forgets these Ideas, that this forgetting is the night preceding the day of consciousness, that it is the point of rest, infinitely vanishing and void, from which the universal determines itself towards the particular.[20] Forgetfulness is consequently the eternally limiting principle infinitely negated by the eternally conjoining principle of recollection. But the fact that the Platonic position requires the two extremes of abstraction, requires the thoroughly abstract pre-existence and the equally abstract post-existence, i.e. immortality, shows precisely that the soul must be conceived absolutely abstractly and negatively even in its temporal existence. The fact that terrestrial life, according to Plato, fades away (this expression taken in both a plastic and musical sense) at either end, should have inclined one to the view that this life was the abundant mean. But this is not the case in the *Phædo*. On the contrary, this life is the imperfect, and the formless the object of longing.*

We end with equally abstract results when, working our way through the other proofs, we arrive at the view of the essence of soul on which these are based. —That which is uncompounded cannot be dissolved or pass away; on the other hand, it pertains to what is compounded to be dissolved in the same way as it was combined. As the soul belongs to what is uncompounded, it follows that it cannot be dissolved. But this whole line of argument is thoroughly specious, for it rests upon the slippery ground of tautology. We must therefore follow Socrates when he explicates the analogies. The uncompounded is that which is always the same and unchanging. Is that essence

---

* As longing constituted the substantial aspect in the *Symposium*, so the same is true of the *Phædo*. But in the *Symposium* it was the longing that desires to possess, while in the *Phædo* it is the longing that desires to lose. Both determinations are equally negative, however, since both longings are ignorant of the *what* into which the one wishes to hurl itself, and into which the other wishes to be dissolved through death.

itself, he asks (78 D), which we in our questions and answers ascribe to true being, always the same and unchanging, or sometimes one thing and sometimes another? Can the in-and-for-itself equal, beautiful, and whatever else has true being, ever undergo any kind of change? 'These things are always the same, formless, and cannot be seen' (79 A). The soul has the greatest affinity with the divine, immortal, rational, uniform, indissoluble, and is always the same and unchanging; the body, on the other hand, has the greatest affinity with the human, mortal, irrational, multiform, dissoluble, and is never the same and unchanging (80 B). But here we have arrived at an equally abstract conception of the existence of the soul and its relation to the body. This consideration is in no wise guilty of materialistically assigning the soul a definite location in the body; on the contrary, it overlooks altogether the relation of the soul to the body, and instead of allowing the soul freely to animate the body which it produced, it is forever contriving to slip away from the body. The image which Cebes subsequently employs as an objection to the immortality of the soul (insofar as this was derived from the consideration that as the body, which is the weaker, survived, so the soul, which is the stronger, must also survive), namely, that this is as if someone were to say of an old weaver who had died: the man is not dead but must surely be somewhere, and as proof for this argue that the cloak he had worn and which he himself had woven was not damaged or destroyed (87 B)—this analogy, I say, when correctly used so as to emphasize the ingeniousness of comparing the soul to a weaver, would itself lead to far more concrete representations. That the soul is uncompounded might be readily admitted, but so long as no more precise answer is given concerning the question in what sense it is uncompounded, and, in another sense, to what extent it is an aggregate of determinations, so naturally the determination of the soul remains wholly negative and its immortality as tedious as the eternal number one.

The last argument is based on the thesis that whatever subsists [bestaaer] does so by virtue of its participation in the Idea, and that every Idea excludes its opposite (104 c: 'must we not say that the number three will endure destruction and anything else rather than submit to becoming an even number while remaining three'), together with the fact that this exclusion applies not merely to Ideas but to everything sub-sumed under the Idea. It will be seen, however, that this argument fares no better than the rest. The soul is the prin-ciple of life, but life is opposed to death. Hence if the soul can never include within itself the opposite (i.e. death) of its Idea (i.e. life), it is therefore immortal. But here the affair heads further and further out on to the deep blue sea of abstraction. For as long as it is not explained what relation of opposition obtains between life and death, so long must the relation of the soul to the body be conceived wholly negatively, and the life of the soul apart from the body remains in every case utterly predicateless and indeterminate.

But when the essence of the soul is conceived so abstractly, one can estimate beforehand what intelligence may be expected with regard to the *how* of the soul's future existence. Here I do not mean chorological and statistical summaries of the new world, nor a fantastic hodgepodge, but speculative trans-parency with regard to this question. The apostle John[21] also says that we do not yet know what we shall become [*vorde*], but this naturally applies to an otherworldly empiricism. The speculative intelligence that there is a resurrection of the body was essential to him, not in order to avoid a difficulty but because he himself found repose in it. By contrast, it is put forward in the mythical part of this dialogue that the resur-rection of the body or continuity is something that only the ungodly have to fear, while those who have been sufficiently purified by philosophy will live in the future wholly without bodies (114 c). The only attempt to stay this unbridled leap of abstraction 'into the wide beyond', and to effect real existence in which thought is not allowed to capsize and life to evaporate, is the ethical harmony, the moral melody that is to furnish the law of nature, as it were, constitutive of every-thing in the new order of things; in a word, the retributive justice that will be the moving principle in all things. And in truth only when this consideration is fully respected will immortality cease to be a shadow existence and eternal life a *Schattenspiel an der Wand*. But not even in the mythical part of the dialogue is this carried out fully. The extent to which it does occur will be investigated later; here it is enough to note that only the mythical part of the dialogue attempts it. —Hence our thought can now return to the point momentarily lost sight of: the negative *what* and the equally negative *how*, which assert themselves in the dialectical development of the *Phædo* as the positive answer to the question concerning the essence of the soul, insofar as this contains a proof for its immortality. The fact that the whole consideration ends negatively, that life fades away in the distant reverberations of a dying echo (*Nachhall*, I would prefer to say), might be due to the subjective standpoint of Platonism, which, dissatisfied with the immediacy of the Idea in existence as given by the happy sufficiency of classicism, now seeks to grasp it in its reflectivity and hence embraces the clouds instead of Juno. This subjective standpoint adds nothing the previous position did not possess, but even deprives it of something, namely, actuality. Rosenkrantz[22] has correctly observed somewhere that the more abundant life is, and the more exuberantly it swells, so much the more pale and scanty is immortality. Homer's hero[23] pines for even the least calling in actual life, and would exchange for it the shadowy realm of the underworld. But with Plato immortality becomes even more ethereal, almost about to blow away, and still the philosopher desires to abandon actuality, yes, to be already dead as far as possible in living life. Such is the grievous self-contradiction of the subjective standpoint.

But so far we have not yet seen the irony in this dialogue, and this is what I want to exhibit as far as possible. That irony may resemble all this to a hair, that with cursory observation it might even be confounded with irony, will surely be admitted by everyone who knows what a minute, invisible personage irony is. Again, this is one of those points of coincidence between Plato and Socrates. Hence, by accentuating the pathos which frequently appears in this dialogue, one may draw everything over to Plato, to that enthusiasm which is so ill-

THE CONCEPT OF IRONY

rewarded in comparison with the results. On the other hand, it will surely not be denied that a species of uncertainty prevails in this dialogue, suggesting in one way or another that irony is at work. For however insignificant the result may be, it could still be expressed with all the conviction of enthusiasm. This uncertainty may be detected in several places in the *Phædo*, and these gain in importance when one relates them to the *Apology*, which, as a historical document, must be accorded pre-eminent place when one is in search of the purely Socratic.

Before proceeding with this documentation, however, I must dwell a little more on this longing for death attributed to the philosopher in the *Phædo*. The view that life essentially consists in dying may be conceived both morally and intellectually. It has been conceived morally by Christianity, which has not remained with the mere negative; for to the extent that a man dies to the one, the 'other' suffers divine increase.[24] When this 'other' has absorbed, appropriated, and thereby ennobled all vitality in this body of sin that must die, when this too becomes gradually shrunken and desiccated so that it bursts and crumbles away, then out of this arises [*hæver*] the full-grown God-Man created according to God in the justice and holiness of truth. Insofar as Christianity also assumes a more perfect knowledge connected with this rebirth, this is only secondary and principally only insofar as knowledge has previously been infected with the blight of sin. Hellenism, on the other hand, has conceived this dying intellectually, that is to say, purely intellectually, and with this one immediately recognizes the sorrowless Pelagianism of paganism. As a precaution, allow me to emphasize what otherwise is undoubtedly clear to most readers. On the one hand, there is in Christianity that which one should be dead to, conceived in its positivity as sin, as a kingdom which only too convincingly proclaims its validity for all who groan under its law; on the other hand, there is that which shall be born and rise again, also conceived positively. With dying conceived intellectually, however, that which one should be dead to is something indifferent, that which shall grow up in its place, something abstract. The relation between these two great views is approximately as follows. The one says: you must refrain from unsound food and master your appetites so that health may develop; the other says: you must give up eating and drinking so that you may entertain the hope of gradually becoming nothing. Thus one sees that the Greek is a greater rigorist than the Christian, but therefore his view is also untrue. In the Christian view the moment of death is the last struggle between day and night, or, as it has been beautifully expressed by the Church,[25] death is our birth. In other words, the Christian does not dwell on the conflict, the doubt, the pain, the negative, but rejoices in the victory, the certainty, the happiness, the positive. Platonism desires that one should be dead to sensible cognition in order by this death to be dissolved into that kingdom of immortality where the in-and-for-itself equal, the in-and-for-itself beautiful, etc., abide in deathly stillness. This is expressed even more forcibly by Socrates' statement[26] that the desire of the philosopher is to die and to be dead. But to long for death thus in and for itself cannot be due to enthusiasm, provided one has any regard for this word and does not use it to describe, for example, that species of madness sometimes seen in a person who desires to come to nought and which is due to a species of ennui or spleen. For so long as one does not actually perceive what is involved in such a wish, it is still possible for enthusiasm to be present; but if this wish is due to a certain apathy, or if the person wishing it is himself conscious of what he wishes, then ennui must predominate. To me, the famous epitaph of Wessel: 'Nor in the end could he be bothered with living,'[27] contains the ironic view of death. But one who dies because he cannot be bothered with living would surely not wish for a new life either, for that would be a contradiction. The listlessness which wishes for death in this sense is obviously a very exclusive sickness and one only at home in the highest circles, but in its perfect homogeneity it is equally as strong as the enthusiasm which sees in death the clarification of life. There are these two poles between which the ordinary human life moves somnolently and unclear: irony is a healthiness insofar as it rescues the soul from the snares of relativity; it is a sickness insofar as it is unable to tolerate the absolute except in the form of nothingness, and yet this sickness is an endemic fever which but few individuals contract, and even fewer overcome.

As regards irony in the *Phædo*, this must be apprehended at the moment when irony as a view breaks through the firmament separating the waters of heaven and earth and unites with the total irony that destroys the individual. This point is as difficult to hold fast as the point between the thaw and the frost, and yet the *Phædo*, if one will use the dimensions of my proposed point of view, lies precisely between these two determinations of irony. I shall now proceed with a documentation as far as possible. In this regard it is not my intention to conceal the fact that every such documentation continually presupposes something, namely, the totality of intuition[28] extending above and beyond the particular, the 'let there be' [*Bliv*] of creation[29] which in every work of man only comes afterwards, at that moment when the invisible becomes intelligible in the visible. If it had been a subjective mysticism—not that Socrates was ensnared in (for this expression would already suggest consciousness)—but a subjective mysticism whose teeming superabundance inundated him as it were, then surely we would not hear in the midst of this dialogue a doubting, uncertain calculation of probability. But that this is so will not be denied by anyone who has read the *Phædo* carefully, much less by anyone who has glanced even superficially at the *Apology*. It must therefore be left to the discretion of each whether such expressions admit of being harmonized with the pathos of a Plato, or what amounts to the same thing, with a Socrates identified to the utmost with Plato, or rather, whether it suggests a difference which is as dissimilar as it is similar, as similar as it is dissimilar. That such is the case with an immediate speculation and irony has already been suggested in the foregoing, and to this our investigation will often return. Socrates announces in the *Phædo* that the main objective of his efforts to demonstrate the immortality of the soul is to become himself thoroughly convinced of this, and then adds (91 B): 'For see, my friend, how selfish is my attitude. If what I say is true, I am the gainer by believing it; but if there be nothing for me after death, at any rate I shall not be burdensome to my friends by my lamentations in these last moments. And this ignorance of mine will not last, for that would be an evil, but will soon end.' Now these words resound from a wholly different world, and it is assuredly not merely the exclamation: 'For see, my friend, how selfish is my attitude' (Θέασαι ὡς πλεονεκτικῶς), that disguises the irony. The thought that he might be reduced to nothingness by death (εἰ δὲ μηδέν ἐστι τελευτήσαντι), *sin post mortem sensus omnis atque ipse animus exstinguitur*[30] (cf. Stallbaum, p. 133) does not hold any terrors for him, nor on the other hand does he include it in order to chase home again the eccentric thought terrified by this consequence. Instead, he deliberately jests [*spøger*] with it and wishes, if it be false, to be disabused of this delusion, 'for that would be an evil,' and thereby to be completely annihilated. But what characterizes the irony most perfectly is the abstract criterion whereby it levels everything, whereby it masters every excessive emotion, and hence does not set the pathos of enthusiasm against the fear of death, but finds it a most curious experiment to become [*blive til*] nothing at all. This must now be a *locus classicus* of the *Phædo*. The scattered sprinklings of a similar character found here and there throughout this dialogue would require too extensive discussion for me to enter upon. Besides, the *Apology* requires our attention.

Apology

The *Apology* will be employed for a twofold purpose: first, the statements it contains concerning the immortality of the soul will serve to reinforce our argumentation in the *Phædo*, which sought to allow the dialectical element in this dialogue to culminate in irony; and secondly, its total design will serve to allow the standpoint of Socrates to become manifest as irony.

If one will but refuse to agree with Ast[1] in supposing that the *Apology* is not by Plato but by an unknown writer, then it is quite immaterial for this investigation whether one holds with Schleiermacher that this defence was actually made in this way by Socrates,* or whether one holds with Stallbaum that it was not made exactly in this way, but that in composing this discourse Plato has endeavoured to approximate as much as possible the historical Socrates. Stallbaum writes (*praefatio ad apologiam Socratis*, p. 4): 'If this (opinion) is correct, surely no one will be surprised that in this work Plato has not exhibited the same sublimity in word and thought as elsewhere. For as he only intended to defend Socrates in the correct manner when he allowed him to address the court as he was in life, he thus could not follow his own opinion but had to consider what agreed with the spirit and character of Socrates, and what accorded with the conditions of time and place.' Should anyone wish to know the large number of authors who have disagreed with Ast on this point, I shall refer him to Stallbaum where their names are gathered together for convenient inspection. The main thing for me, however, is that one comes to see in the *Apology* an authentic image of the actual Socrates. Ast, who considered the sublime and pathetic to predominate in the *Phædo*, naturally cannot be anything but indignant over the way Socrates behaves here, and so among other things declares the *Apology* to be spurious. If it be assumed with the majority of interpreters, yes the absolute majority, that the *Apology* is authentic, then in truth one is compelled to find another solution than merely contenting oneself, as is usually done, with the assurance that there is nothing in the *Apology* which is not consonant with the spirit of Plato, whether this assurance finds its strength in being set forth interrogatively or declamatorily. The objections advanced by Ast are altogether too significant to be brushed aside† in this way, and

* Cf. Schleiermacher, *Platons Werke*, Part One, vol. 2, Berlin, 1818, p. 185: 'Hence nothing is more probable than that we have in this discourse as faithful a transcript from recollection of the actual defence of Socrates as was possible for the practised memory of Plato, together with the necessary differences between a written discourse and one casually delivered.'

† I recall from my early youth how the soul demands the sublime, the paradigmatical, and how in reading the *Apology* I felt disappointed, deceived, and dejected because it seemed to me that all the poetry and courage which triumph over death was here wretchedly displaced by a

if he is right, one is tempted to agree with him in according Xenophon's *Apology* preference over Plato's.[2]

Here there will be no discussion of the entire *Apology*, but only those passages in which Socrates develops his view of death. As the difficulty of explaining them Platonically increases, so the probability of finding the correct explanation in irony likewise increases. All these passages exhibit Socrates' total uncertainty, but this uncertainty, be it noted, does not make him uneasy; on the contrary, this playing with life, this vertigo, inasmuch as death now appears as infinitely significant, now as utter nothingness, is just what pleases him. In the *foreground* is Socrates, yet not as one who rashly dispels the thought of death and clings anxiously to life, not as one who enthusiastically goes forward to meet death and magnanimously offers up his life. No, it is a Socrates who relishes the play of light and shadow entailed in a syllogistic *aut-aut*,[3] when almost at the same instant appear the noontide of day and the pitch black of night, the infinitely real and infinite nothingness. A Socrates who, even on behalf of the listener, gloats over the fact that these two points are fastened together at the top like the pleasant and unpleasant (cf. *Symposium*);[4] yet throughout all this he never once desires certainty with fervent longing of soul, but with a certain curiosity longs instead for the solution to this riddle. Socrates is well enough aware that there is nothing exhaustive in his syllogisms concerning the solution of this problem, and only the speed with which the infinite opposition appears and disappears pleases him. The *background* receding infinitely, on the other hand, is formed by the infinite possibility of death.

In the *Apology* there appears, usually after the most passionate outbursts, an argumentation which blows away the lather of eloquence and reveals nothing underneath. Socrates remarks how disgraceful it would be for him who was appointed by the

---

rather prosaic calculation proceeding in such a way that it seemed as if Socrates would say: this whole affair hardly interests me one way or the other. Since then I have learned to understand it quite differently.

god to live as a lover of wisdom (φιλοσοφοῦντα)[5] and to search out and examine himself and others, how disgraceful it would be for him to desert his post out of fear of death. Then follows the reason (29 A): 'For to fear death, my friends, is only to think ourselves wise without really being wise. for it is to think that we know what we do not know. . . . And what is this but that shameful ignorance of thinking that we know what we do not know?' In this regard Socrates believes he has an advantage over other men: he does not fear death, for he knows nothing about it. Now this is not only a sophism but an irony. Insofar as he emancipates mankind from the fear of death, he gives them in exchange the anxious representation of an inevitable something of which one knows nothing. Accordingly, one must be accustomed to being edified by the reassurance residing in nothingness in order to find repose in this. Hence it would be unreasonable, as he remarks in another place, for him to choose something else which he definitely knows to be an evil (e.g. imprisonment) out of fear for the thing Meletus claims he has deserved: 'about which I say that I do not know whether it is a good or an evil' (37 B).

Towards the end of the *Apology*, however, an attempt is made to show that to die is a good. But this consideration is again an *aut-aut*, and as the view that death is a nothingness appears to accompany the first *aut*, it becomes rather doubtful how far one can share the happiness encircling both these continents like an ocean. Cf. 40 c-E: 'And if we reflect in another way, we shall see that we may well hope that death is a good. For the state of death is one of two things: either the dead man wholly ceases to be and loses all consciousness, or, as we are told, it is a change and a migration of the soul to another place. And if death is the absence of all consciousness, and like the sleep of one whose slumbers are unbroken by any dreams, it will be a wonderful gain. For if a man had to select that night in which he slept so soundly that he did not even dream, and had to compare with it all the other nights and days of his life, and then had to say how many days and nights in his life he had spent better and more pleasantly than this night, I think that a private person, nay, even the Great King of Persia himself, would find them easy to count, compared with the others. If that is the nature of death, I for one count it a gain. For then it appears that all time is nothing more than a single night. But if death is a journey to another place, and what we are told is true—that all who have died are there —what good could be greater than this, my judges?' This second alternative must be especially attractive, for with this one escapes from those who merely pretend to be judges, and is delivered to such judges as Minos, Rhadamanthus, Aeacus, and Triptolemus, who truly deserve to be judges.[6] On the one side of this dilemma, he holds that to be rendered nothing at all by death is a wonderful gain ($\theta\alpha\nu\mu\acute{\alpha}\sigma\iota\sigma\nu$ $\kappa\acute{\epsilon}\rho\delta\sigma\varsigma$); indeed, his discourse becomes rather heated when he remarks that not only a private person but even the Great King himself would have but few days to compare with this. Such a soul slumber and such a nothingness must especially recommend themselves to the ironist, for he here has the absolute in opposition to the relativity of life, yet in a form so light that he cannot possibly strain himself on it, since he has it in the form of nothingness. On the other side of this dilemma, he sets forth statements whose ironic character I have already touched upon,[7] namely, how wonderful it would be to come together in the underworld with the great men of the past and pleasantly converse with them about their fate, but most of all to question and examine them.* Two things are evident from this. First, these statements are not easily reconciled with the expectations expressed in the *Phædo* of existing wholly without a body; and secondly, this happiness is extremely hypothetical since the other possibility lies so near, that is to say, not more than a hair's breadth away. In its entirety this hypothesis is merely a flourish in the air with Socrates making no attempt to actualize one side more than the other. Presumably, the words of the *Phædo* cited previously do make the attempt, for Socrates there holds that his belief is preferable because in this way one will be less burdensome to one's friends; however,

* Immortality and eternal life are here conceived as infinite progress, as an eternal inquiry.[8]

every reader will surely find in this consideration a politeness towards life and an irony which dare even to burlesque death. The conclusion of the *Apology* ends with the same ambiguity (42 A): 'But now the time has come, and we must go away— I to die, and you to live. Which is better is known to the god alone.' Now as this is the case with the view of death even in the *Apology*, so the probability for my conception of the *Phædo* increases accordingly, that is, provided one will grant the possibility that the *Phædo* may be both Socratic and Platonic at the same time.

I shall now undertake a more special consideration of the *Apology* in order to show that its totality is ironic. It is to this end that I shall let Ast speak for a moment, and I hope, with the help of the forceful impression which the weight of his remarks must necessarily have, that the soul of the reader may acquire sufficient elasticity to allow irony to emerge. 'The speaker has so exaggerated in his own way this masculine steadfastness of Socrates (which Ast found in Xenophon's account) that it seems like the most spiritless and heartless indifference. After the verdict he does not allow Socrates to wonder at the pronouncement of the judges, but merely at the number of votes on each side. He then has Socrates make the cold-blooded calculation that he would have been set free if only three[9] votes had fallen the other way, and that if Anytus and Lykon had not come forward with their additional accusations, Meletus would have had to pay a thousand drachmas for not winning a fifth part of the votes. But still more astonishing is this indifference when Socrates speaks of death. He constantly asserts that he is not afraid of death, but upon what is this fearlessness based? On nothing; it is thus empty ostentation. . . . Could Plato, the author of the *Phædo*, have allowed Socrates to speak in this way about death, and could he have attributed to him such a truly vulgar, dull and unfeeling, even ludicrous indifference? . . . And yet this insensitive and spiritless Socrates seeks to play the part of the inspired enthusiast inasmuch as he ventures to prophesy.' (Cf. *op. cit.*, pp. 487, 488.) Now this Astian conception is not meant to stand here and bore itself as a detached and idle quotation; on the contrary, I have hopes that it will become a productive labourer in the vineyard, for I am counting on that perspectival refraction wherein irony will not only become visible to one or another reader, but also show itself to good advantage. For while the pervasive seriousness of Ast advances with its measured gait against the neutral *Apology*, irony sits silently in wait, watching with unblinking eyes, perpetually in motion and active in every encounter, though the reader is perhaps unaware of this before the moment when it casts its net over him and ensnares him. Hence, if my own presentation should turn out to be such a loosely woven net that the reader may easily slip through, or so flimsy that it might not hold him, then certain things in the words of Ast will be both refined and strong enough to bind him fast. Even the vociferousness in the last part of the quotation has its significance, for it will serve as the noise and clamour to drive the reader towards the point where he must be captured. For example, the passage: 'And yet this insensitive and spiritless Socrates seeks to play the part of the inspired enthusiast inasmuch as he ventures to prophesy,' not only surpasses my entire presentation in captivating skill and strength of arm, but I regard it as absolutely overwhelming for everyone who refuses to concur with Ast in rejecting the *Apology*. There is many another Astian remark which will be strengthening to the vacillating and unfortified reader, and perilous for everyone who still crosses himself at the thought that it might be irony which explains the *Apology*. On page 488 he writes: 'The speaker betrays himself in his delivery not only by the antitheses of thought (e.g. "but I am in utter poverty by reason of my devotion to the god,"[10] wherein the lower is so contrasted to the higher, the complaining tone so opposed to the feeling of pride, that the statement almost draws a laugh from us), but also of words; for orators at that time amused themselves with trifling antitheses after the manner of Gorgias and Lysias.'

This seems the appropriate place to discuss the attack upon the ironic conception which Ast makes a little earlier in the same investigation.[11] The consideration that the irony found in the *Apology* might not be Platonic irony is too important to pass over undiscussed. The attentive reader will find in Plato two species of irony: the first is an accelerating force assimilated into the inquiry itself; the second sets itself up whenever possible as lord and master. Hence, if irony is found in the *Apology*, one cannot reject it as a matter of course, as does Ast, simply because it is not Platonic irony. The possibility still remains that the irony of Socrates was different from that of Plato, and hence that the *Apology* was a historical document. In proceeding to a closer examination of Ast's attempt to show that the irony found in the *Apology* is not Platonic, or as one who agrees with Ast would prefer to say, that there is no irony at all in the *Apology*,[12] naturally, I must point out something disadvantageous respecting my own approach, namely, that irony has been handled under a rubric all its own, nor has Ast allowed his various operations of assault to clarify themselves internally and become conscious that they must concentrate themselves at one point, at one decisive battle: whether there is irony in the *Apology* not at this or that point but in its totality.

There is a statement in the *Gorgias* that provides some indication of the significance Socrates would attach to being arraigned before the court of the Athenian people, and what a ludicrous idea he must associate with the thought of having to make a defence before such judges: 'And what I said to Polus can easily be applied to me, for I shall be judged as a physician would be judged who was[13] summoned before a court of little boys on a charge brought by a cook' (521 E).[14] It has been suggested in the foregoing that the total design of the *Apology* must be considered ironic, since the serious accusations about all the new doctrine Socrates introduced into Athens relate in a most curious and quite properly ironic way to his defence, viz., that he knew nothing and could therefore never have introduced new doctrines. Obviously, the irony lies in the fact that there is absolutely no point of connection between the attack and the defence. Had Socrates endeavoured to show that he subscribed to the old, or insofar as he introduced anything new that this was the truth, everything would have been in order. But Socrates does not refute his accusers; instead, he wrests from them the accusation itself. Hence the whole thing turns out to be a false alarm with his accusers' hundred pound cannons, which ordinarily could completely demolish the accused, being fired in vain, since there is nothing at all which may be destroyed.[15] The whole situation is clearly reminiscent of a profoundly witty verse by Baggesen.*[16] But the ironic design in the *Apology* will appear from yet another side. To Socrates—who was accustomed to stick to the question with a stiffneckedness and dauntless courage that was terrifying to the Sophists, and this in spite of their contortions and hobgoblins—what the Athenians had now got up, namely, to put him to death, must have seemed a most ludicrous *argumentum ad hominem*. According to Socrates' point of view, to be sure, either his accusers must convince him that he is wrong or be themselves convinced; whereas all this business about whether he should be put to death or not put to death, or at least fined or not fined, was utterly irrelevant. Thus here again no rational connection remained between the offence and the punishment. Add to this the circumstance that this utterly irrelevant question was to be decided in a wholly external fashion, by the number of votes, a method of settling disputes which had long been the object of Socrates' special affection, and about which he has somewhere remarked[17] that he was completely inept; add this to the foregoing, I say, and one cannot help but approve of that apparently guileless and good-natured yet freezing irony with which he ignores this terrible argument and amicably converses with the Athenians[18] about the probability of his having been acquitted, an eventuality that must naturally have seemed about as ridiculous to

* Og ingen, ingen Moders Sjæl
Kan slaae tilgavns en Død ihjel;
Selv naar han Græset maatte bide,
All Fordeel var paa Tyvens Side.[19]
The reader must particularly note the last two lines, for just as the thief would be benefitted by being put to death, so Socrates, who knew nothing, would have been benefitted in some sense if his accusers could have shown that he not only knew something but even something new.

him as the likelihood that Meletus would be fined. Accordingly, it is only a new irony when in conclusion[20] he wishes to say a few words to those who had voted for his acquittal—for surely these had voted just as ably as the others. And yet there is in the *Apology* an irony higher than the preceding, an irony which engulfs even Socrates himself. The fact that Socrates had so completely and one-sidedly advocated knowledge that every offence became error and every punishment, therefore, something wholly incongruent with error; I say, the polemical force with which he had affirmed this view[21] now reaps the most ironic revenge upon him, since in a way he himself falls for such a ridiculous argument as a death sentence.

That the things here portrayed are clearly ironic situations, and that surely everyone would feel the irony who read the *Apology* with the assumption that Socrates never existed, but that a poet had wanted to illustrate the piquant character inherent in such an accusation and condemnation—all this I regard as indubitable. But let it now concern historical events and many a reader will certainly lack the courage to dare believe it.

The presentation of the irony found scattered throughout the *Apology* places me in a rather awkward position. I might attempt to assemble a multitude from every quarter, but it goes without saying that the extensive argumentation necessary on each point would weary the reader. Moreover, I suspect the entire section, instead of the faint whisper characteristic of irony, would come buzzing forth contrary to its essence. To prove the presence of irony by means of an investigation appended to each particular point would naturally deprive it of the unexpected, the striking; in short, enervate it. Irony requires sharp oppositions and would completely pale away in such stultifying comradeship as argumentation. I shall therefore inscribe once more the words of Ast, who has grasped with extraordinary certainty all the ambiguous points, and by means of these give the reader a fright by proving the unauthenticity of the *Apology*. As I shall insert his pathos into the text, I shall allow myself certain allusions in the notes which I trust will be more than sufficient for the reader. There is a copperplate engraving[22] that portrays the ascension of the Madonna into heaven. In order to exalt the heavens as much as possible there is a black line drawn across the bottom of the picture beneath which two angels stand gazing up at her. Similarly, in inscribing the words of Ast into the text I desire to elevate them as high as possible, and in order to heighten his lofty pathos still more I shall place a line over which the mischievous face of irony is occasionally allowed to peep out. Ast, *op. cit.*, p. 477 ff.: 'The frankness with which he allows Socrates to speak is not the noble kind of frankness flowing from a consciousness of innocence and honesty and which, when irritated by slander, displays itself as pride. No, it is merely boastful self-exaltation. For Socrates only debases himself in order indirectly to exalt himself even more. (In a note to this, Ast remarks: the author of the *Apology* cannot refrain from suggesting this himself: "Do not interrupt me with noise, even if I seem to you to be boasting."*) Now this is not Platonic irony but merely a contempt for others which has the vain intention of exalting[23] itself. Socrates says, for example (17 B), that if they call one who speaks the truth an orator, then by all means he is an orator, but not in the same way as the others (wherein the suggestion is concealed that he is a real or true orator, the others merely apparent orators). Similarly, the reference to his manner of speech (18 A): "For perhaps it might be worse and perhaps better," contains a concealed boast. Even more unmistakable is the false irony in the passage (21 B—22 E) in which Socrates undertakes to demonstrate† the truthfulness of the pronouncement of the oracle, declaring him the wisest of men, for the conceit and boastfulness lies precisely in the thoroughness with which Socrates discusses it. Similarly, Socrates declares himself to be a distinguished and extraordinary person (20 C, 23 A, 34 E),

---

* This is thoroughly analogous to Socrates' decision to prophesy. The frosty seriousness with which he lures the Athenians out on to thin ice is in complete harmony with his subsequent explanation of his significance for the Athenian people, i.e., in what sense he is a divine gift.

† This is Socrates' famous exploration voyage undertaken not in order to discover anything, but to convince himself there was nothing to discover.

and his calling divine* (31 A). He is the greatest benefactor of the city† (30 A, 30 E, 36 D), and on this account am I[24] slandered and envied (28 A), etc. Furthermore, he attributes wisdom to himself‡ (20 D, 20 E, 21 B ff.), and speaks of the wisdom of the Sophists in a sceptical tone§ signifying arrogance. For what is it when one disparages oneself yet at the same time debases all others[25] except an oratorical self-exaltation which, if a serious intention be attributed to it, appears as conceited boasting, while if it be taken as unaffected and unfeigned frankness exhibits a naïveté which, through the unintentional contrast of self-abasement and self-exaltation,‖ readily passes over into the comical (for example, when Socrates declares he is ignorant yet at the same time wiser than all others, and hence exalts himself, the ignorant, as the wisest). If, therefore, the author of the *Apology* intended to portray Socrates as an ironist, he has transformed him into a boastful Sophist, the opposite of the Platonic Socrates; while if he intended to confer upon Socrates an unaffected and undesigning frankness, he has exaggerated the naïveté and failed at his purpose, for the self-exaltation, the opposite of self-abasement, is too obtrusive and glaring for anyone to believe the latter was seriously intended. Thus the modesty is only affected[26] and the self-abasement merely feigned, since it is wholly outweighed by its accompanying self-exaltation. In this phantom, this mere show of being, we recognize for the most part the speaker who, accustomed to the play of antitheses, takes pains to abrogate the first by means of its opposite, the second. Similarly, our apologist has turned [27] into show

* That is, he is like a gadfly.
† Indeed, he even desires to be supported at public expense.
‡ That he knows nothing. § Yet with pre-eminent politeness.
‖ But this is the delicate, ironic rippling of muscles. The fact that he knows that he knows nothing pleases him, and he feels infinitely lightened by this, whereas the rest grind themselves to death for coppers. Ignorance is never conceived speculatively by Socrates, yet it feels so congenial to him, so transportable. He is an *Asmus omnia secum portans*,[28] and this *omnia* is nothingness. Indeed, the happier he is about this nothingness, not as result but as infinite freedom, so much the deeper is the irony.

and pretension the best part of his speech, that which lay before him as a fact, namely, those expressions of the noble and proud frankness and magnanimity of Socrates; for he again abrogates it by means of its opposite, namely, the concern not to anger the judges* upon whose favour everything depended. Accordingly, he always explicates the grounds for his statements so diffusely and with well-nigh anxious solicitation so as not to say anything not self-evident and possibly anger the judges. Does not this anxiety and fear, which is always opposed to the frankness, abrogate the latter and transform it into mere show and deception? A truly free and magnanimous person will speak as consciousness and knowledge bid him without regard for anything but the truth of his statement and untroubled by how it is received. Socrates, by the same token, admits that he fears his accusers and adversaries (18 B, 21 E). Do we recognize in this the Socratic magnanimity and love of truth which fear nothing as exhibited, for example, by Xenophon (*Mem.* 1, 2, 33 ff.) in the conversation with Critias and Charicles whose aim is his ruin? Again, Socrates pretends not to speak in his own defence, but in order to convince his judges that they should not condemn him, lest they offend against the gift of the god (30 D). If you heed

* In a note to this Ast writes (p. 479): 'Therefore the frequent expressions: "cease interrupting,"[29] "do not interrupt,"[30] "and do not be indignant with me for telling the truth." '[31] He holds that the author of the *Apology* had in mind the actual historical fact that Socrates was interrupted several times, but that he now permits Socrates to anticipate these interruptions and thus changes the actual disturbance ($\theta o \rho u \beta \epsilon \tilde{\iota} \nu$) into an imaginary one. He thereby overlooks how genuinely Socratic is this anxious diffidence which continually hushes the Athenians so as not to terrify them by the momentous, the extraordinary, that he has to say. This momentousness is the significance of his person for the Athenians, or to say it clearly, he is a divine gift, which then admits of being determined still further as: he is a gadfly. See also 30 E. Socrates here warns the Athenians not to condemn him, not for his sake but for their own: 'that you may not make a mistake about the gift of the god to you by condemning me. For if you put me to death, you will not easily find another who, if I may use a ludicrous comparison, clings to the state as a sort of gadfly to a horse that is large and well-bred but rather sluggish because of its size, so that it needs to be aroused.'

me, he adds (31 A), then you would preserve me. Now who does not recognize the oratorical expression in this? The request and the wish to be acquitted are concealed and appear as friendly counsel not to offend the gods and reject their gift. Thus the statement of Socrates that he does not speak for himself (in order to bring about his acquittal) but for the Athenians, is again merely oratorical, that is, mere show, deception, and deceit.'*

The Mythical in the earlier Platonic Dialogues as the Indication of a more fulsome Speculation

I am now finished with the presentation of the dialectical in Plato, insofar as this was needful for the present investigation. I have deliberately allowed this whole consideration to end in the *Apology* in order that whatever was uncertain and vacillating in the previous argumentation could there acquire consolidation. The mythical will now be the object of consideration, and if I seek to forget the purpose for which it is undertaken so the deliberation may be as unbiased as possible, I must ask the reader for his part to bear in mind that the duplicity exhibiting itself in the disparity between the dialectical and the mythical is one of the indices, one of the traces, which promise to facilitate the separation of what in time and inwardness appears inseparable.

At first glance one may regard the mythical somewhat indifferently, consider it merely as an alteration in the mode of representation, another species of discourse, without the relation between them being an essential one. Indeed, a suggestion of this may be presumed from certain statements of Plato. In proposing to demonstrate the thesis that virtue can be taught, Protagoras says to Socrates (320 C): 'But what would you like? Shall I, as the elder, speak to you as the younger, and clothe the proof in a myth, or shall I argue out

---

* This is all quite correct, for Socrates is altogether too ironically indifferent to be seriously concerned about the Athenians. Hence he sometimes seems passionately fearless, other times despondent and faint-hearted.

the question?' And when he is finished he remarks (328 c): 'So now, Socrates, I have shown you both by myth and argument that virtue is teachable.' Thus we see that the mythical discourse is here distinguished from the discursive in such a way that the former is considered less perfect, intended for the young, and that these two genres have no necessary relation to each other, since their necessity would only be perceptible in that higher unity in which they themselves would be apparent and actual as discrete moments. These two modes of representation are not viewed in relation to the Idea but in relation to the listener; they are like two languages of which the one is less articulate, more childish and pliable, the other more developed, more incisive and firm. But as they are not seen in relation to the Idea, it is possible to imagine a third language, a fourth, etc., a whole assortment of such forms of representation.

To this must be added that according to this conception the myth lies completely in the power of the narrator. It is his free creation and he may add to it or subtract from it according as he intends to serve the listener. However, this is not at all the case with the mythical in Plato. Here the mythical has a much deeper significance, a fact which becomes evident when one observes that the mythical in Plato has a history. In the first and earliest dialogues it is either wholly absent, in which case its opposite alone prevails, or else it is present in connection with, though in another sense not in connection with, its opposite, the abstract. It then completely disappears throughout a whole cycle of dialogues in which the dialectical alone is present, yet present in quite a different sense than in the earlier dialogues. Finally, it turns up again in the last Platonic works, though in a deeper connection with the dialectical. With regard to the mythical in Plato, therefore, I am immediately referred back to the same dialogues I just left. Here the mythical is found in connection with its opposite, the abstract dialectic. In the *Gorgias*, for example, after the Sophists have struggled with the frenzy of desperation and always less and less 'bashfully,'[1] after Polus has outbid Gorgias, and Callicles Polus in shamelessness, the whole affair concludes[2] with a mythical representation of the condition after death.* But what is the mythical like here? Obviously, in these dialogues it is not so much Plato's free creation, responsive and obedient to his will, but instead something which overwhelms him. It is to be considered not so much an inferior representation for younger or less gifted listeners, but rather as the presentiment of something higher.

Stallbaum,† in his conception of the mythical, clearly embraces the position suggested previously. He considers it

* Incidentally, this myth occurs in three places in Plato. Cf. Stallbaum *ad Phædonem*, p. 177: 'Olympiodorus reports that the third part of this dialogue was called νεκυιαν, a name by which the ancients designated the journey of the Homeric Odysseus. (*Odyssey* XI). As there are in Plato three νεκυιαν, i.e., myths about the underworld: in the *Phædo, Gorgias*, and *Republic*,³ and since they mutually clarify each other, they must all be carefully compared with each other.'

† Cf. *praefatio ad Phædonem* p. 16: 'But as Plato perceived that this difficulty was so great that it seemed much easier to divine with the soul than grasp and articulate clearly with the understanding, it is not to be wondered that myths and fables are woven into the subtle investigation of the question in this dialogue in such a manner as to take the place of proofs and demonstrations. . . . Eberhard appropriately writes (J. A. Eberhard, *Neue vermischte Schriften*, Halle, 1788, p. 384): "It may be regarded as certain that Plato has sometimes employed the myth in opposition to *raisonnements* or the proofs of reason; for example, when the subject under discussion transcends the competence of human reason and experience, or when the proofs of reason were too difficult for him, or when they seemed to him to be too difficult for the comprehension of his listeners." ' Cf. *ad Phædonem* p. 177: 'Often he seems to have used these mythical representations in order to suggest that the topic under discussion was of such a nature that one should give oneself over to presentiments and premonitions, rather than put one's confidence in demonstrations and explanations. When he does this he generally utilizes those myths and fables commonly known among the Greeks, yet in such a way that he not only changes and discards what does not conform to his purpose, but also corrects the superstitiousness of his fellow citizens and attempts to remove it. And here is seen the additional purpose Plato had in his use of myths. He desired gradually to revoke the foolish superstitions of the common people, or at least to correct them. Finally, he seems also to have employed myths for the purpose of gradually preparing the minds of his contemporaries, so oppressed by blind superstition, to receive a purer doctrine of wisdom.'

first to be an accommodation, or to use a more descriptive word in this connection, a condescension (συγκατάβασις), since this suggests that in the mythical Plato descends to the level of the listener, instead of assuming, as we do, that the mythical is something higher, even transcending Plato's own subjective authority. In the second place, he relates it to folk-consciousness, the receptacle by which the Idea was preserved prior to Plato. But neither of these considerations is developed distinctly enough to effect a meaningful separation between what is apprehended through the deductions of reason and what is intuited, nor, in truth, to effect a satisfactory resolution of the disputed limits between tradition and Plato. Baur (*op. cit.*, pp. 90-8) sees in the mythical the significance of tradition, and agrees with Ackermann in relating both the poets and oracular pronouncements to Plato in the same way as the prophets of the Old Testament relate to the apostles and evangelists. We must, on the one hand, see in the mythical of Plato all the faithful veneration and filial piety with which he comprehended the past religious consciousness of his father-land. On the other hand, we must allow for the noble, momentary distrust of his own constructions, which is also the reason he refrained from formulating any laws about worship in the *Republic*,[4] but referred this to the Delphic Apollo. Ast* has a far more elaborate conception, except that it is not based on observation, having not so much the character of an acquisition as wishful thinking.

Both Baur and Ast seem to have overlooked the internal history of the mythical in Plato. While in the earlier dialogues

---

* Cf. *op. cit.*, p. 165: 'The mythical is something like the theological basis of Platonic speculation: knowledge becomes bound and fortified through dogma, and leads the mind out of the sphere of human reflection towards an intuition [*Anschauung*] of the higher life of infinity, where, for-getting its finite and earthly selfhood, it sinks into the unfathomable deep of the divine and eternal. It may be said that in the Platonic dialogue the philosophic representation merely serves to lead the mind to a higher intellection and to prepare for the intuition of the infinite and divine sensuously manifested in the myth, just as in the mysteries the actual con-templation [*Beschauung*] (ἐποπτεία)[5] follows only after preparation and initiation.'

it appears in opposition to the dialectical, inasmuch as the mythical is only heard or rather seen when the dialectical is silent, in the later dialogues it exhibits a more amiable relation to the dialectical, that is, Plato has become master of it, which is to say, the mythical becomes image. To follow Baur in explaining the mythical as the traditional, and to let Plato seek a point of departure for ethical-religious truths in the higher authority deriving from poetry and oracles, is not possible without further proof. For in the first books of the *Republic*,[6] for example, the validity of the pronouncements of the poets is completely disaffirmed, deprecated and polemicized against, while the imitative conception (the poetical) is frowned upon in opposition to the plain and simple narrative conception. Indeed, in the tenth book of the *Republic*[7] Plato seeks to expel the poets from the state altogether. Such an interpretation is impossible without further evidence. The necessary correction is contained in the consideration of a metamorphosis of the mythical in Plato. This appears most distinctly in the earlier dialogues. While the dialectic produces a wholly abstract and sometimes negative result, the mythical seeks to yield much more. But if we next ask what the mythical is, one must surely answer that it is the Idea in a condition of estrangement, its externality,[8] i.e., its immediate temporality and speciality as such. The mythical in the dialogues exhibits this character completely. The enormous span of time traversed by the soul in the *Phædrus*,[9] the spatial infinity illustrated in the *Gorgias* and *Phædo* as representations of the existence of the soul after death, are both myths. The matter is simply explained. The dialectical first clears the terrain of everything extraneous and now attempts to climb up to the Idea; when this attempt fails, however, the imagination reacts. Fatigued by these dialectical exertions the imagination lays itself down to dream, and from this is derived the mythical. In this dream the Idea either hovers swiftly by in an infinite succession of time, or stands stark still and expands itself until infinitely present in space.[10] The mythical is thus the enthusiasm of the imagination in the service of speculation, and, to a certain extent, what Hegel calls the pantheism of the imagination.*[11] It has validity at the moment of contact and is unrelated to any reflection. This may also be seen from an examination of the *Gorgias* and *Phædo*. The mythical representation of the existence of the soul after death is not brought into

* When the mythical is conceived in this way, it might seem that it was being confused with the poetical. In this connection, however, it must be remarked that the poetical is conscious of itself as poetical, has its reality in this ideality, and desires no other reality. The mythical, on the other hand, resides in a condition of negative disunion and doubleness, an intermediary state from which the interests of consciousness have not yet emerged. The poetical is a hypothetical statement in the subjunctive, the mythical a hypothetical statement in the indicative.[12] This duplicity —the indicative pronouncement and the hypothetical form, which vacillates between being neither subjunctive nor indicative and both subjunctive and indicative—is a description of the mythical. So long as the myth is taken for actuality it is not properly myth. It only becomes myth at the moment it comes in contact with a reflective consciousness; and should it now have speculative content and attach itself to the imagination, then the mythical representation appears. But the age of myth is in one sense already past as soon as the question of a mythical representation arises; but as reflection is not yet permitted to destroy it, the myth still exists. And now, in the process of breaking up and departing, it raises itself up from the earth and in farewell reflects itself once more in the imagination[13]—such is the mythical representation. Erdmann remarks (*Zeitschrift für spekulative Theologie*, ed. by Bruno Baur, vol. III, pt. I, p. 26): 'We call a religious myth a fact or complex of facts which *signify* a religious Idea, not *are* one. A religious myth is a fact or complex of facts which represent religious content in sensuous and temporal form, a form which is not a necessary manifestation of the Idea itself (therein lies its difference from history), but merely externally related to it. Hence the myths are not true, though they might contain truth; they are devised, though not by reflection; and they are not actual facts, but feigned and imaginary.' That they are not true, however, is reserved for a later and truer moment of time to perceive. But the imagination, being indifferent to the question whether they are true or not, views them with philosophic interest, and, being fatigued by the exertions of dialectic as in the present case, reposes itself among them. In one sense it poetically produces them itself, and this is the poetical; but in another sense it does not poetically produce them itself, and this is the non-poetical. The unity of both moments is the mythical, that is, the mythical representation. Hence when Socrates says in the *Phædo*[14] that no one can claim the myth is true, this is the moment of freedom, the individual feels free and emancipated from the myth. But when he adds

relation either with a historical reflection, namely, whether it is indeed the case that Aeacus, Minos, and Rhadamanthus sit in judgment, or with a philosophic reflection, namely, whether it is true. If one may characterize the dialectic corresponding to the mythical as longing and desire, as a glance which gazes upon the Idea so as to desire it, then the mythical is the fruitful embrace of the Idea. The Idea descends and hovers above the individual like a benevolent mist. But to the extent that there is at every moment a faint intimation, a distant presentiment, a mysterious almost inaudible whisper of a reflective consciousness in the condition of such an individual, to this extent there is at every moment the possibility that the mythical undergoes a metamorphosis.

As soon as consciousness appears, however, it becomes evident that these mirages were not the Idea. If, after consciousness awakens, the imagination again desires to return to these dreams, the mythical exhibits itself in a new form, that is, as image. A change has now occurred, for the mythical is here taken up into consciousness, that is, the mythical is not the Idea but a reflection of the Idea. This is the case, I believe, with the mythical representations in the constructive dialogues. The mythical is there for the first time assimilated into the dialectical, is no longer in conflict with it, no longer concludes like a partisan; instead, it alternates with the dialectical,* and in this way both are lifted up into a higher order of things. The mythical may well contain traditional elements, for the traditional is the lullaby as it were comprising one moment in the dream. Yet it is most authentically mythical at those moments when the spirit steals away, and

---

that one should venture to believe it, this is the moment of dependency. In the first case he can do with the myth as he pleases, add to it or take from it; but in the second case it overwhelms him and he surrenders himself to it. The unity of both aspects is the mythical representation.

* Because Plato never arrived at the speculative movement of thought, the mythical, or more precisely, the image, may still be a moment in the representation of the Idea. Plato's element is not thought but representation [Forestillingen].[15]

no one knows from whence it came nor whither it goes.[16]

One may arrive at a similar consideration of the mythical by beginning with the image. When in an age of reflection one sees the image protrude ever so slightly and unobserved into a reflective representation, and, like an antediluvian fossil, suggest another species of existence [*Tilvær*] washed away by doubt, one will perhaps be amazed that the image could ever have played such an important role. But when the image permeates more and more, when it is able to accommodate within itself more and more, it then invites the spectator to find repose in it, to anticipate a pleasure which the restless reflection might perhaps only lead him to after an extensive detour. Finally, when the image acquires such scope that the whole of existence becomes visible in it, then this becomes the regressive movement toward the mythical. Natural philosophy often furnishes examples of this, for instance, Henrich Steffen's preface to *Karrikaturen des Heiligsten*[17] is one such splendid image wherein natural existence becomes a myth about the existence of spirit. The image so overwhelms the individual that he loses his freedom, or rather sinks into a state in which it has no reality, for this is not the kind of image freely produced or artistically created. No matter how absorbed thought becomes in accounting for particulars, however ingenious it is at effecting combinations, or how comfortably it establishes its existence in this, still, it is unable to differentiate the whole out from itself and cause it to appear light and easy in the sphere of pure poetry. This is to show how the mythical may assert itself in an isolated individual. Naturally, the prototype of this must have made itself felt in the development of peoples and nations, but one must not forget that it only continues to be mythical so long as this selfsame process repeats itself in the national consciousness, dreamily reproducing the myths of its own past. Every attempt to take the myth historically already shows that reflection is awake and destroys the myth. For myth, like the fairy-tale, prevails only in the twilight of the imagination, although mythical elements may maintain themselves for a time after the historical interest has awakened and the philosophic interest become conscious.

Inasmuch as this is the case with the mythical in Plato, it will not be difficult to answer the question whether the mythical belongs to Plato or Socrates. I think I can answer for myself and the reader that it does not belong to Socrates. If the testimony of antiquity be borne in mind, however, that it was from a productive existence as a poet that Socrates called the twenty-eight-year-old Plato and invested him with a concern for abstract self-knowledge,* then it is quite natural that the poetical element in his active passivity and passive activity must have asserted itself in opposition to the hungry dialectic of Socrates. Furthermore, it must appear strongest and most isolated in the productivity either contemporaneous with Socrates or most closely associated with him. Now this is also the case, for the mythical stands its ground most stubbornly and obstinately in the earlier dialogues, while in the constructive dialogues it has already bowed itself under the mild regimentation of a comprehensive consciousness. The more knowledgeable reader of Plato, therefore, will no doubt agree with me in allowing the more strictly Platonic development to begin with that dialectic appearing in the *Parmenides* and the other dialogues in this cycle, and end with the constructive dialogues. The dialectic contained in these dialogues, as already remarked, is essentially different from the dialectic described thus far. The mythical in the early dialogues, in relation to the entire Platonic development, might be regarded as a kind of pre-existence of the Idea; and to carry the point still further, one might even call the mythical in these dialogues the unripened fruit of speculation, for, as ripening is a process of fermentation, this corresponds quite favourably to the later, authentic Platonic dialectic. That the fruit of speculation never fully ripens in Plato, however, is due to the fact that the dialectical movement is never wholly consummated.[18]

I shall now briefly discuss the mythical portion of a few dialogues. It seems superfluous to call attention to the fact that one cannot call it mythical simply because it contains a

* K. F. Hermann, *Geschichte und System der platonischen Philosophie*, pt. i, Heidelberg, 1839. Cf. p. 30 together with the corresponding note 54.

reference to some myth, for referring to a myth does not make a representation mythical; nor is it mythical because it uses a myth, for this clearly shows one is above it; nor is a representation mythical because one seeks to transform a myth into an object of belief,[19] for the mythical is not addressed primarily to the understanding but to the imagination. The mythical requires that the individual abandon himself to this, and only when the representation oscillates in this way between the production and reproduction of the imagination is the representation mythical. It is generally assumed that the mythical representation in the *Symposium* begins with the narrative of Diotima.[20] But this is not mythical because it refers to the myth about Eros as the offspring of Poros and Penia, for the legends concerning the origin of Eros had not gone unnoticed in the preceding discourses. The determination given to Eros is negative: Eros is an intermediary, is neither rich nor poor. Thus far we have not progressed beyond the Socratic exposition. But now this negative—the perpetual unrest of thought forever separating and combining, which thought is unable to hold fast because it is the forward thrust of thought itself[21]—stops here and unburdens itself for the imagination, enlarges itself for intuition [*Anskuelse*]. Such is the mythical. Everyone who has concerned himself with abstract thought will undoubtedly have noticed how seductive it is in seeking to hold fast that which essentially is not, except insofar as it is abrogated. This is a mythical tendency. What happens is that the Idea is maintained under the determinations of time and space, the latter understood wholly ideally.*
What the mythical representation provides, over and above

* That which gives space reality is the organic process of nature, that which gives time reality is the content of history. But in the mythical representation both time and space have only imaginary reality. This is seen from the myths of India, for example, in the childlike squandering of time, which, attempting to say so much, says nothing at all because the criterion employed is simultaneously deprived of validity. Thus to say that a king reigned for 70,000 years completely abrogates itself, since it uses a determination of time but attributes no reality to it. In such an ideality time and space are arbitrarily confounded and interchanged with each other.[22]

the dialectical movement described earlier, is that it permits the negative to be seen. But in one sense this is also less, for it causes the development of thought to recede, and manifests itself not as a consummation of the process already begun but as an entirely new beginning. Indeed, the more it seeks to enlarge contemplation and render it more comprehensive, the more it exhibits its opposition to the purely negative dialectic; with this, however, it also removes itself more and more from essential thinking, deceives thought, and renders it sentimental and effete. The other way in which the mythical portion of this dialogue provides more than the dialectical is in setting forth the beautiful as the object of Eros. With this we have an authentic Platonic dichotomy, which, as previously remarked, suffers from all the difficulties of a dichotomy, inasmuch as it has the negative outside itself, and the unity attained can never hypostatize itself. If one examines the condition of the beautiful more closely, it becomes apparent that this shuffles off a multitude of determinations through a dialectical movement. The object of love is successively: beautiful bodies—beautiful souls—beautiful discourse—beautiful knowledge—the beautiful. The beautiful is now determined not merely negatively as that which will appear in a far more glorious light than gold, apparel, fair youths and loved ones, but Diotima adds (211 E): 'What if a man had eyes to see the true beauty—the divine beauty, I mean, pure and clear and unalloyed, not infected with the pollutions of the flesh and all the colours and vanities of mortal life—thither looking, and holding converse with the true beauty simple and divine?' Manifestly, the mythical lies in the fact that the in-and-for-itself beautiful shall be seen. And though our feminine expositor has once renounced all mortal vanity and apparel, it is obvious that these will return again in the realm of the imagination to provide the mythical ornamentation. Such will always be the case with *das Ding an sich*[23] when one cannot cast it away or deposit it in the book of forgetfulness; for should one succeed in getting it outside thought, he will then bid the imagination mend and make good the loss.

This position naturally calls to mind the Kantian standpoint. I shall touch briefly upon the difference. Kant, to be sure, stopped with this *an sich* aspect of things; yet either persevered in his effort to grasp it with the aid of subjective thought, and when this turned out to be impossible had the great advantage, the rather ironic good fortune, of always hoping; or else he cast it away, sought to forget it. To the extent that he sometimes endeavours to maintain it, however, he develops the mythical. His entire view of a 'radical evil',[24] for example, is essentially a myth. The evil that thought is unable to cope with is placed outside thought and entrusted to imagination. Similarly, the poet Plato during the mythical portion of the *Symposium* dreams into being all that the dialectician Socrates sought to establish. It is in the world of dreams that irony's unhappy love finds its object. The fact that Plato places this representation in the mouth of Diotima does not make it mythical. Whereas it does pertain to the mythical —a thing imagination is altogether fond of—that the object is placed outside, removed only in order to be brought back again—as when a person does not wish to experience a fairytale himself, and so endeavours to thrust it away by opposing an issue [*Mellemværende*] to it, thereby rendering the presence of imagination all the more appealing. Ast also remarks[25] that this whole affair with Diotima is pure fabrication, while Baur's observation[26] that Plato chose the mythical representation in order to give his *philosophem* positive support in a form familiar to folk-consciousness, not only explains too little but conceives the relation of the mythical to Plato wholly externally.

When we consider the mythical representation of the condition of the soul after death as described in the *Gorgias* and *Phædo*, it is evident that a dissimilarity obtains between these two conceptions. In the *Gorgias* Socrates impresses upon his listeners several times*[27] that he believes this, and acknowledges his belief in opposition to those who perhaps 'might

* The fact that Socrates is also the speaker in the mythical portion of the dialogues proves nothing against the correctness of the distinction between the dialectical and the mythical established here; for it is well known that Plato never introduces himself as a participant, but always employs the name of Socrates.

regard and despise this account as an old wife's tale' (527 A). However, it is apparent from the subsequent lines that he is more concerned to reinforce the Idea of justice than to uphold the myth, since he himself admits that it is natural to despise such tales if by inquiry one can find something better and truer. Again, the mythical consists not so much in references to the legend of Minos, Aeacus, and Rhadamanthus as in holding fast to the decree of judgment as illustrated to the imagination, or such as imagination reproduces it. In the *Phædo*, on the other hand, Socrates himself suggests how the whole conception is to be regarded (114 D): 'A man of sense ought not to assert that the description which I have given of the soul and her abodes is exactly true. But I do say that, inasmuch as the soul is shown to be immortal, he may venture to believe, not improperly or unworthily, that something of the kind is true. The venture is a glorious one, and he ought to charm himself as it were with such things, which is also the reason I have been lengthening out the tale so long.' More-over, the expressions here used are the correct ones, namely, that it is 'a venture' to believe this, and that one ought 'to charm' himself with such things. The representation of the many prolonged epochs through which the soul must pass according to its nature, the vastness of the underworld into which one sees the soul disappear accompanied by its genius, the different characters of the several abodes of the soul, the wave of Tartarus which casts the souls either into Cocytus or Pyriphlegethon, the gathering of these souls in the Acherusian lake from which they lift up their voices and call to those whom they have either slain or wronged—all this is quite properly mythical. But the mythical lies precisely in the power it acquires over the imagination, for in invoking this one conjures forth visions which overwhelm himself. The speculative thought moving busily through this twilight, as it were, is the divine justice, that harmony pervading the intellectual world of which the laws of nature spanning the universe are but an image.

The Republic, Book One

Before I attempt to account for the choice of dialogues discussed, I must add one more selection. The first book of the *Republic* must be briefly considered before leaving the details of Plato. Schleiermacher, in his introduction to the *Republic*, observes of the relation of this dialogue to the earlier ethical dialogues: 'If we would completely understand Plato's meaning, we must not overlook the fact that all the resemblance between the work before us and the other ethical dialogues completely vanishes as the work advances. . . . Even the method is completely changed. Socrates no longer comes forward with questions in the character of a man who is ignorant and only seeking greater ignorance in the service of the god, but as one who has already found what he seeks. He moves forward bearing along with him in strict connection the insights he has acquired. Nay, even in point of style, it is only the immediately succeeding speeches of the two brothers, as constituting the transition, that bear any resemblance to what has gone before. No dialogic embellishment or enticing irony is hereafter to gain the prize, but solid strictness of argument alone. The whole apparatus of the youthful virtuoso glitters here once for all in the introduction and is then extinguished forever, in order to make it as clear as possible that everything beautiful and pleasing of this kind occupies a place in the province of philosophy only in preparatory investigations, the object of which is more to stimulate and excite than to advance and come to satisfactory conclusions; and that when a connected exposition of the results of philosophic investigation is to be given, such embellishments would contribute more to distract the mind than assist the perfect comprehension of the subject.'[1] (*Platons Werke*, Part Three, vol. 1, pp. 9, 10.) Hence it will be helpful to dwell once more on the nature* of this representation, in particular, its relation to the Idea. If one cannot deny that there is an

---

* How it is to be otherwise explained that Plato in one of his last writings concerned himself with the entire Socratic dialectic and irony, which had

essential difference between the first book of the *Republic* and those that follow, and if one agrees with the preceding observations of Schleiermacher, then our attention is once more directed to the earlier dialogues and to that form which must have come under the influence of Socrates. Hence this section of the *Republic* will furnish the occasion for ratifying in all brevity, if possible, the appraisement contained in the foregoing. In particular, there are two things to note: this first book does not merely end without a result, as Schleiermacher claims, but ends with a negative result; secondly, irony is here again an essential moment.

For the sake of completeness we may consider the irony partly in its individual expressions, partly in its definitive endeavour or striving. The latter is naturally the most significant. But it will not be unimportant to see that even its individual expressions do not relate to the Idea, that the destruction of what is distorted and one-sided does not occur in order that the truth may appear, but merely to begin again with something equally distorted and one-sided. This is important in order to see that even the individual expressions of irony have not repudiated their origin and lineage, but are still diligent apprentices, cunning scouts, and incorruptible informers labouring in the service of their master. But this

---

ceased to concern him throughout a not inconsiderable number of intermediary dialogues, and to which he never again returned, will not concern me, since on the whole I subscribe to the observations of Schleiermacher above. As the explanation lies so near at hand, however, I shall make a place for it here. The first book of the *Republic* treats of such questions as constitute the object of inquiry in the earlier dialogues. Hence it was quite natural in this connection for Plato to wish to recall Socrates as vividly as possible, and as he desired to set forth his total-view in the *Republic*, he deemed it appropriate briefly to trace once more the development exhibited in the earliest dialogues, and to provide a kind of introduction, which is far from being an introduction for the reader of the *Republic*, to be sure, but which considered as a recapitulation will always be of interest to the reader of Plato, and which must have had considerable affective value for the grateful disciple himself.[2]

master is none other than the total irony which, when all the minor skirmishes have been fought and all the ramparts levelled, gazes out upon the total desolation and becomes conscious that nothing remains, or rather, that what remains is nothingness. Hence this first book of the *Republic* forcefully reminds one of the earlier dialogues. The outcome suggests the *Protagoras*, the internal arrangement suggests the *Gorgias*, and there is a striking resemblance between Thrasymachus and Callicles. In the *Gorgias* the insolence for which Socrates admires Callicles, who claims that Gorgias and Polus have been overthrown because they lacked the audacity to say directly that most of mankind share the view that to do injustice is the best, if only it is carried out discreetly, but that men have a kind of modesty when it comes to asserting it—as if the weaker had devised this as a mode of defence—this insolence we again find fully developed in Thrasymachus.*
The manner in which Thrasymachus, who has waited impatiently for the opportunity to speak, finally storms forth,[3] reminds one of the forceful attack by Polus and Callicles, while Socrates' first ironic parry suggests a similar passage in the *Gorgias*: 'And I, when I heard him was dismayed, and looking upon him was filled with fear, and I believe that if I had not looked at him before he did at me I should have lost my voice. But as it is, at the very moment when he began to be exasperated by the course of the argument, I glanced at him first, so that I became capable of answering him, and said with a slight tremor: "Thrasymachus, do not be harsh with us" ' (336 D).[4] The caustic way in which Socrates evasively eludes Thrasymachus' thesis ('that justice is nothing else than the interest of the stronger') by sceptically retorting (338 C): 'You cannot mean to say that because Polydamas the pancratiast is stronger than we are, and finds the eating of beef conducive to his bodily strength, that to eat beef is therefore equally for

---

* Cf. 348 D. —To the question whether he would call justice virtue and injustice vice, he answers: no, the opposite, which is later modified, for in answer to the question whether he would then call justice vice, he says: ' "No, I would rather say sublime simplicity." "Then would you call injustice malignity?" "No, I would rather say good counsel." '

our good who are weaker than he is, and right and just for us,' is an unambiguous parallel to the way Socrates ridicules the thesis of Callicles that the strongest (i.e., the wisest, i.e., the best) should have the most.* In general, the irony in this whole first book is so inordinate and uncontrollable, bubbles over with such abundance and romps with so much playfulness and intensity, that one can scarcely imagine what immense muscle power must be possessed by a dialectic corresponding to this. But as all these exertions do not in any way relate to the Idea, so the Sophists together with the involutions of thought in this whole first book bear a certain resemblance to the grotesque figures which perform and the equally grotesque leaps that are executed in a *Schattenspiel an der Wand*.[5] Yet the whole affair is pursued by the Sophists with a seriousness and expenditure of energy that form a biting opposition to the nothingness of the result, and it will be well-nigh impossible to refrain from laughing when one hears Socrates say (350 D): 'Thrasymachus made all these admissions, not as I now lightly narrate them, but with much baulking and reluctance and prodigious sweating—it being summer.' The individual expressions of irony are here not in the service of the Idea, not its emissary gathering the scattered parts together in a whole; for they do not consolidate but disperse, and every new beginning is not the consummation of anything preceding, not an approximation to the Idea, but without any deeper connection with what went before and without any relation to the Idea.

As for the content in this first book, I shall attempt to present a survey complete enough to satisfy our needs and as

---

* Socrates argues that the person with the most knowledge about food and drink should have the most, and when Callicles answers: 'You talk about meats and drinks and physicians and other nonsense; I am not speaking of them,' Socrates continues: 'I understand: then, perhaps, of coats—the skilfullest weaver ought to have the largest coat, and the greatest number of them, and go about clothed in the best and finest of them? *Callicles*: The deuce with coats! *Socrates*: Then the most skilful and best at making shoes ought to have the advantage in shoes; the shoemaker, clearly, should walk about in the largest shoes, and have the greatest number of them?' (*Gorgias* 490 D, E).

compact as I can make it. Socrates and Glaucon are on their way to the Piræus in order to be present at the festival of Bendis.[6] On the way back they are invited to the home of the aged Cephalus. Socrates accepts the invitation and soon a conversation develops between him and Cephalus, a person whose discourse has all the charm of an idyllic pedal point. Socrates expresses his gratitude for the old man's company, for one who has traversed a large part of the journey of life must necessarily be able to advise one who has just begun. The circumstance that Cephalus has partially inherited and partially acquired a not inconsiderable fortune directs Socrates' attention to the problem whether justice wholly consists in speaking the truth and paying one's debts, or whether there are occasions when it would be unjust to repay a debt. (For example, if one were to return to a friend not in his right mind a sword that had been deposited by the friend when in his right mind.) At this point, Cephalus retires and surrenders the discussion to the others, whereupon Polemarchus, his son and heir ('O thou heir of the argument'),[7] takes up the thread. He proposes the thesis that it is just to repay a debt, and expands this so as to mean doing good to friends and evil to enemies, explicating the term 'debt' by the phrase 'to render each his due' (332 B). This last expression, however, furnishes Socrates with the opportunity to develop a sceptical objection derived from the province of knowledge; for as it is evident that to render each his due depends upon knowledge, the sphere of justice becomes severely restricted. He then tilts the whole affair in such a way that justice is seen to be useful only when a thing is not in use, and hence useful by virtue of the useless. Thrasymachus had thus far remained silent, impatiently waiting for the opportunity to break in, but now he storms in upon Socrates with frantic strength, and after first venting his indignation over the way Socrates has duped them, says (338 C): 'I proclaim that justice is nothing else than the interest of the stronger.' Socrates allows himself to appear suitably discountenanced, but after a little teasing designed to distract Thrasymachus' attention from the central question, initiates once more the same tactics so successfully employed against Polemarchus. It is by appeal-

ing to the province of knowledge that Socrates again makes
his escape. The word 'stronger' here becomes the stumbling
block. For if this applies to the stronger without regard to
whether a particular person or the power in the state is meant,
since in either case the laws of the state are calculated according to the appropriate interest, then, as the legislator is not
infallible, it is possible that the laws might not be in the
interest of the stronger but to his injury. Thrasymachus claims,
however, that this objection disappears when one considers
that as a physician is not a physician insofar as he is mistaken
but only insofar as he prescribes correctly, so one who is a
legislator in the true sense of the word will know how to enact
laws truly calculated to serve his own interest. Thrasymachus
is therefore not speaking about an ordinary ruler, but about
a ruler in the strict sense of the word, indeed in the strictest
sense of the word (341 B: 'in the strict sense—a ruler in the
strictest sense'). The fact that the concept is conceived in the
eminent sense provides Socrates with the occasion for a new
doubt, namely, that what holds for every other art must also
hold for the art of the ruler when truly practised: that it
acknowledge no extraneous concern but aim solely and
inflexibly at its own object without having an eye cocked for
any special interest. Socrates had scarcely arrived this far (and
the correctness of his statement about the course of the discussion cannot be denied: 'that the definition of justice had
been completely turned round' (343 A)), when Thrasymachus
was seized with a new attack of rage and like one possessed,
egotistically lost in a monological spawning of words, ridding
himself of a new stream of what Socrates would call insolence,
whose essential content is this: when Thrasymachus speaks of
doing injustice, he does not mean injustice in trivial matters;
quite the contrary, the more grandiose the injustice, the more
perfect it becomes and the more profitable for him who does
it. After he had finished this diatribe he sought to leave, but
the rest of the company prevented him. Socrates returns once
more to his previous conception and shows that each and
every art must be conceived according to its ideal striving,
and that the parasitical growth of finite teleology attempting

to attach itself to this must be rejected. Each particular art has its own characteristic end, its function, which is none other than promoting the interests of those entrusted to its care. Thrasymachus maintains his thesis and further explains that justice is nothing but simplicity, while injustice is discretion. Socrates next moves Thrasymachus to assert that injustice is wisdom and virtue. Thereupon Socrates seizes upon the thesis that injustice is wisdom and, by means of certain analogies drawn from the province of knowledge, once more dislodges Thrasymachus from his entrenchment behind this audacious paradox. The just man does not try to gain any advantage over the just but over the unjust, whereas the unjust man tries to gain an advantage over both the just and the unjust. Similarly, an artisan does not strive to exceed or go beyond what another artisan would do, but beyond what one who is not an artisan would do; a physician does not try to go beyond what another physician would prescribe, but beyond what one who is not a physician would prescribe. In general, the wise do not endeavour to do and say more than another with knowledge, but more than the ignorant; whereas the ignorant seek to do and say more than the wise as well as the ignorant. Hence the just man is wise and good, the unjust ignorant and evil. With this the argument glides on its way, and the subsequent discussion is not lax in predicating every imaginable good of justice. These predicates, however, are more descriptive of the external. They are to be regarded as something like a bulletin calling for the arrest of a criminal, for while this may assist in the capture by furnishing clues, it does not contain the determinations of the concept. While they set thought in motion, they allow it to hover in the abstract and never pacify it with positive content. When, in conclusion, Socrates wishes to have Thrasymachus ratify the result (354 A): 'Never, then, most worshipful Thrasymachus, can injustice be more profitable than justice,' we can in one sense forgive Thrasymachus his contemptuous reply: 'Let this complete your entertainment, Socrates, at the festival of Bendis.' But Socrates has too much insight into the course of the discussion not to notice that the whole procedure has been rather desultory. He therefore concludes with the observation (354 B): 'As a gourmand snatches a taste of every dish which is successively brought to table, without having allowed himself time to enjoy the one before, so have I gone from one subject to another without having discovered what I sought at first, the nature of justice. I left that inquiry and turned away to consider whether justice is virtue and wisdom or evil and folly; and when there arose a further question about the comparative advantages of justice and injustice, I could not refrain from passing on to that. And the result of the whole discussion has been that I know nothing at all. For I know not what justice is, and therefore I am not likely to know whether it is or is not a virtue, nor can I say whether the just man is happy or unhappy.'

In considering the movement throughout this first book, surely everyone will admit that this is not the dialectic of the Idea. Indeed, one might say the question evolves dialectically out of the follies of the speakers. Hence this first book acquires no more than the mere possibility of asking with speculative energy: what is justice. One must therefore agree with Schleiermacher[8] in holding that this first book ends without a result. Yet this might seem wholly accidental. If a work like Plato's *Republic*, consisting of ten books of which the discussion of the Idea of justice is the central issue, does not immediately set forth the result in the first book, this must be deemed quite in order. However, this is not the whole matter. The great difference between the first book and those that follow, the fact that the second book begins all over again, begins from the beginning, must not be lost sight of. If we add to this that the first book is conscious of the fact that it does not arrive at a result, that it does not flee from this consciousness but sustains it and finds repose in it, then it cannot be denied that this first book not only ends without a result,* but ends

---

* That Socrates touches upon one or another positive thought in the course of the discussion cannot be denied. But the positive is here again conceived in its total abstraction, and is to this extent merely a negative determination. Thus to convey every art up into an ideal sphere,[9] into a higher order of things where it is practised only for its own sake unaffected by all earthly profanation, is a very positive thought in and for itself, but

with a negative result. As this in and for itself is ironic, so also Socrates' concluding remarks bear the unmistakable stamp of irony. Hence the consideration of this first book of the *Republic*, if I have not merely been fencing in air, will find support in all that has gone before, while the foregoing, insofar as it was still hovering, will acquire new foothold in this last investigation. Thus my entire edifice need not in any way be precarious, since the one simultaneously supports and is supported by the 'other'.

I must place particular emphasis, however, upon the first book of the *Republic*. In one way or another Plato must have been conscious of the difference between this first book and those that follow; and as a whole cycle of intermediary dialogues do not at all resemble it, so he must have had some definite intention with it. This is the first point. The second is that this first book is thoroughly reminiscent of the earlier dialogues. These must have come under the authority and personal influence of Socrates in quite a different sense than the later dialogues. The result is that it is through these earlier dialogues, together with the first book of the *Republic*, that we can most reliably make our way to a conception of Socrates.

---

also so abstract that in relation to any particular art it becomes a negative determination. The positive thought, the actual content ($\pi\lambda\acute{\eta}\rho\omega\mu\alpha$), would only be given were that wherein it desires itself to become manifest. The negative determination that neither does it desire any 'other' would then follow the positive determination like a shadow, like the possibility of such a desire at every moment abrogated. Here the relation is somewhat reversed, however, for it is asserted as the positive that art is not practised for the sake of an 'other'. It is easy to say that justice ought to be pursued for its own sake, but in order for something actually to be advanced in thought, the first moment of justice must be developed into the second moment of justice, the forward striving unrest of justice in the first place must have found repose and pacification in justice in the second place. So long as it is not known what justice is, therefore, the thought that justice ought to be desired for its own sake naturally remains a negative one.

A confirming retrospect

I have constantly had but one purpose with regard to the selection of dialogues, namely, to restrict myself to those which, according to common consent, would provide me with a view of the actual Socrates, however incomplete this may be. Most scholars in their arrangement of the dialogues have a first group —and this is the main thing for me—which they associate intimately with Socrates, not merely because these are nearest him in time, for this would be a wholly external determination, but because these are presumed to be most akin to him in spirit, though not all scholars are agreed with Ast in explicitly calling them Socratic.* Furthermore, not all scholars are agreed as to which dialogues should be assigned a place in this first group, but, and this is sufficient for me, all include the *Protagoras* and most include the *Gorgias*. Ast[1] also places the *Phædo* in this group, but there are several who oppose him in this. Most are once again agreed in attributing special significance to the *Symposium* and *Phædo* with respect to the conception of Socrates. Inasmuch as Ast[2] declared himself opposed to the view of Schleiermacher presented earlier concerning the connection between the *Symposium* and *Phædo*, his protest places an obstacle in my path. As he still counts the *Phædo* among the 'Socratic' dialogues, however, I can with certain modifications follow Schleiermacher and those agreed with him on this point. Most are agreed in attributing historical significance in a stricter sense to the *Apology*, hence

* 'Plato, in the dialogues constituting the first group, still lived wholly within the Socratic sphere. His aim was to assert the Socratic over against the corrupt principles of the Sophists (*Protagoras*), orators and writers (*Phædrus*), and statesmen (*Gorgias*) of the day; he was concerned to exhibit not only their nothingness and lack of content, but even their perniciousness.' (*Op. cit.*, pp. 53, 54). This observation of Ast can generally be admitted if one bears in mind that the polemic here in question is not a positive polemic thundering down upon false doctrines with the pathos of seriousness, but a negative polemic undermining them in a far subtler yet more emphatic way, coldly and impassively watching them sink down into total nothingness.

particular emphasis must be placed upon this dialogue, and that I have also done. Finally, I have endeavoured under Schleiermacher's auspices to maintain the special significance for this investigation of the first book of the *Republic*.

If I have had an eye for the results of critical scholars regarding the selection of dialogues, accommodated myself to them as much as possible, leaned upon them as much as they allowed, I have nevertheless endeavoured to assure myself of the correctness of these views through an impartial study of a great deal of Plato. That irony and dialectic are the two great forces in Plato will surely be admitted by all; but it is no less obvious that there is a double species of irony and a double species of dialectic. There is an irony that is merely a goad for thought, quickening it when drowsy, disciplining it when dissipated. There is another irony that is both the agent and terminus towards which it strives. There is a dialectic which, in constant movement, is always watching to see that the problem does not become ensnared in an accidental conception; a dialectic which, never fatigued, is always ready to set the problem afloat should it ever go aground; in short, a dialectic which always knows how to keep the problem hovering, and precisely in and through this seeks to solve it. There is another dialectic which, since it begins with the most abstract Ideas, seeks to allow these to unfold themselves in more concrete determinations; a dialectic which seeks to construct actuality by means of the Idea. Finally, there is in Plato still another element which is a necessary supplement to what is lacking in both these two great forces. This is the mythical and the image. To the first species of irony corresponds the first species of dialectic, to the second species of irony the second species of dialectic. To the first pair corresponds the mythical, to the second pair the image, yet not in such a way that the mythical exhibits a necessary relation to the first pair, nor indeed to the second pair, but is instead like an anticipation evoked by the one-sidedness of the first pair, or like a moment of transition, a *confinium*,[3] which properly belongs neither to the one or the other.

Either one must suppose that both these standpoints lie

within the compass of Plato, or that one of them belongs primarily to Socrates and only secondarily to Plato. —In the first case, it must be supposed that Plato has primarily experienced the first stage within himself, allowed it to develop in itself until the second stage began to assert itself, which, after having successively unfolded itself, ended by completely supplanting the first. The first stage is not assimilated into the second, for in the second everything is new. If one ascribes both standpoints to Plato, one must characterize the first as scepticism, as a kind of introduction that leads no further, as an approach that fails to attain its goal. Add to this that under this hypothesis the first standpoint is not accorded its due, not allowed to consolidate itself internally but reduced as much as possible to make the transition to the second stage easier. If one does this, however, one alters the phenomenon; while if one does not do this, the difficulty of accommodating both standpoints primarily within Plato increases. Moreover, the significance of Socrates is in this way thrust aside, and such an attempted interpretation would undoubtedly conflict with history. For in this case the only thing Plato would have Socrates to thank for would be the name 'Socrates', which in this conception would play as accidental a role as the actual influence of Socrates played an essential role. —In the second case, if it be assumed that one of these two standpoints belongs primarily to Socrates and only secondarily to Plato, then it follows that Plato merely reproduced this standpoint. There can be no doubt as to which of these two standpoints belongs to Socrates. It must be the first. Its characteristics, as previously indicated, are irony in its total striving,* and dialectic in its negative, emancipating activity.†

* It might seem that one could characterize the first stage merely as dialectic, and hence conceive Socrates exclusively as a dialectician. This has even been done by Schleiermacher in a well-known essay.[4] But dialectic as such is an altogether too impersonal determination ever to contain a figure like Socrates; for while dialectic infinitely expands itself and flows out in extremities, irony leads the movement back into personality, induces it to round itself off in personality.

† Thus it is quite in order when Aristotle[5] denies dialectic in the proper sense of the word to Socrates.

To the extent that I may not have been entirely successful in justifying this standpoint out of Plato in the foregoing, the reason for this, apart from what my own deficiencies may have occasioned, is that Plato merely reproduced it. As irony must have acquired an exceedingly powerful influence over a poetic disposition like that of Plato, so it became exceedingly difficult for him to understand this influence, to reproduce irony in its totality, and to refrain from any admixture of positive content in order to ensure that it did not become within this standpoint what it later became, namely, a negative power in the service of a positive Idea. If this is now the case, one will perceive in our approach the correctness of allowing those statements in the earlier dialogues that vacillate between a positive and negative standpoint to be ambiguous, momentary glimpses, the mythical portion in these dialogues to be an anticipation, and allow the authentic Platonism to commence with that cycle of dialogues containing the *Parmenides*, *Theaetetus*, *Sophist*, and *Statesman*.

There is, of course, one difficulty always remaining for me, namely, that it is only possible to apprehend the first standpoint through a calculating observation, inasmuch as Plato's reproduction is not entirely free from a certain double illumination. This admits of being the more readily explained as between irony and subjective thought a frequently deceptive similarity obtains. As this first concerns the relation of one personality to another, it is manifest that this relationship, insofar as it is emancipating, may be in part negatively and in part positively emancipating as previously mentioned.[6] Insofar as irony severs the bands restraining speculation, assists it to work itself free from sheer empirical sand banks and venture out upon the deep, this is an emancipating activity in the negative sense. Irony is in no way an interested party in the expedition. But insofar as the speculative individual feels himself emancipated—and now a vast treasure opens before his mind's eye, he might easily believe he owes all this to irony, might in his gratitude wish to owe everything to irony. There is, to be sure, something true in this confusion, since all intellectual property exists only in relation to the consciousness possessing it. For both standpoints, irony and subjective thought, a personality is therefore a necessary point of departure. In both standpoints the activity of personality is emancipating, but whereas that of irony is negative, thought is positive. Hence Plato was emancipating for his pupil in quite another sense than was Socrates for Plato. Still, it became necessary even for the pupil of Plato to think with him in mind, for his speculation remained merely subjective, nor did he allow himself to be eclipsed while the Idea itself confronted the listener. Plato's relation to Socrates did not always remain constant, however, for subsequently he was not so much emancipated by Socrates as he emancipated himself in himself, though his memory was too faithful and his gratitude too intense ever to forget him. Hence insofar as Socrates is still the central figure in the constructive dialogues, this Socrates is but a shadow of the former in the earlier dialogues, a recollection which Plato, however precious to him, nevertheless stood freely above, even freely and poetically created.

As regards form, dialogue is equally necessary for both standpoints. It suggests the self and its relation to the world. But in the first case it is the self which continually swallows the world, while in the second it is the self which seeks to assimilate the world. In the first, the self constantly talks itself out of the world, in the second, into the world. For the first standpoint it is a questioning that devours the answer, for the second, a questioning that unfolds the answer. As regards method, this is dialectical in both standpoints, abstract dialectic. As such it does not exhaust the Idea. What remains in the one standpoint is nothingness, that is, the negative consciousness in which abstract dialectic is assimilated; what remains in the other standpoint is a beyond, an abstract determination, yet one sustained positively. To this extent irony is beyond[7] subjective thought: it is beyond it insofar as it is a completed standpoint which turns back into itself; by contrast, subjective thought has a frailty, a defect through which a higher standpoint must work its way forward. But in another sense irony is an inferior standpoint: it is inferior insofar as it lacks this possibility, remains unresponsive to every demand, will no longer have anything to do with the world, and is sufficient unto itself. As both standpoints are subjective positions, naturally they fall to a certain extent within the province of a philosophy of approximation, yet without losing themselves in this, since they would then degenerate into wholly empirical standpoints. The means by which the one standpoint goes beyond actuality is the negative, i.e., the negation of the validity of experience as assimilated into consciousness; the other standpoint goes beyond actuality in having a positivity in the form of an abstract determination. The one sustains recollection negatively directed backwards in opposition to the movement of life; the other sustains recollection directed forwards in its emanation in actuality.*

But while I am thus engaged in rendering this misunderstanding possible, in developing my investigation of it, perhaps one or another reader is thinking somewhat ironically that it is all a misunderstanding on my part, the whole thing a false alarm. The difficulty such a reader refers to is naturally this: to explain how it is possible for Socrates to have so mystified Plato that the latter could have understood seriously what Socrates said ironically. Indeed, one might make this difficulty even greater for me by recalling the fact that Plato, whatever his last writings show, otherwise understood irony extremely well. As for this last objection, I shall answer that what is at issue here is not the individual expressions of irony, but Socratic irony in its total striving. But to apprehend irony in this way requires a wholly unique intellectual disposition differing qualitatively from every other. In particular, a rich poetic disposition is poorly endowed to conceive such irony in the eminent sense. Such an intellectual disposition might easily feel itself attracted by the individual expressions of irony without ever comprehending the infinity here concealed, might sport with them without any idea of the enormous daamon that inhabits irony's desolate and empty places. As for the first objection I shall answer: partly that it will always

* The reader has found the more extensive treatment of all these similarities and dissimilarities, all these points of coincidence, as they occur in the foregoing.

remain extremely difficult for a Plato wholly to comprehend Socrates; partly, and this is my principal answer, that one cannot look for a simple reduplication of Socrates in Plato, nor has it ever occurred to any reader of Plato to do this. But if Plato, as most scholars agree, has not merely reproduced Socrates but poetically created him, then surely this contains all one might wish respecting the removal of this difficulty. As Plato allows Socrates to do the talking in the later dialogues, yet no one dares to infer from this that the Socratic dialectic actually resembled that found in the *Parmenides*, his development of the concept like that found in the *Republic*; so neither is one justified in inferring from the representation found in the earlier dialogues that the standpoint of Socrates was in actuality exactly as there portrayed. —There might, perhaps, be one or another reader willing to admit this, yes even waiting somewhat impatiently for me to finish this consideration so as to bring a new objection down upon my head. Inasmuch as I have endeavoured in the foregoing to exhibit irony in its total striving within the individual dialogues, surely Plato must also have understood it since it is to be found in his account. To this the following must serve as an answer. In the first place, throughout the foregoing investigation I have merely sought to render my conception of Socrates possible. I have therefore on several occasions allowed the conception to remain hovering, have even suggested it might be regarded in a different way. In the second place, I have argued principally from the *Apology*. In this dialogue, according to the opinion of most, we have a historical rendering of Socrates' actuality; yet even here, characteristically enough, it became necessary for me to conjure forth the spirit of irony as it were, to induce it to collect itself together and become manifest in its complete totality.

Xenophon and Plato

If one were to express in few words the Platonic conception of Socrates, one could say that Plato has given him the Idea. Where empiricism ends, Socrates begins. His activity is to lead speculation out of the determinations of finitude, to lose sight of finitude and steer out upon that Oceanus wherein ideal striving and ideal infinity acknowledge no extraneous concern but are themselves their own infinite destination. As the lower sensation pales beside this higher knowledge, yes, becomes a deception and a deceit by comparison, so every reference to a finite end becomes a belittlement, a profanation of the holy. In short, Socrates has won ideality, conquered those vast regions heretofore an unknown land. Accordingly, he despises the useful, is indifferent towards the established [Bestaaende], an avowed enemy of that mediocrity which empiricism deems highest, even making it an object of pious worship, but which speculation disdains as the changeling of a clan of trolls. If, on the one hand, we call to mind the result arrived at through Xenophon's account, namely, that we there found Socrates feverishly engaged as an apostle of finitude, as an officious drummer for a propaganda of mediocrity, indefatigably proselytizing his own exclusively saving, earthly gospel, that we there found the useful substituted for the good, the serviceable for the beautiful, the established [Bestaaende] for the true, the lucrative for the sympathetic, sobriety for harmonious unity—then one will surely admit that these two conceptions are not easily united. Either we must charge Xenophon with total arbitrariness, with an inconceivable animosity toward Socrates which sought satisfaction through slander; or we must ascribe to Plato an equally mysterious idiosyncrasy for his opposition, one which just as inexplicably realized itself in transforming him into a likeness of himself. If we would allow Socrates' actuality to exist for a moment as an unknown dimension, one might say of these two conceptions that Xenophon has acquired his Socrates by haggling down the price like a huckster, while Plato has created his Socrates in supernatural dimensions like an artist. But what was Socrates actually like, what was the point of departure for his activity? The answer to this would naturally help us out of the distress to which we have thus far been consigned. The answer is: Socrates' existence is irony. As this answer, I believe, cancels the difficulty, so the fact that it cancels the difficulty makes it the correct answer, exhibiting itself at the same moment both as hypothesis and as truth. The point, the stroke rendering the irony into irony, is extremely difficult to catch hold of. With Xenophon one may readily assume that Socrates was fond of going about and talking with every sort of person, because every external thing or event is an occasion for the always battle-ready ironist. With Plato one may readily allow that Socrates touches the Idea, except that the Idea does not open itself to him but is a limit. Each of these two inter-preters has naturally endeavoured to render Socrates com-plete: Xenophon by dragging him down into the shallow regions of the useful, Plato by catching him up into the super-natural regions of the Idea. But irony is the point lying between them, invisible and extremely difficult to hold fast. On the one hand, the manifold of actuality is just the ironist's element; on the other hand, his course through actuality is hovering and ethereal, scarcely touching the ground. As the authentic kingdom of ideality is still alien to him, so he has not yet emigrated but is at every moment, as it were, about to depart. Irony oscillates between the ideal self and the empirical self; the one would make of Socrates a philosopher, the other a Sophist. Still, what makes him more than a Sophist is the fact that his empirical self has universal validity.

ARISTOPHANES

Aristophanes' conception of Socrates will provide the necessary opposition to that of Plato, and by this very opposition bring about the possibility of a new direction in our calculation. Indeed, it would be a great loss if we lacked the Aristophanic evaluation of Socrates. As every development usually ends by parodying itself,[1] and such a parody is a guarantee that this development has outlived itself, so the comic conception is also a moment, in many ways an infinitely correcting moment, in the total illustration of a personality or tendency. Although the immediate testimony concerning Socrates is lacking, though we lack a completely dependable conception of him, still, we have in exchange all the various nuances of misunderstanding, and with such a personality as Socrates I believe this serves us best.[2] Plato and Aristophanes have in common the fact that both their interpretations are ideal, but inverted with respect to each other; Plato has the tragic ideality, Aristophanes the comic. What motivated Aristophanes[3] to conceive Socrates in this manner, whether he was bribed by the accusers of Socrates, whether he was embittered over Socrates' friendship with Euripides, whether he wanted to combat Anaxagoras' speculations on nature through Socrates, whether he identified him with the Sophists, in short, whether there was any earthly or finite reason determining Aristophanes in this matter—all this is wholly irrelevant for this investigation. And insofar as our inquiry might contain an answer, it must of course be a negative one, since it affirms the conviction that the conception of Aristophanes is ideal and hence free from every such consideration, not cowering along the ground but soaring free and easy above it. Merely to conceive Socrates' empirical actuality, to bring him on the stage exactly as he was in life, would have been beneath the stature of Aristophanes and changed his comedy into a satirical poem. On the other hand, to idealize Socrates according to a standard whereby he became wholly unrecognizable would lie entirely outside the interests of Greek comedy. That the latter was not the case is also confirmed by antiquity, which reports[4] that the performance of the *Clouds* was honoured by the presence of its severest critic in this respect, by Socrates himself, who, to the satisfaction of the public, stood up during the performance so the crowd assembled in the theatre could convince itself of the proper resemblance. That a merely eccentric and ideal conception would fall outside the interests of Greek comedy is also confirmed by the penetrating Rötscher,* who brilliantly argues that the essence of Greek comedy lay in apprehending actuality ideally,[5] in bringing an actual personality on the stage in such a way that this is seen as representative of the Idea, and that this is the reason one finds in Aristophanes

* H. Theodor Rötscher, *Aristophanes und sein Zeitalter, eine philologisch-philosophische Abhandlung zur Alterthumsforschung*, Berlin, 1827.

three great comic paradigms: Cleon, Euripides, and Socrates,[6] whose persons comically represent the striving of the age in its threefold direction. Whereas the minutely detailed conception of actuality filled in the distance between audience and theatre, the ideal conception once more estranged these two forces, insofar as art must always do this. Moreover, it is undeniable that Socrates actually presented many comical aspects in his life, or to say it clearly once and for all: he was to a certain extent what one might call an oddity (*Sonderling*).* If one cannot deny that this was already justification for a comic poet, neither can one deny that it would have been too little for an Aristophanes. Though I cannot do otherwise than modestly join the deservedly triumphant Rötscher,[7] who victoriously traces the Idea through and out of its conflict with previous misunderstandings, and though I cannot but agree with him in holding that Socrates was a comic figure for Aristophanes only insofar as he perceived in Socrates the representative of a new principle; still, it is quite another matter whether the seriousness Rötscher vindicates to such a high degree in this drama does not bring him into conflict with the irony he elsewhere attributes to Aristophanes. It is also questionable whether Rötscher has not seen, and made Aristophanes see, too much in Socrates. One might well call Socrates the repre-

* Cf. *Nachträge*[8] *zu Sulzers allgemeiner Theorie der schönen Künste*, vol. 7, pt. 1, p. 162: 'Unfortunately, we know Socrates only from the embellished portraits of Plato and Xenophon, from which a great deal follows that seems strange and suggests an unusual person. The guidance of an invisible daimon in which the philosopher was pleased to believe, his withdrawal and absorption into himself lasting for more than a day even while at camp, to the astonishment of his camp fellows, his conversation whose object, aim, and manner was distinguished by so much that was odd, his neglected exterior and in many respects curious behaviour—all this must have given him the appearance of an oddity in the eyes of the many.' —Similarly, the author remarks that if we knew Socrates better, we would undoubtedly agree with Aristophanes even more (p. 140): 'We would then be unmistakably convinced that in spite of his many virtues and splendid qualities he still had the faults and defects of humanity in great measure, that, as several reliable indications suggest, he belonged in many respects to that class of odd characters, and that his mode of teaching was not free from the reproach of verbosity and pedantry.'

sentative of a new principle, partly because he represented a new standpoint, and partly because his emancipating activity must necessarily incite a new principle. But it does not follow from this that one can safely delimit Socrates any further within such an admission. Socrates looms so large in Rötscher's conception that one altogether loses sight of Plato. But there will be occasion to discuss all this later. If, however, one will suppose that irony was the constitutive factor in Socrates' life, one will have to admit that this presents a much more comic aspect than allowing the Socratic principle to be subjectivity, inwardness, with all the wealth of thought this entails, and locates Aristophanes' authority in the seriousness with which he, as an advocate of the older Hellenism, must endeavour to destroy this modern nuisance. This seriousness is too ponderous, it would limit the comic infinity which as such knows no limit. By contrast, irony is at once a new standpoint and as such absolutely polemical toward the older Hellenism, and also a standpoint which continually cancels itself. It is a nothingness which consumes everything and a something which one can never catch hold of, which both is and is not; yet it is something in its deepest root comical. As irony conquers everything by seeing its disproportion to the Idea, so it also succumbs to itself, since it constantly goes beyond itself while remaining in itself.

The first thing of importance is to become convinced that it is the actual Socrates which Aristophanes has brought on to the stage. As one is reinforced in this conviction by the traditions of antiquity, so a multitude of Socratic traits are to be found in this work which are either historically certain, or appear to be thoroughly analogous to what we otherwise know about Socrates. Süvern, with great philological erudition and much taste, has attempted to prove the unity of the Aristophanic representation and the actual Socrates by just such a series of individual traits.* Rötscher has also submitted a collection of such data, which, though not according to the same criterion, is nevertheless sufficient for our investigation. This material is found in the above-mentioned work on page

* J. W. Süvern, *Über Aristophanes Wolken*, Berlin, 1826, p. 3 *ff.*

277 ff. The next thing of importance is to see the principle, the Idea, which Aristophanes allows us to envisage in Socrates as its transparent representative.

In order to obtain this, however, it is necessary to present a short summary of the work itself, both its plot and action. I can embark upon this investigation so much the more confidently since I have an Hegelian leading the way, and one must always allow that they have a superb talent for making place for things, a constabulary authority knowing instantly how to disperse every sort of learned tumult and suspicious historical conspiracy. To begin with the chorus, which as such represents the ethical substance,[9] this has clad itself in a symbol* in our drama. Rötscher locates the irony in the fact that the chorus is itself conscious of this, that it desires at every moment to spring out from behind this concealment as it were, and which in conclusion it succeeds in doing since it mocks Strepsiades for having been deceived by them. Whether the irony lies in this, or whether the seriousness† defending the substantial consciousness of the state against the vacuity of this modern nuisance does not limit the poetic infinity and wantonness of irony; or whether the whole conclusion of the drama, though it be a just nemesis, does not occur at the expense of irony—except insofar as one will suppose what to my knowledge has never been maintained by anyone, namely, that the revenge Strepsiades reaps by burning down the Thoughtery (φροντιστήριον, 94) was by its very purposelessness a new comic motive, and hence that Strepsiades' not unfunny replies,‡ which in one sense are too good to him, should be explained as a kind of ecstatic madness by which he first phantasized in his head and then with comic ferocity destroyed and stamped out the very disease with which he

* See Rötscher's excellent discussion of the history of the chorus in Aristophanes, *op. cit.*, pp. 50-9.

† Aristophanes acknowledges this seriousness himself in the first parabasis (510 *ff.*).

‡ Cf. 1496: 'Streps. What am I at? I'll tell you. I'm splitting straws with your house-rafters here.'

1503: 'Streps. I walk on air, and contemplate the Sun.'[10]

himself was infected—such questions will not concern me here.* But if we omit all this, it becomes even more important to dwell on the symbol in which the poet has enveloped the chorus, viz., the clouds. Since this could not have been accidentally chosen, it is essential to discover the poet's idea in this connection. Manifestly, it illustrates all the empty and vacuous activity that goes on in the Thoughtery, and it is therefore with deep irony that Aristophanes, in the scene in which Strepsiades is to be initiated into this wisdom, allows Socrates to call upon the clouds,[11] the airy reflex of his own hollow interior. Clouds describe perfectly the completely directionless movement of thought,† which, with incessant fluctuation, without foothold and without immanent laws of motion, configures itself in every which way with the same irregular variation as do the clouds, which now resemble mortal women,[12] now a centaur, a leopard, a wolf, a bull, etc. But resemble them, be it noted, not *are* them, for all this is no more than vapour or the obscure, self-moving, infinite possibility of becoming whatever it becomes, yet too barren to allow anything to become established [*Bestaaende*], a possibility which has an infinite extension and contains the whole

* At any rate, the irony is much more pure and freeborn in an earlier passage where Strepsiades is actually convinced by Phidippides' sophisms that he is right, and that he (Strepsiades) ought to receive a thrashing. Cf. 1437:

   'Streps. Good friends! I really think he has some reason to complain.

           I must concede he has put the case in quite a novel light:

           I really think we should be flogged unless we act aright!'

Similarly, the relation between the two species of discourse, the just and the unjust logics, is conceived with the whole infinity of irony; for when it is remarked that the unjust logic always triumphs, Strepsiades implores Socrates that above all else Phidippides must learn the latter. Cf. 882:

   'Streps. So now I prithee, teach him both your Logics,

           The Better, as you call it, and the Worse

           Which with the worse cause can defeat the Better;

           Or if not both, at all events the Worse.'

† It accords perfectly with this when the ethereal vortex (αἰθέριος δῖνος)[13] is substituted for the plastic shape of the gods as the constitutive principle in nature, and the wholly negative dialectic is excellently characterized as a whirlwind.

world within itself, as it were, but has no content, a possibility able to assimilate everything but retain nothing. To this extent it is sheer arbitrariness for Socrates to give them the predicate 'goddesses', and Strepsiades is naturally far more sensible in supposing them to be fog, mist, and vapour (cf. 330). But while their vacuity is apparent in themselves, it is no less apparent from the community or state which they sustain and protect, and which Socrates describes as a gathering of loafers and idlers singing praises to the clouds.* Indeed, this correspondence between the clouds and the world to which they belong, a fact which it seems to me interpreters have so far overlooked, is expressed even more definitely when it is said: 'These become just what they please' (γίγνονται πανθ' ὅ τι βούλονται). Accordingly, when they spy a fellow with long hair they assume the shape of a centaur, and when they see a thief they assume the shape of a wolf (350-2). In spite of the fact that this is described as an absolute power possessed by the clouds, and despite the fact that Socrates explains that they assume such shapes in order to mock, it might as easily be regarded as a lack of power in them. Here the Aristophanic irony undoubtedly lies in the reciprocal impotence: that of the subject who, in seeking the objective, obtains no more than his own likeness; and that of the clouds, which grasp merely the subject's likeness and produce this

---

* Cf. 331: 'Soc. O, then I declare, you can't be aware that 'tis these
        whom the Sophists protect,
        Prophets sent beyond sea, quacks of every degree,
        fops signet-and-jewel-bedecked,
        Astrological knaves, and fools who their staves of
        dithyrambs proudly rehearse—
        'Tis the Clouds who all these support at their ease,
        because they exalt them in verse.'
Hence their favours also correspond to this. Cf. 316:
        'Soc. No mortals are there, but Clouds of the air, great
        Gods who the indolent fill:
        These grant us discourse, and logical force, and the
        art of persuasion instil,
        And periphrasis strange, and a power to arrange,
        and a marvellous judgment and skill.'

only so long as they continue to see the object. Surely no one will deny that this is an excellent description of the purely negative dialectic which remains for ever in itself and never ventures out into the determinations of life or the Idea, and hence rejoices in a freedom that disdains the shackles imposed by continuity;* a dialectic which is only a power in the most abstract sense, a king without a country who delights in the sheer possibility of renouncing everything at the moment of apparent possession, though both the possession and renunciation are illusory; a dialectic which does not feel restricted by the past nor enveloped by its ironbound consequences, which has no dread of the future because it is so quick to forget that the future is forgotten almost before it is experienced; a dialectic which wants nothing, desires nothing, is sufficient unto itself, which leaps over everything as fickle and wantonly as a runaway child.

The consciousness of this nothingness inherent in the fact that the chorus is at once a symbol and yet ironically aware of being outside this and having quite another reality, Rötscher ascribes only to the chorus, the poet, and the enlightened spectator. He then adds (p. 325): 'The true meaning is necessarily concealed from one who is not aware of this opposition, for he perceives in it merely the symbol, accepts the shape in which it consciously veils itself as its true essence, and confidently and unsuspectingly surrenders himself to it, never grasping that it is merely an appearance that was offered him instead of the truth. The fault of the subject consists in the fact that he gave himself unsuspectingly to these deceptive forces and is ignorant of the essence exhibiting this appearance.' But this concerns the whole inner economy of the work,

* In this description I have been most concerned with the intellectual aspect, since this is obviously nearest Hellenism. That a similar dialectic, in the form of the arbitrary, exhibits itself even more grievously in the moral sphere is also clear; but in this connection I feel there is often too much regard for the features of one's own age when conceiving the transitional period which Greek life was undergoing during the time of Aristophanes. Hegel quite correctly remarks (*Geschichte der Phil.* xviii, 70): 'We must not make criminals of the Sophists because they did not make the good into a principle; this is the vacillation of the age.'

while here it is more important to see whether we can discern in the chorus' symbol, the clouds, as it is presented, something that comes closer to the essence whose image it is. The chorus represents clouds, but the clouds in turn represent various objects as in the beginning of the play they assume the shape of women. But Socrates clearly speaks of these shapes in a very jocular fashion, a fact which sufficiently shows they have no validity for him. Hence what he worships, attributing to it the predicate 'goddess', is the formless nebulosity that Strepsiades quite correctly describes as fog, mist, and vapour.[14] Consequently, what Socrates retains is the formless itself. The shapes which the clouds assume are merely like so many predicates asserted in such a way that they are all co-ordinated without being connected to each other, without inner coherence and without constituting anything, in short, like so many predicates merely reeled off. As in our previous investigation we saw that Socrates arrived at the Idea, but in such a way that no predicate revealed or betrayed what this actually was yet all were silent witnesses to its splendour, so the same thing is suggested, it seems to me, by Aristophanes in the relation of Socrates to the clouds. What remains when one allows the various shapes assumed by the clouds to disappear is nebulosity itself, which is an excellent description of the Socratic Idea. The clouds always appear in a definite shape, but Socrates knows the shape is unessential and that the essential lies behind the shape. Similarly, the Idea is true, and the predicate as such has no significance. But what is true in this way never passes out into any predicate, it never *is*.* If we continue to consider the symbol of the chorus, the clouds, and see in this Socrates' thoughts viewed objectively,† see these as not only produced

* Should it seem to one or another reader that I find too much in Aristophanes, I shall gladly admit this if he in turn will remove the difficulty which always remains when one examines the curious relationship between the subject and the clouds. Obviously, there are two moments to be considered: the chorus has enveloped itself in a symbol, the clouds, but the clouds have in turn assumed the shape of women.

† That this has been set forth as an article of faith, and as such contains both a subjective and objective aspect, may be seen from line 424: 'And

by the individual but also worshipped by him as objective (divine) thoughts, then it is precisely the clouds' hovering above the earth together with their multiplicity even as shapes which suggest the opposition between the subjectivity of the new and the objectivity of the older Hellenism, wherein the divine had a foothold upon the earth in definite, distinct, and eternal shapes. It is therefore a very profound harmony which exists between the clouds and the subject Socrates: the former as the objective power unable to find a permanent location upon the earth, and whose approximation to this always yields distance; and the latter, who, hovering above the earth in a basket,[15] endeavours to elevate himself up into these regions because he fears the force of the earth will draw these thoughts away from him, or to dispense with the imagery, that actuality will absorb and crush his fragile subjectivity (ἡ φροντις λεπτη).* We shall again return to this when, instead of beginning with the chorus, we treat of the character in the action and further explain what relevance Socrates' unique situation has for the Idea.

The chorus illustrates the whole new order of things seeking to displace the older Hellenism, and hence the question whether Aristophanes wanted to mock and ridicule the Sophists under the mask of Socrates can best be answered here. It is obvious that in no case should it be assumed that Aristophanes merely retained Socrates' name, and otherwise presented a portrait which in no way resembled him. If, on the other hand, it is

---

my creed you'll embrace, "*I believe in wide space, in the Clouds* (the objective), *in the eloquent Tongue* (the subjective)." ' Hence it is with the utmost comic force that Aristophanes has Socrates swear by the same powers. Cf. 627: 'Never, by Chaos, Air, and Respiration.'

   * Cf. 227: 'Soc. I could not have searched out celestial matters
                   Without suspending judgment, and infusing
                   My subtle spirit with the kindred air.
                   If from the ground I were to seek these things,
                   I could not find: so surely doth the earth
                   Draw to herself the essence of our thought.
                   The same too is the case with water-cress.'

borne in mind that in one sense Socrates and the Sophists stood for the same position, that it was essentially by carrying through their standpoint and destroying the halfness in which the Sophists came to rest that Socrates undermined them, so that Socrates overcame the Sophists in a certain sense precisely because he himself was the greatest of the Sophists,* then one will surely see in this a possibility for Aristophanes to identify him with the Sophists. This identification also admitted of being carried out with deep irony. For it would certainly be an irony worthy of Aristophanes to conceive Socrates, the Sophists' most spiteful enemy, not as their antagonist but rather as their teacher, which in one sense he certainly was. And the curious confusion that one who combats a particular movement may himself be conceived as its representative, since he himself to some extent partakes of it, conceals in itself so much intentional or unintentional irony that it should not entirely be lost sight of.[16] Finally, it is only when one employs the chorus as a criterion that Socrates disappears among the Sophists, for if we follow the personal characterization of him contained in the work, he stands out sufficiently clear and distinct.

The action of the drama may be presented quite briefly, especially in the present investigation since we are only concerned to reproduce this insofar as the obvious events throw some light upon the Aristophanic conception of Socrates. A respectable landowner, Strepsiades, has got himself into financial difficulties through a miscalculated marriage. His son Phidippides with his love of horses has also been most helpful in contributing to his father's ruin. Constantly troubled by the thought of his debts and perpetually concerned about saving himself from disaster, Strepsiades casts about in vain for a solution when suddenly the thought of the new wisdom that had begun to make itself felt in Athens, and especially its power of proving and disproving everything, awakens with unexpected satisfaction the hope of finding his salvation in this. His first impulse is to let Phidippides enjoy the fruits of

* It is a most descriptive predicate, therefore, which the clouds use in addressing him (359): 'the high-priest of this subtlety feast.'

this modern doctrine, but when the son turns out to be unwilling Strepsiades decides to present himself at the Thoughtery. He then meets one of the disciples who also conveys a favourable impression of the school. Many of Socrates' puzzling characteristics, together with numerous perplexing questions and answers, cause him as a respectable landowner to hesitate, but a masterstroke* of Socrates that comes close to confirming his own inclinations removes all doubt, and with enthusiasm he demands impatiently to be taken to Socrates. Strepsiades obtains permission to enter the Thoughtery only after a preliminary examination, wherein an attempt is made to divest him of the now antiquated thought processes in which he had previously existed (ingeniously characterized by the fact that he

---

* Cf. 177:

'Stud.   He sprinkled on the table—some fine ash—
           He bent a spit—he grasped it compass-wise—
           And—filched a mantle from the Wrestling School.
Strep.   Good Heavens! Why Thales was a fool to this!
           O open, open, wide the study door,
           And show me, show me, show me Socrates.
           I die to be a student. Open, open!'

If the reader will recall that Strepsiades later comes home[17] from the Thoughtery without his cloak, he will surely sense the comedy in this situation. Strepsiades, who had hoped to share in the plunder (a cloak), comes home not merely without a profit, but even without those things formerly his—a cloak. And yet this was to come away rather well, judging from Strepsiades' subsequent remarks, for during his tutoring session he comes to fear that Socrates' speculations will reduce him to nothing at all. Cf. 717:

'Strep.   Why, what can I do?
           Vanished my skin so ruddy of hue,
           Vanished my life-blood, vanished my shoe,
           Vanished my purse, and what is still worse
           As I hummed an old tune till my watch should be past,
           I had very near vanished myself at the last.'

It is also apparent from the chorus' exhortations to Socrates that everything is designed to fleece Strepsiades. Cf. 810:

'Chor.   But now that you have dazzled and elated so your man,
           Make haste and seize whate'er you please as quick as you
           can.'

must first put off his clothes* before entering the Thoughtery).
After a solemn initiation which, if it were able to make any
impression at all on Strepsiades, must necessarily have made
utter confusion of his concepts, he is shown the same way to a
knowledge of the truth as Socrates himself pursued: to immerse
himself in himself† without regard to his surroundings.
Naturally, for Strepsiades this was very meagre sustenance
indeed, and fully as satisfying as the banquet to which the
stork invited the fox,[18] who became a fasting witness to the
way in which his host immersed himself stork-fashion in the
long-necked vase. Strepsiades is therefore deemed incapable
of being transformed by the new wisdom and is presently dismissed. But he has in no wise given up all hope of realizing his
plan. Too modest to believe the failure might lie with the
teacher, he seeks the cause in himself, and soon consoles himself
with the thought of his promising son Phidippides who,
though somewhat sceptical of the specimens of wisdom displayed by his father, finally succumbs to Strepsiades' petitions
and allows himself to be enrolled in the Thoughtery. The
son fares much better and the father brings gifts to Socrates
in gratitude for his splendid progress. Nevertheless, menacing
actuality draws nearer and nearer and finally appears in the
sober shape of two creditors. Overjoyed with Phidippides'
dialectical power of shifting boundary lines,‡ and confident of

* Cf. 497: 'Soc.   Put off your cloak.
         Strep.   Why, what have I done wrong?
         Soc.   O, nothing, nothing: all go in here naked.'

† Here we have the Aristophanic conception of the famous Socratic
trance, his standing still and staring.

‡ Cf. 1178: 'Phid.   What is it ails you?
      Streps.   Why the Old-and-New day.
      Phid.   And is there such a day as Old-and-New?
      Streps.   Yes: that's the day they mean to stake their gauges.
      Phid.   They'll lose them if they stake them. What! do
              you think that one day can be two days, both
              together?
      Streps.   Why, can't it be so?
      Phid.   Surely not; or else a woman might at once be old
              and young.'

the still unforgotten, ingenious questions and answers learned in the Thoughtery, Strepsiades dares to meet these two representatives of calamitous actuality himself. Pasias and Amynias, however, are too much financiers to be put off by such shrewdness. They still have so much confidence in actuality that they doubt not that they will have their day, and if not through dialectic then through the courts. But while Strepsiades is momentarily given to rejoicing over having attained the object of his desire, the poet has reserved for him a little bonus, a quite unexpected dividend resulting from the extraordinary progress made by Phidippides in assimilating the Socratic teaching. For besides the actuality of the due date, Phidippides has outgrown quite another, one which Strepsiades would prefer not to see shaken. Filial respect and obedience to his father fare no better than the due date under this dialectic. Strepsiades is unable to withstand the force of Phidippides' syllogisms which, while previously employed to destroy actuality, are now vigorously employed to posit a new actuality: for thrashings are tangible goods, as the saying goes, and prove themselves in a way that leaves no doubt. And as Phidippides previously had shown himself to be unscrupulous enough to aid his father in avoiding repayment of the borrowed money, so now he develops an almost excessive conscientiousness about repaying an instalment on the debt of thrashings

---

Cf. *Aristophanis Comoedier*, pt. 1, translated by J. Krag, Odense, 1825, p. 233: 'The Athenian month consisted of thirty days. The first twenty were numbered forwards from the first to the twentieth, but the remainder were numbered backwards from the following month. The twenty-first was thus the tenth, the twenty-sixth the fifth, the twenty-ninth the second. The thirtieth was thus the old and the new, and the first was called the new month.' —On this last day of the month interest fell due, and was for this reason dreaded by Strepsiades. But he was now freed from this worry by Phidippides' ingenuity, which had the power to cancel actuality and prove it did not exist. I have deliberately included this sophism as an example of the dialectic taught in the Thoughtery because it parodies the Socratic dialectic based on the principle that one cannot affirm contradictory predicates of the same thing; and also because it insists with so much comic force not only on the validity of the universe of thought, but even presumes the authority to negate actuality.[19]

showered upon him by a loving father. Strepsiades discovers too late the corruption in the new wisdom. Revenge awakens and rushes in over its victim, who once more storms into the Thoughtery, burns it down, and the comedy ends.

This is the briefest possible résumé of the plot. The comic substance lies in that something which Strepsiades desires as the fruit of speculation, a something which to his mind must necessarily result from all these manipulations. But just as Socrates' manipulations in the sphere of intelligence turn out to be without significance, without the capacity to posit anything, so the same exhibits itself even more distinctly in the world of Strepsiades, who has got hold of the hopeless notion that something will actually come of all this* in a finite and

---

* This seems to be the place for an interpretation of the much disputed passage cited earlier[20] concerning the cloak which, according to the statement of the disciple, Socrates snatched from the wrestling school. For the *vita ante acta*[21] of this problem see Rötscher pp. 284 ff. —Süvern has refuted the explanation advanced by Reisig and found in its place a description of the well-known Socratic distraction. As there is some suggestion that it came about through a mathematical demonstration, he associates it with that Socratic illiberality for which we have Xenophon to thank, and according to which he taught that one should only learn so much mathematics as can be employed in everyday living. Rötscher holds that this passage does not refer to any particular fact, but merely represents the cleverest description of the practical inventiveness of which Strepsiades, being hard pressed in life, stood in need. But when in emphasizing the Socratic cunning he insists that Socrates stole the cloak from the Palaestra, for which the law of Solon prescribed the death penalty, I believe he strays from the essential point of these words to which he is so near in other statements. Aristophanes undoubtedly wanted to ironize over this negative dialectic that bleeds to death in wholly vacuous experiments, and so with even deeper irony now attributes to it a creative power, since he allows it to produce an actuality as it were by artificial demonstrations, i.e., in such a way that the production borders upon a theft insofar as this actuality is a finite, earthly thing. The remark consigned by Rötscher to a note[22] is to be understood similarly, viz., that Chaerephon, the friend of Socrates, was frequently honoured by the comic poets with the nickname 'thief' (κλέπτης). The words introducing the incident: 'He sprinkled on the table—some fine ash—He bent a spit—he grasped it compass-wise,' seem to be the prelude to an act of creation; then, with even greater emphasis

worldly sense, or, to take our cue from modern philosophy, who hopes to speculate into existence the Kantian one hundred dollars,[23] or in the absence of them, to speculate away his debts.* The irony lies in the something which, if not immediately then mediately through Phidippides, he speculates into existence: those conscious thrashings which, however unexpected they may be, come with a necessity that is impossible to escape. Strepsiades may well find momentary pleasure in all these ingenious manipulations, but what his sober spirit desires is 'the practical application', nor does this fail to materialize though it comes where least expected. If we inquire into the standpoint shining through this parody, we may not say it is that of subjectivity, for this always yields something, yields the whole world of the abstract ideal. What is characterized here, however, is a purely negative standpoint yielding nothing at all. The profound reflections set forth dissolve

---

and all the surprise of spontaneity, follow the words: 'And—filched a mantle,' etc. —But however one prefers to understand this passage with reference to the significance it must have for the work, there always remains an obscurity in the way this trick relates to the deficiency it is supposed to remedy. The disciple tells Strepsiades that Socrates undertook the above mentioned operation by which he filched a mantle from the wrestling school when they were in need of an evening meal. Yet one does not see how this provided for the evening meal, unless one supposes that Socrates sold the cloak and thereby procured what was needed; nor does one see the significance of the fact that he filched it from the wrestling school. In Hermann's edition[24] (Leipzig, 1799, p. 32) there is another reading of this passage in a note, viz., ἐκ τραπέζης. He also calls attention to the problem that the article here is incorrect, since there is no mention of a specific cloak.[25] This difficulty remains unresolved by Hermann.

* One cannot deny to Strepsiades a commendable perseverance in this matter; in spite of the fact that he comes home from the Thoughtery without having learned a thing (for in this the infirmities of old age were to blame, cf. 855), and in spite of the fact that he has lost both his cloak and his shoes (cf. 857: 'It's very absent sometimes: 'tisn't lost'), still, with confidence in Phidippides' natural ability, he has not abandoned hope and belief in the new wisdom.

like thunder in a vacuum, while following this like a parodying shadow is the fact that Strepsiades seeks to acquire something, but, be it noted, something finite, a finite advantage, which this standpoint is no more able to provide than the intellectual benefit it appears to confer. But if one assumes that Socrates' entire activity consisted in ironizing, one will perceive that Aristophanes has proceeded correctly insofar as he wished to conceive the comical; for irony exhibits itself as comical as soon as one attempts to relate it to a result—though in another sense it frees the individual from the comical. Nor is the dialectic which is illustrated time and time again an authentic philosophic dialectic; unlike the dialectic described earlier as characteristic of Plato, it is an utterly negative dialectic. Had Socrates been in possession of the subjective dialectic of Plato, it would have been completely false for Aristophanes to conceive Socrates in this way; though amusing, it would still not be comical, for the comical must also have a truth. If, on the other hand, the Socratic dialectic was reinforced with sophisms and directed polemically against the Sophists, and at the same time negatively oriented toward the Idea, then the Aristophanic conception is comically correct.[26] The same is true of the symbol of the chorus, the clouds. Had this denoted the ideal realm of the subjective standpoint, then, in spite of the fact that Aristophanes' conception is comical, it would have been untrue to allow the individual to relate himself as accidentally to this as Aristophanes has done. The ironist, by contrast, is extremely lighthearted about the Idea, in this respect he is completely free, since for him the absolute is nothingness.

In considering the second moment of the drama, the *dramatis personæ* and in particular the character of Socrates, it is immediately apparent that Aristophanes has not identified him with the Sophists, for not only has he made Socrates easily recognizable through a multitude of minor traits (this is the point particularly emphasized by Rötscher),[27] but he has chiefly portrayed the Socratic standpoint as one of complete isolation. Now this is perfectly correct. For while Socrates has disciples in this drama as he also had in life, these do not relate to him in any way, or rather, he does not enter into any relationship with them.* Instead of yielding to them, he constantly hovers freely above them, thoroughly analogous to his relationship with Alcibiades described earlier,[28] mysteriously attracting and repelling. The significance of his immersion in himself remains always inexplicable to them, since the subtleties that attempt to reveal something about it bear no relation to it. Aristophanes has made a synthesis of everything belonging to the various moments in Socrates' life, hence even Anaxagoras' speculations on nature come to play a part, since Socrates according to the *Phædo*[29] had once occupied himself with these but afterward abandoned them. I shall disregard the numerous episodes† containing ridiculous subtleties or farcical sleight-of-hand tricks, together with all the fanfare accompanying such feats, in short, the multitude of what might collectively be characterized as sport, since no trace of the Idea is to be found in them. The atheistic observations about nature, which frequently produce an extremely comical effect by their opposition to the rather naïve superstitions of Strepsiades,‡ will subsequently acquire some significance. What is most important, however, is firstly the conception of Socrates as a personality; secondly, the characterization of the central aspect of his teaching, dialectic; and lastly, the portrayal of his standpoint.

As regards the first of these, it will readily be seen that this contains a proof for the fact that Aristophanes has not identified

---

* Hence he says in Plato's *Apology*[30] that he has never been anyone's teacher nor accepted any disciple.

† It deserves to be pointed out, however, that it has been very prudently arranged by Aristophanes so that Socrates plays a much larger role at the beginning of the work than at the end, and that while the education of Phidippides takes place off-stage, the upbringing of Strepsiades is carried out in front of everyone, wherein the old and the modern standpoints, represented by equally comical personalities, yield very little to each other in ludicrousness.

‡ Cf. 368 ff., where Socrates explains how rain is formed, namely, that it is the clouds that rain, and Strepsiades assures him 373: 'Yet before, I had dreamed that the rainwater streamed from Zeus and his chamber-pot sieve.'

Socrates with the Sophists. Sophistry is the wild and dissolute thrashing about of egotistical thought, the Sophist its breathless priest. As the eternal thought in sophistry dissolves itself into an infinity of thoughts, so this swarm of thoughts is illustrated by a corresponding swarm of Sophists.* In other words, there is no necessity whatever to conceive a Sophist in the singular, since the Sophist comes under the concept of species, genus, etc., whereas the ironist is always singular and comes under the determination of personality. The Sophist is ever in feverish activity, ever grasping for something that lies in front of him; the ironist, on the other hand, directs this back into himself at every moment, and such an act with its consequent backward current is a determination of personality. The sophism is therefore a ministering element in irony; and whether the ironist uses the sophism to emancipate himself or to wrest something from another, he nevertheless assimilates both moments into consciousness, i.e., he enjoys. Enjoyment is therefore a determination of personality, even though an ironist's enjoyment is the most abstract of all, the most vacuous, the mere contour, the weakest intimation of that enjoyment possessing absolute content, i.e., happiness. Whereas the Sophist runs about like a harassed merchant, the ironist moves proudly as one terminated in himself—enjoying. This is also suggested by Aristophanes, for when he has the chorus relate how Socrates is the object of its special attention, he also has it distinguish Socrates from another chosen favourite, Prodicus. The chorus makes the following distinction: it yields to Prodicus for his wisdom and insight, and to Socrates 'because he swaggers about the streets, throws his eyes sideways, endures

* After this solemn stillness, by which every new world historical standpoint is represented (for such things come about so unobserved that it is almost as if they never happened in the world but occur outside it), there follows the vociferous chorus of the Sophists, the humming and buzzing of fantastical insects, which, in an infinite series of movements and postures [*Mellemhverandre*],[31] scurry in and over themselves and each other unceasingly in every direction. They usually come in an enormous host like the locusts over Egypt, and they signify that the world spirit is again about to emancipate itself from the restraint of personality in order to lose itself in a formation like that at the mouth of the Rhine.

barefoot much evil, and casts an affectatious glance at us.'* That he becomes a comic personality in Aristophanes' treatment is quite in order. Nevertheless, he is not without that plasticity so characteristic of a personality, that wholeness which has no need of any surroundings but is represented to the eye as a soliloquy.[32] Surely everyone feels it was not an accidental actuality Aristophanes wanted to represent—not Socrates' magnificent body, not the famous big feet which Socrates found apportioned to him by a rare favouritism of nature because they were so perfect for standing on, not the protruding eyes which, as he himself remarks, permitted him to gaze about so effortlessly, not the unfortunate exterior with which nature had so ironically endowed him and which he in turn conceived with so much irony[33]—but that in these words of the chorus Aristophanes wanted to suggest an Idea. Nor is such a conspicuous personality a sign for a wholly subjective speculation, where, precisely because the empirical self recedes and the ideal determinations of the pure self develop, the individual to a certain extent also disappears. No, the ironist is a prophecy of and an abbreviation for a complete personality.

With respect to the Socratic dialectic as portrayed in this work, it must be borne in mind that we are only concerned with this insofar as it can be conceived wholly intellectually; that is to say, we shall not concern ourselves with the immoral behaviour in which such a dialectic may become an effective conspirator when in the service of a corrupt will. To a certain extent Aristophanes must also have been aware of this, for otherwise I do not see how one will be able to save him from

* Cf. 360: 'Chor. Since there is not a sage for whom we'd engage
      our wonders more freely to do,
    Except, it may be, for Prodicus; he for
      his knowledge may claim them, but you,
    For that sideways you throw your eyes as you go,
      and are all affectation and fuss;
    No shoes will you wear, but assume the grand air
      on the strength of your dealing with us.'

the old accusation of having slandered Socrates. Although Socrates was largely and with much justification conceived by Aristophanes as representative for a principle threatening the older Hellenism with destruction, it would nevertheless be unjust to accuse Socrates of having corrupted the morals of the youth, with having introduced a dissoluteness and laxity which both the old and new Hellenism must necessarily abhor. It would be an injustice not only because Socrates had won claim to being the most upright man in Hellas, but principally because the standpoint of Socrates was doubtless so abstractly intellectual (a fact already apparent from the famous conception of sin as ignorance) that I believe it would be more correct as regards conception if one dispensed with some of the bombast about his many virtues and noble heart, yet in addition regarded his life as indifferent to all charges of corrupting ethical norms. Rötscher[34] may emphasize as much as he likes the seriousness with which Aristophanes has conceived his task in the *Clouds*; but Aristophanes is not justified by this, unless one wishes to emphasize the comical inherent in the fact that Aristophanes became so serious about something which could only become as corrupt as it did for a later wrongheadedness. Aristophanes seems also to attribute such an intellectual neutrality to Socrates. When Phidippides is about to be initiated into the Socratic teaching, Aristophanes allows the just and the unjust logics to appear as two opposing forces,[35] and places Socrates outside them both as the indifferent possibility. The dialectic here portrayed is obviously an idle vagabond; sometimes meticulously searching out the most inept things and wasting time and energy on the most foolish hairsplitting ('the nice hairsplittings of subtle logic' 130); sometimes becoming so apathetic and indolent that it assumes the shape of a clever riddle buster, or a certain experimental ingenuity commonly an object for the insipid enthusiasm of unproductive and empty heads; sometimes becoming absorbed in these futilities with such morbid seriousness that the predicate 'deep thinkers' (101) is applied to the whole school; sometimes attempting to grasp something great and significant, but jumping up and running away again the moment this appears.* Between these two extremities lies the dialectical activity whose validity realizes itself in dividing. Whereas the essentially philosophic and speculative dialectic unites, the negative dialectic, since it renounces the Idea, is a broker always negotiating in a lower sphere, that is, it separates.† Hence it presupposes in the pupil only two attributes, those which Socrates seeks to ascertain‡ whether Strepsiades possesses, viz., memory and a natural disposition to talk.§ Strepsiades' answer[36] to the first question—that he possesses memory in a double sense, for if anyone owes him something then his memory is especially good, but if he himself

* Cf. 700. The chorus addresses Strepsiades:
> 'Now then survey in every way,
>   with airy judgment sharp and quick:
> Wrapping thoughts around you thick:
> And if so be in one you stick,
> Never stop to toil and bother,
>   Lightly, lightly, lightly leap,
> To another, to another.'

If it is not reading too much into this, one may find in these words a description of the desultory dialectic that makes of the Idea a solid body incapable of penetration, and from which it therefore runs away. Moreover, the perseverance endorsed by Socrates appears to be one that merely sustains the problem but never solves it. Cf. 743:
> 'Hush: if you meet with any difficulty
> Leave it a moment: then return again
> To the same thought, and think it over again.'

† Hence, when Strepsiades is about to begin his studies, Socrates asks him which thing he desires to learn that he did not know before. Cf. 637:
> 'Attend to me: what shall I teach you first
> That you've not learnt before? Which will you have,
> Measures or rhythms or the right use of words' ($\dot{\epsilon}\pi\tilde{\omega}\nu$).

Although $\ddot{\epsilon}\pi o\varsigma$ [37] (the right use of words) designates grammatical instruction, and though Socrates is set before us as a Per Degn[38] with his minute linguistic hairsplitting, it must nevertheless be remembered that we are here dealing with a forthright comic parody, and that this may well refer to a corresponding concern for dialectical distinctions based on language.

‡ Cf. 482 and 486.

§ Accordingly, the fruits of instruction correspond to this completely, and Socrates promises (260): 'You'll be the flower of talkers, prattlers, gossips.'

owes something then he is very forgetful—contains an appropriate description of this species of dialectic. Of course, this dialectic has no content, and this is finely depicted when Socrates impresses upon Strepsiades[39] that instead of believing in the gods he must believe in nothing but wide empty space and the tongue, a condition describing perfectly all the obstreperous talk about nothing, and which reminds me of a passage in Grimm's *Irish Fairytales*[40] where he speaks of people with an empty head and a tongue like the clapper in a church bell.

Finally, with respect to the standpoint of Socrates, Aristophanes has conceived its peculiar difficulty quite correctly. He has allowed us to see with how much emphasis Socrates was able to say: 'Give me a place to stand' ($\delta o\varsigma$ $\mu o\iota$ $\pi o\upsilon$ $\sigma\tau\omega$).[41] He has therefore assigned Socrates a place in the Thoughtery in a suspended basket, much to Strepsiades' amazement. But whether he hangs from the rafters in a basket or stares omphalopsychically into himself, and in this way frees himself to some extent from earthly gravitation, he still hovers in either case. It is this hovering which is so extremely descriptive: it is the attempted ascension into heaven which fulfils itself in rising to a glimpse of the entire realm of the ideal, when this staring into oneself causes the self to expand to the universal self, pure thought with its content. The ironist, to be sure, is lighter than the world, but he still belongs to the world; he hovers like the coffin of Mohammed between two magnets. Had the standpoint of Socrates been that of subjectivity, inwardness, it would have been comically incorrect to conceive him as Aristophanes has done. Subjectivity is hovering in relation to the substantiality of the older Hellenism, to be sure, yet it is infinitely hovering. Hence it would have been comically more correct to represent Socrates as infinitely vanishing and to have emphasized the comical in the fact that Strepsiades was unable to catch sight of him, than to represent him suspended in a basket. For the basket is the foundation of empirical actuality which the ironist requires, whereas subjectivity in its infinity gravitates towards itself, is infinitely hovering.

In summarizing this discussion of Aristophanes' *Clouds*, it seems to me that if one agrees with Rötscher[42] in characterizing the standpoint of Socrates as subjectivity, then he will find the conception of Aristophanes to be comically more true and hence more just,* as well as be able to remove some of the difficulties otherwise remaining with this Aristophanic work, if he further determines this standpoint as irony, i.e., not to allow subjectivity to overflow in its abundance, but before this occurs allow it egoistically to close itself in irony.

Xenophon, Plato, Aristophanes

As for Aristophanes' relation to Xenophon and Plato, there are elements of both these two conceptions in Aristophanes. Plato has attempted to fill in the mysterious nothingness which constituted the essential point in Socrates' life by giving him the Idea, Xenophon by giving him the diffuseness of the useful. Aristophanes has conceived this nothingness not as the ironical freedom wherein Socrates enjoyed it, but in such a way that he constantly exhibits only the emptiness residing in it. Instead of the eternal fullness of the Idea, Socrates achieves only the most ascetic frugality by this immersion in himself which never fetches anything up from this deep, an immersion which, though it descends into the underworld of the soul, always returns empty handed (one might easily give a psychological meaning to the words Aristophanes applies to the disciples of the new school in a cosmological sense: 'They are sounding the abysses of Tartarus' 192). Instead of the useful,† a kind

---

* Hegel, after having shown how the Socratic dialectic is able to destroy every concrete determination of the good at the expense of and with the help of the good itself, that is, the good as the empty and contentless universal, also remarks that it was Aristophanes who conceived the philosophy of Socrates wholly from its negative side (*Geschichte der Philosophie*, XVIII, 85). It is certain that had there been a Platonic positivity in Socrates, then, no matter how much freedom is allotted the comic poet according to Greek concepts, one cannot deny that Aristophanes has exceeded the limit inherent in the comic itself, the requirement that it be comically true.

† Whereas in Xenophon the useful vacillates between a correspondence to the beautiful and the good, and hence is more an intellectual than a moral concept, in Aristophanes the useful is conceived wholly morally in

of observation nevertheless, there here appears the advantageous (which touches the particular only in its relation to the individual exclusively occupied with his own interest) and the unscrupulous (cf. 177 ff.). Moreover, the speculations on nature with which Aristophanes has outfitted Socrates occasionally suggest the Xenophontic curriculum in natural history when one abstracts from the charge of irreligiosity which shines through in Aristophanes.† In relation to Plato, therefore, Aristophanes has subtracted something; in relation to Xenophon, added something; but as the latter can only involve a negative dimension, this addition is in one sense also a subtraction. Were we now to allow those lines which, throughout the foregoing, have been drawn under the constant surveillance of a calculation based on the reciprocal relation among these three authors, to come clearly into focus and delimit the unknown

---

its opposition to the good and in unity with the bad. Xenophon[43] does not allow Socrates to accept payment for his teaching and suggests by this that his teaching was incommensurable with all such taxation, suggests the ambiguous relation of Socrates' teaching to every kind of external valuation (since in one sense it was too good, in another too bad). Aristophanes, on the other hand, not only permits Socrates to accept payment, but veritably to plunder his disciples.[44] If one does not see in this last feature one of those moral accusations difficult to justify, or a playful exuberance needing some excuse, then one may perhaps see in this an image of the ironist's relation to the individual, since in this relationship the ironist takes more than he gives, since in an intellectual way he does what Socrates did to Strepsiades in a bodily way: he allowed him to come naked into the Thoughtery and run naked out again.[45]

† The fact that I have arranged these three conceptions more according to their relation to the Idea (the plain historical—the ideal—the comical) than according to chronology, will perhaps occasion one or another reader to charge me with an anachronism. Nevertheless, I believe I am right in suspending the chronological consideration. Naturally, I do not by this wish in any way to deprive the Aristophanic conception of any added significance that might accrue to it from the fact that it comes first in time. The significance which it thus acquires in an historical regard is augmented still more by the fact that it is reported that Plato sent the *Clouds* to Dionysius the elder,[46] and gave him to understand that from this he could learn to know the Athenian state.

magnitude or standpoint at once fitting and filling the inter-mediate space; then it will exhibit itself approximately as follows: its relation to the Idea is negative, that is, the Idea is the limit of the dialectic. Constantly engaged in leading the phenomenon up to the Idea (the dialectical activity), the individual is thrust back, or rather, flees back into actuality. But actuality itself has no other validity than to be the constant occasion for wanting to go beyond actuality—except that this never occurs. Whereupon the individual draws these exertions (*molimina*) of subjectivity back into himself, terminates them in himself in personal satisfaction. Such is the standpoint of irony.

The essay has now reached a point of rest, a certain formation of the inquiry has been traversed, and were I to express in a few words its nature and significance as a moment in the whole, I would say that it is a conception of Socrates made possible. Xenophon, Plato, and Aristophanes have not merely conceived Socrates in the usual sense, and this word must be taken in its usual sense when an intellectual phenomenon is at issue, but in a much more special sense they have not repro-duced him but conceived him.* It follows that one must use them with a certain caution, and care must be taken to restrain them at the moment they would run away with one. For this reason, and so as not to be guilty of arbitrariness one-self, it becomes necessary to have assistance from someone. Hence I have constantly sought to be myself the third [*Tredie*] against each.[47] Thus I have allowed the whole to arrive at a finite confrontation. In this way I have secured the possi-bility of being able to explain the disparity among these three conceptions by another conception of Socrates corresponding

* Whenever it is a matter of reconstructing a phenomenon through what must be called conception in the stricter sense, there is a twofold labour: one must explain the phenomenon and through this explain the mis-understanding; one must acquire the phenomenon by means of the mis-understanding, and by means of the phenomenon resolve the sorcery of the misunderstanding.

to this disparity. But with all this I have arrived no further than at the possibility; for while the proposed explanation is able to reconcile the warring powers, it does not follow that this explanation is absolutely correct. If, on the other hand, it were unable to effect a reconciliation, then it would be impossible for it to be correct. Thus it has now been made possible. Throughout this entire investigation I have constantly had something in mind, namely, the final conception, yet without anyone being able to accuse me of a kind of intellectual Jesuitism, or of having hidden, searched, and found what I myself had discovered long ago. The final conception has hovered above every inquiry as mere possibility. Every result has been the unity of that reciprocity whereby it has felt itself drawn towards what it should explain, and what is to be explained drawn in turn toward this. Thus in one sense the final conception has come into existence [*bleven til*] through this deliberation itself, although in another sense it existed [*været til*] before it. But this can scarcely be otherwise, since the whole is prior to its parts.[48] It is, if not generated [*bleven til*], then surely born anew. Still, I believe the open-minded reader will acknowledge this as conscientiousness on my part, even though the whole form of the essay has thereby departed somewhat from the now usual, and in so many ways serviceable scientific method. Had I first set forth the final conception, and within its particular moments assigned each of these three considerations its place, then I would surely have forfeited the moment of contemplation[49] which is always of importance, but doubly so here since by no other way, certainly not by immediate observation, could I have acquired the phenomenon.

From this point on the form of the investigation will also be different. I shall be concerned with certain phenomena which, as historical facts, do not need to be derived from a misunderstanding but merely preserved in their innocence and explained. Here again the final conception is a necessary *prius*, though in another sense it results from this. One might call this section the conception made actual, since it actualizes itself through these historical data.

CHAPTER II

The conception made actual

___

THE DAIMON OF SOCRATES

It will at once be perceived that I have now entered upon a different sphere. In this connection there can be no question of the conception of Plato or Xenophon, unless one will be so unreasonable as to suppose that the daimon of Socrates was a fiction created by Plato and Xenophon. It must be regarded as a fact that Socrates assumed such a daimon, and from the various statements* to be found concerning this phenomenon we must endeavour to form some idea of it and bring this into harmony with our entire conception. This Socratic daimon has always been a *crux philologorum*,[1] a difficulty that has nevertheless operated more enticingly than forbiddingly, and by its mysterious spell even deceptively. Since time immemorial one finds a strong propensity to say something about this thing (for 'what does one hear more eagerly than such fairy tales?'),[2] but there the matter usually ends. The curiosity which is tickled by whatever is mysterious is satisfied as soon as the thing is given a name, and profundity accepts satisfaction when one says with a thoughtful air: ah, what is one to say? Should the reader wish to make the acquaintance of the consummate masterpiece in this field, one that is in itself such a well rounded whole that it goes completely around the subject, I shall refer him to an article found in Funcke,† an article which ends as profoundly as it began and whose middle is no less profound than its beginning and ending. A Dane of

* These statements are to be found in what must be termed historical writings in the strict sense.

† C. Ph. Funcke, *Neues Real-Schullexikon*, Braunschweig, 1800-5, pt. II, p. 643 ff.

kindred spirit, Hr. Magister Block, has likewise been 'unable to resist the temptation to explain this extraordinary phenomenon in the introduction to his translation of Xenophon's *Memorabilia*.[3] He holds that Socrates himself believed he had such a daimon, and 'that this feeling was a presentiment or a kind of enthusiasm which had its cause both in his lively imagination and in his nervous system.'*

But first an account of the facts. Both Xenophon and Plato discuss this Socratic idiosyncrasy. The word τὸ δαιμόνιόν (the daimonion), as Ast correctly observes (p. 483), is not simply adjectival so that one might render it complete by implying function, deed (ἔργον), or sign (σημεῖον), or something of the kind; nor is it substantive in the sense that it describes a particular or unique being. Hence we see that this word is an expression for something utterly abstract, a fact which is also evident from the twofold way it is used and the two contexts in which it occurs. Sometimes it is said: 'the daimonion manifests itself to me' (τὸ δαιμόνιόν μοι σημαίνει), or again: 'something daimonic' (δαιμόνιόν τι), or 'the daimonion occurs' (τὸ δαιμόνιόν γίγνεται). Thus the first thing to be observed is that this word signifies something abstract, something divine, which by its very abstractness is elevated above every determination, unutterable and without predicates, since it admits of no vocalization.[4] If we next inquire into its manner of operation, we learn it is a voice which makes itself heard, yet not in such a way that one would want to insist upon this, as if it manifested itself through words, for it operates wholly instinctively. With regard to its activity, however, the information of Plato and Xenophon disagree. According to Plato it warns, restrains, and urges him to abstain from something, cf. *Phædrus* 242 B, C; *Apology* 31 D; *Alcibiades* 103 A, 124 C; *Theages* 128 D. But according to Xenophon it commands, compels, and urges him to do

---

* There has also been considerable difficulty with this daimon quite recently, and I see from a publication by Heinsius[5] that a psychiatrist in Paris, F. Lelut, has been so self-wise as to claim: 'Socrates was afflicted with that madness which in technical language is called hallucination.' The work is entitled: *Du démon de Socrate*, Paris, 1836.

something, cf. *Memorabilia* I, I, 4; IV, 8, I; *Apology* 12. Ast[6] holds that in this matter one ought to believe Xenophon more than Plato, and seeks thoroughly to confound anyone who cannot be satisfied with this personal prognostication by the following passage (from his point of view quite correct and sufficiently convincing): 'In itself it is unbelievable that the daimon as a divine intimation or presentiment merely warned; for should Socrates have had only a presentiment of injustice, misfortune, etc., and not also a lively presentiment of good tidings, one which not only incited him to action but also filled him with enthusiastic hope?' I shall let Ast answer this for himself. On the other hand, what I must ask the reader to notice is quite significant for the entire conception of Socrates, namely, that the daimonic is represented only as warning and not as commanding, that is, as negative not as positive. If one must choose between Xenophon and Plato, I hold one should sooner side with Plato with whom the constant predicate for the activity of this daimon is that it only warns,* and regard the additional contribution by Xenophon as a Xenophontic thoughtlessness which, without any presentiment of the significance that might be concealed in this, finds in his wisdom that if the daimon warned, then surely it must also instigate and impel. With the latter the condition of the daimonic lapses into the category of the trivial, and the insipid: now here, now there, now this, now that, must naturally have appealed to Xenophon far more. His limpness is much easier to explain than Plato's tautness, inasmuch as the first involves no more than a good-natured simplicity, while the latter entails a considerable degree of audacity and volition. Moreover, it is clear from the passage in the *Apology*,[7] where Socrates refers to this daimonic in order to defend himself against the accusation of Meletus, that Socrates was conscious of the significance of the fact that the daimonic only warned. From this he explains the curious fact that he who

---

* Both Plutarch[8] (*Plutarchi Chaeronensis opuscula*, ed. H. Stephanus. *Tom.* II, pp. 241, 243), and Cicero[9] (*De divinatione* I, 54) have preserved several episodes concerning the activity of this daimon, and in all of them it expresses itself only as warning.

was always ready to advise in private ('though I go about giving this advice privately and meddling in others' affairs')[10] had never occupied himself with the affairs of the state. This is the visible manifestation of the daimonic's negative relation to Socrates, for this in turn caused him to relate himself negatively to actuality, or in the Greek sense, to the state. Had the daimonic also instigated and impelled, then he would surely have been suited to deal with actuality.* This brings us to the question: to what extent was Socrates in conflict with the religion of the state, as his accusers maintained, by his acceptance of this daimonic? Now obviously this was so. It was a thoroughly polemical relation to the religion of the Greek state because he substituted something utterly abstract in place of the concrete individuality of the gods.† Again, it was a polemical relation to the state religion because in place of the god-consciousness permeating everything, even the most insignificant expression of Greek life, in place of this divine eloquence reverberating through all things, he substituted a silence in which a warning voice was only occasionally audible, a voice which (and this contains virtually the deepest polemic) never concerned itself with the substantial interests of the life of the state, never expressed itself concerning these, but merely occupied itself with Socrates' and at most his friend's wholly private and particular affairs.

---

* It must not be lost sight of that this passage is found in the *Apology*, and that on the whole one must suppose it to be historically dependable. This is essential in order to be convinced that I am not concerned here with a Platonic conception but proceed according to factual grounds.

† The attempt made by Socrates[11] to defend himself against this accusation by showing the necessity of assuming daimons if one assumes the daimonical, even when we disregard the ironic form in which he clothes the argument together with the indirect polemic this conceals, scarcely amounts to much. While one must generally admit, hence also here, the correctness of syllogistically deducing theism from pantheism,[12] still, it does not follow that Socrates was justified in relation to the state. For the state had not acquired its gods by way of the syllogism, and what is more, Socrates was clearly able to relate himself indifferently, i.e., irreligiously, toward the result which he was at every moment able to produce upon demand.

If we turn from the previously mentioned pharisaical scholars, who strain at a gnat and swallow a camel,[13] to the efforts of the most recent philosophic discussions of this problem, there immediately appears an essential difference. These have at once directed the question in upon itself and hence seek not so much to explain as to conceive [begribe]. So long as the problem of the daimonic in Socrates is treated in isolation, so long as it is regarded externally, it will naturally remain inexplicable though there be a multitude of conjectures both necessary and indispensable. If, on the other hand, one regards this problem from within, then what presented itself as an insurmountable barrier appears as a necessary limit that restrains the eyes', and with this thought's, hasty flight, forces it back from the peripheral towards what is central and thereby makes it possible to conceive [begribe]. One statement of Hegel* expresses quite simply but with much pregnancy of thought how the daimonic is to be understood: 'Socrates, in assigning to insight and conviction the determination of men's actions, posited the individual as capable of decision in opposition to fatherland and customary morality, and thus made himself an oracle in the Greek sense. He claimed that he had a daimon within, counselling him what to do and revealing to him what was advantageous to his friends.' Rötscher, too, conceives this correctly according to Hegel (p. 254): 'Related to this principle of the free decision of mind in itself, and the momentous consciousness that everything must be drawn before the forum of thought and there be ratified, is the phenomenon of the daimon of Socrates which was so much discussed even in antiquity. In this daimon the above thought of inward decision is brought before our minds.' Hegel also discusses this Socratic daimon in the *Philosophy of Right* (§279):[14] 'In the "divine sign" of Socrates we see the will which formerly had simply transferred itself beyond itself now beginning to apply itself to itself and so to recognize its own inward nature. This is the beginning of a self-knowing and so of authentic freedom.' The place where Hegel discusses this daimon most extensively is naturally in his *Geschichte der Philosophie* (XVIII,

* *The Philosophy of History* (rev. ed.), pp. 269, 270.[15]

94 ff., 103 ff.).[16] Although Hegel engages in a presentation of analogies,* and in this way attempts to resolve the difficulties connected with this phenomenon, the aim and result of his entire discussion is that this phenomenon be conceived [begribes]. The standpoint of Socrates is subjectivity, inwardness reflecting upon itself, and in relation to itself loosens and dissolves the existent [Bestaaende] in a surge of thought that swells up over it and washes it away before itself sinking back into thought once more. In place of the respect (αἰδώς) forcefully yet mysteriously binding the individual to the reins of the state, there now appeared the decisiveness and certainty of subjectivity in itself. Hegel writes (p. 96): 'The standpoint of the Greek mind was determined in its moral aspect as customary or natural morality. Man did not yet have the condition of reflecting into himself, of determining himself.'[17] Under the older Hellenism the laws had the venerableness of tradition for the individual, as that which was sanctioned by the gods, and corresponding to this tradition were time-honoured habits and customs. But while the laws determined the universal, the older Hellenism still required a vehicle of decision in particular events, one which concerned the state as well as the private affairs of citizens. For this they had the oracle (p. 97): 'In essence this moment means the people lacks the power of decision, that the subject is still not determined from within but by an "other", an external; and oracles are everywhere necessary where man does not yet know himself inwardly as being sufficiently free and independent to take it upon himself to decide. This is the lack of subjective freedom.'[18] Now instead of the oracle Socrates had his daimon. This daimonic lies in the transition from the oracle's external relation to the individual to the full inwardness of freedom, and, as still being

* 'It may happen that at death, in illness and catalepsy, men know about circumstances future or present which, in the understood relations of things, are altogether unknown . . . (pp. 95, 96).[19] The further investigation of this daimon, therefore, presents to us a form which passes into somnambulism, into this doubleness of consciousness; and in Socrates there clearly appears to be something of the kind, something magnetic, for he is often said to have fallen into trances (at camp), catalepsy, and raptures' (p. 99).[20]

in this transition, it pertains to representation. Page 95: 'The inwardness of the subject knows and decides in itself, but in Socrates this inwardness had a unique form. The daimon is still the unconscious, the external which decides; yet it is also subjective. The daimon is not Socrates himself, not his opinions and convictions, but unconscious. Socrates is urged. At the same time the oracle is not external but his own oracle. It had the form of knowledge immediately associated with a condition of unconsciousness.'[21] Page 96: 'This is the daimon of Socrates, and it is necessary that this daimon appear in Socrates.'[22] Page 99: 'The daimon is intermediate between the externality of the oracle and the pure inwardness of mind. Although it is something inward, it nevertheless exhibits itself as a separate daimon, not as his wisdom and his will, but separate from human will.'[23] But as this daimon only concerned itself with Socrates' particular situation, Hegel goes on to show that its manifestations are quite insignificant as compared with those of his mind and thought.* Page 106: 'This Socratic daimon did not concern what was most true, being-in-and-for-itself, but mere particularities; hence such daimonic manifestations are far more trivial than those of his mind and thought.'[24]

I am now finished with Hegel's interpretation of this phenomenon, and here as always when one has Hegel aboard (Cæsar and his fortune)[25] I have secured a foothold from which I can safely sally forth upon a digression to see if there might be some particular worth noticing, and to which I can safely return whether I have found anything or not. We have previously seen that the standpoint of Socrates was in many

---

* Cf. p. 98: 'When one foresees the future in somnambulism or at death, one regards these as a higher kind of insight; yet examined more closely they are merely the interests of the individuals concerned, mere particularities. If one wishes to marry or build a house, etc., the outcome is important only for this individual, the content merely particular. The truly divine and universal is the institution of agriculture itself, the state, marriage, legal institutions. As compared with these it is a trivial matter to know that if I go to sea, I shall perish or not. This is a perversion which may easily arise in our representations. To know what is right and ethical is much higher than to know the outcome of such particularities.'[26]

ways that of subjectivity, yet in such a way that subjectivity did not manifest itself in its richness, that the Idea became the limit from which Socrates turned back into himself in ironic satisfaction. Now the daimonic in relation to Hellenism is also a determination of subjectivity, but subjectivity is not fulfilled in this; it still has something external (Hegel remarks that one must not call the daimonic conscience).[27] If we also bear in mind that this daimonic only concerned itself with particular situations and expressed itself only in warnings, then we see that here again subjectivity is stopped in its outward flow, that it terminates itself in a particular personality. The daimonic was sufficient for Socrates, with this he could manage for himself; it is therefore a determination of personality, though naturally only the egoistical satisfaction of a particular personality. Here again Socrates appears as one who stands poised ready to leap into something, yet at every moment instead of leaping into this 'other', he leaps aside and back into himself. If we add to this the polemical consciousness with which Socrates assimilated his entire relationship to his age, the infinite yet negative freedom whereby he breathed light and easy under the vast horizon circumscribed by the Idea as a limit, the certainty he possessed through the daimonic so as not to get tangled up with the multitudinous events of life, then the standpoint of Socrates appears once more as irony. In general, one is accustomed to finding irony conceived ideally, assigned its place as a vanishing moment in the system and for this reason described very briefly. Accordingly, it is not easy to conceive [begribe] how an entire life may be spent in this, especially when the content of this life must be regarded as nothingness. But one forgets that a standpoint is never so ideal in life as it is in the system. We forget that irony, like every other standpoint in life, also has its tribulations, conflicts, defeats, and triumphs. Similarly, doubt is also a vanishing moment in the system, yet in actuality where it fulfils itself in constant conflict with everything that will raise itself up and stand [bestaae] against it ('casting down every high thing that exalteth itself . . . and taking captive every thought into obedience'),[28] it has in another sense much content. This is the wholly personal life with which speculative philosophy has nothing to do, though a little more exact knowledge of this life would free it from the tautological *idem per idem*[29] from which such conceptions often suffer. Be this now as it may, let speculative philosophy be justified in ignoring such things, yet he who wishes to conceive the individual life cannot. As Hegel himself somewhere remarks[30] that with Socrates it is not so much a matter of speculation as individual life, so I shall venture to see in this a sanction for the procedure throughout my whole undertaking, though my own shortcomings might cause this to be quite imperfect.

THE ACCUSATION AND CONVICTION OF SOCRATES

The reader will at once perceive that our present concern is for the factual, hence there can be no question of conception in the same sense as with Xenophon, Plato, and Aristophanes, for whom the actuality of Socrates was merely the occasion for and a moment in a representation attempting ideally to round off[31] and transfigure his person—a thing which the seriousness of the state could not possibly engage in, and whose conception is therefore *sine ira atque studio*.[32] The conception of the state, to be sure, depends in some measure upon that of the accusers; but however hatefully their minds might be disposed towards Socrates, they must have made an effort to stick to the truth as far as possible. Besides, the complaint is but one moment in the state's conception of him; it is the external occasion for the state to become conscious* in a special way of this particular individual's relation to itself. Now whether the Athenian state committed an outrageous injustice by con-

---

* Socrates, too, is fully conscious of this, hence in the *Apology* he makes the indictment the occasion for bringing the question of his activity to the attention of his judges. Cf. 20 c: 'Perhaps some of you may reply: "But, Socrates, what is the trouble with you? What has given rise to these prejudices against you? You must have been doing something out of the ordinary. All these rumours and reports of you would never have arisen if you had not been doing something different from other men. So tell us what it is, that we may not give our verdict arbitrarily." '

demning Socrates, so that we are justified in voluntarily joining that cortège of erudite professional mourners, that insipid host of tearful philanthropists, whose weeping and wailing over the fact that such a noble creature, such an honourable man, a paragon of virtue and cosmopolitanism rolled together in one person, became a sacrifice to the meanest of envies, whose weeping and wailing, I say, still echoes down through the centuries; or whether the Athenian state was wholly right in condemning Socrates; or whether we dare abandon ourselves with a clear conscience to rejoicing over the audacious pen strokes of recent philosophic investigators[33] who sketch Socrates as a tragic hero at once right and wrong and the Greek state as an articulate order of things—all this we need not discuss any further here.

The indictment against Socrates is a historical document.* It contains two accusations, each of which will be the object of a more detailed investigation.

1. Socrates does not accept the gods which the state accepts, and he introduces new gods

The first accusation obviously contains two points: he does not accept the gods of the state, and he introduces new deities. The last point has already been discussed in connection with the daimon of Socrates. We there observed the slight value to be attributed to the dialectical movement by which Socrates in his defence before the court attempts to construct the objective with the determination of personality from the determination of abstract inwardness (the daimonic). I trust the important thing about our discussion there has become sufficiently clear, namely, that the daimonic characterized Socrates' thoroughly negative relation to the established order

* According to Diogenes Laertius, Favorinus, the contemporary and friend of Plutarch, had read the indictment in the Metroön. In the Greek it reads as follows: Τάδε ἐγράψατο καὶ ἀντωμόσατο Μέλιτος Μελίτου Πιτθεὺς Σωκράτει Σωφρονίσκου Ἀλωπεκῆθεν · ἀδικεῖ Σωκράτης, οὓς μὲν ἡ πόλις νομίζει θεοὺς οὐ νομίζων, ἕτερα δὲ χαινὰ δαιμόνια εἰσηγούμενος, ἀδικεῖ δὲ χαὶ τοὺς νέους διαφθείρων · τίμημα θάνατος.[34]

[*Bestaaende*] with respect to religion, not so much because he introduced anything new, since his negativity would then exhibit itself more and more as a shadow following his positivity, but because he rejected the existent [*Bestaaende*], closed himself into himself, and confined himself egoistically to himself. With reference to the first point, we must not see in this rejection of the gods of the state the fruits of a cold, rational, prosaic cosmology, a thing not altogether unknown to the Athenians and which by this time had furnished occasion for several suspected of atheism to be exiled.[35] Socrates did not concern himself with such things, for while he had previously been influenced by Anaxagoras, he soon freed himself from this influence as Plato on several occasions relates,[36] since he abandoned the study of nature for the study of man. Hence when one says that Socrates did not accept the gods which the state accepted, it does not follow that he was an atheist. On the contrary, this Socratic non-acceptance of the gods of the state stems essentially from his whole standpoint theoretically designated by himself as ignorance.* Ignorance is at once an actual philosophic standpoint and also thoroughly negative. The Socratic ignorance was not an empirical ignorance, for he was in possession of much information, had read a great many poets as well as philosophers, and was highly experienced in the affairs of life. No, he was not ignorant in any empirical sense. He was, however, ignorant in a philosophic sense. He was ignorant of the reason underlying all things, the eternal, the divine; that is to say, he knew that it was, but he did not know what it was. He was conscious of it and yet not conscious of it, since the only thing he could predicate of it was that he knew nothing about it. But this is to say no more than we have previously expressed in the words: Socrates had the Idea as a limit. To this extent it must have seemed to him extremely

---

* It will be readily observed how difficult the position of the accusers really was, for each time they presented a positive complaint it was a simple matter for Socrates to refute it by means of this ignorance. Accordingly, his accusers ought to have accused him of this very ignorance, since there is an ignorance which, to a certain extent in every state but especially in the Greek state, must be regarded as a felony.

simple to refute the accusation of his accusers that he did not accept the gods accepted by the state. To this he must give the correctly Socratic reply: How can anyone condemn me for this? Since I know nothing at all, neither do I know whether I accept the gods accepted by the state. Here it becomes apparent how this relates to the question whether a positive knowledge constituted itself behind this ignorance. Schleiermacher, in one of his essays,* calls attention to the fact that when Socrates went about in the service of the oracle proving to his fellow citizens that they knew nothing, it is impossible that the only knowledge he had was a knowledge of his ignorance, since behind this ignorance necessarily lay the conviction that he knew what knowledge was. Schleiermacher next shows that Socrates was the founder of dialectic. But this, too, is a positivity which under closer examination becomes a negativity. Socrates, to recall a previous remark, has arrived at the Idea of dialectic, but does not possess the dialectic of the Idea. And even according to the view of Plato this is still a negative standpoint. Hence in the *Republic*[37] when dialectic appears as one member of a dichotomy, the good also appears as its corresponding positivity. Similarly, in the dichotomy having love as the negative,[38] the beautiful functions as its corresponding positivity. There is, to be sure, a deep positivity with much content in this constantly insinuated, at every moment both posited and recalled, negativity as soon as it is allowed to come to itself; but Socrates continually restrained this as a possibility which never became actuality.

This conclusion may be reached through an attentive reading of Plato's *Apology*, which is so pregnant in its portrayal of the Socratic ignorance that the reader need only be silent and listen when it speaks. He portrays [39] his wisdom in contrast to that of Evenus of Paros who took five minæ for his teaching. He calls him fortunate because of the positivity of which he must have been in possession, seeing he let himself charge so much. He then replies to the question concerning his own wisdom (20 D): 'What kind of wisdom is this? Just that which

* 'Über den Werth des Socrates als Philosophen', in *Abhandlung*[40] *der Königlichen Academie der Wissenschaften*, Berlin, 1814-15, pp. 51-68.

is perhaps human wisdom. In that, it may be, I am really wise.' Nevertheless, he holds that the others must be in possession of a higher wisdom: 'But the men of whom I was speaking just now must be wise in a wisdom which is greater than human wisdom.' The predicate 'human'* here attributed to wisdom in opposition to a wisdom greater than human, is of the utmost significance. When subjectivity with its negative power has broken the spell in which human life reposed under the form of substantiality, when it has emancipated man from his relationship to God just as it liberated him from his relationship to the state, the first form in which this appears is ignorance. The gods flee away taking with them all content, and man is left standing as the form, as that which is to receive content into itself. In the sphere of knowledge such a condition is correctly apprehended as ignorance. Again, this ignorance is quite consistently designated as human wisdom, for with this man has come into his own right: the right not to be, as such.[41] Compared with this the wisdom of the others contained much more, although in another sense it naturally contained much less, and it is not without a certain irony that Socrates speaks of their affluence. He finds this conception also strengthened by the pronouncement of the Delphic oracle, which has seen the same thing from the divine standpoint.† As the oracle generally conformed to the corresponding level of human con-

* This may be compared with the *Apology* of Xenophon where the discussion concerns the same pronouncement of the Delphic oracle to Chairephon, and where we read, §15: 'When the jurors, naturally enough, made a still greater tumult on hearing this statement, he said that Socrates again went on: "And yet, gentlemen, the god uttered in oracles greater things of Lycurgus, the Lacedaemonian law-giver, than he did of me. For there is a legend that, as Lycurgus entered the temple, the god thus addressed him: 'I am pondering whether to call you god or man.' Now Apollo did not compare me to a god; he did, however, judge that I far excelled the rest of mankind." '

† According to the Socratic account the pronouncement of the Delphic oracle meant: 'Human wisdom is worth little or nothing. . . . He among you is the wisest who, like Socrates, knows that this wisdom is really worth nothing at all' (23 A). As the oracle was merely the occasion for the interpreting consciousness, so this pronouncement of the Delphic oracle found its interpretation in Socrates.

sciousness, as in former times it spoke with divine authority and once, during a season of pestilence, concerned itself with posing scientific problems,* so a similar pre-established harmony is to be seen in the pronouncement of the Delphic oracle concerning Socrates. The misunderstanding which insists that he concealed a knowledge behind this ignorance was also perceived by Socrates, yet he regarded it as a misunderstanding. He explains how his efforts to persuade his fellow citizens have incurred many hostilities, and adds (23 A): 'For the bystanders always think that I am wise myself in any matter wherein I refute another.' But we see how he protests against this misunderstanding, and how unwarranted he regards the inference that since he can convince others that they know nothing, so he must therefore know something himself.

What restrained Socrates from immersing himself speculatively in the dimly intimated positivity behind this ignorance was naturally his divine call to convince each individual of his ignorance. He had not come to save the world, but to condemn it.[42] To this end his life was consecrated, and this same activity also restrained him from participating in the affairs of the state.[43] The Athenians might deprive him of life, this he could accept; but he would never accept an acquittal on the condition that he forsake this divine mission, since this would be an attempt to murder him in an intellectual and spiritual sense. He was the eternal counsel for the prosecution who, on behalf of the gods, inflexibly distrained to the last farthing what was owed the divine.[44] What nemesis had previously been in relation to the great and outstanding was now completely and profoundly accomplished by Socrates' ironic

* Cf. Hegel, *Geschichte der Philosophie*, xviii, 173: 'Plato himself soon attained to high proficiency in mathematics. To him is attributed the solution of the Delian or Delphic problem, which was proposed by the oracle, and, like the Pythagorean dogma, has reference to the cube. The problem is to draw a line the cube of which will be equal to the sum of two given cubes. This requires a construction through two curves. The nature of the task then set by the oracle is very curious. On this particular occasion petition had been made to the oracle in a time of pestilence, and it responded by proposing an entirely scientific problem. The change indicated in the spirit of the oracle is highly significant.'[45]

activity in relation to humanity as such. Not content to think about this philosophically, he approached each man individually, deprived him of everything, and sent him away empty-handed. It was as though the angry gods* had turned away from mankind, taken everything with them, and intended to abandon mankind to itself. But in another sense it was mankind who had turned away from the gods and become immersed in itself. Still, this is but a moment of transition. In many respects mankind was on the right path, and one may say of this what Augustine says of sin: *beata culpa*.[46] The heavenly host of the gods lifted themselves up from the earth and disappeared from mortal view, yet such a disappearance was itself the condition for a deeper relationship. Rötscher quite correctly observes (p. 252): 'This clarifies the condition of the much abused Socratic ignorance, which has often served as a good apology for one's own ignorance, no less than a defence against the recognition of true knowledge. The knowledge that he knew nothing is not the pure, empty nothingness it is usually represented as, but the nothingness of the determinate content of the existent [*bestehenden*] world. His wisdom is the knowledge of the negativity of all finite content through which he is drawn into himself, while the investigation of his own inwardness as absolute end expresses the beginning of infinite knowledge, yet merely the beginning, since this consciousness has not fulfilled itself but is only the negation of all that is finite and existent [*bestehenden*].' Hegel also remarks (p. 60): 'Thus Socrates taught those with whom he associated to know that they knew nothing; indeed, what is more, he himself said that he knew nothing and therefore taught nothing. It may actually be said that Socrates knew nothing, for he did not reach the scientific construction of a systematic philosophy. He was conscious of this, nor was it his aim to establish a systematic philosophy.'[47]

Socrates supplied a new direction; indeed, he gave the age its directions (provided one understands this word not so much

* Subsequently, the gods became benevolent again, hence in the *Timæus*[4] Plato derives the origin of the world from the goodness of god, who, knowing no envy, desired to make the world as much like himself as possible.

in a philosophic as a military sense). He approached every man individually in order to assure himself that he was correctly orientated. This activity was not so much calculated to direct their attention to what should come, however, as to wrest from them what they already had. Now this he accomplished, so long as the operation lasted, by shearing away all communication with the besieged: with his questions he starved out that garrison of opinions, ideas, and venerable traditions, etc., which heretofore had been sufficient for the individual. When he had done this to the individual, the consuming flame of envy (this word taken in a metaphysical sense) was then temporarily sated, the destructive enthusiasm of negativity momentarily quenched, and he enjoyed the pleasure of irony to the fullest extent, doubly enjoyed it because he felt divinely authorized, felt busy in his calling. This, of course, lasted but a moment; soon he was back at his function.* The negativity residing in this ignorance was for him not a result, not a point of departure for a deeper speculation;[49] on the contrary, the speculative residing in this thought whereby he had infinitely encircled existence was the divine authority by virtue of which he operated in the particular. This ignorance was the eternal triumph over the phenomenon, a triumph which neither a particular phenomenon nor the sum total of phenomena could wrest from him, but by virtue of which he triumphed at every moment over the phenomenon. In this way he freed the individual from every commitment, freed him in the same way that he himself was free. The others,

* Such is his activity viewed ideally. In his own life, however, this wrathful energy (the word 'wrathful' taken in a metaphysical sense) might easily have been relieved by a certain indolence, a certain lapsing into himself, at which moments he anticipated abstractly the enjoyment expended concretely. This lasted until such time as the divine call again reverberated within, and he was once more ready to lend assistance to the deity by convincing mankind. Accordingly, the Socratic trance which has so often been the object of discussion, and which we have also touched upon previously, is best conceived [begriber] as a dream state wherein negativity became visible to him, and he became intoxicated as it were by its emptiness. While he usually went about engaging both countrymen and strangers, at such moments as this he stood still and stared.

however, could not enjoy this freedom in ironic satisfaction as could Socrates, and it therefore developed in them desire and longing. Whereas his own standpoint culminates in himself, the same standpoint when assimilated into their consciousness is merely the condition for a new standpoint. The reason Socrates could content himself with this ignorance was because he had no deeper speculative need. Instead of pacifying this negativity speculatively, he pacified it far more through the eternal unrest wherein he repeated the same process with each particular individual. But what makes him a personality through all this is irony.

This theoretical ignorance for which the eternal essence of the deity remained a mystery must naturally have had its counterpart in a corresponding religious ignorance respecting divine providence and guidance for mankind. This is a religious ignorance which seeks its edification and manifests its piety in a total ignorance, just as Schleiermacher,[50] for example, in a much more concrete[51] development locates the edifying in a feeling of absolute dependence. This, too, conceals within itself a polemic and becomes a terror for everyone who finds repose in some finite relation[52] to the deity. Here we are reminded of the passage cited earlier[53] from Xenophon's *Memorabilia*, where Socrates relates how the gods have reserved to themselves the most important secrets, namely, the outcome, so that all human endeavour is a vanity accomplishing nothing. It is also apparent in the Platonic dialogue *Alcibiades II*, where Socrates discusses[54] the significance of prayer and warns that one ought to use much caution in asking something of the gods, lest they grant this prayer and it afterward turn out to be anything but a boon to mankind. Now this caution seems to warrant the possibility that in certain situations mankind can perceive what is beneficial and venture to pray accordingly. But one must bear in mind that Socrates, even on the assumption that a man knew what was best for him and prayed accordingly, in no wise supposes that the gods will grant it, a fact suggesting an even profounder doubt respecting what is actually best for mankind. Moreover, this caution deteriorates into an anxiety which ultimately spends itself in

the neutralization of prayer. This may be seen from the fact
that he praises the verse of a poet which reads:

> Give to us what is good, King Zeus,
> whether we pray for it or not;
> Even when we pray for it, do thou
> avert from us the evil.

With this the divine is as far removed from mankind in a
religious regard as it was in a theoretical regard, and the
expression for this is again ignorance.*

In describing the standpoint of Socrates one is accustomed
to think of the well-known expression: 'know thyself' (γνῶθι
σαυτόν).[55] Undeniably, these words contain an ambiguity
which clearly serves to recommend them, for they might as
easily designate a theoretical standpoint as a practical one,
something like the way the word 'truth' functions in Christian
terminology. In recent scientificity,[56] however, these words
have frequently been torn loose from the complex of Ideas to
which they belong and have long wandered like a vagabond
through literature unchallenged. An attempt must therefore be
made to bring them back to their native soil, that is to say, an
attempt to show what they signified with respect to Socrates,
or how Socrates rendered the thought they contain fruitful.
Now it is certainly true that subjectivity in its fullness, inwardness with its infinite richness, may also be designated by the
words: 'know thyself'; but in the case of Socrates this self-
knowledge was scarcely so full of content, for it properly contained no more than the separation and differentiation of that
which only subsequently became the object of knowledge.
The expression 'know thyself' means: separate yourself from
the 'other'.[57] Inasmuch as prior to Socrates this self did not
exist, so the pronouncement of the oracle in turn corresponded
to Socrates' own consciousness in commanding him to know

* In order to prevent any misunderstanding and, if possible, to illuminate
the matter from quite a different standpoint, I shall remind the reader that
prayer has its absolute validity in the Christian consciousness. For the
Christian knows what he should pray for, and knows that when he prays
for this his prayer will be absolutely answered. This, however, is based
on the fact that he knows himself to be in a real relationship to his God.

himself. It was nevertheless reserved for a later age to immerse itself in this self-knowledge. But if one understands in this way what is necessitated by Socrates' opposition to the substantiality of Hellenism, it is evident that Socrates here again has a completely negative result. This principle: know thyself, is therefore wholly congruent with the ignorance described above. The reason he was able to remain poised on this negative point is the same as before, because his life's work and interest was to assert it, not speculatively, for then he would certainly have gone further, but practically against every individual human being.[58] He brought the individual under the force of his dialectical vacuum pump, deprived him of the atmospheric air in which he was accustomed to breathe, and abandoned him. For such individuals everything was now lost, except insofar as they were able to breathe in an ether. Yet Socrates no longer concerned himself with them, but hastened on to new experiments.

If we return for a moment to the event occasioning this inquiry, the accusation against Socrates, it will then be obvious that Socrates was in conflict with the view of the state. Indeed, his attack must be regarded from the standpoint of the state as of the utmost danger, as an attempt to suck the blood out of it and transform it into a phantom. Furthermore, it is clear that Socrates must attract public attention, for it was not a scholarly still life that he pursued; on the contrary, it was with the enormous elasticity of a world historical standpoint that he bobbed one after the other outside the substantial actuality of the state. But as he now stood accused, so neither could the state be satisfied with the defence inherent in his own exploitable ignorance, for this very ignorance must naturally be regarded as a felony from the standpoint of the state.

But if his standpoint was negative in a theoretical regard, it was no less so in a practical regard, for he was incapable of contracting any real relation to the existent [*Bestaaende*].*

---

* Socrates, to be sure, had served the state in three military campaigns[59] (the siege of Potidaea, the campaign in Boeotia near Delium, and the battle of Amphipolis). Subsequently, he was a member of the assembly and wore the robe of an epistates[60]—an event lasting one day. In spite of this he had completely emancipated himself from the true civic relationship to the

This, of course, was due to his theoretical position. He had found his way [found himself] out of the 'other' (for the Greek mind: the state), but in return he could not find his way [find himself] into [come to terms with] the state.[61] In the *Apology* he explains how his divine mission had deprived him of the time and opportunity to concern himself with the affairs of the state, and he declares it is necessary for him to live as a private person.[62]

When one considers that even in our modern states where, precisely because it has undergone a far deeper mediation, the state allows quite a different liberty of action to subjectivity than the Greek state was able to do, when one considers, I say, that even in our modern states the particular individual still always remains a rather ambiguous person, then one can surmise from this with what eyes the Greek state must have looked upon Socrates' attempt to go his own way and live as a private person. Forchhammer remarks on page 6: 'On every porch, at every street corner, on every promenade Socrates seized the Athenian youths by the mantle and interrogated them until they left him not only feeling the humiliation of knowing nothing, but also with doubts about what they had previously regarded as divine, or else devoted themselves entirely to his teaching.' And when Professor Heinsius[63] believes himself to have sufficiently refuted this statement by asking if there is anyone who agrees with Forchhammer in this, then I shall venture to reply to Hr. Professor Heinsius, with all due respect, that I find Forchhammer's description of the activity of Socrates to be both well depicted and correctly conceived as heresy against the state. What I regard as noteworthy in Forchhammer's characterization is his description of the way Socrates loitered around the streets and alleys instead of fulfilling his role in the state or being a citizen in the Greek sense, the way he exempted himself from sharing in the responsi-

---

state. Naturally, Xenophon justifies him[64] in this connection by having Socrates say: 'If I fashion good citizens, then I multiply that service which I owe to the fatherland'; but this is merely part of that Xenophontic stupidity we met with previously.

bilities of the state and was perfectly content to live as a privateer. His position in life was therefore utterly predicate-less,* naturally I do not mean this in the odious sense that he was not Chancellor or First Secretary; but as he did not have any relation to the state, so nothing may be predicated of his entire life and work from the standpoint of the state. Later we see how Plato, too, called the philosopher away from actuality, how he desired the blithe shapes of the Ideas to beckon him away from the tangible, and the philosopher to live far removed from the clamour of the world. But this was not the case with Socrates. To be sure, there was in Socrates something of an enthusiast with respect to knowledge, as surely as it is generally the abstract[65] which offers most temptation to enthusiasm. But this did not remove him from life; on the contrary, he entered into the most vital contact with

* He even boasts of this in the *Apology* when emphasizing that his life has been active though incommensurable with the standards of the state (he obviously intends this to be polemical against the state, and as he blends everything together [*mellem hverandre*] with deep irony, he easily deceives the fleeting attention of his listeners). He relates that he has never bothered about acquiring money, nor about the management of his household, about military, civic, or other offices and positions of authority (now this can scarcely be regarded as so praiseworthy from the standpoint of the state), nor about political parties and conspiracies (here we have a confusion, for naturally the state must regard the fact that he has never participated in the latter as commendable, yet the irony is evident from the loose way he lumps together an authentic civic life in the state with mobs and partisan dissensions). By contrast, he has privately en-deavoured to confer the greatest benefit upon the individual, but this is to say that he merely contracted a wholly personal relationship to individuals. Cf. *Apology* 36 B, C. —A similar attempt to blend everything together [*mellemhverandre*] occurs at another place in the *Apology*[66] when Socrates passionately asserts that everyone ought to remain at that post which either he himself has chosen, in the thought that it was best for him, or which the state has chosen for him. But it is this arbitrary liberty of action here postulated that must be considerably restricted from the standpoint of the state. The confusion becomes even greater when next he proceeds to argue from those few instances when he remained at the post assigned to him in the service of the state. For the state will always know how to appreciate this, but the fact that he has taken it upon himself to choose a post, this is what is fishy.

it. His relation to this, however, was his purely personal relationship to individuals, an interaction consummating itself as irony. Human beings were therefore of infinite significance* to Socrates, and if he was uncompromising in his refusal to subordinate himself to the state, then he was equally compromising and pliable in his association with people, equally a virtuoso of the casual encounter. He conversed equally well with tanners, tailors, Sophists, statesmen, poets, with young and old, conversed with them equally well about everything, for he everywhere found a task for his irony.† But with all this he was not a good citizen, and he assuredly did not make others so.‡ Whether the standpoint which Socrates represented was in actuality higher than that of the state, whether he was in truth divinely authorized, must be adjudicated by world history. But if it is to judge fairly, it must also admit that the state was within its rights in judging Socrates. In a certain

* While Cicero writes[67] that Socrates brought philosophy down from the skies and into the houses of men, it was even more the case that he brought men out of their houses and up from the underworld in which they had previously lived. All his virtuosity notwithstanding, it was still possible for him occasionally to bog down in this undertaking, to miss the irony amidst his long-winded conversations with every Tom, Dick, and Harry, to lose sight of the thread of irony and momentarily lapse into a certain triviality. So much for a previous remark concerning Xenophon's conception.[68]

† When Phædrus (in the dialogue of the same name) expresses his surprise that Socrates is so little acquainted with the countryside that he must be led around like a stranger, indeed, that he almost seems never to have been outside the city gates, Socrates answers (230 D): 'Very true, my good friend; and I hope that you will excuse me when you hear the reason, which is, that I am a lover of knowledge, and the men who dwell in the city are my teachers, and not the trees or the country.'

‡ The method he employed: 'For I tried to persuade each one of you not to think of his affairs until he had thought of himself . . . not to think of the affairs of Athens until he had thought of Athens herself' (*Apology* 36 C), was obviously completely backwards with respect to Hellenism. Similarly, the thesis: concern yourself first with the state before you concern yourself with its particular affairs, suggests those revolutionary tendencies in our age[69] expressing themselves not so much in tangible things as in thoughts (naturally the thoughts of particular individuals) and their usurped sovereignty.

sense he was revolutionary, yet not so much by what he did as by what he omitted to do. But a partisan or head of a conspiracy he was not, his irony saved him from this. For while it deprived him of true civic sympathy for the state, the true civic pathos, so it also freed him from the sickliness and excitement requisite for a partisan. His position was altogether too personally isolated, every relationship contracted too loosely conjoined to be anything more than a significant contact. He stood ironically outside every relationship, and the law governing it was a perpetual attraction and repulsion. His connection with a particular individual was only momentary, while high above all this he hovered in ironic satisfaction. This relates to an accusation urged against Socrates in recent times, for he has been accused of being an aristocrat (Forchhammer).[70] This, of course, must be understood in an intellectual sense, and here one is unable to acquit Socrates. The ironic freedom he enjoyed, for as no relationship had sufficient strength to hold him he constantly felt freely above it; the satisfaction in being sufficient unto himself, to which he surrendered, all this suggests something aristocratic. It is well known that some have compared Socrates to Diogenes the Cynic, and called Diogenes an 'angry Socrates'. Schleiermacher[71] was of the opinion that the latter ought rather to be called a caricatured Socrates, and sought the similarity between them in the independence of sensual enjoyment which both endeavoured to acquire. But surely this is far too little. For if one recalls that Cynicism is the negative enjoyment (in relation to Epicureanism), that Cynicism enjoys the privation and deficiency, that it is not unacquainted with desire but seeks its satisfaction in not surrendering to it, that instead of issuing in desire it turns back into itself at every moment and enjoys the lack of enjoyment, an enjoyment vividly suggesting what ironic satisfaction is in the intellectual sphere—when one considers all this and applies it intellectually to the manifold life of the state, then the similarity between these two will not be so insignificant. True freedom consists in indulging in pleasure and yet preserving the soul unharmed. In the life of the state true freedom consists in being involved in the relations of life in such a way that these have objective validity for one, and through all this preserving the innermost and deepest personal life, which may well animate all these relationships, but which to a certain extent is still incommensurable with them.

But if we return for a moment to the event furnishing the occasion for this inquiry, the accusation against Socrates, it will then be evident that Socrates as citizen was not a point on the periphery of the state gravitating toward its centre, but instead a tangent constantly touching only the peripheral manifold of the state. It is no less clear that in relation to the state one may not venture to attribute to him the negative virtue of not doing evil (a negativity which must be regarded by the Greek mind as an offence), but by bringing others into the same situation he actually did do evil. And there is one thing more. He did not contract any deeper relationship with those whom he had raised out of their natural station (he was not a partisan), but was at the same moment ironically above them.

But if it was impossible for Socrates to accommodate himself and find his way back into the manifold concretion of the state, and if it was doubtful how much he could accomplish with the average Athenian citizen, whose life had been formed during the course of years by the life of the state; still, he had in the youth to whom the state jealously looked for its future a nursery wherein his Ideas could thrive, since youth always lives more universally than manhood. It was therefore quite natural for Socrates to direct his attention especially to the youth. With this we make our transition to the second accusation.

2. Socrates corrupts the youth

The defence advanced by Socrates in Plato's *Apology* (26 A) is that either he corrupts the youth voluntarily or involuntarily (ἑκων-ἀκων). As it would be foolish to suppose he did this voluntarily, however, because even he must see that sooner or later he himself would come to suffer for this, so it must be assumed that he does this involuntarily, in which case it is irrational to order him punished, since his accusers ought to take steps to instruct and admonish him. That this defence does not amount to much is clearly seen by all, for in this way one could explain away every offence and transform it into error.*

Hegel[72] has discussed this accusation so expertly that I shall be as brief as possible respecting those points in which I can agree with him so as not to fatigue more knowledgeable readers with what they already know. Against the broad accusation of Meletus that he corrupts the youth, Socrates places his entire life. The charge then becomes more specifically that he undermines the respect of the youth for their parents.† This is considerably illuminated by a special incident between Socrates and Anytus concerning the latter's son.‡ Socrates' defence rests on the general thesis that the most skilful, i.e., the most discerning, i.e., the wisest, ought to be preferred to the less wise. Hence in the choice of a military commander one would not prefer parents to those skilled in warfare.§ Hegel next identifies the indefensible feature in Socrates' behaviour as the moral intervention of a third person into the absolute relationship between parents and children, an intervention which, to keep to a single instance of factual evidence, seems to have caused the young man in question, the son of Anytus, to become dissatisfied with his situation.¶ This is as far as Hegel takes us. Moreover, we have actually come quite far with this Hegelian conception. But the matter may be viewed from another aspect. The state has naturally been in complete agreement with Socrates in holding that the wisest should be preferred to the less wise; but it does not follow that the state can relinquish to each individual the decision whether or to what extent he is the wisest, much less allow the individual to disseminate his wisdom unchecked by the state

* I have deliberately emphasized this *raisonnement* because it provides a clue to how Socrates' moral doctrine was constituted (a feature to be investigated later), and shows that his moral doctrine suffered from the defect of being based upon an utterly abstract theory of knowledge.

† Xenoph., *Mem.* 1, 2, 49; Xenoph. *Apology* §20. To this may be compared the conduct of Phidippides towards his father in Aristophanes' *Clouds*.

‡ Xenoph. *Apology* §29-31.

§ Xenoph. *Apology* §20, 21; *Mem.* 1, 2, 51.

¶ Cf. Hegel, *op. cit.*, p. 109.[73]

merely because in his own judgment he is the wisest. The state as the totality in which the family lives and moves may partially suspend the absolute relationship between parents and children, for example, it may use its authority to establish requirements concerning the education of children. This is due to the fact that the state is higher than the family within the state. But the family is in turn higher than the individual, especially concerning his own affairs. In opposition to the family the individual as such is not authorized to disseminate his wisdom on his own responsibility merely because he believes himself to be the wisest. In opposition to the individual, therefore, the relation of children to parents is absolute.* But as Socrates through his irony had risen above the validity of the substantial life of the state, so the life of the family likewise had no validity for him. The state and family were for him a sum of individuals, and he related himself to the members of the family and state as individuals, every other relationship being to him a matter of indifference. Hence we see how the thesis that the wisest should be preferred to the less wise, precisely by its utter abstractness, becomes essentially immoral (the thesis should have read: whoever thinks himself the wisest should place himself in charge of those he thinks are less wise, for surely Socrates was never preferred except perhaps by the youth, who could have no voice in the matter since they were the very ones to be instructed). Thus we have here another example of how the celebrated moral doctrine of Socrates was constituted. The error clearly lies in the abstract position he assumed respecting knowledge.

Perhaps Socrates meant to compensate for the mischief he caused through this unauthorized intervention by refusing to

* I have limited myself to the relationship between Socrates and the youth he endeavoured to instruct. I have not been concerned with the harmful features which his teaching might have, since whatever can be said in this respect has been discussed in the foregoing. What I wish to emphasize is the unauthorized way in which Socrates set himself up as a teacher simply as a matter of course. The divine authority to which he laid claim can have no value from the standpoint of the state, for in assuming a position of complete isolation he again deprived himself of the sanction of the state.

accept money for his teaching. For it is well known that there was one thing of which Socrates was not a little proud and which he often discusses with much bravado,[74] namely, that he did not accept money for his teaching.* This most often entails a deep irony directed at the Sophists, for these were so exorbitantly paid that their teaching also became incommensurable with money and monetary value—in the opposite sense. But if one will look closer, perhaps something else may be seen in this. It might also derive from the irony with which he conceived his own teaching, for as his wisdom by his own statement was of an ambiguous sort, so also was his teaching. He says of the pilot in the *Gorgias* (511 E): 'And he who is the master of this art (the art of the pilot), and has done us this great service (transported us unharmed), gets out and walks about on the seashore by his ship in an unassuming way. For he is able to reflect and is aware that he cannot tell which of his fellow passengers he has benefitted, and which of them he has injured, in not allowing them to be drowned.' Similarly, one could say the same thing about the teaching of Socrates by which he transported the individual from one continent to another. And just as in the same passage he praises the art of the pilot in contrast to the art of the orator for accepting a small payment though the same service is performed, so he, too, can boast that in contrast to the Sophists he accepts no payment whatsoever. Thus the fact that he did not accept money for his teaching can scarcely be regarded as something in and for itself so exceptionally praiseworthy, nor can it be regarded without further qualification as an absolute sign for the absolute value of his teaching. To be sure, all true teaching is incommensurable with money, and it certainly becomes infinitely ludicrous when payment is allowed to have a decisive influence upon teaching, as though one who taught logic, for example, were to offer logic for three thalers and logic for four thalers. But it does not follow from this that to take money for one's instruction is in and for itself wrong. It is clear that the practice of accepting payment for teaching began

* Aristophanes is of a different opinion, for he not only allows him to accept money for his teaching but even sacks of flour.[75]

with the Sophists, and to this extent one can easily account for Socrates' behaviour and ironic polemic against this practice. As previously mentioned, however, it might be that Socrates' behaviour in this respect concealed an irony towards his own teaching, as if he were to say: frankly speaking, this is peculiarly related to my kind of knowledge, for since I know nothing neither can I very well accept payment for imparting this wisdom to others.

If we return for a moment to the event that furnished the occasion for entering upon this investigation, the accusation against Socrates, it will readily be seen that his offence (considered from the standpoint of the state) consisted in neutralizing the validity of family life, in dissolving the determinations of natural law by which the individual member of the family reposed in the whole family—piety.

We could stop here were our purpose merely to trace this accusation, but one who makes the conception of Socrates the object of investigation must go a step further. In spite of the fact that Socrates committed an offence against the state by his unauthorized intrusion into the family, it is conceivable that through the absolute significance of his teaching together with the intimate way in which he related himself to his disciples with their best interest at heart, he still could have made good again the damage wrought by his inopportune meddling. We would now inquire whether his relationship to his disciples exhibits the seriousness, whether his teaching knows the pathos one has a right to expect from such a teacher. But we miss this completely in Socrates. It is impossible to imagine Socrates in such a relationship as one who uplifted his disciples under the vaulted heaven of the Ideas through a contemplation of their eternal essences, or as one who impregnated the youth with the fullness of an intuitive view, or as one who laid a great moral responsibility upon his own shoulders by watching over them with fatherly concern, releasing them only reluctantly from his hold while his eyes never wholly lost sight of them, or as one who, to recall a previous expression, loved them in the Idea. In relation to others Socrates was too negatively circumscribed in his own person for this ever to happen. An eroticist he certainly was to the fullest extent; the enthusiasm for knowledge was his on an extraordinary scale; in short, he possessed all the seductive gifts of the spirit. But communicate, fill, enrich, this he could not do. In this sense one might possibly call him a seducer,[76] for he deceived the youth and awakened longings which he never satisfied, allowed them to become inflamed by the subtle pleasures of anticipation yet never gave them solid and nourishing food. He deceived them all in the same way as he deceived Alcibiades, who, as previously mentioned, observes that instead of the lover, Socrates became the beloved.[77] And what else will this say except that he attracted the youth to him, but when they looked up to him, when they sought repose in him, when forgetting all else they sought a safe abode in his love, when they themselves ceased to exist and lived only in being loved by him—then he was gone, then the enchantment was over, then they felt the deep pangs of unrequited love, felt that they had been deceived and that it was not Socrates who loved them but they who loved Socrates, and yet they were unable to break with him. Naturally, for more gifted natures this could neither have been so noticeable nor so distressing. He had turned the gaze of his disciples inwards, and the more gifted ones must gratefully feel that it was to him they were indebted for this. Indeed, they must become even more grateful the more they recognized that they were not indebted to Socrates for the treasure itself. His relation to his disciples was therefore stimulating, to be sure, but not at all personal in a positive sense. What restrained him in this regard was once again his irony. Should anyone wish to urge against this the love with which Xenophon and Plato comprehended Socrates, I shall answer: first, it has already been shown that the disciples might easily love him, indeed, might be unable to tear themselves loose from this love; and secondly, and this is the more concrete answer, that Xenophon was too constricted to notice this, Plato too full. Whenever Plato sensed how much he possessed, involuntarily he must think of Socrates; he therefore loved Socrates in the Idea, which he did not owe to Socrates, to be sure, but which Socrates assisted him to reach. Hence Socrates asserts quite correctly in the

Apology (33 A): 'But I was never anyone's teacher. I have never withheld myself from anyone, young or old, who was anxious to hear me converse while I was making my investigation.'*

As for the more intimate relationship between Socrates and his disciples, his relation to Alcibiades must serve as the typical example. This rash, sensuous, ambitious, and gifted young man must naturally have been a most inflammable tinder for Socrates' ironical flint. We have previously seen how through Socrates' irony this relationship constantly remained the same, how it was kept at the abstract, spineless beginning of a relationship, held at the point of zero and never grew in strength and inwardness. For while the power was increased on both sides, the increase was so equally proportioned that the relationship remained the same, with Alcibiades' growing impetuosity always meeting its master in Socrates' irony. In an intellectual sense one may say that Socrates looked upon the youth to desire them.[78] But as his desire did not aim at possessing the youth, so neither did his advances. He did not proceed by eloquent speeches and long oratorical outpourings, nor by vociferously trumpeting forth his own wisdom; on the contrary, he went about unassumingly and was apparently indifferent towards young men. His questions did not concern his relationship to them, but he discussed various topics of importance to them personally, all the while acting quite objectively. Yet in the midst of all this indifference they felt more than they saw of that penetrating side glance which instantaneously pierced their souls like a dagger thrust. It was as though he had spied upon the innermost thoughts of their souls which somehow forced them to speak about them in his presence. He became their confidant without their ever understanding how it had come about, and whereas they were greatly changed by all this, he remained immovably the same. And now when all the ties of

* Socrates most likely says this in order to refute the objection that he taught wholly different things in the intimate circle of his disciples than he did when someone else was present. In this regard one may safely admit that Socrates was always the same. Beyond this, however, his words show how slack was his relation to the youth, that it was never consolidated by other than accidental contacts with knowledge.

prejudice were loosened, when all intellectual rigidity had been made soft, when his questions had put all things aright and made the transformation possible, then the relationship consummated itself in that momentous instant, that gleam of pure silver[79] instantly illuminating the world of their consciousness, when he spun everything round them in and for a split second, when everything was changed for them 'in a moment, in the twinkling of an eye'.[80] It is related that an Englishman[81] travelled about in order to enjoy various natural prospects, and if he came upon a spot in some virgin forest from which an unusual prospect could be opened up by having the intervening trees removed, he then hired men to saw down the offending members. When everything was ready, when the trees were sawed through, he climbed up to this designated point, took out his eyepiece, and gave the signal—the trees fell, and for a moment his eye delighted in the enchantment of the prospect, an enchantment that was the more beguiling because at the self-same moment he almost experienced the opposite. The same is true of Socrates. By means of his questions he sawed through the virgin forest of substantial consciousness in all quietude, and when everything was ready, all these formations suddenly disappeared and his mind's eye enjoyed a prospect such as it had never before seen. But, more accurately, it was the youth who enjoyed this pleasure while Socrates stood aside as the ironic observer enjoying their surprise. This work of sawing through the forest often required considerable time, and in this regard Socrates was indefatigable. But the relationship had already been consummated the moment this was accomplished, for Socrates gave no more. With the youth now feeling indissolubly bound to him there supervened that condition which Alcibiades so aptly describes as Socrates' transition from the lover to the beloved. If one will conceive his relation to the youth in this way, then one is forcefully reminded of the art of midwifery which he claimed to possess. He assisted the individual to an intellectual delivery, severed the umbilical cord of substantiality. As an *accoucheur* Socrates was unsurpassed, but more than this he was not. He assumed no real responsibility for his disciples' subsequent lives, and Alcibiades is once again the typical example.*

If one understands the word in an intellectual sense, one may call Socrates an eroticist, and express it even more emphatically by recalling the celebrated words of the *Phædrus* (249 A): 'to love young boys according to the love of wisdom' (παιδεραστεῖν μετὰ φιλοσοφίας). Here we might possibly touch briefly upon the charge of pederasty directed against Socrates, a charge which in the course of time has never been allowed to die out because there has usually been one or another scholar in every generation who felt obliged to defend Socrates' honour in this respect. Now it is not my intention to present a defence for Socrates, since it does not even interest me to reflect upon the accusation; but if the reader will understand it as an image,† then I believe one will see in this new evidence for Socrates' irony. In the panegyric delivered by Pausanias in the *Symposium*,[82] there occurs the following statement: 'This Eros (the common whose worshippers love women as well as youths, and with those they love, love the body more than the soul) is the offspring of the goddess who is far younger than the other, and owes its existence [*Tilværelse*] to a union of the male and female. But the other Eros is the offspring of the heavenly goddess, in whose birth the female has no part but only the male . . . Those who are inspired by this love turn to the male because they love that which by nature possesses more power and a larger share of mind' (181 c). With these words we already have an adequate description of that intellectual love which must of necessity occur among such an æsthetically developed people as the Greeks, where individuality was not infinitely reflected in itself, but was instead what Hegel has so aptly called 'beautiful individuality',[83] where the opposition within individuality was not cleft deep enough to allow true love to be the higher unity. As this intellectual love seeks its object among the youth, so this suggests that it loves possibility but

* Cf. Forchhammer, *op. cit.*, p. 42 ff.

† Those who are unable to understand this intellectually are referred to Johannes M. Gesner's: 'Socrates sanctus Paederasta', in *Commentarii societatis regiae scientiarum Gottingensis. Tom.* II, *ad annum* MDCCLII, pp. 1-31.

flees actuality. This adequately exhibits its negative character. In spite of this it may still possess a high degree of enthusiasm; indeed, it may have enthusiasm precisely because of this. Enthusiasm is not always conjoined with fortitude; quite the contrary, enthusiasm is a consuming excitement in the service of possibility. An ironist is therefore always an enthusiast, except that his enthusiasm accomplishes nothing, for he never goes beyond the determination possibility. It is in this sense that Socrates loved the youth. But it will now have become evident that this is a negative love. His relationship to the youth was obviously not without significance, but, as previously remarked, in the sense of acquiring deeper significance such a relationship was already past, that is to say, his relation to the youth was the beginning of a relationship. That such a condition might easily endure for a time, that the youth might easily feel bound to Socrates even after he had detached himself from them, all this I have endeavoured to show in the foregoing. But if one will consider that the relation of Socrates to the youth is the last possibility of finding a positive relationship, if one considers how much one might expect in this regard from the man who, after emancipating himself from every real relationship, concentrated himself solely upon this, if one considers all this, I say, then one will be unable to explain the negativity here described unless one assumes that the standpoint of Socrates was irony.*

But let us return to the accusation against Socrates and the conviction this occasioned. The judges pronounced him guilty, and if one were to characterize his crime with a single word without too much concern for the points of the indictment, then it could be called *apragmosyne* or indifferentism. For while

* History has preserved yet another relationship contracted by Socrates: his relationship with Xantippe. But that Socrates was not quite the model husband is surely felt by all. The conception of his relationship to her—attributed to Socrates by Xenophon[84]—that he had the same benefit from this shrewish wife as trainers of wild horses, namely, learning how to manage them, that she was for him an exercise in mastering people, inasmuch as when he had done with her he could easily put up with other people—this conception, I say, does not evince much connubial love but a high degree of irony. Cf. Forchhammer, p. 49 and note 43.

he was not inactive, and while he was not indifferent towards everything, still, in relation to the state he was this by virtue of his private practice. Socrates was therefore found guilty, but the sentence was as yet undetermined. With Greek humanity it fell to the condemned to propose an alternative punishment, naturally within certain limits. Hegel gives a detailed account in this connection of what was reprehensible in the behaviour of Socrates. He shows that Socrates was deservedly condemned to death, and that his crime lay in refusing to acknowledge the sovereignty of the people, in asserting his own subjective conviction in opposition to the objective judgment of the state. His refusal in this matter might possibly be construed as moral stature, but his death was still self-inflicted. The state was as much justified in condemning Socrates as he was in seeking to emancipate himself from the state, and so he became a tragic hero.* So much for Hegel. Inasmuch as I hold myself to the *Apology*, however, I shall attempt to give a more detailed account of his behaviour. One would think that the opportunity to determine his punishment should have been desperately welcomed by Socrates, for as his conduct had shown itself to be incommensurable with ordinary determinations, so also must be the punishment. Now Socrates is rigorously consistent when maintaining[85] that the only punishment he can impose upon himself is a fine, since if he had any money it would be no loss for him to forfeit it, in other words, because the punishment in this case cancelled itself. It is again thoroughly consistent when he proposes to the judges that they be satisfied with the pittance he can pay, thoroughly consistent, for as money had no reality for him, so the punishment remained the same whether he paid much or little, that is to say, because the punishment was nothing. The only punishment he considered suitable was one which was no punishment at all. But let us pursue this informative passage[86] from the *Apology* in more detail. He begins by expressing his surprise at being found guilty by so small a majority, a fact which sufficiently indicates he does not see in the judgment of the state an objective conception valid

* Cf. Hegel, *op. cit.*, pp. 113 ff.[87]

in opposition to the particular subject. To a certain extent the state does not even exist for him, for he dwells merely upon the numerical. That a quantitative determination might pass over into a qualitative determination seems never to have occurred to him.[88] He dwells upon how extraordinary it is that three[89] votes should have decided the outcome, and, in order to emphasize the extraordinary still more, sets forth the most extreme opposition: if, he says, Anytus and Lycon had not come forward, Meletus himself would have been fined a thousand drachmæ. Here again we see how the irony of Socrates causes him to reject every objective determination of his life. The judges are only a number of individuals, their decision has merely numerical value, and when the majority finds him guilty Socrates holds that this is to say neither more nor less than that so and so many individuals have condemned him. Here everyone sees the completely negative conception of the state. Next, an ironic fate desires that Socrates himself determine the punishment. What gives this situation such extraordinary ironic elasticity is the prodigious opposition: the sword of the law is suspended above Socrates' head by a hair, a human life hangs in the balance, the people are grave and circumspect, the horizon dark and overcast—and then Socrates as absorbed as an old geometer in trying to solve the problem of making his life congrue with the conception of the state, a problem as difficult as trying to square the circle inasmuch as Socrates and the state exhibit themselves as absolutely incongruous figures. It would indeed be comical to see Socrates attempt to conjugate his life according to the paradigm of the state, since his life was wholly irregular; but the situation becomes still more comical by the *dira necessitas*[90] which under pain of death bids him find a similarity in this dissimilarity. It is always comical when one conjoins two things which can have no possible agreement. But it becomes even more comical when it is said: make no mistake about it, unless you discover an agreement you must die. The life of Socrates in its complete isolation must appear wholly incongruous with every determination of the state. Similarly, the movement of thought, the dialectic by which Socrates seeks to bring about a relationship, must also exhibit the most extreme oppositions. He is pronounced guilty by the state, the question concerns what punishment he deserves. But as Socrates feels his life can in no wise be comprehended by the state, it would appear that he might just as well merit a reward. He proposes therefore meals in the prytaneum at public expense.* Should the state not feel called upon to reward him in this fashion, he will then concentrate harder and consider what punishment he might deserve. In order to escape the death penalty demanded by Meletus he could choose either a fine or banishment. But he is unable to arrive at any decision in the matter, for what could induce him to choose one of these two alternatives? Could it be the fear of death? This would surely be irrational, for he does not know whether death be a good or an evil. Hence it would appear that Socrates himself was of the opinion that death was the most fitting punishment, and this because no one knows that it is an evil, that is to say, because the punishment here again, as previously in the case of the fine, cancels itself. He could not choose either a fine or banishment, since in the first case he would be imprisoned because his financial situation would not allow him to pay, and in the second case he clearly saw that he was even less suited to live in a state other than Athens, for within a short time he would again be exiled from this state, etc. Hence he could choose neither a fine or banishment. And why not? Because they would entail suffering, and he could not agree to this because it was undeserved, for as he himself says (38 A): 'And, what is more, I am not accustomed to think that I deserve anything evil.' Insofar as there can be any question of what punishment he deserved, his constant answer is: whatever is no punishment at all, namely, either death, since no one knows whether it be a good or an evil, or a fine, provided they will be satisfied with an amount such as he can pay, since money is of no value to him. But as for punishment in a more concrete sense, a per-

---

* As his life as such is incommensurable with its conception by the state, and as he is no more deserving of a reward than a punishment from the state, so he therefore provides a second reason for this: he is a poor man in need of peace and quiet.

ceptible punishment, then he holds that every such is improper.

Thus we clearly see how the standpoint of Socrates is thoroughly negative towards the state, how he was wholly incompatible with it; but we see it still more clearly at that moment when, indicted for his way of life, he surely must have become conscious of his disproportion to the state. Yet undismayed he carries through his standpoint with sword over head. His discourse is not the mighty pathos of enthusiasm, his appearance not the absolute authority of personality, his indifference not a blissful reposing in his own fullness. We find none of these things. Instead, we have an irony carried through to its utmost limit, an irony that allows the objective power of the state to crush itself against the rock-like negativity of irony. The objective power of the state, its restraints upon the activity of the individual, its laws, its courts, everything loses its absolute validity for him, all are stripped away as imperfect forms. Thus he elevates himself higher and higher, becoming ever lighter as he rises, seeing all things disappear beneath him from his ironical bird's eye perspective, while he himself hovers above them in ironic satisfaction borne by the absolute self-consistency of the infinite negativity within him. Thus he becomes estranged from the whole world to which he belongs (however much he may still belong to it in another sense), the contemporary consciousness affords him no predicates, ineffable and indeterminate he belongs to a different formation.[91] But that which sustains him is a negativity which as yet has fashioned no positivity. And here it becomes explicable how even life and death have lost their absolute validity for him. Thus we have in Socrates not the apparent but the actual zenith of irony, because Socrates was the first to arrive at the Idea of the good, the beautiful, and the true as a limit, that is, to arrive at ideal infinity in the form of possibility. In a much later age, however, after these Ideas have acquired their actuality, personality its absolute fullness (*plērōma*), when subjectivity again seeks to isolate itself and infinite negativity once more exposes its abyss in order to engulf the actuality of this mind or spirit, irony will then exhibit itself in an even more dangerous and precarious shape.[92]

CHAPTER III

The conception made necessary

The life of Socrates is for the observer like a majestic pause in the course of history: one does not hear him at all, a deep stillness prevails until this is suddenly broken off by the discordant attempts of several different schools of disciples to trace their origins back to this hidden and mysterious source. With Socrates the stream of the historical narrative plunges underground for a time like the river Guadalquivir, but only in order to burst forth again with renewed force.[1] He functions in world history like a dash[2] in punctuation, and the ignorance concerning him, which is due to the lack of opportunity for immediate observation, does not so much invite us to pass him by as to conjure him forth by means of the Idea, to allow him to become visible in his ideal configuration, in other words, to become conscious of that thought which is the meaning of his existence in the world, that moment in the development of the world spirit[3] symbolically denoted by the unique character of his existence in history. As in a certain sense he is and is not in world history, so his significance for the development of the world spirit is just to be and not to be, or not to be and yet to be: he is the nothingness from which a beginning must be made. He is not for he does not exist for immediate conception, and corresponding to this in an intellectual sense is the negation of the immediacy of substantiality. He is, for he exists for thought, and corresponding to this in the world of mind is the appearance of the Idea, but, be it noted, in its abstract form, its infinite negativity. To this extent the form of his existence in history is not a perfectly adequate image of his intellectual significance. If in the first part of this dissertation I therefore endeavoured to obtain a hold on Socrates *via negationis*,[4] then this last part of the dissertation will endeavour

222

to maintain that hold on him, *via eminentiæ*.[5] Naturally, our intention is not to tear Socrates loose from his historical context; on the contrary, it is essential to see him wholly in this. Nor do we intend Socrates to become so divine and exalted that he is unable to secure a foothold on the earth, for such personages are as useless to the historian who has arrived at the age of discretion as they were to the Indian maiden.* 'Socrates did not grow out of the earth like a mushroom, but stands in a determinate continuity with his time,' says a wise man.[6] In spite of this continuity, one must bear in mind that he does not admit of being absolutely explained through the past, or if one will regard him as a conclusion to the premises of the past, that there was more in him than in the premises, the *Ursprüngliche*, the latter being necessary in order for him truly to be a turning point.[7] Plato has expressed this on several occasions[8] by calling Socrates a divine gift, and Socrates himself says in the *Apology* (30 D): 'And now, Athenians, I am not arguing in my own defence at all, as you might expect me to do, but rather in yours in order that you may not make a mistake about the gift of the god to you by condemning me'; and again (31 A): 'And you may easily see that it is the god who has given me to your city.' This expression that Socrates was a divine gift is particularly descriptive, inasmuch as it not only points to the fact that Socrates was wholly suited for his age (for should not the gods give good gifts), but in addition suggests that he was more than the age could give itself.

Inasmuch as Socrates affords a turning point, it becomes necessary to consider the period before and after him. It seems somewhat superfluous here to present a historical account of the decline of the Athenian state, and on this point surely

* 'In the episode Nala, in the poem of Mahabhárata, we have a story of a virgin who in her twenty-first year—the age at which the maidens themselves have a right to choose a husband—makes selection from among her wooers. There are five of them, but the maiden remarks that four of them do not stand firmly on their feet, and thence correctly infers that they are gods. She therefore chooses the fifth who is a veritable man.' Cf. Hegel, *Philosophy of History* (rev. ed.), p. 151.[9]

everyone will agree with me who is not afflicted with that lunacy from which a great many of the younger votaries of systematic philosophy seem to suffer, a lunacy expressing itself not comically but tragically in continually recounting the same story.[10] Because it is a turning point in history, Hegel discusses it time and time again, sometimes when his purpose is to explain it, other times when it is employed as an example. Anyone with even a slight acquaintance with Hegel will necessarily be familiar with his view on this, and I shall not plague anyone by repeating what no one can say so well as Hegel himself.[11] Should the reader desire an attractive and more detailed account of how Athens increasingly declined after Pericles, who in one sense was an abnormal phenomenon checking and restraining the evil during his own lifetime, an account which traces the principle of decline through the various spheres of the state, I shall refer him to Rötscher, *op. cit.*, pp. 85 ff. However, I am unable to resist one observation. In many ways the Athens of this period resembles what Rome later became. In an intellectual sense Athens was the heart of Greece. Now when Hellenism approached its dissolution all the blood flowed violently back into the chambers of its heart. Everything gathered in Athens: wealth, luxury, splendour, art, science, wantonness, the enjoyment of life,* in short, everything which, by hastening its ruin, might also serve to glorify and illuminate one of the most brilliant intellectual dramas that can be imagined. There is a certain nervousness in the life of Athens, a heart palpitation hinting that the hour of dissolution is near. But that which was the condition for the destruction of the state exhibits itself from the other side as that which has infinite significance for the new principle yet to appear, hence the dissolution and decay become the fertile soil of the new principle. The evil principle in the Greek state was the arbitrary freedom of finite subjectivity (unjustified subjectivity) in all its many variegated forms.[12] Only one of these, however, will be the object of closer investigation, namely, sophistry. This is the troll which haunts the landscape

* 'Wheresoever the carcass is, there will the eagles be gathered together.' *Matt.* 24 : 28.

of reflection and its name is legion.[13] We are concerned with
the Sophists because in them Socrates perceived the present
or past which had to be destroyed. We wish to see how this
was constituted and then calculate how Socrates must have
been constituted so as to be able to destroy them. Reflection
begins with the Sophists, and to this extent Socrates will
always have something in common with them. In relation to
Socrates, therefore, one might characterize the Sophists as
false Messiahs.

The Sophists* represent knowledge in a condition of frag-

* Hegel has again provided an excellent account of this. The more
extensive treatment found in his *Geschichte der Philosophie*, so it seems to me,
is not always in agreement with itself, and occasionally bears the character
of a collection of desultory remarks exhibiting lack of subordination to the
divisions suggested by the various headings.[14] As for the relation of this
more extensive account to the short sketch found in his *Philosophy of History*,
one may appropriately apply the remark which Hegel[15] has somewhere
made to the effect that mind is the best epitomist. This sketch is so per-
tinent and illustrative that I shall include it here (pp. 268, 269): 'With
the Sophists began the process of reflection on the existing state of things,
and of ratiocination. That very diligence and activity which we observed
among the Greeks in their practical life, and in the achievement of works
of art, showed itself also in the turns and windings which these ideas took;
so that, as material things are changed, worked up and used for other than
their original purposes, similarly the essential being of mind—what is
thought and known—is variously handled; it is made an object about
which the mind can employ itself, and this occupation becomes an interest
in and for itself. The movement of thought and that which goes on within
its sphere, a process which had formerly no interest, acquires attractive-
ness on its own account. The cultivated Sophists, who were not erudite
or scientific men, but masters of subtle turns of thought, excited the admira-
tion of the Greeks. For all questions they had an answer; for all interest
of a political or religious order they had general points of view; and in
the ultimate development of their art, they claimed the ability to prove
everything, to discover a justifiable side in every position. In a democracy
it is a matter of the first importance to be able to speak in popular assemblies
—to urge one's opinions on public matters. Now this demands the power
of duly presenting before them that point of view which we desire them to
regard as essential. For such a purpose intellectual culture is needed, and
this discipline the Greeks acquired under their Sophists. In the hands of
those who possessed it, this mental culture then became the means of

mented multiplicity tearing itself loose from the substantial ethic through dawning reflection. They represented a detached culture for which everyone felt a need, that is, everyone for whom the enchantment of immediacy had vanished. Their wisdom was '*ein fliegendes Blatt*'[16] which was neither prevented from circulating about by some important person nor assimilated into a coherent system of knowledge. Their external appearance corresponds perfectly to this. They were everywhere, as we say, like bogus money. They wandered from city to city like troubadours and itinerant scholastics[17] in the Middle Ages, set up their schools and began enticing the youth, who were drawn to them by the report trumpeted abroad that these men both knew and could prove everything.* What they promised to impart to mankind was a broad culture rather than insight into the particular sciences, and the advertisements of Protagoras[18] clearly resemble the Mephistophelian counsel to the student in Goethe's *Faust*[19] against enrolling in any of the several faculties. He assures the youth they need have no fear that he and the other Sophists will return them against their will to the very studies they wished to avoid. He does not intend to instruct them in arithmetic, astronomy, etc., but will make them men of culture, impart to them the appropriate instruction for becoming accomplished statesmen no less than skilful men in their private affairs. In the *Gorgias*[20] we see how this universal culture presents itself as that which in public life is able to surpass all the sciences, so that one who is in posses-

---

enforcing their views and interests on the people: the expert Sophist knew how to turn the subject of discussion this way or that way at pleasure, and thus the doors were thrown wide open to all human passions. A leading principle of the Sophists was that "man is the measure of all things"; but in this, as in all their apothegms, lurks an ambiguity, since the term "man" may denote spirit in its depth and truth, or in the aspect of mere caprice and private interest. The Sophists meant man simply as subjective, and intended in this dictum of theirs, that mere liking was the principle of right, and that advantage to the individual was the ground of final appeal.'[21]

* The introduction of Plato's *Protagoras*[22] contains a graphic account of some of the modes of sophistic behaviour.

sion of this has a master key with which to open all doors. This general culture resembles what in our age has so often been auctioned off by our learned hucksters of indulgences under the name of information. As the chief interest of the Sophists, after acquiring money, was to acquire influence in the affairs of the state, their travels resemble the sacred pilgrimages and pious processions which now belong to the order of the day in the political world, whereby our political drummers endeavour to impart to others in the shortest possible time the requisite political culture with which to discuss things. That life is full of contradictions seems to escape the notice of immediate consciousness, and it confidently and trustingly clings to its inheritance from the past like a sacred relic; reflection, by contrast, discovers this fact at once. It discovers that what should be absolutely certain, the determining principle for men (laws, statutes, etc.), brings the individual into contradiction with himself. It also discovers that all this is external to man and as such cannot be accepted. But if it exposes the fault, it also has a remedy near at hand: it teaches how to give reasons for everything. It imparts to men an agility and dexterity in subsuming each particular case under certain universals, that is, it distributes to each man a rosary of *loci communes*[23] by whose frequent recitation he is always able to say something about the particular, make some observations concerning it, adduce some reason for or against it. Indeed, the more such categories one possesses and the more skilled one becomes in using them, the more cultivated he is. Such was the culture imparted by the Sophists. Although they did not concern themselves with instruction in the particular sciences, it nevertheless seems appropriate to liken the general culture they practised, the cramming they trained people in, to the résumé of knowledge which a tutor seeks to impart to those whom he tutors.[24] In one sense this general culture is quite rich, in another sense quite impoverished; for it deceives both itself and others in never perceiving that it continually utilizes the same quantities, deceives both itself and others the same way that Tordenskjold deceived others when he caused the same troops, as soon as they had paraded down one street, to parade again through the next. In relation to immediate consciousness, which in all innocence accepts with childlike simplicity whatever is given, this culture is negative and too clever to be innocent. In relation to reflection, however, it is positive to a high degree. In its initial form this culture causes everything to become vacillating, but in its second form it enables every right thinking disciple to render everything secure again.[25] The Sophist demonstrates therefore that everything is true. In a certain sense the thesis that everything is true was valid for the older Hellenism, for actuality had absolute validity. But with sophistry reflection is awake, and it in turn causes everything else to become vacillating; but sophistry next proceeds to lull everything back to sleep again by means of argumentation: by *raisonnements*[26] this hungry monster is sated. Hence with the Sophists the thinker finds himself able to demonstrate everything, for they were able to give reasons for everything, and by means of these anything whatsoever could be made true at every moment.

Now it is certainly true that the thesis, 'everything is true', when asserted within the sphere of reflection, at the next moment passes over into its opposite: nothing is true. But this next moment never came for the Sophists because they lived in the moment. What made sophistry able to repose in this was the fact that it lacked a comprehensive consciousness, lacked the eternal moment wherein it must render an account of the whole. Since reflection had made everything vacillating, sophistry took it upon itself to remedy the need of the moment. Hence in sophistry reflection was stopped in its crucial outward movement, was mastered at every moment, and the surety binding it was the particular subject. It must have seemed, therefore, that sophistry was able to coerce the very spirit which it had conjured forth. But when everything has become vacillating, what then can be the surety that shall save? Either it is the universal (the good, etc.), or it is the finite subject, its will, desire, etc. The Sophists seized upon the latter alternative. The free thought, which already announces itself to a certain extent in reflection when not arbitrarily restrained, lives like a slave under sophistry; and every time it raises its head in order to gaze freely about it is seized and harnessed by the individual in the service of the moment. The Sophist has clipped its tendons so it cannot run from him, and reflection must now mould tiles,[27] erect buildings, and do other slave labour, for it lives stunted and oppressed under the yoke of the thirty tyrants (the Sophists). Hegel remarks in his *Geschichte der Philosophie* (xviii, 5): 'The concept which reason has found in Anaxagoras to be essence, is the simple negative into which all determination sinks, including all that is existent and individual. Before the concept nothing can endure [*bestehen*], for it is simply the predicateless absolute to which everything is clearly only a moment; with this there is nothing, so to speak, permanently fixed and bound. The concept is the constant change of Heraclitus, the movement, the causticity, which nothing can resist. Thus the concept which finds itself becomes the absolute power before which everything vanishes; and with this all things, everything established [*bestehen*], everything held to be secure, is made vacillating. This surety—whether it be the surety of being or the surety of determinate concepts, principles, customs and laws—becomes vacillation and loses its stability. Such principles, etc., themselves belong to the concept and are posited as universal; but this universality is only their form, for the content which they possess, as determinate, falls into movement. It is this movement we see arising in the so-called Sophists. . . .'[28] It would seem, however, that Hegel made too much of the sophistic movement, and the reservations one may have concerning the correctness of his interpretation is strengthened still more by the fact that there follows in his discussion of sophistry much that cannot easily be harmonized with it, just as in his conception of Socrates there is much which, were his conception of sophistry correct, would make it necessary to identify Socrates with the Sophists. Sophistry, to be sure, nourishes within itself a secret most damaging to itself, but this it refuses to acknowledge; and the pompous and self-assured procession of the Sophists, their incomparable sufficiency (all of which we learn from Plato) clearly shows that they believed themselves able to satisfy the exigencies of the age, not so much by causing everything to become vacillating, but after having done this to render it all secure again. The oft repeated sophistic thesis: πάντων χρημάτων μέτρον ἄνθρωπον εἶναι,*[29] contains a positivity for finite reflection, though deeper consideration will discover it to be ultimately negative. The Sophists obviously considered themselves the physicians of the age. Hence one sees in Plato that every time the Sophists are constrained to give an account of their art their constant reply is: the art of the orator. It is precisely in this sphere that the positivity of the Sophists is to be seen. But the orator is always concerned with the particular case, hence it is important to view the matter from before and after, and to speak in a prescribed manner; on the other hand, he is also concerned with a multitude of individuals, and with this in mind the Sophists taught one how to play upon the passions and emotions. The important thing was always the particular case, to win it meant everything. Perhaps an analogy might serve to illumine the positivity in sophistry. Casuistry conceals within itself a secret quite similar to that of sophistry. In casuistry the nascent reflection is likewise stopped, for as soon as reflection is allowed

---

* This sophistic thesis provides an interesting example of the fate of quotations in their oftimes long and tortuous journey through life. Certain quotations are like stock characters in comedies: one needs only to have their existence [Tilværelse] insinuated and one recognizes them at once. The reader who snatches his wisdom from periodicals, journals, prefaces to books, and publisher's advertisements, readily acquires a great multitude of what might be called 'nodding acquaintances'. As is usually the case with these, however, one knows the external man, but is most often completely ignorant of his origin, history, situation, etc.—Now this sophistic thesis is a stock figure in modern literature's world of quotations. Hegel has nevertheless presumed the liberty of conceiving it as if its meaning were: man is the end towards which all things strive.[30] This was indeed a bold rape, but one for which I dare say Hegel can be forgiven, since he frequently calls attention to the meaning it had in the mouth of the Sophists. Nevertheless, a multitude of Hegelians, who, not having been conspirators in the good, have elected to become conspirators in the evil, have caused this false coin to gain wide circulation. In Danish the ambiguity of the word 'Maal'[31] is tempting for one who is not aware that it is a Sophistic thesis. Accordingly, I have chosen to cite it in the Greek according to the Theatetus 152 A.

to break forth it immediately overruns casuistry. Although a deeper consideration will perceive its negativity, casuistry still retains a positivity of sorts. The casuist is calm and confident, believing himself not only able to help himself but others as well. Should one fall into doubt[32] and turn to a casuist, therefore, one will always find him with seven precepts and seven solutions ready at hand. This is indeed a high degree of positivity—and yet it is illusory, for the casuist nourishes the self-same disease he attempts to cure, without being aware of it. In discussing the *Protagoras* I have sufficiently emphasized the relation between the conception of Socrates and that of the Sophist. Protagoras has a multitude of virtues, a positive assortment, whereas for Socrates virtue is one. This Socratic thesis is clearly negative in relation to the affluence of Protagoras, and yet it is also speculative: it is the negative infinity wherein each particular virtue is free. The Protagorean thesis that virtue can be taught is clearly positive and contains a high degree of confidence towards both existence and the sophistic art. By contrast, the Socratic thesis that virtue cannot be taught is negative, yet it is also speculative insofar as it is a description of the eternal self-positing infinity wherein all teaching is assimilated. Protagoras is therefore constantly positive, though this is merely apparent; Socrates is constantly negative, though this, too, is to some extent merely apparent. Socrates is positive insofar as infinite negativity contains within itself an infinity; he is negative because for him infinity is not a manifestation but a limit.*

---

* Even Gorgias, who incidentally refused the title of Sophist,[33] is to a certain extent more positive than Socrates, although his dialectic develops the sophistic scepticism still further. The three well-known theses[34] advanced in his work on nature contain a scepticism concerned not merely to show the relativity of determinate being [*Værende*] or its non-being [*Ikke-Væren*] in itself, i.e., its being [*Væren*] for an 'other', but even intrudes itself into the determinations of determinate being [*Værende*]. Nevertheless, the way he conceives determinate being [*Værende*] is still infected with a positivity compared to absolute infinite negativity. Hegel says of the dialectic of Gorgias generally (p. 41): 'This dialectic is clearly impregnable for anyone who affirms (sensuous) being [*Seyende*] to be real.'[35] The positivity which I have generally ascribed to the Sophists has here, to be

It was from such a positivity as this that Hellenism was to be emancipated, a positivity that was as insipid in a theoretical regard as it was corrupting in practical affairs. In order for this to occur beneficially, however, a radical cure was necessary, one allowing the disease to burn itself out in order that no such disposition might remain in the body. The Sophists were thus Socrates' arch-enemies, and if we inquire how he must have been constituted in order to be able to hold them in check, it is impossible not to be momentarily overjoyed by the ingenuity to be found in world history, for Socrates and the Sophists were made for each other, as we say, to a degree rarely seen. Socrates is endowed and fitted out in such a way that it is impossible to mistake the fact that he was meant to do battle with the Sophists. Had Socrates had a positivity of his own to assert, the result would have been that he and the Sophists had come to speak all at once—for the wisdom of the Sophists was surely as tolerant as the piety of the Romans and had no objection to there being one more Sophist, one more stall in the market-place. But such was not the case. The holy was not to be taken in vain, the temple must first be purified before the divine would again dwell there. Truth demanded a silence before again lifting up its voice, and it was Socrates who should occasion this silence. Thus he was exclusively negative. Had he possessed a positivity of his own, he would never have been so unmerciful, never so cannibalistic as he

---

sure, acquired a somewhat different significance. It must be borne in mind, however, that Gorgias was foremost among the Sophists so that one cannot deny him a certain philosophic stature. But he becomes positive in relation to Socrates precisely because he possessed a presupposition, whereas for Socrates infinite negativity is the pressure imbuing subjectivity with the elasticity to become the condition for ideal positivity. In Plato's *Gorgias* the theses advanced by Gorgias, Polus, and Callicles 'with increasing arrogance'[36] are also positive in relation to Socrates, positive in the sense in which I have usually attributed this to the Sophists. The thesis[37] that justice is the interest of the stronger is positive in relation to the negativity wherein the inward infinity of the good is first apprehended. The thesis that it is better to do injustice than suffer injustice is positive in relation to the negativity wherein slumbers the divine providence.

was and as he necessarily had to be in order not to fail his mission in the world. To this end he was perfectly endowed. If the Sophists could answer everything, then he could question everything; if they knew all things, he knew nothing at all; if they could speak without cessation, he could keep silent, i.e., converse.* If the Sophists were pompous and demanding, Socrates was modest and unassuming; if the Sophistic mode of living was luxurious and pleasure-seeking, the Socratic was simple and temperate; if the aim of the Sophists was to acquire influence in the state, Socrates was wholly disinclined towards the affairs of the state. If the teaching of the Sophists was invaluable, then so was Socrates'—in the opposite sense; if the Sophists desired to dine as guests of honour, Socrates was content to sit furthest removed; and if the Sophists wished to amount to something, then Socrates would rather be nothing at all. While all this may certainly be conceived as indicative of Socrates' moral fibre, it might perhaps be more correct to see in this an indirect polemic against all the abuses of the Sophists, a polemic born of the inward infinity of irony. We may certainly speak of the moral strength of Socrates in one sense, but the point he arrived at in this connection was rather the negative determination that subjectivity determines itself. What he lacked, on the other hand, was the objectivity wherein subjectivity is free in itself, the objectivity which is not the constricting but the expanding limit of subjectivity.[38]   The point he arrived at was the internal self-consistency of ideal infinity itself, but in the form of an abstraction that was as much a metaphysical as an æsthetic and moral determination. The thesis so often propounded by Socrates that sin is ignorance already indicates this sufficiently.   What we see in Socrates is the infinitely exuberant freedom of subjectivity, that is, irony.

I trust that two things have become clear from this discussion: first, that irony has world historical validity; and secondly, that Socrates is not belittled by my conception but properly becomes a hero,[39] so that one sees him actively

* The verbosity and diffuse speeches of the Sophists are rather descriptive of the positivity in their possession.

engaged in his element, and that he becomes visible for those with eyes to see, audible for those with ears to hear.[40] Classical Hellenism had outlived itself, a new principle must come forth; but for this to appear in its truth all the fertile weeds of corrupt anticipations and misunderstandings must be ploughed under, destroyed at their deepest root. The new principle must struggle, and world history requires the services of an *accoucheur*. This role was filled by Socrates. He was not the one to introduce the new principle in its fullness, for in him it was only present cryptically (κατὰ κρύψιν);[41] instead, he must render its appearance possible. This intermediate state, which is and is not the new principle, which is potentially but not actually the new principle (*potentia non actu*), is irony. Thus irony is the brand, the two-edged sword, which he wielded over Hellas like a destroying angel. Socrates has also conceived this with the right irony when he says in the *Apology*[42] that he is like a gift of the gods, but then determines this more accurately as: he is a gadfly which the Greek state, like a large and noble but sluggish horse, had need of. The way in which his behaviour thoroughly conformed to this has been sufficiently discussed in the foregoing. Irony is the incitement to subjectivity, and in Socrates this is in truth a world historical passion. In Socrates one development ends and a new development begins. He is the last classical figure, and yet he consumes this authenticity and natural fullness in that service to the god whereby he destroys classicism. His own classicism is what makes it possible for him to sustain irony. This is what I have previously characterized as the divine healthiness possessed by Socrates. For reflective individuality,* on the

* It might seem that Socrates was a reflected individuality, and the curious design suggested by his bodily features seems to suggest that he was not so much what he was as that he became [*blev*] what he was. It should be possible, however, to conceive this analogously with the homely exterior which he himself describes with so much irony. It is well known that Zopyrus[43] made physiognomic studies regarding Socrates. Now all physiognomic truth rests upon the thesis that essence is and only is insofar as it is in appearance, or that appearance is the truth of essence, essence the truth of appearance. The fact of the matter, however, is that essence is the negation of appearance, though not its absolute negation, for then

other hand, every natural determination is a task, and through and out of the dialectic of life emerges the clarified[44] individuality as the personality which at every moment triumphs and struggles still. Reflective individuality never attains the repose pervading beautiful individuality, since the latter is to a certain extent a product of nature containing the sensual within itself as a necessary moment. The harmonious unity of beautiful individuality is disturbed by irony, and to a certain extent it is disturbed in Socrates, destroyed in him at every moment, negated. It is here that the view of death discussed earlier becomes explicable. But above this destruction rises the ironic ataraxy[45] (to recall an expression from Greek Scepticism) elevating itself ever higher and higher.

With respect to the chosen people, the Jews, it was necessary

---

essence would essentially have vanished. Now to a certain extent this is irony: it negates the phenomenal, not in order to posit anything by means of this negation, but negates the phenomenal altogether. It flees back into itself instead of going out of itself, it is not in the phenomenon but seeks to deceive by means of the phenomenon, the phenomenon is not in order to manifest essence but to conceal essence. If one recalls that in happy Hellas essence and phenomenon constituted a unity as an immediate natural determination, then one will also perceive that when this harmony is cancelled the separation must be cleft deeper and deeper until unity in a higher form is achieved. To this extent it seems possible that Socrates conceived the opposition between his essence and appearance ironically. He found it quite in order that his exterior should suggest something completely other than his interior. And however much one emphasizes the moral freedom negating all these imperfect natural features, the opposition still remains insofar as his moral endeavour was unable to change his exterior. Socrates will therefore always remain an extremely difficult problem for physiognomy; for if one emphasizes the element of self-determination, the difficulty remains that his exterior was essentially unchanged, while if one emphasizes the element of heredity, Socrates becomes a stumbling block for all physiognomy. (Mehring's article, '*Ideen zur wissensch. Begründung d. Physiognomik*', appearing in the periodical published by Fichte[46] (vol. II, pt. 2, p. 244, 1840), stresses the moment of self-determination without mentioning the difficulty). However, if one keeps sight of the ironic satisfaction Socrates had in being so endowed by nature that everyone was mistaken about him, then one will have no need to delve any further into physiognomic profundities.

for the scepticism of the Law to prepare the way, by means of its negativity to consume and burn away the natural man, as it were, in order that grace should not be taken in vain.[47] It is the same with the Greeks—who might well be called the chosen people in a worldly sense, a happy[48] people of fortune whose native soil was harmony and beauty, a people in whose development the purely human traversed its determinations, a people of freedom—so also with the Greeks, I say, in their intellectual world void of sorrow it was necessary for the silence of irony to become the negativity preventing subjectivity from being taken in vain. Irony, like the Law, is a demand; indeed, irony is an enormous demand, for it disdains reality and demands ideality.* It is evident that ideality is already present in this desire, if only as possibility, for intellectually the object of desire is present in desire, the latter being the stirring of the object in the desiring subject. And as irony resembles the Law, so the Sophists resemble the Pharisees, for the latter operated in the province of the will exactly like the Sophists in the sphere of knowledge. What Socrates did for the Sophists was to confront them with the next moment, a moment wherein their momentary truth dissolved itself into nothingness, that is to say, he allowed infinity to swallow up finitude. The irony of Socrates was not only directed against the Sophists, however, but against everything existent [*Bestaaende*]; from all this he demanded ideality, and this demand was the judgment which condemned and doomed Hellenism. His irony is not an instrument that he employed in the service of the Idea; irony is his standpoint, for more than this he had not. If he had possessed the Idea, his destructive activity would never have been so drastic. He who proclaimed the Law was not the one to bring grace, and he who asserted the demand in all its severity was not the one able to fulfil it. It must be borne in mind, however, that

* The irony of Socrates is world historically warranted because the demand of the age was true in world history. Hence it did not partake of the sickly and egotistical as did irony at a much later period,[49] when after ideality had already been given in its fullest measure, it claimed the form of an eccentric sublimation.[50]

between this Socratic demand and its fulfilment was not the same abyss[51] as between the Law and grace. In this Socratic demand the fulfilment was potentially present (κατὰ δύναμιν), and here a world historical formation acquires a high degree of culmination. Schleiermacher, in the previously cited[52] essay (p. 54), takes the position that Plato is much too complete for an initial beginning, takes this position in opposition to both Krug[53] and Ast who overlooked Socrates and began with Plato. But irony is the beginning, yet no more than a beginning; it is and it is not. Moreover, its polemic is a beginning that is equally a conclusion, for the destruction of the previous development is as much its conclusion as is the beginning of the new development, since this destruction is only possible because the new principle is already present as possibility.

To be consistent with the bifrontic character inherent in every historical beginning, we must next consider Socrates from the other side, namely, his relation to the development tracing its origin back to him.* It is well known that not only Plato but a multitude of schools derive their wisdom from this point.† In order to explain this phenomenon it might seem necessary to presuppose a high degree of positivity in Socrates. I have previously attempted to show, however, that even his relation to Alcibiades can be explained without assuming such

---

* Plato has conceived his relation to Socrates with as much beauty as piety in the famous statement[54] that he thanked the gods for four things: that he had been born a human being and not an animal, a man and not a woman, a Greek and not a barbarian, but most of all because he had been born an Athenian and contemporary of Socrates.

† Cf. Christian A. Brandis, 'Grundlinien der Lehre des Socrates', *Rheinisches Museum*,[55] Bonn, 1827, p. 119. 'No philosopher of antiquity has won for himself and for the pursuit of truth such a great number of extremely gifted men as did Socrates, only he has given rise to a multitude of schools so different from one another in doctrine and mode of teaching, yet united in the conviction that they owe their guiding principles to Socrates. Among these philosophical schools, of which some have characterized ten (others nine) as ethical, i.e. Socratic, scarcely one, except perhaps the Epicurean, would have found such a characterization disdainful.' (The nine Socratic schools are the Academic, Megaric, Eretrean, Elean, Peripatetic, Cyrenaic, Cynic, Stoic, and Epicurean).

a positivity, indeed, that it only becomes explicable when one assumes it was not present. I also attempted to show the kind of sorcery possessed by irony in order to captivate the sensibilities. It is to similar considerations that I shall now proceed in order to show how irony can once again explain this phenomenon, indeed, that this phenomenon demands irony as its explanation. Hegel remarks in *Geschichte der Philosophie* (XVIII, 126)[56] that Socrates has been reproached because such discrepant philosophies derived from his teaching, and replies that this was due to the indefiniteness and abstractness of his principle. But to reproach him for this merely shows that one wishes him to have been other than he actually was. If the Socratic standpoint had possessed the limitation which every intermediate position necessarily must have, then it would certainly have been impossible for so many descendants to attempt to claim their birthright at this source. If, on the other hand, his standpoint was infinite negativity, then it is easily explained, for this contains within itself the possibility of everything, the possibility of the whole infinitude of subjectivity. Hegel, in discussing the three Socratic schools (Megaric, Cyrenaic, and Cynic), further remarks (p. 127) that these schools are quite different from each other, and adds that this clearly shows that Socrates was devoid of any positive system.[57] But he was not only devoid of any positive system, but devoid of any positivity whatsoever. Subsequently, I shall attempt to show this with reference to the way in which Hegel has vindicated for Socrates the Idea of the good. Here it is enough to say that he had the good merely as infinite negativity. With the good subjectivity is in lawful possession of an absolutely valid end for its activity. Yet Socrates did not proceed from the good but arrived at the good, ended with the good, and this is why it was wholly abstract for him.* But if one must

* Hegel, too, seems to agree with this, though he is not constant on this point (p. 124): 'Socrates did not get further than expressing for consciousness generally the simple essence of self-thought, the good, expressing and investigating the determinate concepts of the good as to whether they properly expressed that essence which they were supposed to express, and whether the matter was in fact determined by them. The good was made

constrict Hegel's statements in this way, one must also expand them by emphasizing the enormous elasticity inherent in this infinite negativity. It is not enough to say that one may conclude from the disparity among the Socratic schools that Socrates was devoid of any positive system, for one must add that it was the pressure of infinite negativity which made all positivity possible, that this was an infinite incitement and stimulation for positivity. As in life Socrates began wherever he found himself, so his significance for the world historical development is to be an infinite beginning which contains within itself a multitude of beginnings. As beginning, therefore, he is positive, but as mere beginning he is negative. His relation to this development is the reverse of his relation to the Sophists; the unity in both, however, is irony. It will also be seen that these three Socratic schools are united in the abstract universal,* however differently they may have conceived it. This entails the ambiguity that it may direct itself polemically against the finite, and yet be instigating for the infinite. As Socrates in associating with his disciples (if I may be permitted to use such a word)[58] was indispensable for keeping the inquiry afloat, so in a world historical sense he has the significance of having launched the ship of speculation. This entails an infinite polemic, a power to remove every obstacle that might hinder its course. Yet Socrates does not himself venture on board, but merely dispatches it. He belongs to an older formation despite the fact that a new formation begins with him.† He discovers within himself another hemisphere in the same sense that Columbus had discovered America

---

the end of human action. With this he left aside the whole world of representation, objective being in general, without seeking a transition from the good as the essence of the conscious as such to the thing, and without recognizing that essence as the essence of things'.[59]

* Hegel's account of the principles of these schools may be found on pp. 127, 128.[60]

† Compare this with our concluding remarks above on page 221: 'Thus he (Socrates) becomes estranged from the whole world to which he belongs, the contemporary consciousness affords him no predicates, ineffable and indeterminate he belongs to a different formation.'

before he went on board and actually discovered it. His negativity precludes every setback as much as it precipitates the actual discovery. As his intellectual mobility and enthusiasm in daily intercourse were inspiring for his disciples, so the enthusiasm of his standpoint is the moving energy in the ensuing positivity.

It has been shown in the foregoing that Socrates was completely negative in his relation to the existent [*Bestaaende*], that he hovered in ironic satisfaction above all the determinations of substantial life. It has also been shown that in relation to the positivity advanced by the Sophists, a positivity which they sought to secure and transform into something enduring [*Bestaaende*] through their manifold reasons, he once again related himself negatively and in his ironic freedom knew himself to be above this. His entire standpoint, therefore, culminates in infinite negativity, for it exhibits itself as negative both in relation to the past development and the subsequent development, though in another sense it is positive in both instances, that is to say, it is infinitely ambiguous.[61] His whole life was a protest against the establishment [*Bestaaende*], the substantial life of the state. His interest in the activity of the Sophists concerns their attempt to bring about a surrogate for the existent [*Bestaaende*]. But their manifold reasons were unable to withstand the whirlwind of his infinite negativity which instantaneously tore away all the polypous tendrils with which the particular empirical subject sought to secure himself, and which now swept them out upon that infinite Oceanus where the good, the true, the beautiful, etc., confine [delimit] themselves in infinite negativity. So much for the historical conditions under which his irony expressed itself. As for the manner in which it manifested itself, we must say that it appeared partially as a mastered moment in discourse, and totally in its complete infinity whereby it finally swept away even Socrates himself.

Hegel's conception of Socrates

It now remains to show how the conception of Socrates developed in this essay relates to earlier views of him, that is, it remains to let this conception make its own way in the world. It is not my intention, however, to run through all possible conceptions, nor by means of such an historical survey to fashion myself in the likeness of the youngest disciples of a certain new school—who have once more chosen the form of the fairy-tale[1] —by continually repeating with each successive link the entire exercise as a model. Surely everyone feels it would be unreasonable to go back so far as to concern oneself with the conceptions of Brucker[2] and Tychsen,[3] or so conscientious as to include the reminiscences of Krug.[4] To begin with the well-known essay[5] of Schleiermacher* was already a beginning, although

* The task which Schleiermacher has set for himself already shows one cannot expect to find there any absolutely exhaustive result. With Socrates —to recall once more a previously cited[6] observation of Hegel, which, curiously enough, is really by Hegel—it is not so much a matter of philosophy as of individual life. What Schleiermacher vindicates for Socrates is the Idea of knowledge, and this is the positivity which, as previously remarked, concealed itself behind his ignorance. He writes on page 61: 'For otherwise how was he able to declare that the things which others professed to know were merely ignorance except by virtue of a more correct conception of knowledge and a more correct procedure based on this? Wherever he demonstrates this ignorance it will be seen that he proceeds by way of these two criteria: first, knowledge in all true thought is the same, and consequently every such thought must have the same characteristic form; and secondly, all knowledge forms a totality. Hence his demonstrations always depend upon the fact that whoever proceeds from a true thought cannot become entangled in a contradiction with another true thought, and that knowledge derived through valid inferences from one point cannot contradict knowledge discovered in the same way from another point. Because Socrates uncovered such contradictions in the customary ideas of mankind, he sought to stir up this fundamental

I cannot agree with Brandis[7] in holding that it was Schleiermacher who first succeeded in breaking through.

---

thought in everyone who could in any way understand or comprehend
him.' Subsequently, Schleiermacher attributes method to Socrates and
conceives this according to the *Phædrus*[8] as having a twofold task (p. 63):
'to know how one correctly comprehends scattered particulars in a unity,
and in turn how to divide a composite unity into diverse parts in conformity with its nature.' If we consider what is suggested here, we see that
this contains nothing which may not agree [*bestaae*] with our entire conception. What is emphasized here is the idea of consistency, the law upon
which rests the realm of knowledge; yet it is conceived so negatively that
the principle it contains, and which Socrates also employed, is none other
than *principium exclusi medii inter duo contradictoria*.[9] The totality which all
knowledge should form is in turn conceived so negatively that it is essentially infinite negativity. Similarly, the twofold task of the method is
negative, for the unity by which the many is comprehended is the negative
unity into which it disappears, and the division by which the unity is
resolved is the discursive negativity. But this is precisely what we have
conceived as the essential aspect in the Socratic dialectic, namely, the fact
that it brings about the infinite self-consistency of the ideal. What is lacking
in Schleiermacher, however, is the consciousness of Socrates' significance
as a personality, although to a certain extent one cannot fairly require this
of him, since he has consciously limited his task. In this regard, Baur, in
his frequently mentioned work, has much merit, and the consideration
that the similarity between Socrates and Christ must first be sought in the
validity which they both had as personalities, is a very fruitful consideration.[10] The important thing, however, is to retain the infinite dissimilarity
remaining within this similarity.[11] I have often remarked in the foregoing
that irony is a determination of personality. It has the movement of turning
back into itself which is characteristic of personality, of seeking back
into itself, terminating in itself—except that in this movement irony returns
empty-handed. Its relation to the world is not such that this relation is a
moment in the content of personality. Its relation to the world is never at
any moment to be in relation to the world, its relation is such that at the
moment this is about to commence, it draws itself back with a sceptical
closedness (ἐποχή).[12] But this reserve is the reflex of personality into
itself that is clearly abstract and void of content. The ironical personality
is therefore merely the outline of a personality. Hence one sees that there
is an absolute dissimilarity between Socrates and Christ; for in Christ dwelt
the immediate fullness of the godhead,[13] and his relation to the world is an
absolutely real relationship, so that the Church is conscious of itself as the
members of his body.[14]

Hegel obviously provides a turning point in the conception of Socrates. I shall therefore begin with Hegel and end with Hegel without considering either his predecessors or his successors, since the former insofar as they have any significance have found their consolidation in his conception, while the latter have only relative value with respect to Hegel.[15] Generally speaking, as Hegel's representation of history may not be accused of wasting time quibbling about the particular, so it concentrates with enormous intellectual intensity upon certain decisive campaigns. Hegel grasps and conceives [*begriber*] history in its larger formations. Hence Socrates is not allowed to stand there like a *Ding an sich*,[16] but must come forth whether he likes it or not.

The difficulty involved in obtaining certainty regarding the phenomenal aspect of the existence of Socrates does not disturb Hegel in the least. Such trifles are wholly unknown to him. And when the perplexed augurs deliver the report that the sacred fowls will not eat, he answers with Appius Claudius Pulcher:[17] then let them drink, and straightaway casts them overboard. In his treatment of Socrates in *Geschichte der Philosophie* there is nothing to illuminate the relation between the three different conceptions of Socrates by his contemporaries,* and this in spite of the fact that Hegel himself remarks that with Socrates it is not so much a matter of philosophy as of individual life. He employs but a single Platonic dialogue†[18] as an example of the Socratic method, yet without a word as to why he chose precisely this one. Xenophon's *Memorabilia* and *Apology*, as well as the *Apology* of Plato, are utilized wholly as a matter of course. He is not fond of a lot of fuss [*Ophævelser*],[19] and not even Schleiermacher's attempt to arrange the dialogues so that one great Idea moves in successive development

* Aristophanes constitutes an exception to this, but more of this later.

† In introducing this dialogue he makes the general observation (p. 69): 'A number of Xenophontic and Platonic dialogues end in the same manner, leaving us quite unsatisfied as to the result (content). This is the case with the *Lysis*, where Plato inquires what love and friendship secure for men; similarly, the *Republic* begins by inquiring into justice. This confusion has the effect of bringing about reflection, and this is the aim of Socrates. This completely negative aspect is central.'[20]

THE CONCEPT OF IRONY

through them all finds grace in his eyes. He remarks (p. 179):
'To treat Plato from a literary point of view, as Schleiermacher
does, critically examining whether one or another minor
dialogue is authentic or not—as for the more important dialogues the testimony of the ancients leaves not the slightest
doubt—is wholly superfluous for philosophy and belongs to
the hypercriticism of our age.'[21]   All such investigations are
wasted energy on Hegel, and when the phenomena are presented on parade he is in too much haste and too aware of
his role as commanding general in world history to have time
for anything more than the regal glance he lets sweep over
them.   Although he is freed in this way from much prolixity,
he nevertheless misses one thing or another that would be a
necessary moment in a complete account.   Hence that which
suffered the injustice of being overlooked in this way occasionally asserts its right and interposes itself at another place.
In Hegel's account of the Platonic system, therefore, one finds
various remarks strewn loosely about advanced with the claim
to be absolute, since the entire context in which they would
have appeared in their relative (hence so much the more
warranted) truth is destroyed.   Page 184: 'There is no need
to inquire further as to what belongs to Socrates and what
belongs to Plato in the representation of the dialogues.   So
much is certain: we are perfectly able to understand the
system of Plato from his dialogues.'[22]   Page 222: 'We find this
dialectic (whose result is merely negative) quite often in
Plato, both in the more essentially Socratic* and moralizing
dialogues, and in the many dialogues relating to the conception
of the Sophists with regard to science.'[23]   Page 226: 'Dialectic
in this higher sense (as that which resolves opposites through
the universal in such a way that the resolution of this contradiction is the affirmative) is the essentially Platonic dialectic.'†[24]

* Hegel here makes a distinction between the dialogues by means of the
predicate 'more essentially Socratic', but without indicating to what
extent he is satisfied with the philological inquiries.

† When he calls this dialectic 'the essentially Platonic dialectic,' he
thereby forms an opposition to that other dialectic not so essentially
Platonic.

Page 230: 'Many dialogues contain merely negative dialectic, and this is the Socratic conversation.'[25] These particular statements are in complete agreement with what I have advanced in the first part of this essay, but it is impossible for me to adduce them any further since they are strewn about so loosely in Hegel's account.

The main presentation of Socrates is found in his *Geschichte der Philosophie* (xviii, 42-122).[26] It is to this that I shall now turn. —The extraordinary thing about this Hegelian conception is that it begins and ends with Socrates' person. Although Hegel in several places seems to want to vindicate a positivity for Socrates, and though he attributes to him the Idea of the good, still, it appears that in relation to the good the individual remains arbitrarily determined, and the good as such has no absolutely binding power. It is remarked on page 93: 'The subject is the determining and deciding principle. Whether the mind deciding is good or bad is now determined by the subject.'[27] (That is to say: the subject stands freely above that which must be regarded as determining him; he stands freely above it not merely at the instant of choice but at every moment, for the arbitrary will [*Vilkaarlighed*] constitutes no law, no constancy, no content). 'The point of deciding within oneself began to unfold with Socrates; for the Greeks this was an unconscious determination. With Socrates the deciding mind is placed in the subjective consciousness of man, and the important question is: how does this subjectivity appear in Socrates himself. Because the person, the individual, makes the decision, we come back to Socrates as a person, and what follows is a discussion of his personal relations.'[28] Now the form in which subjectivity appears in Socrates is the daimonic. But as Hegel correctly enjoins that the daimonic is not yet conscience, it is apparent that in Socrates subjectivity vacillates between finite and infinite subjectivity, for in conscience the finite subject renders himself infinite. Page 95: 'Conscience is the representation of universal individuality, of the mind certain of itself, which at the same time is universal truth. The daimon of Socrates is the entirely necessary other aspect of his universality. As he became conscious of this, so he became conscious of the other aspect, the individuality of mind. His pure consciousness, however, stands above both aspects. We shall now determine the deficiency in this aspect: the defect in the universal was itself replaced in a defective way, in a particular way; hence, that which was corrupted did not find restitution as the negative.'[29] But the fact that his pure consciousness stood above both aspects is obviously what I have expressed as follows: Socrates had the Idea of the good as infinite negativity.

It would be difficult to present a coherent discussion of the many excellent, individual observations found in this section of Hegel, together with that pregnancy of thought so characteristic of him, because there is often so much brought together that it is difficult to find any coherence.[30] Much of it, therefore, has already been utilized in the foregoing part of my essay. But when I consider the totality of the Hegelian interpretation, consider it in relation to the modification[31] which I have argued for, then I believe the whole matter can best be treated under one head: in what sense is Socrates the founder of morality. In this connection the most important moments in Hegel's conception will also come in for discussion.

IN WHAT SENSE IS SOCRATES THE FOUNDER OF MORALITY?

Hegel describes Socrates' significance in general terms as follows (p. 43): 'Socrates expresses essence as the universal self, as the good, the consciousness which rests in itself. But this is the good as such, free from determinate [*seyenden*] reality, free from the relation of consciousness to determine reality—individual sensuous consciousness (feeling and inclination)—or free finally from the theoretically speculative thought about nature, which, while it is indeed thought, nevertheless has the form of being in which I am not certain of my self.'[32] Socrates has arrived at being-in-and-for-itself as being-in-and-for-itself for thought. This is the first moment; the second is that this good, this universality, must be known by me.

In order not to make more of this than Hegel does, however, it becomes necessary to say something about the Socratic teaching. That according to Hegel the Socratic teaching was negative, had the negative as its end, that it was calculated to render vacillating and not to render secure, that in Socrates the negative was not immanent in a positivity but self-purposive, all this clearly follows from the various individual statements cited above as well as from a multitude of observations found in the section properly dealing with Socrates. But it becomes even more obvious from the way Hegel discusses the Aristophanic conception of Socrates. He remarks on page 85 that it was Aristophanes who conceived the Socratic philosophy from its negative aspect, whereby everything existent [Bestaaende] disappears in the indeterminate universal. He adds that it does not occur to him to justify or excuse Aristophanes. Page 89: 'The exaggeration which may be ascribed to Aristophanes is that he drove this dialectic to its bitter end; yet it cannot be said that injustice is done to Socrates by this representation. Aristophanes was not unjust in this; indeed, one must admire his depth in having recognized the dialectical aspect in Socrates as being negative and in having presented it (although after his own fashion) so forcibly. . . . Socrates' universality had the negative aspect of the abrogation of truth (law) as it appears in natural consciousness. This consciousness thus became the pure freedom over determinate content which for him was valid in itself.'[33] The fact that the Socratic teaching was negative is expressed in still another way by Hegel when he remarks that the philosophy of Socrates is not properly speculative philosophy, but 'an individual activity' (p. 53).[34] In order to bring about this individual activity he moralized. 'It was not, however, a species and manner of preaching, exhortation, lecturing, not a dry morality' (p. 58),[35] for all this was contrary to Greek urbanity. Instead, this moralizing expressed itself in the fact that he caused every man to reflect upon his duties. With young and old, cobblers, smiths, Sophists, statesmen, citizens of every sort, he fell in with their interests, be they domestic interests (the rearing of children) or cognitive interests, and directed their thinking away from the determinate case to the universal, that which concerns the true and beautiful in and for itself (p. 59).

Here we have the significance of his moralizing, and here it becomes apparent what Hegel understands when, following the tradition of antiquity, he calls Socrates the founder of morality. But in this connection we must not overlook the well-known meaning of 'morality' to be found in Hegel. He distinguishes between morality and a concrete ethic.[36] The latter may be either a natural concrete ethic, such as that found in the older Hellenism, or it may be a higher determination of this, such as reappears after having come to itself in morality. In his *Philosophy of Right*,[37] therefore, he discusses morality before taking up the higher concrete ethic. While under morality, in the section on 'Good and Conscience', he discusses the moral forms of evil: hypocrisy, probabilism, Jesuitism, the appeal to conscience, and irony.[38] The moral individual is here the negatively free individual. He is free because he is not bound by an 'other', yet he is negatively free because he is not limited in an 'other'. When the individual, because he is in his 'other', is in his own, only then is he in truth, i.e., positively free, affirmatively free. Moral freedom is therefore arbitrariness, the possibility of good and evil. Hence Hegel remarks in the *Philosophy of Right* (p. 92): 'To have conscience, if conscience is only formal subjectivity, is simply to be on the verge of slipping into evil.'[39] In the older Hellenism the individual was not at all free in this sense, but was implicated in the substantial concrete ethic; he had not yet taken himself, not yet separated himself from this condition of immediacy, did not yet know himself. This was accomplished by Socrates, although not in the same sense as the Sophists who taught the individual to contract himself into his own particular interests. Socrates, on the other hand, brought the individual to this by universalizing subjectivity, and to this extent he is the founder of morality. He asserted the significance of consciousness, not sophistically but speculatively. He arrived at being-in-and-for-itself as being-in-and-for-itself for thought, arrived at the determination of knowledge which estranged the individual from the immediacy in which he had heretofore lived. The individual must no longer act out of respect for the law, but must consciously know why he acts. But this, as anyone can see, is a negative determination: it is negative towards the established [*Bestaaende*] as well as negative towards that deeper positivity, that which conditions both negatively and speculatively.

This is also apparent with regard to the determination of the concept of virtue. Hegel advances Aristotle's conception of the Socratic definition of virtue. On page 77 he credits Aristotle with the following statement: ' "Socrates spoke better of virtue than did Pythagoras, but not quite correctly, for he made the virtues into knowledge ($\epsilon\pi\iota\sigma\tau\dot{\eta}\mu\eta$). But this is impossible. All knowledge is connected with a reason ($\lambda\dot{o}\gamma o\varsigma$), and this reason exists only in thought; hence he placed all the virtues in insight (knowledge). It turns out, therefore, that he abrogates the irrational—affective—part of the soul: passion ($\pi\dot{a}\theta o\varsigma$) and custom ($\ddot{\eta}\theta o\varsigma$)." '[40] Hegel next remarks that this is an excellent criticism: 'We see that what Aristotle misses in the Socratic definition of virtue is the aspect of subjective actuality, or that which we now call the heart.'[41] What virtue lacks, therefore, is a determination of being, whether this be conceived with reference to the particular subject or whether in a higher sense it is seen to be realized in the state. But Socrates destroyed the immediate, substantial consciousness of the state, and never arrived at the Idea of the state. Consequently, virtue can only be determined in this abstract fashion, having its reality neither in the state nor in the consummated personality* given only through the

---

* One is accustomed to regarding Socrates as a paragon of virtue, and even Hegel advances this view when he remarks (p. 58): 'Socrates was a model of the moral virtues: wisdom, modesty, moderation, temperance, justice, courage, steadfastness, a firm sense of rectitude in relation to tyrants and the people, removed from cupidity and ambition.'[42] Now this is certainly true, but even the predicate 'moral' which Hegel applies to these virtues already suggests they still lacked that deep seriousness which every virtue only acquires by being assimilated into a totality.[43] As the state had lost its significance for Socrates, so his virtues are not civic virtues but personal virtues. Indeed, if one wished to characterize them in the sharpest terms, then he might call them experimental virtues. The individual stands

state. He credits another statement to Aristotle on page 78:
' "In one respect Socrates proceeded correctly but not in the
other. While it is untrue that virtue is science, he was nevertheless correct in holding that it is not without insight (without
knowledge). . . . He made virtue into logos. We say, however,
that virtue is with logos." '*[44] Hegel again says that this is an

---

freely above them. If Socrates is therefore free from the prudishness that
so often expresses itself in stark moralists, and if we must agree with Hegel
when he asserts (p. 56): 'we do not have to think of Socrates entirely after
the fashion of the litany of moral virtues,'[45] then it is no less certain that
all these virtues have reality for the individual merely as an experiment.
He stands freely above them and can dispense with them whenever he
wishes; and if he does not do so it is merely because he does not wish to,
while the fact that he does not wish to is again merely because he wishes
not to. Hence they never acquire any deeper sense of obligation for him.
To this extent one may certainly say that the individual is not serious about
these virtues, though he takes the matter ever so seriously, that is, if one
will not deny that every arbitrary exercise essentially lacks seriousness and
is nothing but sophistry in the sphere of action.

* The thesis that virtue is knowledge may be illuminated from still
another aspect with reference to Socrates when one recalls the other thesis
that sin is ignorance, a Socratic thesis to which we have often referred in
the foregoing.[46] The thesis that virtue is knowledge contains not merely
what is discussed above, a negative determination over against a natural
concrete ethic which in all innocence knows not what it does; in addition,
it contains a description of this infinite self-consistency of the good whose
abstract movement goes beyond every determination of finitude. This is
seen even more clearly from the thesis that sin is ignorance, for this implies
that sin is inconsistency. At some point sin stops, deviates, and does not
remain in the infinity possessed by the good. When virtue as a determination of knowing tears itself loose from the immediate concrete ethic, it
assumes an ideal configuration corresponding to the ideal infinity of the
good. In the substantial concrete ethic virtue is at every moment limited,
but in the concrete ethic of ideality virtue knows itself as caught up in the
infinity of the good, knows itself in the same infinity wherein the good
knows itself. But all these determinations are merely abstract and negative
so long as one remains at the determination of pure knowing, notwithstanding the fact that it is infinite absolute negativity. The thesis that sin
is ignorance and inconsistency is true from a thoroughly abstract, metaphysical standpoint which regards everything under the aspect of its infinite
self-consistency.

extremely accurate observation. The one aspect is that the universal begins with thought, but it pertains to virtue as character that man *is* this himself, and this entails the heart, temperament, etc. Thus there are two aspects: the universal and the realizing individuality, real mind.

Once again we have arrived at the point where it will become apparent in what sense Socrates was in possession of a positivity. We have now returned to the point we left when we took up the question of his teaching. This consisted in causing the universal to appear in opposition to the particular. With reference to the Socratic principle, therefore, the first determination is the most important even though it is merely formal, namely, that consciousness draws from itself what is truth (p. 71). The fact that one bears consciousness in himself is the principle of subjective freedom. With this the universal has become visible. But the universal has both a positive and a negative aspect (p. 79). We shall now see to what extent Hegel is successful in establishing a positive aspect in Socrates' conception of the universal, or whether we ought not to return to another remark by Hegel, which, as a kind of caption (p. 70): 'This, in short, is the method and the philosophy of Socrates,'[47] already proclaims itself as an observation to which special significance should be attributed. He then adds: 'It seems as if we had not yet exhibited much of the Socratic philosophy, for we have merely kept to the principle. But the main thing with Socrates is that his consciousness for the first time reached this abstraction. The good is the universal. . . . It is a principle concrete in itself, but not yet manifest in its concrete determination. In this abstract attitude lies the deficiency of the Socratic principle. Affirmatively it cannot be articulated, for it has no further development.'[48] In relation to the Sophists Socrates has made an enormous advance. Whereas the Sophists were content to remain at the infinite refraction of the good within the manifold of the useful and advantageous, Socrates arrived at the good in and for itself. But, be it noted, he arrived at this, he did not begin with it. The universal has both a positive and a negative aspect. The reality of the concrete ethic had become vacillating, and this came to consciousness in Socrates. He elevated the concrete ethic to insight, but this is to bring to consciousness the fact that concrete ethical customs and laws are vacillating with respect to their determinateness and immediacy. 'It is the power of the concept which abrogates their immediate existence and value, abrogates the sacredness of their being-in-itself.'[49] As an example of the fact that the universal had a positive aspect in Socrates ('he showed the young men the good and true in what was determined, returning to it because he did not want to remain in mere abstraction'),[50] Hegel cites Socrates' conversation with the Sophist Hippias (*Memorabilia* IV, 4, 12-16, 25). Here Socrates advances the thesis that the just obey the laws, and against the objection that the laws are not absolute, inasmuch as peoples and rulers often change them, he submits the analogy that those who wage war in turn contract peace. He maintains that the best and happiest state is one in which the citizens are of one mind and obey the laws. Now Hegel sees in this an affirmative content. But the reason Socrates exhibits something positive here is because he does not carry through his standpoint, does not advance to the point he had essentially arrived at, the good in and for itself. Here he permits the established [*Bestaaende*] to endure [*bestaae*], hence it is not a positivity following upon his infinite negation but a positivity preceding it.[51] But even with this movement he has already advanced beyond immediate Hellenism, for he clearly assimilates the laws into reflection and thereby removes them from the condition of the immediately given. This, however, is only a feigned movement, not the authentic Socratic movement. The positivity discussed here, therefore, can decide nothing with reference to the question: to what extent did Socrates assert a positivity, or to what extent did the universal become concrete for him? Hegel seems also to have been aware of this, as may be seen from his statements on pp. 79, 81, and 82. Examples of the negative aspect are also furnished by Hegel, but as we have seen that the positive aspect was not positive in the same sense as the other was negative, so now we see that Socrates only asserted the universal as negative. Hegel cites another example from Xenophon and adds (p. 83):

'Here we see the negative aspect, namely, that Socrates rendered vacillating what had formerly been stable and secure for reflection. To refrain from lying, deceit and stealing was regarded as right for natural reflection, as fixed for thought. The comparison of this with other things equally true and established, however, showed that they contradicted each other. Hence what had formerly been stable became vacillating and no longer regarded as secure. The positive which Socrates set in place of what had been stable was partly in opposition to this, namely, to obey the laws. Here we see the universal, the indeterminate; and in the phrase: "obey the laws," everyone who hears it understands the laws expressed just as universal reflection is conscious of them, namely: do not lie, do not deceive. Yet these laws say simply that lying, deceit and stealing are universally set forth as wrong, as determinations which do not suffice for the concept.'[52] Page 85: 'Here we see the universal determined and realized: a general articulation of the laws. But as these are vanishing moments, we see in truth the indeterminate universal, and the deficiency of its indeterminateness not yet satisfied.'[53] Hegel next proceeds to show (p. 90) 'how the realization of the universal appeared in Socrates himself.'[54] Here the subject appears as deciding, as that which arbitrarily determines itself in itself. Yet the limitation which the universal acquires in this way is one which at every moment is arbitrarily posited by the subject. For this constriction of the universal to be stable and not accidental, for the universal to become known in its determinateness, however, is only possible in a total system of actuality.[55] But this is what Socrates lacks. He negated the state without ever arriving again at the higher form of the state wherein infinity is affirmed, as he negatively required.

Thus we see that Socrates may well be called the founder of morality in the sense Hegel intends it, and that his standpoint could still have been irony. To the moral, i.e. the negatively free subject, corresponds the good as task when conceived as infinitely negative. The moral individual can never realize the good; only the positively free subject can have the good as infinitely positive, as his task, and realize it. If one wishes to include the determination of irony so often emphasized by Hegel, namely, that for irony nothing is serious,[56] then this may also be asserted with reference to the negatively free subject. For he is not at all serious about the virtues he practises, insofar as true seriousness is only possible in a totality, as will certainly be affirmed by Hegel, a totality wherein the subject no longer arbitrarily determines himself at each moment to continue his experiment, where he feels the task not as something which he has set himself, but as something which has been set for him.*

It is towards this point of exhibiting Socrates as the founder of morality that Hegel unilaterally allows his conception of Socrates to gravitate. It is the Idea of the good that he seeks to claim for Socrates, but this causes him some embarrassment when he attempts to show how Socrates has conceived the good.[57] It is essentially here that the difficulty with Hegel's conception of Socrates lies, namely, the attempt is constantly made to show how Socrates has conceived the good. But what is even worse, so it seems to me, is that the direction of the current in Socrates' life is not faithfully maintained. The movement in Socrates is to come to the good. His significance for the development of the world is to arrive at this (not at one point to have arrived at this). His significance for his contemporaries is that they arrived at this. Now this does not mean that he arrived at this towards the end of his life, as it were, but that his life was constantly to come to this and to cause others to do the same. In this respect he also arrived at the true, i.e. the true in and for itself, the beautiful, i.e. the beautiful in and for itself, and in general at being-in-and-for-itself as being-in-and-for-itself for thought. He came to this and he constantly came to this. He did not just moralize, therefore, but caused being-in-and-for-itself to become visible out of the determinateness of the manifold. He conversed with

* In Plato's *Republic*[58] dialectic corresponds to the good (as love corresponds to the beautiful). Hence it is quite in order when Aristotle refuses[59] to attribute dialectic to Socrates. He lacked the dialectic which can allow oppositions to endure [*bestaae*], yet it is precisely this dialectic which is necessary if the good is to exhibit itself as infinitely positive.

artisans about the beautiful, and assisted the beautiful in and for itself to extricate itself (*via negationis*)[60] from those determinations of being in which it had heretofore been available. The same applies to the true. He did not do this once and for all, but he did this with every individual. He began wherever the individual might find himself, and soon he was thoroughly involved in issuing clearance papers for each one of them. But as soon as he had ferried one of them over he immediately turned back for another. No actuality could withstand him, yet that which became visible was ideality in the most fleeting suggestion of its faintest configuration, that is, as infinitely abstract. As Charon[61] ferried men over from the fullness of life to the sombre land of the underworld, and in order that his shallow barque might not be overburdened made the voyagers divest themselves of all the manifold determinations of a concrete life: titles, honours, purples, great speeches, sorrows, and tribulations, etc., so that only the pure man remained, so also Socrates ferried the individual from reality over to ideality, and ideal infinity, as infinite negativity, became the nothingness into which he made the whole manifold of reality disappear. Insofar as Socrates continually caused being-in-and-for itself to become visible, it might seem that surely here was his seriousness; but because he merely came to it, merely had being-in-and-for-itself as infinitely abstract, he therefore had the absolute in the form of nothingness. Actuality, by means of the absolute, became [*blev til*] nothingness, but the absolute was in turn nothingness. In order to be able to maintain Socrates at this point, in order never to forget that the content of his life was to undertake this movement at every moment, one must bear in mind his significance as a divine missionary. Yet this has been ignored by Hegel, although Socrates himself places much emphasis upon it. Insofar as one still feels tempted to attribute to him something more, such an inclination is due to the fact that one forgets that world historical individualities are great because their whole lives belong to the world, that they have nothing for themselves as it were. But for this the world has so much the more reason to thank them.

In Hegel's account of the Socratic method[62] there are two

PART TWO

THE CONCEPT OF IRONY

Introduction

The object of investigation in this part of the essay has to a certain extent already been given in the foregoing, inasmuch as one aspect of the concept has already become visible under the form of contemplation.[1] In the previous part of this essay I have not so much presupposed the concept as I have allowed it to come into existence [*blive til*], since I sought to orient myself in the phenomenon. I have thereby found an unknown dimension, a standpoint, which exhibited itself as that which must have been characteristic of Socrates. I have called this standpoint irony, but the name of it in the first part of the essay is of less importance. The main thing is that no moment, no feature, has been overlooked, and that all of them have been ordered together in a totality.[2] Whether this standpoint is irony will now be determined, since in the development of the concept I shall come to that moment which must conform to Socrates as surely as his standpoint was irony. As in the first part of the essay I was concerned solely with Socrates, so in the development of the concept it will become apparent in what sense he is a moment in the development of the concept, in other words, it will become apparent whether the concept of irony is absolutely exhausted in him, or whether there are not other forms of appearance which must also be taken into account before we can say that the concept is adequately conceived. As in the first part the concept continually hovered in the background with a constant need to take form in the phenomenon, so in this part the phenomenal appearance of the concept will accompany the discussion as a pervasive possibility of dwelling among us.[3] These two moments are inseparable: for if the concept were not in the phenomenon, or rather, if it were not the case that the phenomenon is only intelligible and actual in and with the concept, and if the phenomenon were not in the concept, or rather, if it were not the case that the concept is only intelligible and actual in and with the phenomenon, then all knowledge would be impossible; since in the one case I would lack truth, and in the other, actuality. Now if irony is a determination of subjectivity, one will immediately perceive the necessity of two appearances of this concept. Moreover, actuality has given the name of irony to both of them. The first is naturally where subjectivity for the first time asserts its right in world history. Here we have Socrates, that is to say, by this we are shown where to seek the concept in its historical appearance. But after subjectivity had exhibited itself in the world it did not disappear without a trace, the world did not sink back into its previous form of development; on the contrary, the old disappeared and everything became new. Should a new manifestation of irony appear, moreover, it must be insofar as subjectivity asserts itself in a still higher form. It must be a subjectivity raised to the second power, a subjectivity of subjectivity, corresponding to reflection on reflection. With this we are once again world historically oriented, that is, we are referred to that development which modern philosophy acquired in Kant and consummated in Fichte, and even more to those positions after Fichte which endeavoured to assert subjectivity in its second potentiality. That this is indeed the case is also shown by actuality, for here again we meet irony. But as this standpoint is an intensified subjective consciousness, it follows that it must become clearly and distinctly conscious of irony, that it affirm irony as its standpoint.[4] This occurred in Friedrich Schlegel who asserted it in relation to actuality, in Tieck who asserted it in poetry, and in Solger who became æsthetically and philosophically conscious of irony. Finally, irony here met its master in Hegel. Whereas the first form of irony was not combated but pacified in that subjectivity received its due, the second form of irony was both combated and destroyed, for since it was unjustified it could only receive its due by being abrogated.[5]

While these considerations sufficiently orient us with reference to the history of this concept, this is not to say that a conception of this concept, insofar as it seeks confirmation and support in the foregoing, does not involve difficulties. To the extent that one seeks a complete and coherent discussion of this concept, one will soon convince himself that it has a problematic history, or to be more precise, no history at all. In the period after Fichte where it was particularly important, one finds it mentioned again and again, suggested again and again, presupposed again and again. But if one searches for a lucid discussion one searches in vain. Solger complains that A. W. Schlegel in his *Vorlesungen über dramatische Kunst und Literatur*,[6] where one would certainly expect to find an adequate exposition of it, mentions it only briefly in a single passage.* Hegel† complains that the same is true of Solger, and finds it no better with Tieck. And now since all complain, why should not I also complain? I shall complain that the opposite is the case with Hegel. At the point in his system where one would expect to find an explanation of irony, we find it merely talked about instead. And in spite of the fact that if one were to copy out everything said of irony, he would have to admit it is not inconsiderable,[7] still, in another sense it is not very much for he says about the same thing on every occasion. To this must be added that he directs his attack against the several, frequently different notions which have been associated with this word, with the result that since the terminology is not

* *Solgers nachgelassene Schriften und Briefwechsel*, ed. by Ludwig Tieck and Friedrich Raumer, vol. II, p. 514 (from a review of A. W. Schlegel's lectures): 'It was most strange for the reviewer to find irony (which I regard as the true basis of all dramatic art and not to be excluded even from the philosophical dialogue if this is to be properly dramatic) mentioned only once in the entire work (pt. II, sec. 2, p. 72), and all intermingling of irony in the properly tragic forbidden. And yet the reviewer can recall previous statements of this author which at least appear to approximate this idea. But irony is the exact opposite of that view of life which, as the author supposes, is rooted in seriousness and jest.'

† Hegel, xx, 188 (in a review of *Solgers nachgelassene Schriften*): 'The same occurred to Solger. In the speculative exposition of the highest Idea which is presented in the above-mentioned work with the most intense earnestness, he does not even mention irony, which is supposed to be intimately united to enthusiasm and in whose depth art, religion, and philosophy are identical. Here, if anywhere, one would have expected to find the exclusive secret, the great unknown—irony—set forth in its philosophic significance with clarity.' See the same place for Hegel's comments concerning Tieck.

constant his polemic is not always perfectly clear. It is not the case, however, that I may justifiably complain about Hegel in the same way that he complains about his predecessors. In particular, there are excellent observations in Hegel's review of Solger's posthumous writings to be found in volume twenty of his collected works. Although the presentation and portrayal of negative standpoints is not so exhaustive and rich in content as one might wish (for in the portrayal of these one must apply the following: *loquere, ut videam te*[8]), still, Hegel understands so much the better how to manage them, and to this extent one will find in the positivity he asserts an indirect contribution to their portrayal. Whereas the Schlegels and Tieck had their greatest significance through the polemic by which they destroyed a previous development, and whereas for this very reason their standpoint became rather diffuse, for it was not a major battle they won but a multitude of encounters, so Hegel, on the other hand, has absolute significance through his positive total view whereby he conquers that polemical prudishness, which, like the virginity of Queen Brunhilde,[9] required a more than average man, a Siegfried, in order to be subdued. There is also frequent mention of irony in the writings of Jean Paul, and various things are to be found in his *Aesthetik*[10] but without philosophic or genuine æsthetic competence. He talks altogether like an æsthete, more from a rich æsthetic experience than actually substantiating his æsthetic standpoint. For him irony, humour, and caprice are like different languages, and his exposition is limited to expressing the same thought ironically, humorously, and in the language of caprice—something like the way Franz Baader[11] first gives an exposition of certain mystical theses, and then proceeds to translate them into the language of mysticism.[12]

But as the concept of irony has so often acquired a different meaning, it is essential that one does not come to use it consciously or unconsciously in a wholly arbitrary fashion. To the extent that one subscribes to the ordinary use of language, therefore, it is essential for one to see that the various meanings it has acquired in the course of time can all be accommodated here.

For orientation

There was a time not so long ago when a man could make his fortune here with a morsel of irony,[1] one which compensated for all defects in other respects and helped a man to make his way honourably through the world, which gave one the appearance of being cultivated and having had a look at life and some understanding of the world, which signified to the initiated that one was a member of a widespread intellectual Freemasonry. One still encounters an occasional representative of this bygone age who has preserved that delicate and meaningful smile ambiguously revealing so much, that intellectual air of nobility with which he was so successful in his youth and upon which he built his future in the belief that he had overcome the world.[2] But alas, this was a disappointment! His searching eye looks in vain for a kindred spirit, and were not his golden age still a fresh memory for some, the play of his countenance would remain a mysterious hieroglyph for his contemporaries, among whom he lives as a stranger and alien.[3] Our age demands something more: it demands, if not lofty[4] then at least loud-voiced pathos, if not speculation then surely results, if not truth then conviction, if not honesty then certainly affidavits to that effect, if not emotion then incessant talk about it. It therefore mints quite a different species of privileged faces. It will not tolerate the mouth to be closed defiantly nor the upper lip to quiver prankishly. No, it demands that the mouth drop open, for how else is one to visualize a true and genuine patriot except he be making speeches, how else should one visualize the dogmatic face of a profound thinker except with a mouth able to swallow the whole world, how else could one imagine a virtuoso on the cornucopia of the living word except with a mouth wide open? It will not tolerate a man to stand still and become immersed in himself, to walk slowly is already suspect, and how could one even think of such a thing in the animated moment in which we live, this fateful hour which everyone agrees is pregnant with the extraordinary?[5] It despises isolation, and how could it possibly tolerate a human being getting the preposterous idea of going through life alone, an age which, hand in hand and arm in arm (like itinerant journeymen and mercenaries), lives for the Idea of community?*

While irony is far from being especially familiar to our age, it does not follow that it has completely vanished. Neither is our age an age of doubt, yet there are still many expressions of doubt remaining from which one can study doubt, as it were, although there remains a qualitative difference between a speculative doubt and a vulgar doubt about this or that.[6] In oratorical discourse there frequently occurs a figure of speech which bears the name of irony and whose characteristic is this: to say the opposite of what is meant. With this we already have a determination present in all forms of irony, namely, the phenomenon is not the essence but the opposite of the essence. When I speak the thought or meaning is the essence, the word the phenomenon. These two moments are absolutely necessary, and it is in this sense that Plato has remarked that all thinking is a dialogue.[7] Now truth demands identity, for if I have the thought without the word, I do not have the thought; and if I have the word without the thought, I do not have the word, since it may not be said that infants and the demented speak. When next I consider the speaking subject, I again have a determination present in all forms of irony, namely, the subject is negatively free. If I am conscious when I speak that what I say is my meaning, and that what is said is an adequate expression for my meaning, and I assume that the person with whom I am speaking comprehends perfectly the meaning in what is said, then I am bound by what is said, that is, I am here positively free. Here applies the ancient line: *semel emissum volat irrevocabile verbum.*[8] Furthermore, I am bound in relation to myself and cannot detach myself

* This is not intended to disparage or belittle the serious pursuits of the age, yet it is certainly to be wished that the age were more serious about its seriousness.

whenever I choose. If, on the other hand, what is said is not my meaning, or the opposite of my meaning, then I am free both in relation to others and in relation to myself.

The ironic figure of speech cancels itself, however, for the speaker presupposes his listeners understand him, hence through a negation of the immediate phenomenon the essence remains identical with the phenomenon. When it sometimes happens that such an ironic figure of speech is misunderstood, this is not the fault of the speaker, except insofar as he has taken up with such an underhanded patron as irony which is as fond of playing pranks on its friends as its enemies. We say of such an ironic turn of speech: it is not serious about its seriousness. The expression may be serious enough to strike terror, yet the knowing listener is initiated into the secret concealed behind it, and precisely through this the irony is again cancelled. The most common form of irony is when one says something seriously which is not seriously intended. The other form of irony is when one says something facetiously, as a jest, which is intended seriously, although this occurs more seldom.* As previously remarked, however, the ironic figure of speech cancels itself. It is like a riddle and its solution possessed simultaneously. The ironic figure of speech also contains an attribute characteristic of all forms of irony, namely, a certain exclusiveness[9] deriving from the fact that although it is understood, it is not directly[10] understood. Hence this figure of speech looks down, as it were, on plain and ordinary discourse immediately understood by everyone; it travels in an exclusive incognito, as it were, and looks down from its exalted station with compassion on ordinary pedestrian speech. In everyday affairs this ironic figure of speech occurs chiefly in the higher circles as a prerogative belonging to the same category as that *bon ton*[11] requiring one to smile at innocence and regard virtue as a kind of prudishness, although one still believes in it to a certain extent.

* This most often occurs in connection with a certain despair, and is therefore usually found in humorists; for example, when Heine in the most facetious tone deliberates upon which is worse: a toothache or a bad conscience, and decides in favour of the first.[12]

Insofar as the higher circles (naturally this must be understood according to an intellectual protocol) speak ironically—just as kings and rulers speak French so as not to be understood by commoners—to this extent irony is in the process of isolating itself, for it does not generally wish to be understood.[13] Here the irony does not cancel itself. It is, furthermore, merely an inferior form of the ironic conceit[14] which desires witnesses in order to convince and reassure itself, for it is merely an inconsistency which irony has in common with every negative standpoint that while according to its concept it is isolation, it nevertheless seeks to constitute a society, and, when it cannot elevate itself to the Idea of community, seeks to realize itself in conventicles. But there is as little social unity in a coterie of ironists as there is truly honesty among a band of thieves. If we now disregard that aspect of irony which it opens to the conspirators and consider it in relation to the uninitiated, in relation to those against whom its polemic is directed,[15] in relation to the existence [*Tilværelse*] it conceives ironically, then it usually expresses itself in two ways. Either the ironist identifies himself with the nuisance he wishes to attack, or he enters into a relation of opposition[16] to it, but in such a way, of course, that he is always conscious that his appearance is the opposite of what he himself subscribes to, and that he experiences a satisfaction in this disparity.

In relation to a foolishly inflated wisdom which knows about everything it is ironically correct to go along with it, to be transported by all this knowledge, to goad it on with jubilant applause into rising ever higher and higher in an always greater and greater lunacy, although through all this the ironist is himself aware that the whole thing is empty and void of content. In relation to an insipid and inane enthusiasm it is ironically correct to outbid this with ever more and more elated exultation and praise, although the ironist is himself aware that this enthusiasm is the greatest foolishness in the world. Now the more the ironist succeeds in deceiving and the better his falsification progresses, so much the greater is his satisfaction. But he experiences this satisfaction in solitude, and his concern is precisely that no one notices his deception.

—This is a form of irony which occurs more seldom, though it is equally profound and easier to effect than the irony appearing in the form of an opposition. In particular, one sometimes sees it employed against a man who is on his way toward suffering from some fixed idea, against a man who deludes himself into thinking he is handsome or has especially handsome side-whiskers, or imagines he is witty or that he once said something so funny that it cannot be repeated often enough, or against a man whose whole life is contained in a single event, as it were, which he constantly reverts to and which anyone can induce him to relate at any moment if one but knows the right spring to press, etc. In all these instances it is the ironist's pleasure to seem ensnared by the same prejudice imprisoning the other person.[17] It is one of the ironist's chief satisfactions to discover such weaknesses everywhere, and the more distinguished the person in whom they are found, so much the more does it please the ironist to make a fool of him unawares. Hence even a distinguished individual becomes for the ironist at times like a puppet, a marionette, to which he has attached strings and which he can cause to perform whatever movements he wishes according to the way he manipulates the strings. And curiously enough, it is the weaker aspects in man that come much closer to being Chladni figures[18] and which constantly become visible when one bows correctly, rather than his better aspects; for the former seem to bear in themselves a natural necessity, whereas one so often has cause to lament the fact that the better aspects are subject to inconsistencies.

It is equally characteristic of irony, however, to make its appearance through a relation of opposition. In relation to a superabundance of wisdom, to be so ignorant, so stupid, to be as much of a bumpkin[19] as possible, yet always so amiable and eager to learn that the landlords of wisdom take pleasure in letting one poach on their well-stocked preserves. In relation to a sentimental and inane enthusiasm, to be too dense to grasp the sublime which inspires others, yet all the while to evince the good will which so earnestly desires to grasp and comprehend what has heretofore remained a mystery—these, I say, are perfectly normal expressions of irony. And the more guile-less the stupidity of the ironist seems, and the more honest and unfeigned his efforts appear, so much the greater is his joy. It will be seen from this that it is as ironic to appear wise though one is ignorant as to appear ignorant though one is wise. —Irony may exhibit itself through a relation of opposition in a still more indirect fashion when it chooses the simplest and most limited human beings, not in order to mock them, but in order to mock the wise.[20]

In all these instances irony exhibits itself most nearly as conceiving the world, as attempting to mystify the surround-ing world not so much in order to conceal itself as to induce others to reveal themselves. But irony may also manifest itself when the ironist seeks to lead the outside world astray respecting himself. In our time when the social situation makes a secret love affair almost impossible, when the city or commune most often has already had the banns of the happy couple read several times from the pulpit before the parson has done it once; in our time when society would consider itself robbed of one of its dearest prerogatives did it not have the power to fasten the knot of love, and, at its own invitation (not the parson's)[21] to have much to say about it, so that a love affair only acquires its validity by being publicly discussed, while an understanding entered into without the knowledge of the community is almost regarded as invalid, or at least as a shameful invasion of its prerogatives—just as a sexton regards suicide as a disgraceful stratagem designed to sneak oneself out of the world—in our time, I say, it may occasionally seem necessary for a person to play false if he does not wish the city to take upon itself the honourable task of proposing for him, so that he need only present himself with the customary facial expression of one about to propose in the manner of Peder Erik Madsen[22] with white gloves and a written sketch of his future prospects in his hand, together with other magical charms (not to mention a trustworthy *aide-memoire*) to be used in the final assault. If there be still other external circum-stances that make a certain secrecy necessary, such mystifica-tion becomes increasingly pure and simple dissemblance. But the more the individual conceives these mystifications as episodes in his own love affair, and the more abandoned his joy at having directed everyone's attention to a wholly different object, so much the more does irony manifest itself. The ironist enjoys the whole infinity of love, and the amplification which others seek by having confidants, this he induces by having trusted intimates who yet know nothing.[23] Similar mystifications are sometimes also necessary in literature when one is everywhere surrounded by a multitude of vigilant literati who discover authors about the same way that Poly Panderer[24] arranges matches. Indeed, the less it is an external reason determining one to play hide and seek (family considerations, concern for promotion, timidity, etc.), and the more it is a certain inward infinity which seeks to emancipate one's work from every finite relation to oneself, desires to be absolved from all the condolences of fellow sufferers and all the congratulations of that endearing brotherhood of authors—so much the more does irony manifest itself. And should it progress so far that it is possible to induce some crowing rooster, who would so dearly love to lay an egg, to allow the paternity to be imputed to him, half averting and half reinforcing people in their delusion, then the ironist has won the day.[25] If one wishes on occasion to divest himself of the habit which everyone must dutifully put on and wear according to his social position —and in our time one might very easily be tempted, if now and then one wishes to know he is at least better off than a convicted criminal and dares to show himself attired in other than the clothes of the work-house—then here too a certain mystification will be necessary. But the more it is a finite consideration that determines one to engage in such mystifications, as when a merchant travels incognito in order to expedite the successful outcome of an investment, a king in order to surprise his custom house functionaries, a police inspector to come for once as a thief—in the night,[26] a person in the most subordinate position in the state with fear for high-ranking superiors, etc., then the more it approximates plain and simple dissemblance. On the other hand, the more it is the need once in a while to be a human being and not always and forever chancellor, and the more poetic infinity inherent in it together with the more artfully the mystification is accomplished, then so much the more does irony manifest itself. And should he wholly succeed in leading people astray, perhaps to be arrested as a suspicious character or involved in interesting domestic situations, then the ironist has attained his wish.

But the outstanding feature of irony in these and similar instances is the subjective freedom which at every moment has within its power the possibility of a beginning and is not generated from previous conditions.[27] There is something seductive about every beginning because the subject is still free, and this is the satisfaction the ironist longs for. At such moments actuality loses its validity for him; he is free and above it. This is something which the Roman Catholic Church understood in certain points, and on various occasions during the Middle Ages it used to elevate itself above its absolute reality and conceive itself ironically, e.g., in The Feast of the Ass,[28] The Feast of Fools,[29] Easter Humour,[30] etc. A similar sentiment was the basis for allowing Roman soldiers the liberty of reciting satirical verses over the triumphator. Here one was conscious both of the majesty of life and the reality of glory, yet at the same time ironically above it. Similarly, there was much irony concealed in the life of the gods of Greece without ever needing the railleries of a Lucian, for not even the heavenly actuality of the gods was spared the piercing blasts of irony. As certain as it is that there is much existence [*Tilværelse*] which is not actuality, and that there is something in personality which is at least momentarily incommensurable with actuality, so also it is certain that there resides a truth in irony.[31] Add to this that thus far we have merely conceived irony as a momentary expression, so that in all these instances we may still not speak of pure irony, or irony as a standpoint. On the other hand, the more the consideration of the relation between actuality and subject, as occasionally asserted here, draws into its orbit, the more we approach the point where irony exhibits itself in its usurped totality.[32]

A diplomat's conception of the world is in many respects ironical, and the famous statement of Talleyrand that man was given speech not in order to reveal his thoughts but to conceal them[33] expresses a deep irony against the world, and from the perspective of statecraft corresponds perfectly to another authentic diplomatic thesis: *mundus vult decipi, decipiatur ergo*.[34] But it does not at all follow that the diplomatic world regards existence ironically; on the contrary, there are many things it would seriously maintain. —The difference between all the expressions of irony suggested here is therefore merely a quantitative one, a more or a less. On the other hand, irony in the eminent sense differs qualitatively[35] from the kind of irony described here, just as a speculative doubt differs qualitatively from a vulgar and empirical doubt. Irony in the eminent sense directs itself not against this or that particular existence [*Tilværende*] but against the whole given actuality of a certain time and situation. It has, therefore, an apriority in itself, and it is not by successively destroying one segment of actuality after the other that it arrives at its total view, but by virtue of this[36] that it destroys in the particular. It is not this or that phenomenon but the totality of existence [*Tilværelse*] which it considers *sub specie ironiæ*.[37] To this extent one sees the propriety of the Hegelian characterization of irony as infinite absolute negativity.[38]

Before we proceed to a closer discussion of this, however, it seems appropriate to orient ourselves in the conceptual landscape wherein irony has its abode. In this regard one must distinguish between what we shall call an executive irony* and a contemplative irony.

* Belonging to executive irony, or dramatic irony as it might be called, is also the irony of nature, since this is not conscious in nature except for one who has an eye for it, for whom it is then as if nature were like a person playing tricks on him, or confiding to him its pain and sorrow. This disparity is not present in nature for one who is too natural and too naïve, but only exhibits itself for one who is himself ironically developed. Schubert (*Symbolik des Traumes*, Bamberg, 1821) has a judicious selection of a multitude of such ironic features in nature. He remarks that nature has with deep mockery . . . 'strangely conjoined mirth with lament, joy with sorrow, like the voice of nature in the music of the wind on Ceylon, which sings frightfully merry minuets in tones of a deep, wailing, heart-rending voice' (p. 38). He calls attention to the fact that nature has ironically juxta-

We shall begin[39] with what I have ventured to call executive irony. Insofar as irony asserts a relation of opposition in all its various nuances, it might seem that irony were identical with dissembling,* and for the sake of brevity one usually translates the word 'irony' as dissemblance.[40] But whereas dissemblance describes more the objective act by which the disparity between essence and phenomenon is effected, irony is also descriptive of a subjective satisfaction, for it is by means of irony that the subject emancipates himself from the constraint

---

posed the most remote extremes (p. 41): 'Following immediately after the rational and moderate human being—in the free association of ideas of natural species—comes the absurd ape, after the intelligent and immaculate elephant the unclean swine, after the horse the ass, after the repulsive camel the slender deer, and after the bat, which, being dissatisfied with the usual lot of the mammal, imitates the bird, comes the mouse, which, being dissatisfied in the opposite sense, scarcely ventures forth from the deep.' Now all such features are not in nature, but the ironic subject perceives them in nature. Similarly, one may also regard every deception of the senses as an irony of nature. But to become conscious of this requires a consciousness which is itself ironical. Indeed, the more polemically developed an individual is, the more irony he will find in nature. Such a view of nature belongs, therefore, more to the romantic than the classical development. Allow me to illustrate this point by means of an example. In happy Hellas nature was seldom witness to anything but the gentle and mild harmonies of an evenly tempered soul, for even the Greek sorrow was beautiful, hence echo was a friendly nymph. In Nordic mythology, however, where nature resounded with wild shrieks, where the night was not luminous and clear but dark and overcast, full of dread and terror, where grief was not assuaged by quiet recollection but by a deep sigh and an eternal forgetting, there echo became a troll. Thus in Nordic mythology echo is called *Dvergmaal* or *Bergmaal*.[41] Cf. Grimm: *Irische Elfenmärchen*, p. LXXVIII. *Færoiske Quæder*, Randers, 1822, p. 464. This irony in nature has here been accorded a place in a footnote because it is essentially only apparent for an individual oriented in humour, since it is essentially only through a consideration of sin in the world that the ironic conception of nature makes its appearance.[42]

* Irony is conceived in this way by Theophrastus, cf. *Theophrasti Characteres*, ed. by Ast, p. 4, ch. 1: περὶ εἰρωνείας. Here irony is defined as follows: προσποίησις ἐπὶ χεῖρον πράξεων καὶ λόγων (*simulatio dissimulatioque fallax et fraudulenta*).[43]

imposed upon him by the continuity of life, whence it may be said of the ironist that he 'cuts loose.' To this must be added that dissemblance, insofar as one wishes to relate it to the subject, has a purpose, an external purpose foreign to dissemblance itself. Irony, on the other hand, has no purpose, its purpose is immanent in itself, a metaphysical purpose. The purpose is none other than irony itself. When an ironist exhibits himself as other than he actually is, it might seem that his purpose were to induce others to believe this. His actual purpose, however, is merely to feel free, and this he is through irony. Irony has, therefore, no external purpose but is self-purposive. It follows that irony is quite different from Jesuitism,[44] for in Jesuitism the subject is free regarding the choice of means with which to accomplish his purpose, but not at all free in the ironic sense where the subject has no purpose.

Insofar as it is essential for irony to have an external which is the opposite of the internal, it might seem that irony were identical with hypocrisy.[45] In Danish one occasionally finds irony translated as *Skalkagtighed* [mischievousness], and a hypocrite is usually called an *Øienskalk* [fraud]. But hypocrisy properly belongs to the moral sphere, for the hypocrite constantly strives to seem good though he is evil. Irony, on the other hand, belongs to the metaphysical sphere, for the concern of the ironist is merely to seem other than he actually is. As he therefore conceals his jest in seriousness and his seriousness in jest (like the music of the wind on Ceylon), so it may also occur to him to seem evil though he is good. It must be borne in mind, however, that moral determinations are essentially too concrete for irony.

But irony has a theoretical or contemplative aspect. Were we to consider irony an inferior moment, we might allow it to be a sharp eye for what is crooked, wry, distorted, for what is erroneous, the vain in existence [*Tilværelse*]. In conceiving this it might seem that irony were identical with ridicule, satire, persiflage, etc. Naturally, it has an affinity with this insofar as it, too, perceives what is vain, but it differs in setting forth its observation. It does not destroy vanity, it is not what punitive justice is in relation to vice, nor does it have the power of reconciliation within itself as does the comic. On the contrary, it reinforces vanity in its vanity and renders madness more mad. This is what might be called irony's attempt to mediate the discrete moments, not in a higher unity but in a higher madness.[46]

If we consider irony as it directs itself against the whole of existence [*Tilværelse*], it here again sustains the opposition between essence and phenomenon, between the internal and the external. It might seem that as absolute negativity it were identical with doubt.[47] It must be borne in mind, however, that doubt is a conceptual determination while irony is the being-for-itself of subjectivity. Again, it must be remembered that irony is essentially practical, that it is only theoretical in order to become practical again, in other words, it is not concerned with the irony of the situation but only with that of itself. Hence when irony gets wind of the fact that there must be something concealed behind the phenomenon other than what is contained in the phenomenon, this is merely what irony has always been so keen about telling everybody, namely, that the subject feels free, and so the phenomenon never acquires any reality for the subject. The movement is the direct opposite. With doubt the subject constantly seeks to penetrate the object, and his misfortune consists in the fact that the object constantly eludes him. With irony, on the other hand, the subject is always seeking to get outside the object, and this he attains by becoming conscious at every moment that the object has no reality. With doubt the subject is witness to a war of conquest in which every phenomenon is destroyed, because the essence always resides behind the phenomenon. But with irony the subject constantly retires from the field and proceeds to talk every phenomenon out of its reality in order to save himself, that is, in order to preserve himself in his negative independence of everything.

Finally, insofar as irony becomes conscious of the fact that existence [*Tilværelse*] has no reality, thereby expressing the same thesis as the pious disposition, it might seem that irony were a species of religious devotion.[48] In religious devotion, if I may be permitted to put it this way, the lesser actuality, that is to say, the relationship to the world, also loses its validity; but this only occurs insofar as the relationship to God at the same moment asserts its absolute reality. The devout mind also affirms that all is vanity, but this is only insofar as this negation thrusts aside all interference and allows the eternally existent [*Bestaaende*] to become manifest. Add to this that when the devout mind perceives all is vanity, it makes no exception regarding its own person, makes no fuss [*Ophævelser*][49] respecting itself; on the contrary, this, too, must be thrust aside so the divine will not be impeded by its resistance, but pour itself out in the mind made receptive by religious devotion. Indeed, we see from the more penetrating writings for edification that the pious mind regards its own finite personality as the most wretched of all. With irony, on the other hand, when everything else becomes vain, subjectivity becomes free. And the more vain everything becomes, so much the lighter, more vacuous, more evanescent becomes subjectivity. Whereas everything else becomes vain, the ironic subject does not himself become vain but saves his own vanity. For irony everything becomes nothingness, but nothingness may be taken in several ways. The speculative nothingness is that which at every moment is vanishing for concretion, since it is itself the demand for the concrete, its *nisus formativus*.[50] The mystical nothingness is a nothingness for representation, a nothingness which yet is as full of content as the silence of the night is eloquent for one who has ears to hear.[51] Finally, the ironic nothingness is that deathly stillness in which irony returns to 'haunt and jest' [*spøger*][52] (this last word taken wholly ambiguously).

The world historical validity of irony.
The irony of Socrates

If we return to the general designation of irony given above as infinite absolute negativity, this will sufficiently indicate that irony no longer directs itself against this or that particular phenomenon, against a particular thing [*Tilværende*], but that the whole of existence [*Tilværelse*] has become alien to the ironic subject, that he in turn has become estranged from existence [*Tilværelse*], and that because actuality has lost its validity for him, so he, too, is to a certain extent no longer actual. The word 'actuality' must primarily be taken to mean historical actuality, that is to say, the actuality given at a certain time and under certain conditions. This word may be taken not only in a metaphysical sense, as when one treats the metaphysical problem of the relation of the Idea to actuality, where there can be no question of this or that actuality but only of the Idea's concretion, i.e. its actuality; but the word 'actuality' may also be used with respect to the historically actualized Idea. This last-named actuality is different at various times. By this we do not mean that historical actuality in the sum total of its existence does not have an eternal coherence in itself, but only that for peoples separated by time and space the given actuality is different. Although the world spirit throughout every development is constantly in itself, this is not the case with the people of a certain age nor with the given individuals of that age. For these a given actuality presents itself which it is not in their power to reject, for the world process leads those who go willingly but drags those who do not.[1] But insofar as the Idea is concrete in itself, it is necessary for it constantly to become [*blive*] what it is—to become concrete. This, however, it can only become through peoples and individuals.

With this there appears a contradiction through which the development of the world occurs.[2] The given actuality of a certain age is valid for a people and the individuals constituting that people. To the extent that one does not wish to say that this development is past, however, this actuality must be displaced by another actuality, and this must take place through this people and these individuals. For the people contemporaneous with the Reformation Catholicism was the given actuality, and yet it was an actuality which no longer had validity as such. Hence one actuality here collided with another, and herein lies the deeply tragic aspect of world history. An individual may be world historically justified and at the same time without authority. Insofar as he is the latter he must become a sacrifice, while insofar as he is the former he must triumph, that is to say, he triumphs by becoming a sacrifice. Here it is apparent how self-consistent is the development of the world, for as the truer actuality comes forth, it respects even the past. It is not a revolution but an evolution. The past shows it is still justified by demanding a sacrifice, the new by providing a sacrifice. But a sacrifice there must be because a new moment shall actually come forth, and because the new actuality is not a mere conclusion to the past but contains something more, not merely a corrective to the past but also a new beginning.

With every such turning point in history there are two movements to be observed. On the one hand, the new shall come forth; on the other, the old must be displaced. Insofar as the new shall come forth, we here meet the prophetic individual envisaging the new in the distance, in dark and indefinite shapes. The prophetic individual does not possess the future, he merely intimates it. He cannot assert it, yet he is lost to the actuality to which he belongs. His relation to this is a peaceful one, however, for the given actuality is not aware of any opposition. Next comes the authentic tragic hero. He fights for the new and endeavours to destroy what for him is a vanishing actuality; yet his calling is not so much to destroy as to assert the new, and thereby to destroy the past indirectly. Still, the old must be displaced and seen in all its imperfection, and here we meet the ironic subject.[3] For the ironic subject the given actuality has completely lost its validity; it has become for him an imperfect form which everywhere constrains. He does not possess the new, however, he only knows the present does not correspond to the Idea. He it is who has come to render judgment. The ironist is in one sense prophetic, to be sure, for he constantly points to something future; but what it is he knows not. While he is prophetic in this sense, his position and situation are nevertheless the opposite of the prophetic. The prophet goes hand in hand with his age, and from this standpoint envisages that which shall come; and if he is lost to his age, as remarked above, he is only this because he has become absorbed in his visions. The ironist, on the other hand, has advanced beyond the reach of his age and opened a front against it. That which shall come is hidden from him, concealed behind his back, but the actuality he hostilely opposes is the one he shall destroy. Towards this he directs his consuming gaze, and concerning his relation to his age one may apply the words: 'Behold, the feet of them who shall carry thee away.'[4] The ironist is also a sacrifice required by the world process, not strictly speaking as if he needed to fall as a sacrifice, but zeal in the service of the world spirit consumes him.[5]

Thus we here have irony as infinite absolute negativity. It is negativity because it only negates; it is infinite because it negates not this or that phenomenon; and it is absolute because it negates by virtue of a higher which is not. Irony establishes nothing, for that which is to be established lies behind it. It is a divine madness which rages like a Tamerlane and leaves not one stone standing upon another in its wake. Here, then, we have irony. To a certain extent every world historical turning point must also exhibit this formation, and it would certainly not be without historical interest to trace such a formation throughout world history. Without attempting this, however, I shall merely cite Cardanus, Campanella, and Bruno[6] as examples from the age nearest the Reformation. Erasmus of Rotterdam to a certain extent was also irony. The significance of this formation, I believe, has heretofore not been sufficiently recognized; and this is so much the more curious since Hegel has treated the negative with such decided partiality. But corresponding to the negative in the system is irony in historical actuality; moreover, the negative exists [er til] in historical actuality, which it never does [er] in the system.[7]

Irony is a determination of subjectivity. With irony the subject is negatively free. The actuality which shall give him content is not, hence he is free from the restraint in which the given actuality binds him, yet negatively free and as such hovering, because there nothing is which binds him. It is this very freedom, this hovering, which gives the ironist a certain enthusiasm, for he becomes intoxicated as it were by the infinity of possibles; and should he require consolation for all that has passed away, then let him take refuge in the enormous reserves of the possible. But he does not surrender himself to this enthusiasm; on the contrary, it merely inspires and nourishes the enthusiasm for destruction already within him. —As the ironist does not have the new within his power, it might be asked how he destroys the old, and to this it must be answered: he destroys the given actuality by the given actuality itself. Still, it must not be forgotten that the new principle is present in him κατὰ δύναμιν, as possibility.* In destroying actuality through itself, however, he places himself in the service of the irony of the world. Hegel remarks in his *Geschichte der Philosophie* (xviii, 62): 'All dialectic accepts as valid what shall become valid as if it were valid, and allows the internal destruction to develop within it. Such is the universal irony of the world'.[8] Here the irony of the world is quite correctly conceived. Inasmuch as each particular historical actuality is but a moment in the actualization of the Idea, it bears within itself the seeds of its own dissolution. This is seen quite clearly in Judaism, whose significance as a moment of transition is particularly striking. Accordingly, it was

---

* The negative is like water in relation to whatever is reflected in it: it has the property of making whatever it gives birth to appear as high above itself as it makes whatever it opposes appear far beneath itself. The negative, however, is no more aware of this than is the water.[9]

already a deep irony against the world when the Law,[10] after having proclaimed the commandments, added the promise: if you obey these, you shall be happy, for it soon became apparent that mankind was unable to fulfil the Law, hence a happiness attaching itself to this condition became rather more than hypothetical.[11] But the fact that Judaism was destroyed through itself is also apparent from its historical relation to Christianity. If, without going further into an investigation of the significance of the advent of Christ, we seek merely to maintain this as a turning point in world history, then here, too, one cannot miss the ironic formation. This is provided by John the Baptist. He was not the one who should come,[12] did not have a knowledge of what should come, and yet he destroyed Judaism. He destroyed it not with the new but through itself. He demanded of Judaism what Judaism professed to give— righteousness. But this it was unable to provide and hence it perished. He allowed Judaism to endure [*bestaae*], and at the same time developed the seeds of its own dissolution inherent within it. In the case of John the Baptist, however, his personality undergoes a total eclipse, and in him is seen the irony of the world in its objective configuration, as it were, so that he becomes merely an instrument in its hand. But for the ironic formation to be perfectly developed, it is essential for the subject to become conscious of his irony, to feel negatively free when he condemns the given actuality and to enjoy this negative freedom. In order for this to occur, however, subjectivity must be developed; or rather, when subjectivity asserts itself, irony appears. Subjectivity feels itself confronted by the given actuality, feels its own power, its own validity and significance. But in feeling this it saves itself as it were from the relativity in which the given actuality seeks to hold it. To the extent that this irony is world historically justified, the emancipation of subjectivity takes place in the service of the Idea, even though the ironic subject is not clearly conscious of this. This is the genial quality of an irony that is warranted. As for an unwarranted irony, on the other hand, it may be said that whosoever shall save his life shall lose it.[13] But whether irony is warranted or not can only be adjudicated by history.

Because the subject regards actuality ironically, it does not follow that in asserting such a conception of actuality he also proceeds ironically. In recent times there has been considerable discussion of irony and the ironic conception of actuality, but only occasionally has this conception fashioned itself ironically.[14] The more this occurs, however, so much the more certain and inevitable is the destruction of actuality, so much the greater is the preponderance of the ironic subject over the actuality he wishes to destroy, and so much the greater is his freedom. In the utmost stillness he performs the same operation as the irony of the world. He allows the existent [*Bestaaende*] to exist [*bestaae*] though it has no validity for him, yet he pretends that it has [15] and under this guise leads it on towards its certain dissolution. Insofar as the ironic subject is world historically justified, there is in this a unity of what is genial with artistic sobriety and discretion.[16]

But if irony is a determination of subjectivity, it must exhibit itself the first time subjectivity appears in world history. Irony is itself the first and most abstract determination of subjectivity.[17] This points to the historical turning point at which subjectivity appeared for the first time, and with this we have arrived at Socrates.

It has been sufficiently shown in the preceding part of this essay how the irony of Socrates was constituted. The whole given actuality had lost its validity for him, and he had become estranged from the actuality of substantiality.[18] This is the one aspect of irony; the other is that he employed irony even in destroying Hellenism. His behaviour towards it was always ironical; he was ignorant and knew nothing, constantly seeking enlightenment from others. But in thus allowing the established [*Bestaaende*] to endure [*bestaae*], it therefore perished. This tactic he maintained to the last, a fact which was especially apparent when he stood accused. But his zeal in its service consumed him, and at last he, too, was seized with irony: everything spins round him, he becomes giddy, and all things lose their reality. This view of Socrates and the significance of his standpoint in world history seems to me to culminate so naturally in itself that it will, I hope, find acceptance with one or another of my readers. Inasmuch as Hegel[19] declares himself opposed to conceiving the standpoint of Socrates as irony, it becomes necessary to take account of the objections found here and there in his writings.

Before proceeding with this, however, I shall first attempt to illuminate as best I can a weakness from which Hegel's entire conception of the concept of irony seems to suffer. Hegel always discusses irony in a most contemptuous fashion, indeed irony is an abomination in his sight. Now concurrent with the appearance of Hegel occurred Schlegel's most brilliant period. As the irony of the Schlegels had condemned an ever increasing sentimentality in æsthetics, so Hegel was the one to correct what was deceptive in irony. It is one of Hegel's great merits that he halted, or at least tried to halt, the prodigal sons of speculation on their way to damnation. He did not always use the gentlest means, however, and when he called to them his voice was not always mild and fatherly but often harsh and pedantic. Naturally, it was the disciples of irony who caused him most consternation, and he soon abandoned all hope for their salvation and treated them like incorrigible and perverse sinners. On every occasion Hegel seizes the opportunity to talk about these ironists, and always discusses them in the most sarcastic fashion; indeed, he looks down with intense scorn and superiority on these 'superior persons,' as he often calls them. But the fact that Hegel has become infatuated with the form of irony nearest him has naturally distorted his conception of the concept.[20] And if the reader seldom gets a discussion, Schlegel, on the other hand, always gets a drubbing.[21] But this does not mean that Hegel was wrong regarding the Schlegels or that the Schlegelian irony was not an extremely serious error. Nor does this deny that Hegel has certainly brought about much benefit through the seriousness with which he opposes every isolation, a seriousness which makes it possible to read many a Hegelian discussion with much edification[22] and fortification. This does mean, on the other hand, that Hegel in one-sidedly focusing on post-Fichtian irony has overlooked the truth of irony, and as he identifies all irony with this, so he has done irony an injustice.

As soon as Hegel pronounces the word 'irony' he immediately thinks of Schlegel and Tieck, and his style instantly takes on the features of a certain indignation. But what is erroneous and illegitimate in the irony of Schlegel, together with Hegel's merit in this respect, will be discussed in their proper place. Here we must return to his mode of regarding the irony of Socrates.

We have previously pointed out that Hegel emphasized two features in his account of the Socratic method: irony and midwifery. His presentation of this material is to be found in *Geschichte der Philosophie*, xviii, 59-67.[23] The discussion of Socratic irony is very brief, however, and Hegel uses the occasion to disclaim against irony as a general principle before adding (p. 62): 'It was Friedrich Schlegel who first advanced this thought, and Ast has repeated it';[24] then follows the 'serious' words[25] Hegel usually pronounces on these occasions. Socrates pretends to be ignorant, and under the guise of being taught he teaches others. Page 60: 'This aspect is the celebrated Socratic irony. It acquires in Socrates a subjective form of dialectic, and is a manner of carrying on with people. Dialectic proper has to do with the reasons for things, but this irony is a particular mode of behaviour between one person and another.'[26] But as Hegel had previously remarked that Socrates uses the same irony 'when he wished to bring the manner of the Sophists into disrepute,'[27] we are here confronted with a difficulty; for in the one instance he wished to instruct, in the other merely to disgrace. Hegel next calls attention to the fact that this Socratic irony seems to contain something untrue, but then proceeds to show the correctness of Socrates' behaviour. Finally, he arrives at the true significance of Socratic irony, its essential greatness. This is the fact that it endeavours to make abstract ideas concrete and effect their development. He then adds (p. 62): 'When I say that I know what reason, what belief, are, these are only quite abstract representations; for them to become concrete, however, it is necessary that they be explained, and this presupposes that what they really are is unknown. The explication of such representations was effected by Socrates, and this is

the truth in the irony of Socrates.'[28] But this confuses everything. The account of the Socratic irony completely loses its
historical substance, and the passage cited is so modern that
it scarcely resembles Socrates in the least. It was not at all
the concern of Socrates to make the abstract concrete. Moreover, the examples Hegel submits are obviously rather poorly
chosen, for I do not think he will be able to adduce analogies
for this unless he takes the whole of Plato and appeals to the
fact that Socrates' name is employed continuously throughout
the dialogues, whereby he will then contradict himself and
everyone else. The Socratic concern was not to make the
abstract concrete, but through the immediately concrete to
cause the abstract to become visible. Against these Hegelian
considerations it will therefore be sufficient to bear in mind
both the twofold species of irony which we identified in Plato
(for it is obviously what we called the Platonic irony that
Hegel meant, and which on page 64 he identifies with Socrates),
and that the laws of motion exhibited throughout Socrates'
life were not oriented to begin with the abstract so as to arrive
at the concrete, but to begin with the concrete in order to
arrive at the abstract, and constantly to arrive at this. Thus
when Hegel's entire discussion of Socratic irony terminates by
becoming identical with Platonic irony, with both Socratic
and Platonic irony becoming (p. 67) 'more a manner of conversation, a social pleasantness, and not pure negation, not
the negative attitude',[29] then such remarks will already have
been answered in the foregoing. —Hegel's account of Socrates'
midwifery does not fare a great deal better. Here he mentions
the significance of the fact that Socrates asked questions, and
his discussion is both fine and true; but the distinction emphasized in the foregoing between questioning in order to obtain
an answer and questioning in order to shame and humiliate
has been ignored. Hegel's concluding example[30] of the concept of becoming [at vorde] is again thoroughly unsocratic,
unless he means to find a Socratic development in the *Parmenides*.[31] —Finally, in the Hegelian presentation of Socrates'
tragic irony,[32] one must bear in mind that this is not the irony
of Socrates but the irony of the world with Socrates. Hence it

can explain nothing with respect to the problem of Socratic irony.

In a review of the posthumous writings of Solger, Hegel again calls attention to the difference between the Schlegelian and Socratic ironies.[33] That there is a difference we have everywhere maintained, and will clarify this further in its proper place. But it does not follow from this that the standpoint of Socrates was not irony. He reproaches Friedrich Schlegel because, having no understanding of speculation and disregarding this, he has torn the Fichtian thesis concerning the constitutive validity of the ego out of its metaphysical context, torn it out of the sphere of thought and applied it directly to actuality 'with the consequent denial of the vitality of reason and truth, and with the consequent corruption of this into mere appearance in the subject as well as into mere appearance for others.'[34] He calls attention to the fact that in order to describe this corruption of truth into mere appearance, one has taken the liberty of corrupting the name of the innocent Socratic irony. When the similarity with respect to the principle has been posited in the fact that Socrates always entered into his investigations with the assurance that he knew nothing in order to humiliate and disgrace the Sophists, then the result of this behaviour is always something negative and without systematic results. To this extent the assurances of Socrates that he knew nothing were given in dead earnest, and are therefore not ironic. I shall here concern myself no further with the difficulty that arises when Hegel here shows that the Socratic teaching ended without a result, when this is compared with what was previously developed from Hegel, viz., that through his ironic teaching Socrates rendered the abstract concrete.[35] Instead, I shall inquire a little more into how far Socrates was serious about his ignorance.

It has been shown in the foregoing that when Socrates said he was ignorant, he was nevertheless in possession of knowledge, for he had a knowledge of his ignorance. This knowledge, however, was not a knowledge of something, that is, it had no positive content, and to this extent his ignorance was ironic. Finally, as Hegel has sought in vain, so it seems to me, to vindicate a positive content for Socrates, so now I think the reader will have to side with me in this matter. Had his knowledge been a knowledge of something, his ignorance would merely have been a form of conversation. Thus his irony is now complete in itself. To this extent his ignorance is both to be taken seriously and not to be taken seriously, and upon this point Socrates is to be maintained. To know that one is ignorant is the beginning of wisdom, but if one knows no more than this, it is only a beginning. It is this knowledge which holds Socrates ironically aloft. But when Hegel next calls attention to the fact that Socrates was serious about his ignorance, and from this tries to show that his ignorance was not irony, it seems that here again Hegel is not constant. The fact is that when irony is about to set forth a supreme thesis, it proceeds like every negative standpoint: it expresses something positive, and this is the seriousness of what it says. For irony nothing is an existent [*Bestaaende*], it does as it pleases *ad libitum*[36] with everything. But when it attempts to express this, it says something positive and with this its sovereignty is at an end. Hence when Schlegel or Solger affirms that actuality is mere appearance, mere illusion, mere vanity, a nothingness, they manifestly intend it seriously, yet Hegel supposes that this is irony. The difficulty here encountered is essentially that irony in a strict sense can never set forth a thesis, because irony is a determination of the being-for-himself subject, who, with perpetual agility, allows nothing to endure [*bestaae*], and because of this agility is unable to consolidate himself in the total view that he causes nothingness to exist [*bestaae*]. The consciousness of Schlegel and Solger that finitude is a nothingness is manifestly just as seriously intended as the Socratic ignorance. In the last analysis the ironist must always posit something, but what he posits in this way is nothingness. Now it is impossible to take nothingness seriously without either arriving at something (this happens when one takes it speculatively seriously), or without despairing (this happens when one takes it personally seriously). But the ironist does neither of these, and to this extent one may say he is not really serious about it. Irony is the infinitely delicate play with nothingness,

286

a playing which is not terrified by it but still pokes its head into the air.[37] But if one takes nothingness neither speculatively nor personally seriously, then one obviously takes it frivolously and to this extent not seriously. If Hegel means that Schlegel was not serious about existence [*Tilværelse*] being a nothingness without reality, then there must have been something which had validity for him, but in that case his irony would have been sheer form. It may therefore be said of irony that it is the seriousness with nothingness insofar as it is not the seriousness with something. It conceives nothingness continually in opposition to something, and in order to emancipate itself seriously [for seriousness] with something, seizes upon nothingness. But it does not become at all serious about nothingness, except insofar as it is not the seriousness with something. The same is true with Socrates' ignorance: it is the nothingness whereby he destroys every knowledge. This can best be seen from his conception of death. He is ignorant of what death is and what is after death, whether there be something or nothing at all, completely ignorant. But he does not take this ignorance any further to heart; on the contrary, he feels quite properly free in this ignorance. He is not serious about this ignorance, and yet he is dead serious about the fact that he is ignorant. —I warrant the reader will therefore agree with me in holding that nothing is advanced through these Hegelian considerations which prevents us from supposing that the standpoint of Socrates was irony.[38]

Let us summarize what has been emphasized in the first part of this essay as characteristic of the standpoint of Socrates: the whole substantial life of Hellenism had lost its validity for him, that is to say, the established [*bestaaende*] actuality had become unreal to him, not in some particular aspect but in its totality as such. In relation to this invalid actuality he allowed the established [*Bestaaende*] to feign existence [*bestaae*] and thereby brought on its destruction. Through all this he became ever lighter and lighter, always more negatively free. Hence we see from the present discussion that the standpoint of Socrates was irony as infinite absolute negativity. However, it was not actuality altogether that he negated, but the given

Irony after Fichte

It was in Kant, to recall a rather well-known fact, that modern speculation, now feeling itself full grown and of age, became tired of the tutelage in which it heretofore had lived under Dogmatism and went like the Prodigal Son to his father to demand that he divide and apportion to him his inheritance.[1] The outcome of this settlement is well known, as is also the fact that speculation did not need to go abroad in order to squander its fortune, for prosperity was nowhere to be found. Indeed, the more the ego became absorbed in scrutinizing the ego in the Critical philosophy, the more emaciated the ego became, until it ended by becoming a *Gespenst* as immortal as the husband[2] of Aurora. The ego was like the crow, which, deceived by the fox's praise of its person, lost the cheese.[3] Thought had gone astray in that reflection continually reflected upon reflection, and every step forward naturally led further and further away from all content. Here it became apparent, and it will ever be so, that when one begins to speculate it is essential to be pointed in the right direction. It failed to notice that what it sought for was in the search itself, and since it refused to look for it there, it was not in all eternity to be found. Philosophy was like a man who has his spectacles on but goes on searching for them; he searches for what is right in front of his nose, but he never looks there and so never finds them.

Now that which is external to experience, that which collided with the experiencing subject like a solid body, after which each recoiled from the force of the impact in its own direction; *das Ding an sich*, which constantly persisted in tempting the experiencing subject (as a certain school[4] in the Middle Ages believed the visible emblems in the Eucharist were present in order to tempt the believer); this externality, this *Ding an sich* was what constituted the weakness[5] in Kant's system. It even

289

became a problem whether the ego itself was not a *Ding an sich*. This problem was raised and resolved by Fichte.[6] He removed the difficulty connected with this *an sich* by placing it within thought, that is, he rendered the ego infinite as $I=I$. The producing ego is the same as the produced ego; $I=I$ is the abstract identity. With this he emancipated infinite thought. But this infinity of thought in Fichte is like every other Fichtian infinity (his ethical infinity is incessant striving for striving's own sake, his æsthetic infinity is perpetual production for production's own sake, God's infinity is continual development for development's own sake), that is, a negative infinity, an infinity without finitude, an infinity void of all content. Hence when Fichte rendered the ego infinite he asserted an Idealism in relation to which all actuality became pale, an acosmism in relation to which his Idealism became actuality, notwithstanding the fact that it was docetism. With Fichte thought was rendered infinite, and subjectivity became infinite absolute negativity, infinite tension and longing. Fichte hereby acquired a significance for knowing. His *Wissenschaftslehre*[7] rendered knowledge infinite. But that which he rendered infinite was the negative, hence in place of truth he acquired certainty, not positive but negative infinity in the infinite identity of the ego with itself. Instead of positive endeavour, i.e. happiness, he obtained negative endeavour, i.e. an *ought*. Inasmuch as Fichte had the negative his standpoint acquired an infinite enthusiasm, an infinite elasticity. Kant lacks the negative infinity, Fichte the positive. In this way Fichte receives an absolute return on his method, for knowledge here becomes a whole out of a part. But because Fichte maintained the abstract identity as $I=I$, and in his Idealistic realm would have nothing to do with actuality, he thus acquired the absolute beginning from which, as has so often been discussed, he sought to construct the world. The ego became the constitutive principle. But as the ego is merely formally hence negatively conceived, Fichte essentially got no further than the infinite, elastic *molimina*[8] towards a beginning. He has the infinite longing of the negative, its *nisus formativus*,[9] but has it as an urgency which cannot get under way, has it as a divine and absolute impatience, as an infinite power which yet accomplishes nothing because there is nothing to which it can be applied. It is a potentiality and an exaltation mighty like a god, which is able to lift the whole world but has nothing to lift. With this the starting point of philosophy is brought to consciousness, the presuppositionless with which it begins, and yet the enormous energy of this beginning brings it no further. In order for thought, subjectivity, to acquire truth and content it must allow itself to be born: it must sink down into the depths of the substantial life and allow itself to be concealed in this as the Church is concealed in Christ.[10] It must—half anxiously, half sympathetically, half shrinking backwards, half surrendering itself—allow the waves of the substantial ocean to close over itself, just as in the moment of enthusiasm the subject almost becomes absent to himself and sinks down into that which inspires, yet all the while experiencing a quiet shudder because it concerns his very life. But this requires courage, and yet it is necessary; for everyone who shall save his soul shall lose it. Nor is this the courage of desperation, for as Tauler[11] has so beautifully expressed it in a more concrete context:

> *Doch dieses Verlieren, dies Entschwinden*
> *Ist eben das echte und rechte Finden.*

It is well known that Fichte later abandoned this position, which found many admirers and few disciples, and in various writings sought in a more edifying fashion to pacify and diminish this earlier full assurance ($\pi\lambda\eta\rho o\phi o\rho i\alpha$).[12] On the other hand, it would appear from the posthumous works published by his son[13] that he also sought to become lord and master over this negative infinity by immersing himself in the very essence of consciousness. As this does not concern this investigation, however, I shall confine myself to one of the standpoints attaching itself to the earlier Fichte, namely, with the irony of Schlegel and Tieck.

In Fichte subjectivity had become free, infinite, and negative. But in order for it to emerge from this movement of emptiness, wherein it moved in infinite abstraction, it had to be negated; in order for thought to become actual it had to become concrete. With this there emerges the question of metaphysical actuality. The Fichtian principle that subjectivity, the ego, has constitutive validity, that it alone is the almighty, was seized upon by Schlegel and Tieck and with this they proceeded to operate in the world. But this involved a double predicament: first, it was to confound the empirical and finite ego with the eternal ego; and secondly, it was to confuse metaphysical actuality with historical actuality. Thus it was to apply an abortive metaphysical standpoint directly to actuality. Fichte would construct the world, but what he meant was a systematic construction; Schlegel and Tieck, on the other hand, would dispose of a world.*

Here it is evident that this irony was not in the service of the world spirit. It was not a moment of the given actuality that was to be negated and displaced by a new moment; no, all historical actuality was negated to make room for a self-created actuality. It was not subjectivity that was here to appear, for subjectivity was already given by the conditions of the world; no, it was an eccentric subjectivity, a subjectivity raised to the second power. It will be seen from this that such an irony was wholly unwarranted, and that Hegel's efforts to oppose it were quite in order.

Irony† now appeared as that for which nothingness was an existent [*Bestaaende*], as that which was through with everything, yet at the same time as that which had absolute power to do everything. If it allowed something to stand [*bestaae*], it knew it had the power to destroy it, and it knew this at the same moment it allowed it to endure [*bestaae*]. If it posited

* This ironic endeavour did not end with Schlegel and Tieck, but has found an extensive following in the Young Germany. In the general discussion of this standpoint, therefore, many a consideration is directed at Young Germany.[14]

† Throughout this discussion I use the expressions: *irony* and the *ironist*, but I could as easily say: *romanticism* and the *romanticist*. Both expressions designate the same thing. The one suggests more the name with which the movement christened itself, the other the name with which Hegel christened it.

something, it knew it had the authority to abrogate it, and it knew this at the same moment it posited it. It knew itself to be in complete possession of the absolute power to bind and to loose.[15] It was as much lord over the Idea as over the phenomenon, and it destroyed the one by the other. It destroyed the phenomenon by showing that it did not correspond to the Idea, and it destroyed the Idea by showing that it did not correspond to the phenomenon. Moreover, it was quite correct in both cases, since the Idea and the phenomenon are only in and with each other. But through all this irony rescued its sorrowless life. To do all this was given to the subject man: Behold, who is great like unto Allah, and who can stand [bestaae] before him?

But actuality (the historical actuality) relates in a twofold way to the subject: partly as a gift which will not admit of being rejected, and partly as a task to be realized. The disparate way in which irony related to actuality is sufficiently indicated by the fact that the ironic orientation is essentially critical. Both its philosopher (Schlegel) as well as its poet (Tieck) are critical. Hence the Sabbath—which our age believes in so many ways has already arrived—was not used in order to rest from historical labours but to criticize. But criticism usually excludes sympathy, and there is a criticism for which there is no more anything abiding [Bestaaende] than there is anything innocent to a suspicious policeman. But one did not criticize the old classics, nor did one criticize consciousness as did Kant; no, one criticized actuality itself. Now there might well have been much in actuality in need of a critique, and evil in the Fichtian sense of indolence and laziness might well have become rampant and its *vis inertiæ*[16] in need of a rebuke, in other words, there might well have been much in existence [Tilværende] which, precisely because it was not actuality, must be sheared away. But it was in no way defensible to direct its critical onslaught against the whole of actuality. I need scarcely remind the reader that Schlegel was critical, but that Tieck was no less critical will surely be admitted if one will consider that his polemic against the world is deposited in his dramas, and that these presuppose a polemi-

cally developed individual in order to be understood—a fact
which has caused them to become proportionately less
popular than they deserve to be in light of their genius.

When in the foregoing I said that actuality offers itself partly
as a gift, this was intended to express the relation of the
individual to the past. This past will have validity for the
individual, will not be overlooked or ignored. Irony, however,
has no past. This is due to the fact that it sprang from metaphysical investigations. It had confounded the temporal ego
with the eternal ego, and as the eternal ego has no past, so
neither does the temporal. Insofar as irony should be so conventional as to accept a past, this past must then be of such a
nature that irony can retain its freedom over it, continue to
play its pranks on it. It was therefore the mythical aspect of
history, saga and fairy-tale, which especially found grace in its
eyes. Authentic history, on the other hand, wherein the true
individual has his positive freedom because in this he has his
premises, must be dispensed with. To this end irony behaved
like Hercules wrestling with Antæus, for the latter could not be
overcome so long as he stood firmly on the ground; but
Hercules lifted Antæus off his feet and in this way over-
powered him. Irony did the same to all historical actuality.
With a twist of the wrist all history became myth, poetry, saga,
fairy-tale—irony was free once more. Now it took its choice,
had its own way, and did exactly as it pleased. It was particularly fond of Greece and the Middle Ages, but without
becoming lost in historical conceptions which it knew were
Dichtung und Wahrheit.[17] At one moment it dwelt in Greece
beneath the beautiful Hellenic sky, lost in the presentational
enjoyment of the harmonious Hellenic life, dwelt there in such
a way that it had its actuality in this. But when it grew tired
of this arbitrarily posited actuality it thrust it away so far that
it wholly disappeared. Hellenism had no validity for it as a
world historical moment, but it had validity, even absolute
validity, because irony was pleased to have it so. At the next
moment it concealed itself in the virgin forests of the Middle
Ages, listened to the mysterious whisperings of the trees and
built nests in their leafy tops, or hid itself in dark hollows, in

short, sought its actuality in the company of knights and troubadours, became enamoured of a noble maiden on a snorting horse with a falcon trained for hunting perched on her outstretched right forearm. But no sooner had this love affair lost its validity than the Middle Ages were spirited away back into infinity, dying away in ever weakening contours on the undercloth of consciousness. The Middle Ages had no validity for it as a world historical moment, but it had validity, even absolute validity, because irony was pleased to have it so. The same thing repeats itself in every theoretical domain. A particular religion was momentarily absolute for it, yet it knew full well that the reason it was absolute was merely because irony was pleased to have it so. At the next moment it chose something else. It therefore taught with *Nathan der Weise*[18] that all religions were equally good, Christianity perhaps the worst, and for a change it even fancied becoming a Christian. It behaved in identical fashion with philosophic matters. It condemned and denounced every philosophic standpoint, was for ever passing sentence, always in the judgment seat, yet never investigated any of them. It always placed itself above the object, which was also quite natural, for only now should actuality really begin. Irony had sprung from the metaphysical problem concerning the relation of the Idea to actuality, but metaphysical actuality is beyond time, hence it was impossible for the actuality desired by irony to be given in time. It is this condemning and denouncing behaviour of irony that Hegel particularly censures in Friedrich Schlegel (cf. xx, 161). In this respect one cannot overrate Hegel's great contribution to the conception of the historical past. He does not reject the past but conceives [*begriber*] it; he does not dismiss other philosophic standpoints but overcomes them. Hegel has therefore put a stop to all that incessant chatter to the effect that only now shall world history begin, as if it should begin precisely at four o'clock or in any event certainly before five. And if one or another Hegelian has got up such enormous world historical momentum that he cannot stop, but strikes out devil-may-care with awesome speed, then Hegel is not to blame for this.[19] While more can be accomplished with respect to contemplation than Hegel has done, still, no one who has any concept of the significance of actuality will be so ungrateful as to go beyond Hegel so hastily as to forget what he owes him, that is, if he has ever really understood Hegel. But if it be asked what gives irony the right to behave in this way, it must be answered that this is because irony knows the phenomenon is not the essence. The Idea is [er] concrete and must therefore become [blive] concrete, but this becoming [Bliven] concrete of the Idea is the historical actuality. Within this historical actuality every particular segment has its validity as a moment. This relative validity, however, is not acknowledged by irony. At one moment historical actuality has absolute validity for irony, at the next moment none at all, for irony has itself assumed the momentous task of providing actuality.

But actuality for the individual is also a task to be realized. In this connection one would think that irony would show itself to advantage, for since it had gone beyond every given actuality, surely it must have something good to set in its place. But this is not the case. As irony contrives to overcome historical actuality by making it hover, so irony itself has in turn become hovering. Its actuality is sheer possibility. In order for the acting individual to be able to fulfil his task in realizing actuality, he must feel himself assimilated into a larger context, must feel the seriousness of responsibility, must feel and respect every rational consequence. But irony is free from all this. It knows itself to be in possession of the power to begin from the beginning whenever it pleases, for nothing in the past is binding upon it. Moreover, as irony enjoys a critical satisfaction in theoretical concerns, so in practical affairs it relishes a similar divine freedom acknowledging no bonds, no chains, but, abandoning itself heedlessly to reckless play, romps like a leviathan[20] in the deep. Irony is free, to be sure, free from all the cares of actuality, but free from its joys as well, free from its blessings. For if it has nothing higher than itself, it may receive no blessing, for it is ever the lesser that is blessed of a greater.[21] This is the freedom for which irony longs. It therefore keeps watch over itself, and fears nothing so much as that one or another impression may overwhelm it. For when the individual is free in this way, only then does he live poetically, and it is well known that irony's great demand was that one should live poetically. But by living poetically irony understood something other, something more, than what this signifies to every rational person with some regard for the worth of a human being, some sense for what is original in man. It did not understand by this the artistic seriousness which lends assistance to the divine in man, which listens hushed and silently to the voice of what is unique in individuality, disclosing to it its movements so as to predominate in the individual, and so cause the whole of individuality to develop harmoniously into a plastic shape culminating in itself. It did not understand by this what the pious Christian understands when he becomes conscious of the fact that life is an upbringing, an education, which, to be sure, is not going to make him other than he is (for the Christian God is not in possession of the infinite negative omnipotence of the Mohammedan God, for whom a man as huge as a mountain and a flea as large as an elephant are as possible as a mountain as small as a man and an elephant as minute as a flea, because all things might easily be quite other than they are), but which shall develop the very seeds God has planted in man, since the Christian knows himself as that which has reality for God. Here the Christian lends assistance to God and becomes his accomplice as it were in perfecting the good work God has begun.[22] By living poetically irony did not merely intend to lodge a protest against all that baseness which is no more than a wretched product of its environment, a protest against all the mediocre types with which the world is unfortunately rich enough. No, irony desired something more. It is one thing poetically to produce oneself, quite another to allow oneself to be poetically produced.[23] The Christian allows himself to be poetically produced, and in this respect a simple Christian lives far more poetically than many a gifted head. But even one who poetically produces himself in the Greek sense acknowledges that he has been assigned a task. It is also of the utmost importance for him to become conscious of what

297

is original in him, and this originality is the limit within which
he poetically produces, within which he is poetically free.
Individuality has a purpose which is absolute, therefore, and
its activity consists in realizing this purpose, and in and through
this realization to enjoy itself, that is to say, its activity is to
become *für sich* what it is *an sich*.[24] But as the average person
has no *an sich* but becomes whatever he becomes, so neither
does the ironist. This is not because he is merely the product
of his environment; on the contrary, he stands completely
above his environment. No, to be able to live poetically, to be
able poetically to create himself to advantage, the ironist
must have no *an sich*. Hence irony lapses into the very thing
it most opposes, for the ironist acquires a certain similarity to
a thoroughly prosaic person, except that he retains the negative
freedom whereby he stands poetically creating above himself.
Accordingly, the ironist most often comes to [*bliver til*] nothing,
for it is the case with man, unlike God, that only nothing can
be created [*bliver*] out of nothing. But the ironist constantly
preserves his poetic freedom, and when he notices that he is
becoming [*bliver til*] nothing, he includes even this in his
poetizing. For it is well known that to become [*bliver til*]
nothing at all was one of those poetic attitudes and vocations
in life made valid by irony, indeed it was the most distinguished
of them all. In the poetry of the romantic school, therefore, a
Taugenichts[25] is always the most poetic character; and what
the Christian talks so much about during agitated seasons,
namely, to become a fool in the world,[26] this the ironist
realizes in his own fashion—except that he feels no martyrdom
but the highest poetic enjoyment. But this infinite poetic
freedom, already suggested by the fact that to become [*blive
til*] nothing at all is itself included, is expressed in a still more
positive way, for the ironic individual has most often traversed
a multitude of determinations in the form of possibility,
poetically lived through them, before he ends in nothingness.
For irony, as for the Pythagorean doctrine,[27] the soul is constantly on a pilgrimage, except irony does not require such a
long time to complete it. But if irony is a little skimpy with
time, it doubtless excels in the multiplicity of determinations.

And there is many an ironist who, before finding repose in nothingness, has traversed a far more extraordinary fate than the cock in Lucian,[28] which had first been Pythagoras himself, then Aspasia the ambiguous beauty from Miletus, Crates the Cynic, a king, a beggar, a satrap, a horse, a jackdaw, a frog, and a thousand other things too long to tell, and finally a cock, and this more than once because it found most satisfaction in this. All things are possible for the ironist. Our God is in the heavens: he hath done whatsoever he hath pleased;[29] the ironist is on earth, and does just as he likes. Still, one cannot blame the ironist because he finds it so difficult to become [*blive til*] something, for it is not easy to choose when one has such an enormous range of possibles. For a change he even deems it appropriate to let fate and accident decide for him. He therefore counts on his fingers like a child: rich man, poor man, beggar man,[30] etc. As all these determinations merely have the validity of possibility, he can even run through the whole lot almost as quickly as a child. What costs the ironist time, however, is the care he lavishes on selecting the proper costume for the poetic personage he has poetized himself to be. In this matter the ironist has great skill, not to mention a considerable assortment of masquerade costumes from which to make a judicious selection. Now he strolls about with the proud mien of a Roman patrician in trimmed toga, now he is sitting in the *sella curulis*[31] with weighty Roman seriousness, now he disguises himself in the humble cloth of a penitent pilgrim, now he crosses his legs like a Turkish pasha in his harem, flits airily about like a bird, a lovesick cyther player. This is what the ironist means when he maintains that one should live poetically, and this is what he attains by poetically producing himself.

But let us return to our previous remark that it is one thing poetically to produce oneself, quite another to let oneself be poetically produced. The man who allows himself to be poetically produced also has a specific given context to which he must accommodate himself, and hence is not a word without meaning for having been divested of connection and context. But for the ironist this context (this pretext he would say) has no validity, and as he is not inclined to fashion himself to suit his environment, so his environment must be fashioned to suit him, that is, he not only poetically produces himself but his environment as well. The ironist is reserved and stands aloof; he lets mankind pass before him, as did Adam the animals, and finds no companionship for himself. By this he constantly comes into collision with the actuality to which he belongs. It is therefore essential for him to suspend what is constitutive of actuality, that which orders and sustains it: ethics and morals. Here we have arrived at the point which has been the special object of Hegel's attack. Whatever is substantial [Bestaaende] in the given actuality has only poetic validity for the ironist, indeed he even lives poetically. When the given actuality loses its validity for the ironist, therefore, this is not because it is an outlived actuality which shall be displaced by a truer, but because the ironist is the eternal ego for whom no actuality is adequate. Here it is evident how this relates to the fact that the ironist sets himself above ethics and morals, a thing even Solger disclaims against[32] when he asserts that this is not what he means by irony. Still, it cannot properly be said that the ironist sets himself above ethics and morals, for he lives much too abstractly, much too metaphysically and æsthetically ever to arrive at the concretion formed by ethics and morals. Life is for him a drama, and what engrosses him is the ingenious unfolding of this drama. He is himself a spectator even when performing some act. He renders his ego infinite, volatizes it metaphysically and æsthetically, and should it sometimes contract as egoistically and shallowly as possible, at other times it unfurls so loosely and dissolutely that the whole world may be accommodated within it. He is inspired by the virtues of self-sacrifice as a spectator is inspired by them in a theatre, and he is a severe critic who well knows when such virtues become insipid and false. He even feels remorse, but æsthetically not morally. At the moment of remorse he is æsthetically above his remorse examining whether it be poetically correct, whether it might be a suitable reply in the mouth of some poetic character.

Because the ironist poetically produces himself as well as his environment with the greatest possible poetic licence, because he lives completely hypothetically and subjunctively, his life finally loses all continuity. With this he wholly lapses under the sway of his moods and feelings. His life is sheer emotion. Now certain it is that to have feeling may be most true, and surely no earthly life is so absolute as to be unacquainted with the oppositions inherent in this. But in a healthy life feeling is merely an intensification of what otherwise animates and moves a human being. A serious Christian well knows that there are moments when he is more deeply and forcefully affected by the Christian life than others, but he does not become a heathen when this feeling has passed. Indeed, the more healthy and seriously he lives, so much the more will he become master over feeling,[33] that is to say, so much the more will he humble himself through this and thereby save his soul. But as the ironist has no continuity, so the most contrary feelings are allowed to displace each other. Now he is a god, now a grain of sand. His feelings are as accidental as the incarnations of the Brahma. Although thinking himself free, the ironist succumbs to the terrible law of the irony of the world and toils in the most awful bondage. But the ironist is a poet, and so it does not always appear that he is a ball for the irony of the world to sport with. He poetizes everything, especially his feelings. To be truly free he must have control over feeling, one must instantly displace another. When it sometimes happens that his feelings displace one another so preposterously that even he notices all is not right, he poetizes further. He poetizes that it is he who evokes the feeling, and he keeps on poetizing until he becomes so spiritually palsied that he must cease. Feeling has therefore no reality for the ironist, and he seldom gives expression to his feelings except in the form of an opposition. His grief conceals itself in the exclusive incognito of the jest, his joy is enveloped in lament. Now he is on his way to the cloister, but en route he visits the mount of Venus;[34] now he is journeying to the mount of Venus, but stops at a cloister long enough to pray. The philosophic pursuits of irony are likewise dissolved in feeling. It is this which Hegel censures in Tieck,[35] and which is particularly apparent in the latter's correspondence with Solger: at one moment he is absolutely certain, at the next he conducts further inquiries, now he is a dogmatist, now a doubter, now it is Jacob Böhme who excites him, now the Greeks, etc., sheer feeling. As there must always be a bond uniting these oppositions, a unity into which these intense dissonances of feeling resolve themselves, so upon closer examination one will even find such a unity in the ironist. Boredom is the only continuity the ironist has. Yes, boredom: this eternity void of content, this bliss without enjoyment, this superficial profundity, this hungry satiety. But boredom is the negative unity assimilated into personal consciousness, the negative unity in which opposites disappear. That both Germany and France at this moment have only too great a number of such ironists, and no longer need to be initiated into the secrets of boredom by some English lord, the travelling member of a spleen club; and furthermore, that one or another youthful ward of the Young Germany and France would long ago have died of boredom had not their respective governments been so fatherly as to arrest them in order to give them something to think about—all this will scarcely be denied by anyone. If anyone wishes to have a splendid image of such an ironist, who, by his very doubleness in existence, lacked existence, then let me remind him of Asa-Loke.[36]

It is evident from this how irony remains thoroughly negative: in a theoretical dimension it establishes a disparity between Idea and actuality, actuality and Idea; and in a practical dimension between possibility and actuality, actuality and possibility. In order to exhibit this further in the historical appearance of irony, I shall examine its most important representatives a little closer.

FRIEDRICH SCHLEGEL

Friedrich Schlegel's celebrated novel *Lucinde*,* which became the gospel of the Young Germany and the system for its

* Friedrich Schlegel, *Lucinde*, second unabridged edition, Stuttgart, 1835.

Rehabilitation des Fleisches,[1] and which was an abomination to Hegel,[2] will here be the object of investigation. This discussion is not without difficulties, however, for *Lucinde*, as everyone knows, is a very obscene book, and by including certain passages for closer examination I shall be incurring the risk of making it impossible for even the purest reader to come away wholly unscathed. I shall therefore be as provident and sparing as possible.[3]

In order not to do Schlegel an injustice one must recall the numerous errors which have crept into the many relationships in life, and in particular which have been relentless in making love as tame, well-behaved, sluggish and apathetic, as utilitarian and serviceable as any other domesticated animal, in short, as unerotic as possible. To this extent one must be extremely beholden to Schlegel should he succeed in finding a solution. But alas, the only climate he discovers in which love can thrive is even worse, not a climate somewhat further south in relation to our northern climate, but an ideal climate that exists nowhere. Accordingly, it is not only the tame ducks and geese of a domesticated love which beat their wings and utter a terrifying cry when they hear the wild birds of love whistling by overhead. No, it is every more deeply poetic person, whose longings are too strong to be bound by romantic cobwebs, whose demands on life are too great to be satisfied through writing a novel, who here, precisely on behalf of poetry, must lay down his protest and endeavour to show that it was not a solution Friedrich Schlegel discovered but a delusion he strayed into, must endeavour to show that to live is something different from to dream. When we consider more closely what Schlegel opposed with his irony, it will surely not be denied that there both was and is much in the ingress, progress, and egress of marriage deserving such a correction, and which makes it natural for the subject to seek to emancipate himself from such things. There is an extremely constricted seriousness, a purposiveness, a wretched teleology worshipped by many like an idol, which demands every infinite pursuit as its rightful sacrifice. Love is thus nothing in and through itself, but only becomes something through the purpose whereby it is accommodated to that pettiness whose success creates such a furore in the private theatre of the family. 'To have purposes, to carry out purposes, to interweave purposes artfully with purposes into a new purpose: this ridiculous habit is so deeply rooted in the foolish nature of godlike man that if once he wishes to move freely without any purpose, on the inner stream of ever flowing images and feelings, he must actually resolve to do it and make it a set purpose (p. 153). . . . It is, to be sure, a different matter with people who love in the ordinary way. The man loves in his wife only the race, the woman in her husband only the degree of his natural qualities and social position, and both love in their children only their own creation and property (p. 55). . . . Oh, it is true, my friend, man is by nature a most serious animal (p. 57).'[4] There is a moral prudishness, a strait-jacket in which no rational human being can move. In God's name let it be sundered! There is, on the other hand, the moonlit kind of theatre marriages[5] of an overwrought romanticism for which nature, at least, has no purpose, and whose barren breezes and impotent embraces profit a Christian state no more than a pagan one. Against all these let irony rage! But it is not merely against untruths such as these that Schlegel directs his attack. There is a Christian view of marriage which, at the very hour of the nuptials, has had the audacity to proclaim the curse even before it pronounces the benediction.[6] There is a Christian view that places all things under sin, that recognizes no exception, spares nothing, not the child in the womb nor the most beautiful among women.[7] There is a seriousness in this view too high to be grasped by the harassed toilers of prosaic daily life, too severe to be mocked by marital improvisors. —Thus those times are now past when mankind lived so happily and innocently without sorrow and tribulation, when everything was so like man, when the gods themselves set the fashion and sometimes laid aside their heavenly dignity in order to steal the love of some earthly woman; when one who quietly, furtively sneaked away to a rendezvous could fear or flatter himself by finding a god among his rivals; those times when the sky arched itself proudly and beautifully over

happy love like a friendly witness, or with quiet gravity concealed it in the solemn peace of the night; when everything
lived only for love, and everything was in turn only a myth
about love for the happy lovers. But there lies the difficulty,
and it is from this perspective that one must evaluate the
efforts of Schlegel and all earlier and later romanticism: *those
times are past*, and still the longing of romanticism draws back
to them. But in so doing it undertakes no *peregrinationes sacras*[8]
but *profanus*. Were it possible to reconstruct a bygone age,
one must reconstruct it in its purity, hence Hellenism in all its
naïveté. But this is what romanticism refuses to do. It is not
properly Hellenism it reconstructs, but an unknown continent
it discovers. But what is more, its enjoyments are refined to a
high degree; for it does not merely seek to enjoy naïvely, but
in this enjoyment desires to become conscious of the destruction
of the given ethic. This is just the point of its enjoyment, as it
were, that it smiles at the ethic under which it believes others
groan, and in this lies the free play of ironic arbitrariness.
Christianity by means of the spirit has established a dissension
between the spirit and the flesh,* and either the spirit must
negate the flesh or the flesh negate the spirit. Romanticism
desires the latter, and is different from Hellenism in that along
with the enjoyment of the flesh it also enjoys the negation of
spirit. This it claims is to live poetically. I trust it will become
apparent, however, that poetry is precisely what it misses,
for true inward infinity proceeds only from resignation, and
only this inward infinity is in truth infinite and in truth
poetic.

Schlegel's *Lucinde* seeks to suspend the established ethic, or
as Erdmann not infelicitously expresses it: 'All moral determinations are mere sport, and it is accidental to the lover
whether marriage is monogamous or whether *en quatre*,[9] etc.'†

---

* Christianity in no wise seeks by this to destroy sensuousness, for it
teaches[10] that it is only in the resurrection that none shall be taken in
marriage nor given in marriage. But it also calls to mind[11] the man who
had no time to attend the great marriage feast because he was holding
his own.

† J. E. Erdmann, *Vorlesungen über Glauben und Wissen*, Berlin, 1837, p. 86.

Were it possible to imagine that the whole of *Lucinde* were merely a caprice, an arbitrarily fashioned child of whim and fancy gesticulating with both her legs like the little Wilhelmine without a care for her dress or the world's judgment; were it but a light-headed whimsicality that found pleasure in setting everything on its head, in turning everything upside down; were it merely a witty irony over the total ethic identified with custom and use: who then would be so ridiculous as not to laugh at it, who would be such a distempered grouch that he could not even gloat over it? But this is not the case. Quite the contrary, *Lucinde* has a most doctrinaire character and a certain melancholy seriousness pervading it which seems to derive from the fact that its hero has arrived at this glorious knowledge of the truth so late that a part of his life has gone unutilized. The audacity which this novel so often reverts to, which it clamours for, as it were, is therefore not a momentary whimsical suspension of that which is objectively valid, so that the expression 'audacity' as used here would itself have been capricious in using so strong an expression with deliberate abandon. No, this audacity is just what one calls audacity, but which is so amiable and interesting that ethics, modesty, and decency, which at first glance have some attraction, seem rather insignificant entities by comparison. Surely everyone who has read *Lucinde* will agree that it does have such a doctrinaire character. But should anyone wish to deny it, I must then ask him to explain how the Young Germany could have been so completely mistaken about it; and should he succeed in answering this, I shall then remind him that it is well known that Schlegel later became a Catholic and as such discovered the Reformation to have been the second fall of man, a fact which sufficiently shows that *Lucinde* was seriously intended.

Lucinde seeks to abrogate all ethics, not simply in the sense of custom and usage, but that ethical totality which is the validity of mind, the dominion of the spirit over the flesh. Hence it corresponds fully to what we have previously designated as the special pursuit of irony: to cancel all actuality and set in its place an actuality that is no actuality. In the first place, therefore, it is quite in order that the girl, or rather, the wife in whose arms Julian finds repose, that Lucinde 'was also one of those who have a decided inclination for the romantic, and who do not live in the ordinary world but in one self-created and self-conceived' (p. 90), one of those, therefore, who properly have no other actuality than the sensual; quite in order, secondly, that it is one of Julian's great tasks to bring before his imagination an eternal embrace —presumably as the only true actuality.

If we consider *Lucinde* as such a catechism of love, it requires of its disciples 'what Diderot calls the perception of the flesh,' 'a rare gift,' and pledges them to develop it into that higher sense of artistic voluptuousness (pp. 29, 30). Naturally, Julian appears as priest in this worship 'not without unction', that is, as one 'to whom the spirit itself spake through a voice from heaven, saying: "Thou art my beloved son in whom I am well pleased" ' (p. 35); as one who cries out to himself and others: 'Consecrate thyself and proclaim that only nature is venerable and only health agreeable' (p. 27). What it seeks is a naked sensuality in which the spirit is a negated moment; what it opposes is a spirituality in which sensuality is an assimilated moment. To this extent it is incorrect when it takes as its ideal the little two-year-old Wilhelmine, 'for her years the most clever [*geistreichste*] person of her time' (p. 15), since in her sensuality the spirit is not negated because it is not yet present. It desires nakedness altogether and so despises the northern coldness, and it seeks to ridicule that narrow-mindedness unable to tolerate nakedness. However, I shall not concern myself any further whether this is a narrow-mindedness, or whether the veil of attire is still not a beautiful image of how all sensuality ought to be, since when sensuality is intellectually mastered it is never naked. Instead, I shall merely call attention to the fact that the world still forgives Archimedes for running stark naked through the streets of Syracuse, and this surely not because of the mild southern climate, but because his spiritual exaltation, his 'eureka, eureka'[12] was a sufficient attire.

The confusion and disorder that *Lucinde* seeks to introduce into the established order [*Bestaaende*] it illustrates itself by means of the most perfect confusion in its design and structure. At the very outset Julian explains that along with the other conventions of reason and ethics he has also dispensed with chronology (p. 3). He then adds: 'For me and for this book, for my love of it and for its internal formation, there is no purpose more purposive than that right at the start I begin by abolishing what we call order, keep myself entirely aloof from it, and appropriate to myself in word and deed the right to a charming confusion' (p. 5). With this he seeks to attain what is truly poetical, and as he renounces all understanding and allows the phantasy alone to rule,* it may well be possible for him and the reader, should the latter wish to do likewise, to let the imagination maintain this confusion [*Mellemhverandre*] in a single perpetually moving image. —In spite of this confusion, however, I shall endeavour to bring a kind of order into my presentation and let the whole consolidate itself at one definite point.

Julian, the hero of this novel, is no Don Juan (who by his sensual genius casts a spell over everything like a sorcerer; who steps forth with an immediate authority showing himself lord and ruler, an authority which words cannot describe but of which some representation may be had from a few imperious bars[13] of Mozart; a being who does not seduce but by whom all would like to be seduced, and were their innocence restored to them would desire nothing more than to be seduced again;

---

* That the imagination alone rules is repeated throughout the whole of *Lucinde*. Now who is such a monster that he is unable to delight in the free play of the imagination? But it does not follow from this that the whole of life should be given over to imagination. When the imagination is allowed to rule in this way it prostrates and anæsthetizes the soul, robs it of all moral tension, and makes of life a dream. Yet this is exactly what *Lucinde* seeks to accomplish, and its standpoint is essentially designated as follows (p. 153): 'The supreme insight of the understanding is to choose the role of silence, to restore the soul to imagination, and not to disturb the sweet cooings of the young mother with her child.' This obviously means that when the understanding has reached its zenith, its formation must give way to the imagination, which shall then rule and no longer be an interlude in the enterprise of life.

a dæmon who has no past, no history of development, but springs forth at once fully endowed like Minerva), but a personality ensnared in reflection who develops only successively. In the 'Apprenticeship of Manhood' we learn more of his history. 'To play faro with the appearance of the most violent passion, and yet to be distracted and absent-minded; to venture everything in a heated instant and as soon as it is lost to turn away indifferently: this was just one of the vicious habits by which Julian fulminated away his youth' (p. 59). The author thinks that by this single characteristic he has adequately portrayed Julian's life. In this we fully agree. Julian is a young man who, intensely torn asunder within, has by this very sundering acquired a living idea of that sorcery which in a few moments is able to make a man many, many years older; a young man who by this very sundering is in apparent possession of an enormous power, just as surely as the excitement of desperation produces athletic prowess; a young man who long ago had already begun the grand finale,[14] but who nevertheless flourishes the goblet[15] with a certain dignity and grace, with an air of intellectual ease in the world, and now summons all his strength in a single breath in order by a brilliant exit to cast a glorifying nimbus over a life which has had no value and leaves no bereavement behind; a young man who has long been familiar with the thought of suicide, but whose stormy soul has begrudged him time to reach a decision. Surely love must be that which shall save him! After having been on the verge of seducing a young and innocent girl (a fairy-tale, however, which has no further significance for him, since she was obviously too innocent to satisfy his thirst for knowledge), he discovers in Lisette the very teacher he needs, an instructress who has long been initiated into the nocturnal mysteries of love, and whose public instruction Julian tries in vain to restrict to a private instruction for himself alone.

The portrait of Lisette is perhaps the most accomplished in the whole novel, and the author has treated her with a visible partiality and spared nothing in order to cast a poetic glow over her. As a child she was more melancholy [*tung-*

sindig] than light-minded [*letsindig*], but even then she had been daemonically excited by sensuality (p. 78). Later she had been an actress, but only for a short time, and she always poked fun at her lack of talent and at all the boredom she had endured. Finally, she had offered herself completely to the service of sensuality. Next to independence she had an immense love for money, which she nevertheless knew how to use with taste. Her favours she allowed to be repaid sometimes by sums of money, sometimes by the satisfaction of a whimsical infatuation for some particular person. Her boudoir was open and wholly without conventional furniture, for on every side there were large, expensive mirrors, and alternating with these superb paintings by Correggio and Titian. In place of chairs she had genuine oriental carpets and some groups of marble in half life-size. Here she often sat Turkish fashion the whole day long, alone, her hands folded idly in her lap, for she despised all womanly tasks. She refreshed herself from time to time with sweet-scented perfumes, and had stories, travelogues, and fairy-tales read to her by her jockey, a plastically fair youth whom she had seduced in his fourteenth year. But she paid little heed to what was read, except when there was something ridiculous or some platitude which she, too, found true; for she esteemed nothing but reality, had no sense for anything else, and found all poetry ridiculous. Such is Schlegel's portrayal of a life, which, however corrupt it may be, nevertheless seems to put forward the claim to be poetical. The thing particularly prominent here is the exclusive indolence which bothers about nothing, which cannot be bothered with working but despises every womanly pursuit, which cannot be bothered with occupying the mind but merely lets it be occupied, which dissolves and exhausts every power of the soul in enervating enjoyments and causes consciousness itself to evaporate in a nauseous twilight.[16] But enjoyment it was nonetheless, and surely to enjoy is to live poetically. The author seems also to want to find something poetical in the fact that Lisette did not always consider only money when distributing her favours. At such moments he seems to want to illuminate her wretched love with a reflection of that devotion belonging to innocent love, as if it were more poetical to be a slave to one's caprice than to money. So there she sits in this luxurious room with external consciousness slipping away from her, the huge mirrors reflecting her image from every angle produce the only consciousness she has remaining. When referring to her own person she usually called herself 'Lisette', and often said that were she able to write she would then treat her story as though it were another's, altogether preferring to speak of herself in third person. This, evidently, was not because her earthly exploits were as world historical as a Caesar's,[17] so that her life was not her own because it belonged to the world. It was simply because the weight of this *vita ante acta*[18] was too heavy for her to bear. To come to herself concerning it, to allow its menacing shapes to pass judgment upon her, this would indeed be too serious to be poetical. But to allow this wretched life to dissolve itself in indefinite contours, to stare at it as though it were something indifferent to her, this she liked to do. She might grieve over this lost and unhappy girl, she might offer her a tear, perhaps, but that this girl was herself she wanted to forget. But it is weak to seek to forget, although on occasion there may be stirring in this an energy foreshadowing something better. But to seek to relive oneself poetically in such a way that remorse can have no sting because it concerns another, all the while allowing enjoyment to become intensified through a secret complicity, this is a most effeminate cowardice. Throughout the whole of *Lucinde*, however, it is this lapsing into an æsthetic stupor* which appears as the designation for

---

* This is set forth especially in the section entitled 'An Idyl of Idleness,' where the highest perfection is posited as pure and unadulterated passivity. 'The more beautiful the climate we live in, the more passive we are. Only the Italians know how to walk, only the Orientals how to recline, and where do we find the human spirit developed more delicately and lusciously than in India? It is the privilege of being idle which is the true principle of nobility, and which everywhere distinguishes the noble from the common' (p. 42). 'The highest and most perfect life is simply to vegetate' (p. 43). Plant life is the ideal to which it aspires, and so Julian writes to Lucinde: 'The time is coming when we two shall intuit in one mind that we are blossoms of one plant or petals of one flower. Then shall we know

what it is to live poetically, and which, since it lulls the deeper ego into a somnambulant state, permits the arbitrary ego free latitude in ironic self-satisfaction.

But let us examine this more closely. There have been many attempts to show that such books as *Lucinde* are immoral, and there have been frequent cries of shame and ignominy over them. But so long as the author is allowed overtly to claim and the reader covertly to believe that such works are poetical, there is not much to be gained by this, and this so much the less since man has as great a claim on the poetical as the moral has claim on him. Be it therefore said, as it shall also be shown, that they are not only immoral but unpoetical, and this because they are irreligious. Let it be said first and last that every man can live poetically who in truth desires to.[19] If we next inquire what poetry is, we might answer with the general characterization that poetry is victory over the world. It is through a negation of the imperfect actuality that poetry opens up a higher actuality, expands and transfigures the imperfect into the perfect, and thereby softens and mitigates that deep pain which would darken and obscure all things. To this extent poetry is a kind of reconciliation, though not the true reconciliation;[20] it does not reconcile me with the actuality in which I live, for no transubstantiation of the given actuality occurs. Instead, it reconciles me with the given actuality by giving me another actuality, a higher and more perfect. Indeed, the greater the opposition, so much the more imperfect is the reconciliation, so that it often becomes no reconciliation at all but rather animosity. Only the religious, therefore, is capable of effecting the true reconciliation, for it

---

with laughter that what we now call only hope was properly recollection' (p. 11). Hence longing itself assumes the form of vegetative still life. ' "Julian," asked Lucinde, "why do I feel a deep longing in this serene peace?" "Because it is only in longing that we find peace," answered Julian. "Yes, peace is only when the mind, being disturbed by nothing, is moved to long and seek itself, where it can find nothing higher than its own longing" ' (p. 148). '*Julian*: Divine peace, dear friend, I have found only in this longing. *Lucinde*: And that divine longing I have found in this beautiful peace' (p. 150).

renders actuality infinite for me. The poetical may well be a sort of victory over actuality, but the process whereby it is rendered infinite is more like an abandonment of, than a continuation in, actuality. To live poetically is therefore to live infinitely. But infinity may be either an external or an internal infinity. The person who would have an infinitely poetical enjoyment also has an infinity before him, but it is an external infinity. When I enjoy I am constantly outside myself in the 'other'. But such an infinity must cancel itself. Only if I am not outside myself in what I enjoy but in myself, only then is my enjoyment infinite, for it is inwardly infinite. He who enjoys poetically, were he to enjoy the whole world, would still lack one enjoyment: he does not enjoy himself. To enjoy oneself (naturally not in a Stoic or egotistical sense, for here again there is no true infinity, but in a religious sense) is alone the true infinity.

If after these considerations we return to the claim that to live poetically is the same as to enjoy (and this opposition between poetic actuality and the given actuality, precisely because our age is so deeply penetrated by reflection, must exhibit itself in a much deeper form than it has ever before appeared in the world; for previously the poetic development went hand in hand with the given actuality, but now it is in truth a matter of to be or not to be, now one is not satisfied to live poetically once in a while, but demands that the whole of life should be poetic), then it readily appears that this utterly fails to secure the highest enjoyment, the true happiness wherein the subject no longer dreams but possesses himself in infinite clarity, is absolutely transparent to himself. This is only possible for the religious individual who does not have his infinity outside himself but within himself. To revenge oneself is accordingly a poetic enjoyment, and the pagans believed that the gods had reserved all vengeance unto themselves because it was sweet.[21] But though I were to have my revenge absolutely sated, though I were a god in the pagan sense before whom all things trembled and whose fiery anger were able to consume everything, still, I would in revenge merely be enjoying myself egotistically, my enjoyment would be merely an external infinity.[22] To this extent the simplest human being who did not permit his vengeance to rage but mastered his anger was much nearer to having overcome the world, and only he enjoyed himself in truth, only he possessed inward infinity, only he lived poetically. If from this standpoint we would consider the life set forth in *Lucinde* as a poetic life, then we might allow it every possible enjoyment—but the right to use one predicate in describing it will surely not be denied us: it is an infinitely cowardly life. And provided one will not claim that to be cowardly is to live poetically, it might well be possible for this poetic life to exhibit itself rather unpoetically, that is to say, wholly unpoetically. For to live poetically cannot mean to remain obscure to oneself, to work oneself up into a disgusting suggestiveness, but to become clear and transparent to oneself, not in finite and egotistical satisfaction, but in one's absolute and eternal validity. And if this be not possible for every human being then life is madness, in which case it is a matchless foolhardiness for the individual—though he be the most gifted who has ever lived in the world—to delude himself in thinking that what was denied all others was reserved for him alone. Either to be a human being is absolute, or the whole of life is nonsense—despair the only thing awaiting everyone not so demented, not so uncharitable and haughty, not so desperate as to believe himself the chosen one. Hence one should not restrict himself to reciting certain moralisms against the whole tendency after *Lucinde*, which, often with much talent and often enchantingly enough, has taken it upon itself not to lead but to lead astray. One must not allow it to deceive itself and others that it is poetic, or that it is through this way that one attains what every human being has an imperative demand for—to live poetically.

But let us return to Julian and Lisette. Lisette ends her life as she began it, fulfilling what Julian never had enough time to resolve, and through the act of suicide seeks to attain the goal of all her aspirations—to be rid of her self. However, she preserves her æsthetic tact to the very end, and the last words which, according to her servant, she pronounced in a shrill voice: 'Lisette must die, must die now! An inexorable fate requires it!' must be regarded as a kind of dramatic silliness quite natural for one who had formerly been an actress on the stage and who subsequently became one in life as well. —Now the death of Lisette must naturally have made an impression on Julian. I shall let Schlegel speak for himself, however, lest anyone think I distort. 'The first effect of the death of Lisette was that Julian idolized her memory with fanatical veneration' (p. 77). Yet not even this event was sufficient to develop Julian: 'This exception to what Julian regarded as ordinary among the female sex (the average woman, according to Julian, did not possess the same "high energy" as Lisette) was too unique, and the circumstances in which he found her too sordid for him to acquire true perspective through this' (p. 78).

Julian, after withdrawing in loneliness for a time, is again allowed by Schlegel to come into contact with society, and in a more intellectual relation to certain of this life's feminine members once more runs through several love affairs, until he finally discovers in Lucinde the unity of all these discrete moments, discovers as much sensuousness as cleverness [*Aandrighed*]. But as this love affair has no deeper foundation than intellectual sensuousness, as it embraces no moment of resignation, in other words, since it is no marriage, and as it asserts the view that passivity and vegetating constitute perfection; so here again the ethical integrity is negated. Accordingly, this love affair can acquire no content, can achieve no history in a deeper sense; and so their amusements can only be the same *en deux* as those with which Julian had formerly occupied his loneliness, namely, in considering what some clever lady would say or reply on some piquant occasion. It is a love without real content, and the eternity so often mentioned is none other than what might be called the eternal pleasure instant, an infinity without infinity and as such unpoetic. One can hardly refrain from smiling, therefore, when such a frail and fragile love fancies itself able to withstand the storms of life, fancies itself in possession of a strength sufficient to look upon 'the harshest whim of chance as an excellent jest and a frolicsome caprice' (p. 9). For this love is not at home in the actual world, but belongs to an imaginary world where the lovers are themselves lords over storms and hurricanes. Moreover, as everything in this alliance is calculated in terms of enjoyment, so naturally it conceives its relation to the generation deriving its existence [*Tilværelse*] from it equally egotistically (p. 11): 'Thus the religion of love weaves our love ever more closely and firmly together, for the child doubles the happiness of its gentle parents like an echo.' Occasionally, one comes across parents who with foolish seriousness wish to see their children well settled as soon as possible, perhaps even to see them well settled in the grave. Julian and Lucinde, on the other hand, seem to want to keep their offspring always at the same age as the little Wilhelmine so as to derive amusement from them.

Now what is problematic about *Lucinde* and the whole tendency connected with it is that although beginning with the freedom and constitutive authority of the ego, it does not go on to arrive at a still higher aspect of mind but instead at sensuality, and consequently at its opposite. Ethics imply a relation of mind to mind, but as the ego seeks a higher freedom, seeks to negate ethical mind, it thereby succumbs to the law of the flesh and the appetites. But as this sensuality is not naïve, it follows that the same arbitrariness that established sensuality in its supposed privileges may at the next moment pass over to assert an abstract and eccentric aspect of mind. These vibrations may be conceived partly as the play of the irony of the world with the individual, partly as an attempt by the individual to mimic the irony of the world.

TIECK

We shall here discuss some of the satirical dramas and lyrical poetry of Tieck. His earlier novelle[1] were written before he was brought to a knowledge of the truth by the Schlegels, while his later novelle approximate actuality more and more, and not infrequently seek by a certain breadth to congrue with it completely. With Tieck I already breathe a little easier, and when I once more look back at *Lucinde* it seems that I had just awakened from an anxious and disturbing dream in which were heard at once the seductive tones of sensuality and the wild, brutish howls that sound in their midst. For it seems as if someone had offered me the loathsome preparation brewed in a witch's cauldron that robs one of all taste and appetite for life. Schlegel lectures and attacks actuality directly. This is not the case with Tieck, however, who abandons himself to a poetical exuberance while preserving its indifference towards actuality. It is only when he does not do this that he comes near to attacking actuality, yet even then his attack is always more indirect. That such a poetic exuberance wholly beside itself in the most inordinately ironic 'tra-la-la',[2] also has a validity will surely not be denied. To this extent Hegel has often done Tieck an injustice,[3] and I must wholly agree with an otherwise zealous Hegelian when he observes: 'Hegel was equally at home with jest and witticism, but the ultimate depths of humour remained partially closed to him. Moreover, the most recent form of irony was so much opposed to his own orientation that he completely lacked the wherewithal with which to recognize or appreciate what was authentic in it.'[*][4] But the nearer such poetry approaches actuality, the more it becomes understandable only through a rupture with actuality; the more polemic it conceals in itself, the more it makes a polemical development a condition for the reader's sympathy, slips out of its poetical indifference, loses its innocence and acquires a purpose. It is then no longer that poetic licence which, like Münchhausen, takes itself by the nape of the neck and in this way, hovering in the air without any foothold, makes the one lump of coal more significant than the next. It is then no longer the pantheistic infinity of poetry, but instead the finite subject applying an ironic lever in order to wrench the whole of existence [*Tilværelse*] out of its fixed juncture. Now all existence [*Tilværelse*] becomes mere sport for a poetic arbitrariness which disdains nothing, not even what is most insignificant, and which retains [*bestaaer*] nothing, not even what is most significant. In this connection one need

* H. G. Hotho, *Vorstudien für Leben und Kunst*, Stuttgart and Tübingen, 1835, p. 394.[5]

317

only read through the list of characters in a work by Tieck or any other romantic poet in order to get an idea of what unheard of and highly improbable things happen in their poetic world. Animals talk like humans, humans talk like cattle, chairs and tables become conscious of their significance in existence [*Tilværelse*], men feel existence [*Tilværelse*] as a thing without meaning, nothing becomes [*blive til*] everything and everything nothing, all things are possible even the impossible, all things are rational even the irrational.

It must be borne in mind, however, that Tieck and the whole romantic school related or thought they related to an age in which men had become ossified, as it were, within the finite social situation. Everything had become perfected and consummated in a divine Chinese optimism that allowed no rational longing to go unsatisfied, no rational wish unfulfilled. Those glorious assumptions and maxims drawn from custom and convention had been made the objects of a pious idolatry. Everything was absolute—even the absolute. One refrained from polygamy, one wore a steeple crown hat. Everything had its predetermined significance. Everyone felt the magnitude of his accomplishment, naturally according to his station in life, with finely nuanced dignity. Everyone felt the immense significance of his own tireless efforts for himself and for the whole. One did not live with Quakerish frivolity without concern for the time of day or the stroke of the hour. Such ungodliness would seek to insinuate itself in vain. Each thing proceeded according to its own measured gait, even he who went with a proposal of marriage, for he knew unquestioningly that he was attending to a lawful errand and was taking a most weighty step. Everything took place on the stroke of the hour. One was inspired by nature on Midsummer Day. One was full of contrition on the fourth Friday after Easter. One fell in love when he reached his twentieth year. One went to bed at ten o'clock. One married, one lived for domesticity, one filled his position in the state. One had children and family cares. One stood erect like a man. One was seen in holy places attending to his blessed duties. One was an associate of the pastor under whose eye he epically cultivated the many fine features of an honourable, posthumous reputation, which he also knew this same pastor would one day with heavy heart seek in vain to stammer forth. One was a friend in the true and proper sense of the word, a real friend, just as one was a real chancellor. One understood the world, one raised his children to know the same. One was inspired one night a week by the poet's eulogy on the beauty of existence [*Tilværelse*]. One meant everything to his own, year in and year out with a certainty and precision always correct to the very minute. The world was becoming childish, it had to be rejuvenated. To this extent romanticism was beneficial. There runs through romanticism a chilling wind, a refreshing morning zephyr from the virgin forests of the Middle Ages or the pure ether of Greece; it sends a cold shiver down the back of the Philistine, and yet it is necessary in order to dispel the brutish miasma in which man had heretofore breathed. The centuries become vagrant, the enchanted castle rises, its inhabitants all awaken, the forests breathe easy, birds sing, the beautiful princess surrounds herself with suitors, the woods echo the sound of hunting horns and baying hounds, the meadows shed fragrance, poetry and song tear themselves loose from nature to flutter about—and no one knows from whence they come or whither they go. The world is rejuvenated, but as Heine has so wittily observed,[6] it was rejuvenated by romanticism to the extent that it became a little child again. The calamity of romanticism is that what it grasps is not actuality. Poetry awakens, forceful longings, mysterious presentiments, exciting emotions all awaken, nature awakens, the enchanted princess awakens—the romanticist falls asleep. It is in a dream that he experiences all this. Whereas everything around him formerly slept, so everything now awakens but he sleeps. But dreams do not satisfy. Faint and weary he rises unrefreshed, but only to lay himself down to sleep once more, and soon art is required to summon the somnambulant state. But the more art this requires, the more eccentric becomes the ideal which the romanticist conjures forth.

It is between these two poles that romantic poetry moves. On the one hand, there is the given actuality with all its wretched Philistinism; on the other hand, there is the ideal actuality in dawning shapes. These two moments are related necessarily to each other. The more caricatured actuality becomes, the higher gushes the ideal—except the fountain which here gushes forth does not flow unto everlasting life.[7] The fact that this poetry vacillates between opposites shows that in a deeper sense it is not true poetry. The true ideal is not in any way beyond: it is *behind* us insofar as it is a driving force, in *front* of us insofar as it is an inspiring goal, but through all this it is *within* us and this is its truth.[8]

Accordingly, the reader can have no truly poetic relation to this genre of poetry, since the poet himself has no authentically poetic relation to his poem. The poetic standpoint assumed by the poet is the poetic arbitrariness, the total impression left by the poem is an emptiness wherein nothing remains. This arbitrariness is apparent throughout the entire structure. Now the piece hastens forward, now it stands still and stagnates in an episode, now it goes backward; now we are in Peder Madsen's Lane,[9] now in heaven; now there occurs something extremely improbable, but which the poet well knows is improbable; now bells sound in the distance, it is the pious procession of the three holy kings; now there follows a solo for French horn;* now something is advanced seriously but immediately twisted inside out—and the unity in laughter shall reconcile all oppositions, yet this laughter is in turn accompanied by the distant flute tones of a deep sadness, etc., etc.

Inasmuch as the whole design fails to order itself into a poetic totality, since what is poetical for the poet is the freedom with which he rules all things, while what is poetical for the

* This may be compared with the excellent account by Hotho, *op. cit.*, p. 412: 'Here the adventurous licence of the imagination retained unlimited room for every species of image: daring episodes swirl forth at will, arabesque-like curiosities twist themselves into teasing laughter through the loose, spangled fabric, allegory expands the otherwise constricted shapes until nebulous, here and there the parodic jest hovers in topsy-turvy abandonment. And this genial pleasure is wedded to a feeble indulgence unable to refuse any idle invention which springs from its own bosom.'

reader is the freedom with which he mimics the poet's caprices; inasmuch as the whole design, I say, fails to order itself into a poetic totality, the discrete elements stand [*staae*] isolated, or rather, because the discrete elements consist in [*bestaae i*] an isolated striving, there can therefore be no poetic unity. The polemical striving never finds any rest, for the poetic element in this poetry consists in constantly liberating itself by means of a new polemic, and it is as difficult for the poet to find the ideal as the caricature. Every polemical stroke contains something more, the possibility of transcending itself in a still more ingenious portrayal. The ideal striving in turn has no ideal, for every ideal is at the same moment only an allegory concealing an even higher ideal, and so on *ad infinitum*. The poet affords neither himself nor the reader any repose, for repose is the very opposite of such poetry. The only repose it has is the poetic eternity wherein it envisages the ideal, but this eternity is an absurdity without time, and so at the next moment the ideal becomes allegory.

As Tieck was in possession of a unique inventiveness in apprehending Philistinism, an amazing virtuosity in the perspective of the bizarre, so his ideal striving has such artesian[10] depth that the image supposed to become visible on the horizon vanishes in the infinite. He has an unusual talent for making one feel strange, and the ideal human shapes occasionally to be seen are so extraordinary as actually to make one rather apprehensive; for they resemble those curious geological formations in nature occasionally to be seen, and their steadfast, knowing eyes infuse not so much confidence as a certain *unheimlich*[11] anxiety.*

Inasmuch as the whole aim of this poetry is to approach by means of a constant approximation that mood which can never find its perfectly adequate expression, whereby this poetry is poetry about poetry in the infinite, and furthermore, to put the reader in a mood incommensurable with the very offerings of this poetry, so naturally such poetry has its strength in the

* Should the reader desire a visual representation of such a personage, I shall refer him to the illustration[12] found in *Das Knaben Wunderhorn, alte deutsche Lieder*, vol. 3, Heidelberg, 1808.

lyrical. This lyricism must not become heavy and burdensome by having a deeper content, but become fainter and fainter until it vanishes like the distant soundings of a fading echo. In lyricism the subjective moment is the musical element, and this is here developed to the exclusion of everything else. In this regard everything depends on the ring in the verse, the resonance with which the one stanza calls to and answers the other, the graceful windings of the verse in lithe and easy dance steps, all the while humming its own accompaniment as it were.[13] The rhyme itself becomes a wandering knight in search of adventure, and what Tieck and the rest of romanticism have been at such pains to effect (that the reader suddenly sees a strange face which yet looks so familiar that it seems as though he had once seen this face far back in time—in a past transcending the historical consciousness), this now happens to the rhyme, which suddenly confronts an old acquaintance from better days and now begins to feel quite uneasy. Tired and bored with its usual comrades, the rhyme casts about for new and more interesting acquaintances. Finally, the musical element isolates itself completely, for occasionally romanticism is actually successful in reconstructing that genre of poetry which everyone remembers from his childhood in the fine verse: ' 'Twas brillig, and the slithy toves . . .'[14] Such poetry must be considered most perfect, for here the mood, and presumably this is what everything turns on, predominates completely and is utterly uninhibited, since all content is negated.[15]

Although Tieck did not negate actuality with as much seriousness as Schlegel, still, his eccentric and impotent ideal floating about like a cloud in the sky, or like the shadow of one racing elusively over the ground, shows he had gone astray. Schlegel later pacified himself in Catholicism, and Tieck found occasional repose in a sort of deification of all existence [Tilværelse] whereby everything became equally poetic.

It was Solger who sought to become philosophically conscious of irony. His views are set forth in his æsthetic lectures published posthumously,* together with certain essays to be found in his posthumous writings.† Hegel has paid much attention to the account of Solger and treats him with decided partiality. In the frequently mentioned review of *Solgers nachgelassene Schriften*, Hegel expresses himself as follows (xx, 182 f.): 'As it usually appears, irony is to be regarded more as a celebrated hobgoblin with aristocratic pretensions. With respect to Solger, however, it may be treated as a principle.' Hegel again refers to Solger in the introduction to his *Philosophy of Fine Art*, vol. I, p. 93:[1] 'Solger was not, as the others were, satisfied with superficial philosophic insight. An authentically speculative impulse and inward compulsion forced him to desce...d to the depths of the philosophic Idea,' and complains that Solger died too early to bring this to its concrete fulfilment.

To give an account of the standpoint of Solger is extremely difficult, for he has developed his views, as Hotho correctly observes, with '*schwerbegreifbarer philosophischer Klarheit.*'[2] The matter is simply this: Solger has got himself lost in the negative. Hence it is not without certain misgivings that I embark upon this stormy sea, not because I fear so much for my life, but because it will be next to impossible to give the reader any sort of reliable information about what has become of me or where I find myself at any given moment.[3] Inasmuch as the negative only becomes visible through the positive, and since the negative is here autonomous and present in all its barrenness, so the reader is completely confounded. The moment one expects the possibility of a determination by which to orient oneself, everything disappears once more, since upon closer

* K. W. F. Solger, *Vorlesungen über Aesthetik*, edited by K. W. L. Heyse, Leipzig, 1829.

† *Solgers nachgelassene Schriften und Briefwechsel*, edited by Ludwig Tieck and Friedrich Raumer, 2 vols., Leipzig, 1826.

323

inspection the positive envisaged in the distance turns out to be a new negation.[4] Solger may well have significance for the development of speculation, but it will no doubt be best to regard him as a sacrifice to Hegel's positive system. Here Hegel's partiality towards Solger also becomes explicable. Solger is the metaphysical knight of the negative. He does not collide with actuality in the same sense as the other ironists, for his irony did not in any way fashion itself in opposition to actuality.* The irony of Solger is contemplative irony, and he sees the nothingness of all things. Thus irony is an organon, a sense for the negative.

The activity of Solger lies in the sphere of speculation. As he nowhere gives a coherent, progressive, and strictly philosophic account, but only aphoristic utterances sometimes of a purely metaphysical nature, sometimes involving historical-philosophical, æsthetic, and ethical investigations, utterances tangent to the whole domain of philosophy, so we are soon involved in great difficulty. Add to this that his diction is often more poetic than philosophic, and that he fails to give the reader a clear idea of the direction in which the movement proceeds. (When, for example, he says that God,[5] in revealing himself, sacrifices himself—now I am well aware that this expression could have a meaning analogous to the metaphysical significance accorded by recent speculation to the expression that God is reconciled with the world. But as the latter is itself a dilution of the concept compared to Christian terminology, such recent abuses can hardly provide an acceptable defence for Solger's behaviour towards an even more concrete concept.) Such expressions as *to negate*, *to destroy*, *to abrogate* occur frequently, but for the reader to be correctly oriented he must first understand the laws of motion. The negative has a double function: it renders the finite infinite,

---

* It is quite correct when Solger remarks (*Nachgelassene Schriften*, vol. II, p. 514): 'Is this irony an insolent disregard for whatever essentially and seriously interests man, a total disregard for the schism in his nature? Not at all. This would be a vulgar mockery which has not advanced beyond seriousness and jest, but combating them on their own level with their own weapons.'

and it renders the infinite finite. But if one does not know which movement he is involved in, or rather, if he is now in one movement and now in the other, so naturally everything is confused. Moreover, one must agree on the significance of that which is said to be negated, for otherwise the negation (like the cæsura in that well-known verse)[6] may fall at the wrong place. When it is said that actuality must be destroyed, must be negated, one ought to know what is understood by actuality; for in one sense actuality has itself come about through a negation. But this is never clarified, and so one comes across such confusions as the following: man is the *Nichtige** (already one must be careful to agree about the sense in which man is the *Nichtige*, and to what extent there is something positive and valid in this *Nichtige*); the *Nichtige* must be destroyed (here again one must first hold a little consultation to decide how far man is able to destroy the *Nichtige* in himself, whereby in another sense he does not remain the *Nichtige*); yet the *Nichtige* in us is the divine (cf. *Solgers nachgelassene Schriften*, vol. I, p. 511).

Solger seeks to bring about the absolute identity of the finite and the infinite, seeks to destroy the boundary which in many ways would hold them apart. He works towards the absolute, presuppositionless beginning, and his activity is therefore speculative. We read in his *Nachgelassene Schriften*, vol. I, p. 507: 'It is well known that the science of the philosopher differs essentially from every other in that it is self-contained. Every other science presupposes something as given, either a determinate form of knowledge as in mathematics, or a determinate subject matter as in history, natural science, and the like. Philosophy alone must create itself.' His contemplative irony sees the finite as the *Nichtige*, as that which must be abrogated.† But the infinite, too, must be negated, must not

---

* I have retained this German word because I know of no Danish word meaning exactly the same thing. Although the reader may find himself disturbed by this word, still, he may find some profit in having a constant memento of Solger.

† The essential difference between the irony of Solger and that described earlier will be seen at once. The irony of Solger is a kind of contemplative,

consist in an otherworldly *an sich*. With this the true actuality is effected (cf. *Nachgelassene Schriften*, vol. 1, p. 600): 'The finite, the simple fact, is no more true actuality than the infinite, the relation to concepts and shifting oppositions, is the eternal. True actuality is a moment of intuition [*Anschauung*] wherein the finite and the infinite, which our ordinary understanding apprehends only in relation to each other, are completely abrogated, since it is in this that God or the eternal manifests itself.' Here we have the Idea at the point of absolute beginning, as infinite absolute negativity. If something is to come of [*blive til*] this, however, the negative must again assert itself and render the Idea finite, make it concrete. The negative is the unrest of thought, but this unrest must appear, must become visible: its desire must exhibit itself as the desire which drives the work, its pain must exhibit itself as the pain which begets. Should this fail to come about, we have merely the unauthentic actuality of contemplation, religious devotion, and pantheism. And whether one maintains devotion as a moment or allows the whole of life to become devotion, the true actuality nevertheless fails to appear. If it is only a moment, there is nothing to do but instantly evoke it again; while if it is to fill the whole of life, then in truth actuality never comes into existence [*bliver til*]. Hence it is to no avail when Solger explains[7] that one must not imagine the Idea in a heavenly or supra-heavenly place like Plato; to no avail when Solger reassures us he does not allow finitude to disappear as a mere *modus* like Spinoza; to no avail that he refuses to let the Idea come into existence [*tilblive*] through an eternal becoming [*Vorden*] like Fichte; and no less futile that he disapproves of Schelling's attempt to show perfect being is in existence [*Tilværelse*]. All such things are but preliminary studies. Solger is at the beginning. As this beginning is utterly abstract, however, it is essential that the dualism in existence manifest itself in its truth. But this does not happen; quite

religious devotion, and it does not occur to him to preserve the being-for-himself subject in his prudishness. All finitude must be negated, including the observing subject; indeed, he is already negated in this contemplation.

the contrary, it becomes evident that Solger actually is unable to grant the finite any validity, unable to render the infinite concrete. He sees the finite as the *Nichtige*, as vanishing, as the *nichtige* universe. Moral determinations have no validity, therefore, and all finitude together with its moral and immoral endeavour vanishes in a metaphysical contemplation that regards this as nothingness. He writes (*Nachgelassene Schriften*, vol. I, p. 512): 'That we can be evil is due to the fact that we have a phenomenal appearance, a vulgar existence which in itself is neither good nor evil, neither something nor nothing, but instead the mere shadow which essence in its divided existence [*Daseyn*] casts upon itself, and upon which we in turn may cast the image of good and evil as upon a film of smoke. All our moral virtues are but such reflected images of the good, and woe to them who trust in them! All our moral vices are but such reflections of evil, and woe to them who despair over them or regard them as actual and true, not believing in that before which they are nothing and which alone is able to cancel [*heben*] them in us!' Here the weakness in Solger is readily apparent. While it is true that moral virtues have no value in and for themselves, but only through the humility which allows God to produce them in us, and while it is true that a man's vices can only be cancelled by God and not by his own powers, still, it does not follow that one must metaphysically abandon himself, and in the one case ignore that synergism[8] which lends assistance to the divine, and in the other that contrition which will not let go[9] of God. The finite in this connection is undoubtedly the *Nichtige*, but there is still something in it to give it a hold.

The philosophic endeavour apparent throughout all this is not consummated; hence one has not a speculative exposition, but a pantheistic abandonment of that abstract *an sich* in the absolute identity of the finite with the infinite. Pantheism may occur in two ways: either by accentuating man or by accentuating God, either through anthropocentric or theocentric reflection. If I allow humanity to produce God, there is no conflict between God and man; if I allow man to disappear in God, there is again no conflict. Solger evidently does the latter. Naturally, he does not think of God Spino-zistically as substance, but this is because he will not abrogate the pietistical identity of the human and divine.

These metaphysical investigations are pursued no further. We shall therefore turn to another cycle of considerations concerning a more speculative-dogmatic sphere. Solger employs as a matter of course such concrete ideas as God, to sacrifice oneself, to surrender oneself out of love, etc. One finds constant allusion to such notions as God's creating out of nothingness, his atonement, etc. This part has been thoroughly treated by Hegel so I can attach myself to him. First a few citations from Solger. It is notably in two letters from the first volume of *Nachgelassene Schriften*, one to Tieck and another to Abeken, that most of these speculative flashes occur. Page 603: 'Since God exists or manifests himself in our finitude, he sacrifices and annihilates himself in us, for we are nothingness.' Page 511: 'It is not our relative weakness that constitutes our imperfection, and not our essential being that constitutes our truth. We are *nichtige* phenomena because God has assumed existence in us and thereby separated himself from himself. And is this not the greatest love: that he has betaken himself to nothingness in order that we might be, that he has sacrificed himself and annihilated his nothingness, killed his death, in order that we might not remain mere nothingness but return to him and have our being in him? The *Nichtige* in us is itself the divine, insofar as we apprehend it as the *Nichtige* and know ourselves as this. In this sense it is also the good, and we can in truth only be good before God through self-sacrifice.' Hegel discusses this material in xx, 165 ff.* It will at once be seen that Solger, in spite of his speculative energy, does not orient us so much as he disorients us, and that since every intermediate determination is wanting, it becomes extremely difficult to ascertain whether the negations occur correctly. When it is affirmed: 'since God exists or manifests himself in our finitide,' we must first know in what sense God exists in finitude,

---

* Incidentally, Hegel's discussion of the observations of Solger furnish a most interesting contribution to the question: how does Hegel relate to the Christian view.

that is, we here lack the concept of creation. When next it is asserted that he sacrificed himself by existing in finitude, it might seem that creation were being articulated. But if this is what is meant, it is not very clearly expressed. Indeed, it ought to have read: in that God sacrifices himself, he creates. This would seem to be strengthened by the fact that the corresponding predicate affirms that God annihilates himself. When we say that God annihilates himself, we have obviously expressed a negation, but, be it noted, a negation whereby the infinite is rendered finite and concrete. On the other hand, the expression that God sacrifices himself, as well as that God annihilates himself, might tend rather to direct our thought to the atonement. This is reinforced by the very next words: we are nothingness, for here the finite is clearly posited and posited in its finitude, its nothingness, yet it is this nothingness which must be negated, and this negation whereby the infinite is rendered finite. However, we lack the intermediate determinations to show in what sense man is nothingness, intermediate determinations[10] of such a scope that the significance of sin would find a place within this conception. Thus we here have a speculative obscurity according neither the creation nor the atonement, neither finitude nor sin their due. Should we compare this with the statements contained in the letter to Tieck, the same sort of speculative twilight emerges. We here learn that we 'are *nichtige* phenomena because God has assumed existence in us and thereby separated himself from himself.' Here the concept of creation is intimated. But not to mention the fact that the intermediate determinations requisite to maintain the act of creation are wanting, not even the pantheistic thought is distinctly articulated. For it may not properly be said that we are *nichtige* phenomena because God has assumed existence in us. According to the view and terminology of Solger, it ought to be formulated: insofar as God annihilates himself, the nothingness of all finitude comes into existence [*bliver til*]. To say that God assumes existence in this, however, is not to say that God is separated from himself (for he is this in the moment of creation) but in himself, and the nothingness again cancelled. When in the following it is said: 'And is this

not the greatest love: that he has betaken himself to nothingness in order that we might be,' creation and atonement are
again confused and confounded with each other. God has not
betaken himself to nothingness in order that we might be,
for we are nothingness; rather, he has betaken himself to
nothingness in order that we might cease to be nothingness.
As for Solger's attempt to see the love of God in this, it must
be remarked that the intermediate determinations are again
wanting; for the concept of creation must always be given so
that God's love does not become self-love. Solger subsequently
uses still more concrete expressions when he says that God
has sacrificed himself and annihilated his nothingness, killed
his death. With this one must naturally think of the atonement, of the negation of finitude and the return to God and
in God. But as it has been previously affirmed that God
annihilates himself by existing in our finitude, so now we
have had the same expression for both the creation and the
atonement. The expression 'God sacrifices himself' seems
rather difficult to comprehend when it is explained by the
words: he annihilates his nothingness. But the confusion
becomes even greater when we learn that the *Nichtige* in us is
the divine. For we are the *Nichtige*, and how then can the
Nichtige in us be the divine (for this seems to suggest that there
is some 'other' in us not the *Nichtige*). Finally, it is asserted
that we can apprehend the *Nichtige* in ourselves. But should
this mean that we can negate it ourselves through this knowledge, then manifestly we here have a Pelagian concept of
atonement.

What Solger seems vaguely to have grasped throughout this
whole inquiry is the negation of negation containing in itself
the true affirmation. Inasmuch as the whole movement of
thought is never worked out, however, the one negation runs
erroneously into the next, and the true affirmation never
results. Hegel has clearly perceived this and so remarks (p.
470): 'At one point we are presupposed as nothingness (that
which is evil). The harsh, abstract expression: he annihilates
himself, is then predicated of God. Hence it is God who posits
himself as nothingness, and this in order that we might be.

Accordingly, the *Nichtige* in us is called the divine, insofar as we apprehend it as the *Nichtige*.'

Were I to give the reader some idea of the view of Solger, which, by accommodating itself to his favourite concept irony, might in this way perhaps approach him nearest, then I would say that Solger has made God's existence into irony: God posits himself constantly over into nothingness, takes himself back again, then posits himself over once more, etc., a divine pastime which, like all irony, posits the most fearful oppositions. In the enormous oscillation of this double movement (the centrifugal as well as the centripetal) finitude is also a participant, and at the moment of separation man becomes the shadow of the divine, sketching his moral virtues and vices upon this shadow existence as only one with an eye for irony can perceive as nothingness. Now since all finitude is nothingness, the person perceiving it as such by means of irony lends assistance to the divine. Beyond this point I am unable to develop this, since I find no information in Solger about the kind of reality finitude acquires through irony. Solger, to be sure, in certain passages[11] speaks of a mysticism which, when looking towards actuality is the mother of irony, but when looking towards the eternal world is the child of enthusiasm and inspiration. He also mentions an immediate presence of the divine exhibiting itself through the fact that our actuality disappears. But here again we lack the intermediate determinations requisite for any deeper, positive total-view to be constructed of this.

We shall next inquire how Solger carried through his standpoint in the sphere of æsthetics. In this regard he came to the assistance of the romanticists and became the philosophic spokesman for romanticism and romantic irony. Once again we meet the same fundamental view that finitude is a nothingness, that it must be destroyed as an untrue actuality in order for the true to become visible. I have already emphasized the truth this contains, and also tried to show what is abortive in this view. Accordingly, one does not see which actuality is to be destroyed: whether it is an untrue actuality (to this Solger would naturally answer affirmatively, but if this is not to be a mere tautology one must know something more of this untrue actuality), that is to say, whether it is the egotism of the discrete moments which is to be negated in order that the true actuality may become visible, the actuality of mind, not as a beyond but as a present; or whether this divine pastime is, in fact, able to allow any actuality to endure [bestaae]. It is in art[12] and poetry that Solger seems to find the higher actuality that becomes visible through the negation of finite actuality. Here a new difficulty arises: inasmuch as the poetry so frequently alleged by Solger[13] in his correspondence with Tieck to be the highest, romantic poetry, is unable to pacify the negation in this higher actuality, since its essential striving is to bring to consciousness the fact that the given actuality is the imperfect, while the higher actuality only allows itself to be envisaged in the infinite approximation of presentiment and intimation; so it seems necessary once more to relate oneself ironically to every particular production inasmuch as each individual product is but an approximation. To this extent it is evident that the higher actuality to become visible in poetry is nevertheless not in poetry but constantly becoming [vorder]. And here one must not misunderstand me, as if I meant that becoming [Vordelse] were not a necessary moment in the actuality of mind. But true actuality becomes [vorder] what it is, whereas the actuality of romanticism merely becomes [vorder]. Similarly, faith is a victory of the world,[14] yet it is also a struggle; for only when it has striven has it been victorious over the world, although it was victorious before it had striven. Thus faith becomes [bliver] what it is; it is not an eternal struggle but a victory which struggles still. In faith the higher actuality of spirit is not merely becoming [vordende], but present while yet becoming [vorder].

Irony is often mentioned in Solger's lectures on æsthetics, especially in the section dealing with the 'Organism of the Artistic Spirit.'[15] Irony and enthusiasm are there set forth as the two factors necessary for artistic production, the two necessary conditions for the artist. What is to be understood by this will be discussed in its proper place.[16] Here I shall only say that this entire approach essentially belongs to a wholly different standpoint, unless one intends to allow irony to manifest itself in destroying its own work of art, enthusiasm to designate the attitude which intimates a higher.

On the other hand, certain remarks from Solger's review of A. W. Schlegel's *Vorlesungen über dramatische Kunst und Literatur* will here be examined more closely. They are found in the second volume of Solger's posthumous writings.[17] A considerable obscurity prevails in these pages. In certain passages Solger says that irony exhibits itself as a limiting power teaching man to abide in actuality, teaching man to seek his truth in limitation. After protesting on page 514 against the position that irony teaches man to set himself above everything, Solger adds: 'True irony derives from the point of view that so long as man lives in the present world, it is only in this world that he can fulfil his determination, and this in the highest sense of the word [vocation]. The striving for the infinite does not actually lead man beyond this life as the author maintains, but merely into indeterminateness and emptiness. It is inspired, as the author also admits, by the feeling of earthly limitation to which we have been restricted once and for all. Everything by which we think to go beyond finite ends is vain and empty conceit.' This contains a profound truth to which I shall return subsequently, but surely everyone will agree with me when I say that one would sooner have thought it was Goethe who spoke than Solger. Already the following words sound rather curious, therefore, when it is asserted that the highest as well as the lowest in finite existence perish. Indeed, it will not be easy to harmonize this with his previous assertion that man can only fulfil his determination or vocation by limiting himself, unless it be assumed that the vocation of man is merely to perish, a vocation which the person who dissolves himself in infinite vacuity may as easily attain. Yes, he even appears to lend assistance to the divine, while the other seems to place obstacles in the way.

His view of actuality as that which must be destroyed is often mentioned (p. 502): 'The earthly must be consumed as such if we are to apprehend how the eternal and essential is present in it.' It would be of interest to see how far Solger is successful in allowing the higher actuality in art and poetry to manifest itself in truth, to what extent the true repose, according to Solger's conception, occurs in the universe of poetry. I shall include a passage in which Solger discusses our relation to poetry (p. 512): 'If we examine ourselves carefully as to what we perceive in true tragic or comic masterpieces, it is evident that what they have in common, in addition to their dramatic form, is a more internal basis. The whole conflict between the imperfection in man and his higher vocation appears to arise in us as something *Nichtige*, wherein something appears to prevail quite other than this schism alone. We see heroes beginning to wonder whether they have erred in the noblest and finest elements of their feelings and sentiments, not only as regards their successful issue, but even as regards their source and worth. Indeed, what exalts us is the destruction of the best itself, and this not merely because we take refuge in an infinite hope. Moreover, what pleases us in comedy is this same nothingness of human affairs, since this appears to us as the lot to which we have been assigned once and for all. . . . That mood wherein contradictions annihilate themselves and by this comprise our essentiality we call irony, or, in the comic sphere, caprice and humour.' Here it is evident to what extent the negation destructive of actuality is pacified in a higher actuality. We are exalted by the destruction of the best, but this exaltation is of an extremely negative character. It is the exaltation of irony which here fashions itself in similitude with the divine envy, yet which is not only envy of the great and eminent but even of the small and insignificant, thoroughly envious of all finitude. When the great perish in this world this is tragedy, but poetry reconciles us to this by showing us that it is the true which is victorious.[18] It is in this that exaltation and edification consist. We are not exalted by the destruction of the great, we are reconciled to its destruction by the fact that truth is victorious, and we are exalted by its victory. If, however, I see in tragedy merely the destruction of the hero and am exalted by this, if in tragedy I merely become conscious of the nothingness of human affairs, if tragedy pleases me in the same way as comedy: by showing me the nothingness of the great as comedy shows me the nothingness of the small, then, manifestly, the higher actuality is not yet present. Indeed, the author seems not even willing to let that mood remain which affords some presentiment of the higher actuality, for he expressly says that we are exalted by the destruction of the best, and this not merely because we take refuge in an infinite hope. For the more there can be in this migration into infinite hope is merely the happiness residing in the destruction of all things, the desolation and emptiness wherein there is assuredly too much peace.

To summarize what has been advanced concerning Solger, it will appear that his standpoint was irony as he himself designated, except that his irony was of a speculative nature. With Solger infinite absolute negativity is a speculative moment. He has the negation of negation, and yet it is a veil before his eyes preventing him from seeing the affirmation. It is well known that Solger died prematurely, and I shall not attempt to decide whether he would have been successful in consummating the speculative thought grasped by him with so much energy, or whether his energy was not already consumed in asserting negativity. It seems most appropriate to me, however, to regard Solger as a sacrifice for Hegel's positive system.

Irony as a mastered moment.
The truth of irony

It was mentioned in the foregoing that Solger in his lectures on æsthetics makes irony a condition for every artistic production.[1] But in the present context when we say that the poet must relate himself ironically to his poem, this means something other than it meant in the foregoing. Shakespeare has often been praised as the great master of irony, and there can scarcely be any doubt that this is correct. Shakespeare, however, in no wise allows the substantial content to evaporate in an ever more volatile sublimation, and insofar as his lyricism sometimes culminates in madness there is in this madness nevertheless an extraordinary degree of objectivity.[2] Accordingly, when Shakespeare relates himself ironically to his work, this is simply in order to let the objective prevail. Irony is now pervasive, ratifying each particular feature so there is neither too much nor too little, so that everything receives its due, so that the true equilibrium may be effected in the microcosmic situation of the poem whereby it gravitates towards itself. The greater the oppositions involved in this movement, so much the more irony is required to control and master those spirits[3] which obstinately seek to storm forth; while the more irony is present, so much the more freely and poetically does the poet hover above his composition. Irony is not present at some particular point in the poem but omnipresent in it, so that the visible irony in the poem is in turn ironically mastered. Thus irony renders both the poem and the poet free. For this to occur, however, the poet must himself be master over irony. It is not always the case that the poet is master over irony in the actuality to which he belongs merely because he is successful in mastering irony in the moment of artistic production. One is accustomed to say that the personal life of the poet does not concern us, and this is also quite correct. In the present inquiry, however, it will not be inappropriate to bear in mind the disparity in this matter which may often occur.

Add to this that such a disparity acquires ever greater significance the more the poet has not continued in the immediate standpoint of genius. Indeed, the more the poet has departed from this standpoint, the more necessary it becomes for him to have a total-view of the world, and in his own individual existence to be master over irony, that is, the more necessary it becomes for him to be in some measure a philosopher.[4] If this is the case, the particular poetic production will not have a mere external relation to the poet, but he will see in the particular poem a moment in his own development. It was in this respect that Goethe's existence as a poet [Digter-Existents] was so great: he succeeded in making his existence as a poet [Digter-Tilværelse] congrue with his actuality. This again requires irony, but, be it noted, mastered irony.[5] For the romanticist, on the other hand, the particular poetic production is either a darling with which he is wholly infatuated and which he is unable to explain how it has been possible for him to call to life, or it is an object which awakens disgust. Both alternatives are naturally untrue. The truth is that the particular poetic production is simply a moment. For Goethe irony was in the strictest sense a mastered moment, a spirit ministering to the poet. In the first place, the particular poem culminates in itself by means of irony; in the second place, the particular poetic production exhibits itself as a moment, and so his whole existence as a poet [Digter-Existents] culminates in itself by means of irony. As a poet Professor Heiberg represents the same standpoint, for while almost every line he has written affords an example of irony's inner economy in the work, there is also present throughout all his works a self-conscious endeavour to order and assign each particular its place in the whole.[6] Thus irony is here mastered, reduced to a moment: the essence is none other than the phenomenon,

337

the phenomenon none other than the essence;[7] possibility is not so prudish as not to betake itself to actuality, but actuality is possibility. Goethe, both as struggling and as victorious, has always acknowledged this view, has constantly professed this view with an enormous energy.

But what is valid for an existence as a poet [*Digter-Existents*] is to a certain extent also valid in the life of every particular individual. The poet does not live poetically in that he creates a work of poetry, for should this have no conscious and inward relation to him, his life will then lack that inward infinity which is the absolute condition for living poetically (hence one discovers that poetry often vents itself through unhappy individualities, and that the painful annihilation of the poet becomes a condition for the poetic production).[8] On the contrary, the poet only lives poetically when oriented and thus assimilated into the age in which he lives, when he is positively free within the actuality to which he belongs. But to live poetically in this way is attainable for every other individual. The seldom gift, the divine happiness of allowing what is poetically experienced to fashion itself poetically, however, naturally remains the enviable lot of the chosen few.

When irony has been mastered in this way, when the wild infinity wherein it storms consumingly forth has been restrained, it does not follow that it should then lose its significance or be wholly abandoned. On the contrary, when the individual is correctly oriented, and he is this insofar as irony is mastered, only then does irony acquire its proper significance and true validity. In our day there is much talk about the significance of doubt for philosophy,[9] but doubt is for philosophy what irony is for the personal life. As philosophers claim that no true philosophy is possible without doubt, so by the same token one may claim that no authentic human life is possible without irony. When irony has first been mastered it undertakes a movement directly opposed to that wherein it proclaimed its life as unmastered. Irony now limits, renders finite, defines, and thereby yields truth, actuality, and content; it chastens and punishes and thereby imparts stability, character, and consistency. Irony is a disciplinarian feared only by those who do not know it, but cherished by those who do. He who does not understand irony and has no ear for its whisperings lacks *eo ipso* what might be called the absolute beginning of the personal life. He lacks what at moments is indispensable for the personal life, lacks the bath of regeneration and rejuvenation, the cleansing baptism of irony that redeems the soul from having its life in finitude though living boldly and energetically in finitude. He does not know the invigoration and fortification which, should the atmosphere become too oppressive, comes from lifting oneself up and plunging into the ocean of irony, not in order to remain there, of course, but healthily, gladly, lightly to clad oneself again.

Thus when one occasionally hears someone discussing irony with an air of superiority respecting the infinite striving wherein it runs riot, one may well agree with him. But insofar as the speaker is himself unacquainted with the infinity that stirs itself in irony, to this extent his standpoint is not above irony but beneath it and still subject to irony. This is the case wherever one overlooks the dialectic of life. It requires courage not to surrender oneself to the ingenious or compassionate counsels of despair that would induce a man to eliminate himself from the ranks of the living; but it does not follow from this that every huckster who is fattened and nourished in self-confidence has more courage than the man who yielded to despair. It requires courage when sorrow seeks to deceive one, when it would teach one to adulterate all joy into melancholy, all longing into privation, every hope into recollection, I say, it then requires courage to want to be glad; but it does not follow from this that every overgrown child with his insipid smile, his pleasure-drunken eye, has more courage than the man who bowed himself in sorrow and forgot to smile. The same is true of irony. Hence if one must warn against irony as a seducer, one must also praise it as a guide—and precisely in our day one must praise it. In our age philosophy has come into possession of such an enormous result that all can scarcely be right with it. Insights not only into man's secrets but into

God's secrets are sold at such a bargain that it all begins to look rather suspicious. In our joy over the result we have forgotten that a result has no value if it has not actually been acquired. But woe to him who cannot tolerate the fact that irony seeks to balance the accounts! Irony is like the negative way, not the truth but the way.[10] Everyone who has a result merely as such does not possess it, for he has not the way. When irony appears on the scene it brings the way, though not the way whereby one who imagines himself to have a result comes to possess it, but the way whereby the result forsakes him. Add to this that the task of our age must surely be seen to be that of translating the results of philosophy into the personal life, personally to appropriate these results. Hence when philosophy teaches that actuality has absolute validity, it is essential that it in truth acquire validity. For one cannot deny that it would be utterly ludicrous if a person who learned in his youth, perhaps even taught others, that actuality had absolute validity, if such a person, I say, became old and died without actuality having acquired any other validity for him than that season in and season out he had proclaimed the wisdom that actuality had validity. Thus if philosophy mediates all opposites, then it is essential that this abundant actuality in truth become visible. There is a different tendency in our age that exhibits an enormous enthusiasm, and, curiously enough, what excites it seems to be enormously little. How beneficial irony could be here. There is an impatience that would reap before it has sown. By all means let irony chasten it. There is in every personal life so much that must be repudiated, so many wild shoots that must be sheared away. Here again irony is an excellent surgeon. For when irony has been mastered, as previously remarked, its function is then of the utmost importance in order for the personal life to acquire health and truth.

Irony as a mastered moment exhibits itself in its truth precisely by the fact that it teaches us to actualize actuality, by the fact that it places due emphasis upon actuality. This cannot mean that it wishes quite St. Simonistically[11] to idolize actuality, nor does it deny that there is, or at least that there ought to be, in every human being a longing for a higher and more perfect. But this longing must not hollow out actuality; on the contrary, the content of life must become a true and meaningful moment in the higher actuality whose fullness the soul desires. Actuality in this way acquires its validity—not as a purgatory, for the soul is not to be purified in such a way that it flees blank, bare, and stark naked out of life—but as a history wherein consciousness successively outlives itself, though in such a way that happiness consists not in forgetting all this but becomes present in it. Actuality will therefore not be rejected and longing shall be a healthy love, not a cowardly, effeminate ruse for sneaking oneself out of the world. Accordingly, when romanticism longs for a higher, this may well be true; but as man shall not put asunder what God has joined together,[12] so neither shall man join together what God has put asunder, for such a sickly longing is simply an attempt to have the perfect before its time. Thus actuality acquires its validity through action. Yet action must not degenerate into a kind of stupid perseverance, but must have an apriority in itself so as not to become lost in a vacuous infinity.

So much for the practical. In a theoretical regard the essence must exhibit itself as the phenomenon. When irony has been mastered it no longer believes, as do certain clever people in daily life, that something must always be concealed behind the phenomenon. Yet it also prevents all idolatry with the phenomenon, for as it teaches us to esteem contemplation, so it rescues us from the prolixity which holds that to give an account of world history, for example, would require as much time as the world has taken to live through it.

Finally, insofar as there can be any question of the 'eternal validity'[13] of irony, this can only find its answer through an investigation of the sphere of humour. Humour contains a much deeper scepticism than irony, for here it is not finitude but sinfulness that everything turns upon. The scepticism of humour relates to the scepticism of irony as ignorance relates to the old thesis: *credo quia absurdum*;[14] but humour also contains a much deeper positivity than irony, for it does not move itself in humanistic determinations but in the anthropic deter-

APPENDIX

TRANSLATOR'S NOTES

GLOSSARY

INDEX

Appendix

A translation of the Latin formulæ and theses for the oral defence appended to Kierkegaard's original essay, and of his Petition to the King. These were omitted when the book was later published for the general public. See Introduction, pages 38-9.

APPENDIX

Dissertationem hanc inauguralem Philosophorum in Universitate Hafniensi Ordo dignam censuit, quae una cum thesibus adjectis rite defensa auctori gradum Magisterii artium acquirat.

Dabam d. XVI Julii MDCCCXLI

F. C. SIBBERN,
h. a. Decanus fac. philos.

THESES,
DISSERTATIONI DANICAE DE NOTIONE IRONIAE
annexæ
quas
AD JURA MAGISTRI ARTIUM
in Universitate Hafniensi Rite Obtinenda
die xxix Septemb.
hora 10
PUBLICO COLLOQUIO DEFENDERE CONABITUR
SEVERINUS AABYE KIERKEGAARD,
theol. cand.
MDCCCXLI

The Faculty of Philosophy in the University of Copenhagen has declared this inaugural dissertation as worthy of securing the author the degree of Master of Arts, after it, together with the accompanying theses, has been defended in the usual manner.

16th July 1841

F. C. SIBBERN,
Dean of the Fac. of Philos.

THESES,
attached to
THE DANISH DISSERTATION ON THE CONCEPT OF IRONY
which
SØREN AABYE KIERKEGAARD
theological candidate
WILL ENDEAVOUR TO DEFEND PUBLICLY
on 29th September
at 10 o'clock
in order to obtain in the usual manner
THE DEGREE OF MASTER OF ARTS
in the University of Copenhagen
1841

APPENDIX

I. *Similitudo Christum inter et Socratem in dissimilitudine præcipue est posita.*

II. *Xenophonticus Socrates in utilitate inculcanda subsistit, nunquam empiriam egreditur nunquam ad ideam pervenit.*

III. *Si quis comparationem inter Xenophontem et Platonem instituerit, inveniet, alterum nimium de Socrate detraxisse, alterum nimium eum evexisse, neutrum verum invenisse.*

IV. *Forma interrogationis, quam adhibuit Plato, refert negativum illud, quod est apud Hegelium.*

V. *Apologia Socratis, quam exhibuit Plato aut spuria est, aut tota ironice explicanda.*

VI. *Socrates non solum ironia usus est, sed adeo fuit ironiæ deditus, ut ipse illi succumberet.*

VII. *Aristophanes in Socrate depingendo proxime ad verum accessit.*

VIII. *Ironia, ut infinita et absoluta negativitas, est levissima et maxime exigua subjectivitatis significatio.*

IX. *Socrates omnes æquales ex substantialitate tanquam ex naufragio nudos expulit, realitatem subvertit, idealitatem eminus prospexit, attigit non occupavit.*

X. *Socrates primus ironiam introduxit.*

XI. *Recentior ironia inprimis ad ethicen revocanda est.*

XII. *Hegelius in ironia describenda modo ad recentiorem non ita ad veterem attendit.*

XIII. *Ironia non tam ipsa est sensus expers, tenerioribus animi motibus destituta, quam ægritudo habenda ex eo, quod alter quoque potiatur eo, quod ipsa concupierit.*

XIV. *Solgerus non animi pietate commotus, sed mentis invidia seductus, quum negativum cogitare et cogitando subigere nequiret, acosmismum effecit.*

XV. *Ut a dubitatione philosophia sic ab ironia vita digna, quæ humana vocetur, incipit.*

I. The similarity between Christ and Socrates consists essentially in dissimilarity.

II. The Xenophontic Socrates is content to emphasize the useful; he never goes beyond the empirical, never arrives at the Idea.

III. If one makes a comparison between Xenophon and Plato, one will find that the first takes too much from Socrates, the second adds too much to him; neither of them found the truth.

IV. The form of the question employed by Plato corresponds to the negative in Hegel.

V. Socrates' apology, as presented by Plato, is either spurious, or else to be explained wholly ironically.

VI. Socrates did not merely use irony, but was so completely dedicated to irony that he himself succumbed to it.

VII. Aristophanes has come very close to the truth in his portrayal of Socrates.

VIII. Irony as infinite and absolute negativity is the lightest and weakest intimation of subjectivity.

IX. Socrates drove all his contemporaries out of substantiality as if naked from a shipwreck, undermined actuality, envisaged ideality in the distance, touched it, but did not acquire it.

X. Socrates was the first to introduce irony.

XI. The recent manifestations of irony are primarily to be subsumed under ethics.

XII. Hegel in his characterization of irony has considered only the modern, not so much the ancient form.

XIII. Irony is not so much apathy, divested of all tender emotions of the soul; instead, it is more like vexation over the fact that others also enjoy what it desires for itself.

XIV. Solger adopted acosmism not out of piety, but seduced by envy because he could not think the negative nor subdue it by thought.

XV. As philosophy begins with doubt, so also that life which may be called worthy of man begins with irony.[1]

PETITION TO THE KING

To the King!

The undersigned ventures to appear before Your Majesty with the humble petition for permission to present his essay prepared for the master's degree 'On the Concept of Irony with Constant Reference to Socrates' in the mother tongue, yet so that Latin theses be appended to the same and that the oral defence be conducted in Latin.

2nd June 1841, Copenhagen.

Søren Aabye Kierkegaard, candidate in theology with *Laudabilis* from June, 1840, respectfully seeks permission to present his essay prepared for the master's degree 'On the Concept of Irony with Constant Reference to Socrates' in the mother tongue, yet so that there be appended to the same Latin theses and that the oral defence be conducted in Latin.

6th June 1841

In respectfully venturing to direct Your Majesty's royal attention to this my petition, it is principally with the idea that by royal favour a similar dispensation has been allowed both Mag. Hammerich and Mag. Adler which gives me courage to hope, and this so much the more since the external circumstances appear to be wholly uniform. As for the subject which I have undertaken to discuss, the concept of irony, to be sure, belongs in a sense to antiquity, but it essentially belongs to it only insofar as the modern age takes its beginning with it, so that the apprehension of this concept must in the strictest sense be claimed by modernity. Add to this that this concept has most recently asserted itself in a wealth of individual manifestations. Accordingly, its appearance in our time must also come in for discussion. In this connection, I shall permit myself respectfully to call Your Majesty's attention to how difficult, indeed impossible, it would be to discuss this subject exhaustively in the language which has thus far been that of scholarship, not to mention that the free and personal presentation would suffer too much. But as the nature of the subject must recommend this my application, so I hope by my examinations, all of which have been completed with the best character and the *Examen philologico-philosophorum* with distinction, to have given evidence of being in possession of sufficient competence in the language of scholarship that I may not be regarded as having made myself unworthy of such a dispensation. In addition, I have for some time occupied myself with teaching the Latin language and thereby had occasion not to forget what I have learned but perhaps even to learn more. In this connection, I shall permit myself to include a copy of a confirmatory letter from Hr. Professor Nielsen, Director of the Borgerdyd's Gymnasium.

Your Majesty's most humble and loyal subject,
SØREN AABYE KIERKEGAARD,
Candidate in Theology

Translator's Notes

In preparing the notes to accompany this English translation, I have availed myself of the Danish notes of A. B. Drachmann, editor of the essay in *Samlede Værker*, and the German notes of E. Hirsch, translator of the most recent German edition of the essay. In this connection, I wish to thank dr. phil. A. G. Drachmann and cand. jur. G. M. Drachmann, Copenhagen, and Prof. E. Hirsch and the firm of Eugen Diederichs Verlag, Düsseldorf-Köln, respectively, for generous permission to make extensive use of this material. In the case of bibliographical, historical, and interpretive notes merely reproduced in translation, I have indicated my indebtedness by appending (D) or (H) to the note to signify the source as Drachmann or Hirsch respectively. The use of an occasional note by other editors is acknowledged without abbreviation. It has not been possible to verify all bibliographical references, especially in the case of older Danish material. All references to Kierkegaard's *Samlede Værker* (cited by volume and page) are to the second edition, Copenhagen, 1920-36; while references to Kierkegaard's *Papirer* (cited by volume and entry) are to the second edition, Copenhagen, 1909-48. The German references to Hegel's *Werke* (cited by volume and page) are to the *Jubiläumsausgabe*, Stuttgart, re-issued in 1958.

Historical Introduction (pages 7-41)

1. Georg Brandes, *Søren Kierkegaard. En kritisk Fremstilling i Grundrids*, Copenhagen, 1877, p. 187. Brandes also mentions that Kierkegaard's only close friend at that time, Emil Boesen, related that it was during the composition of the essay on irony that Kierkegaard came to clarity about what he wanted and was able to do in the world (p. 59).

2. At the risk of giving a one-sided and distorted picture of much significant scholarship, I shall here include a brief survey of some of the highlights of previous interpretation of the essay on irony for those who might find it helpful. The fact that the essay would eventually have to be dealt with seriously was clear when **A. B. Drachmann** argued ('Hedenskab og Christendom hos S. K.,' in *Udvalgte Afhandlinger*, Copenhagen, 1911, pp. 124-40) that Kierkegaard's grasp of the specifically Christian dimension on such questions as dogma, authority, and community was a consequence of his appreciation for Socrates and the Socratic ignorance which isolates and equalizes the individual, and that Kierkegaard's view of a paradoxical

Christianity was derived, as it were, from a commitment to 'paganism.' While the figure of Socrates was here recognized as crucial for understanding Kierkegaard, it was nevertheless the Socrates of *Philosophical Fragments* and the *Postscript* that interested scholars. The decisive rejection of the essay came at the hands of **Harald Høffding** when he practically ignored it in *Søren Kierkegaard som Filosof*, Copenhagen, 1892. In *Den Store Humor*, Copenhagen, 1916, he further dismissed the essay by maintaining that Kierkegaard was here so influenced by the Hegelian oriented speculation of the period that it caused him to misunderstand completely the positive character of Socratic irony so that the portrait of Socrates in the essay had to be subsequently corrected. This same Hegelian allegiance was also responsible for misreading the social situation within which the irony of Friedrich Schlegel, according to Høffding, appeared as beneficial (p. 64*ff*.). In **Vilhelm Andersen's** substantial study of Humanism in Danish letters (*Tider og Typer af Dansk Aands Historie*, first series, part two, vol. II, Copenhagen, 1916, pp. 65-108) we again have a more appreciative view of the essay wherein he finds all the fundamental ideas of the entire authorship already present. There are two ways into Kierkegaard: with Socrates where he began, or with Christianity where he ended. Socrates remains the type for Kierkegaard's intellectual relationship to Humanism and to the world. Nor is the Hegelianism of the essay ignored by Andersen, for Kierkegaard, like his whole generation, found that for them the 'way to the Greeks' went through Hegel, and he sees the *Phenomenology of Mind* behind Kierkegaard's earliest projects as the search for types with which to represent and embody the stages of consciousness in still more concrete form than in Hegel. A significant breakthrough occurred, however, when **Torsten Bohlin** asserted (*Søren Kierkegaards etiska åskådning*, Stockholm, 1918, pp. 12, 29) that Kierkegaard's relation to Hegelian speculation as well as to romanticism was, in Kierkegaard's own sense of the term, dialectical. 'His struggle to liberate his contemporaries from the diluting effect on actual problems and tasks in life both on the part of Hegelian speculation and romanticism is essentially his own struggle to emancipate himself, and one which he achieves for the sake of his own personality.' In the essay on irony Bohlin finds a double polemic, finds that Kierkegaard uses romanticism polemically against Hegel, and Hegel polemically against romanticism. The real significance of the essay, however, is not its value as a scholarly work, but as a mirror for the young Kierkegaard's intellectual personality.'

In the dissertation of **Jens Himmelstrup** (*Søren Kierkegaards Opfattelse af Sokrates*, Copenhagen, 1924, pp. 9, 11, 69, 80, 107, 172, 174*ff*.) the problem is squarely faced for the first time. While 'Socrates' is one of the three most important themes throughout Kierkegaard's writings, the fact remains that its most extensive treatment is to be found in the early academic essay on irony. The work is discussed in its own terms and as part of an effort to trace the development and ramifications of this theme. Himmelstrup shows that while new moments are subsequently added to the initial portrait of Socrates, and while the nature of this development is generally from negativity towards greater positivity, viewed formally, Kierkegaard continues to conceive the standpoint of Socrates as irony. The concept of irony therefore undergoes a similar development. The Hegelianism of the essay is thoroughly discussed and for the first time acquires real substance, for Himmelstrup steadfastly argues that the essay discloses that Kierkegaard, while an opponent of the system as such, was at this time nevertheless committed to the Hegelian ethic, the essay itself being written from such an ethical standpoint. The essay, no less than any of his other works, relates intimately to his personality, his whole situation in life being such that he sought theoretical support from Hegel for a practical problem. It follows from Himmelstrup's argument that Kierkegaard changed this personal commitment to the Hegelian ethic soon after defending the essay on irony (after the final rupture with Regine Olsen) to embrace the ethical individualism he so consistently developed throughout his subsequent writings. In this interpretation the excessive Hegelian detail of the essay becomes intelligible, though Himmelstrup goes on to show that there remain significant differences between the Socrates of Hegel and Kierkegaard, permitting them to be distinguished. The attitude of **Eduard Geismar** (*Søren Kierkegaard. Livsudvikling og Forfatter-virksomhed*, 2 vols., Copenhagen, 1926-27, pt. 1, pp. 95-103) towards the Hegelianism of the essay is essentially one of puzzlement. He begins by remarking that it is 'extremely curious that in the master's essay Kierkegaard still moves mainly within an Hegelian framework,' both formally in the arrangement of the chapters (the conception of Socrates' standpoint as irony made possible, actual, and necessary), and in its content as well: the entire discussion is based on the Hegelian principle that there are negative critical ages, yet such a negativity is the cunning of the Idea in preparation for a deeper and truer formation. The age of Socrates was one such critical age, and he himself negatively incarnated. The reason this arch-Hegelianism is so curious, according to Geismar, is because 'we know that two years previously Kierkegaard had renounced Hegelianism. As early as 1835 he knew that within the total-view sought by the modern Faust there was no room for Christianity; and in 1838 he had made up his mind that paradox is higher than philosophy, which relates to it merely as propædeutic.' Geismar then raises the question: 'How, then, can he in 1840-41 have fallen back into Hegelianism?' He rejects Himmelstrup's explanation as insufficient and proposes his own: Kierkegaard's thought contained two levels, a Humanistic level and a Christian level, and that the former moves within an Hegelian framework. The essay on irony is limited to expressing this single dimension of his thought with the Christian level only perceptible through an occasional hint. Kierkegaard's own position at the time was such a partial Hegelianism, a positive Idealism together with reservations for the dimensions of sin and grace. **Emanuel Hirsch** (*Kierkegaardstudien*, 2 vols., Gütersloh, 1930-33) rejects the postulate of a radical shift in Kierkegaard's development between 1838 and 1840, and finds an essential agreement between the standpoint in his first book, *From the Papers of One Still Living* (1838), and the essay on irony, particularly in the relation between his æsthetic theories and his ethical-religious views. As for the Hegelianism of the essay, Hirsch takes the position that in spite of the Hegelian detail ('so pervasive that without a parallel reading of Hegel's discussion of Socrates and pronouncements on irony an incorrect image of Kierkegaard's intellectual independence must result,' vol. II, p. 146), Kierkegaard was in no significant sense an Hegelian. The use of the dialectical triad is kept within the limits set by an affirmation of freedom, personality, and the miracle of grace. Against the pro-Hegelian statements of the essay Hirsch matches anti-Hegelian statements from the essay, reinforced by passages from the Journal (p. 135*ff*.). Kierkegaard's own standpoint at the time was that of the speculative theism of Karl Daub and I. H. Fichte. As for the thorough rejection of romanticism evidenced in the essay, Hirsch posits a positive reappraisal of romanticism in its relation to Christianity immediately after the essay and already enacted in *Either/Or* (1842).

In the post-war discussion of the essay, **Pierre Mesnard** (*Le vrai visage du Kierkegaard*, Paris, 1948) popularized the hypothesis that the essay on irony was itself an ironic work. Mesnard reaches back to the insight of Torsten Bohlin that the work has its own dialectic, and that Kierkegaard has allowed Hegel and the romantics reciprocally to negate or determine each other. According to Mesnard, Hegel represented the 'seriousness' of rational thought for the young Kierkegaard, and he willingly embraced him as a weapon against the 'cult of the flesh' he perceived in Schlegel's *Lucinde*. But as to what this seriousness ultimately entails, Mesnard finds that Kierkegaard once more identifies it with a 'poetic existence' which, unlike that of the romantics, 'endeavours to realize itself in an authentic personality.' He concludes his discussion of the essay and the issue of its Hegelianism by recalling the view of Wilhelm Kütemeyer, translator of the essay into German (1929), who concluded that in the master's essay 'the examination turns out badly for Hegel,' and who suspected a concealed perfidy on the part of this 'innocent candidate' whose attitude he, too, deemed ironic. In an effort to concretize the irony, Kütemeyer simply holds with the consensus that the work contains Kierkegaard's most personal views at that time, but finds it somehow ironic that he should have submitted them to the faculty in the form of an academic essay. Mesnard finds it doubly ironic that the representatives of Hegelian philosophy and bourgeoise society should have voted for its approval. Unfortunately, Mesnard's discussion leaves the erroneous impression that the work was submitted to a pro-Hegelian faculty (just as Kierkegaard's subsequent writings often give the modern reader the mistaken impression that he was surrounded by a sea of Hegel enthusiasts, the only opponent of Hegel in the entire realm—which is merely to say that he was an effective polemicist and to this extent writing for a limited public). This view of Kierkegaard's local intellectual milieu prevailed until 1957, when Niels Thulstrup ('Kierkegaards Verhältnis zu Hegel,' in *Theologische Zeitschrift*, Basel, 1957) supplied the historical information needed to correct this tendency. He writes: 'If one considers the clergy as a whole, the bishops with J. P. Mynster as guiding personality, the only theological faculty in the country at that time (Copenhagen), the original thinker N. F. S. Grundtvig (1783-1872) and the circle of young, often able but argumentative theologians who surrounded him, or if one will consider the faculty of philosophy, in this respect quite significant, or even the Danish poets and wits from the 1830s and 40s; then one will always arrive at the result that there is to be found only one single representative spokesman for Hegelianism in the strict sense (ignoring, of course, the usual partisans, factionists, and unindependent epigones)—and that is J. L. Heiberg.' The latter, of course, was not one of Kierkegaard's academic readers and never affiliated with the University of Copenhagen, whose faculty was generally oriented against the Hegelian philosophy. Paul Martin Møller had made a conscientious study of Hegel which culminated in an open disavowal of Hegelianism, while Sibbern, head of the department of philosophy, wrote a substantial critique of Hegelian principles in 1838, for which his published works were conspicuously consigned to the satirical Hell in Heiberg's poem 'A Soul After Death. An Apocalyptical Comedy' (1840). Generally speaking, a clearly anti-Hegelian contribution by the young Kierkegaard would have been welcomed by Sibbern and the faculty. And yet to discuss the historical issue of Hegelianism in Denmark apart from Kierkegaard's contribution is like discussing the conquest of Gaul without Cæsar. If the conflict began with Heiberg, Møller, Sibbern, and Mynster, it was only resolved in the next generation with Heiberg, Martensen, Nielsen, and Kierkegaard. Strategically, it might be worth remarking that Sibbern, when reminiscing about the young Kierkegaard, clearly regarded him as a disciple of Hegel during this period, a judgment undoubtedly influenced to some extent by his appraisal of the essay on irony—a judgment shared by three generations of Copenhagen philosophers.

Hermann Diem's important study of Kierkegaard's dialectic naturally makes the discussion of Socrates in the essay on irony its point of departure. As this work is now available in English (*Kierkegaard's Dialectic of Existence,*

Edinburgh and London, Oliver and Boyd, 1959), I need not venture upon a summary here. **Wilhelm Anz** ('Die religiöse Unterscheidung,' in *Symposium Kierkegaardianum*, Copenhagen, 1955) has accepted the suggestion of Mesnard that the essay is ironical, and appears to want to remedy Kierkegaard's omission of the essay from his 'authorship' by applying the perspective of *The Point of View*, as it were, that the æsthetic works are only to be understood by reference to the religious production. For he argues that Kierkegaard—in direct opposition to the pervasive interpenetration of the æsthetic and religious spheres so characteristic of Idealism—is vitally concerned to distinguish and differentiate the religious from the æsthetic. As his æsthetic views are essentially those of his age, however, the differentiation occurs in two distinct phases, and that the first is best represented by the section of the essay on irony entitled 'Irony As a Mastered Moment,' where Kierkegaard, according to Anz, forms an alliance with German classicism in the figure of Goethe (who by virtue of possessing a *Lebensanschauung* is deemed a master of irony) in opposition to the victims of irony in the struggle against the nihilistic consequences of the age of reflection. For Anz the 'sovereign irony of Kierkegaard is to be seen in the fact that in the essay on irony he does not go beyond his provisional union with Goethe. It suffices to show that the delimitation of infinite subjectivity is a task which the incipient *Existenzdialektiker* can refer to the classical poet. Such a conclusion, which poses the problem in its most acute form for the author, though still concealed from the reader, is wholly commensurate with the polemical geniality of Kierkegaard. Goethe as vanquisher of the Socratic *aporie*—this thought seen in the perspective of a dialectic of existence advances against a wholly ironic background.' The essay then closes by alluding to this ironic background under the rubric 'the eternal validity of irony.' At this point one almost thinks of Geismar's puzzlement in the wake of Himmelstrup's conclusions, for it is the case with Goethe no less than Hegel that Kierkegaard keeps up a running negative critique against Goethe both before and after the essay on irony. **Edo Pivčević** has recently held (*Ironie als Daseinsform bei Søren Kierkegaard*, Gütersloh, 1960, pp. 48-52) that the central problem throughout Kierkegaard's production derives from his romantic heritage, the problem of overcoming the ethical solipsism latent in romantic individualism. Naturally, the essay on irony becomes central in determining this dominant concern. According to Pivčević, 'the main purpose of the dissertation was the polemic against the Socratic-romantic nothingness; and only on a subordinate level, in various veiled allusions, does the polemic against the nothingness of absolute speculation (Hegel) assert itself.' Finally, **E. Hirsch** in his German translation of the essay (1961), has recently argued that the plan for the essay on irony was conceived as early as 1837, and the first third actually written in 1838. One is convinced that Hirsch is right on this point by his argument that

Kierkegaard was simply involved in too many demanding pursuits during 1840-41 to have written the whole of such an essay in the eleven months available, and that the essay itself exhibits a marked bifurcation of style between its two parts. While the style of the earliest sections does not quite reproduce the intricate syntax of the first book (138), as Hirsch suggests, it is true that if one omits the section on Solger in Part Two there is a recognizable development of style throughout the essay. It is probably true, as Billeskov Jansen pointed out in 1951 (*Studier i Søren Kierkegaards Litterære Kunst*, Copenhagen, 1951, pp. 14, 15) that from the beginning Kierkegaard had two styles: the one extremely formal, rather artificial, and distinguished mostly by its tortuous syntax and unbearable to read; the other a more intimate, conversational style reserved for his Journal. The essay would thus exhibit the gradual enactment of a resolve to make the latter the style of his published work. It is true, as Hirsch points out, that by the end of the essay on irony we have seen the birth of Kierkegaard as a mature writer.

In the course of this obviously superficial sketch of previous interpretations, disclosing as it does such divers opinions, many a reader will no doubt have entertained the suspicion that Kierkegaard was perhaps performing as his own pseudonym when writing the essay on irony.

3. Cf. *Postscript*, pp. 449, 275 (VII, 493 297).

4. Cf. *Papirer*, X^3 A 477: '*A Passage in My Dissertation.* Influenced as I was by Hegel and whatever was modern, without sufficient maturity truly to appreciate what was great, I have somewhere in my dissertation been unable to refrain from taxing Socrates with the imperfection that he had no eye for the totality but merely regarded the individual numerically. —Oh, what a Hegelian fool I was! Precisely this is positive proof for how great an ethicist Socrates really was.' Cf. also *Papirer*, X^2 A 108.

5. *Berlingske Tidende*, nr. 227, 29th September 1841; *Dagen*, nr. 227-8, 29th, 30th September 1841.

6. Cf. 'Om den menneskelige Frihed,' in *Prosaiske Skrifter*, vol. 1, pp. 1-110. On the occasion of a controversy between Professor Howitz and an anonymous reviewer on the juridical problem of arriving at a satisfactory legal definition of insanity and responsibility, Heiberg, as Lecturer in Danish language and literature in the University of Kiel, seized the opportunity to reconcile the opposing standpoints by means of the Hegelian philosophy which he had recently appropriated. The essay was originally published in Kiel in December 1824, and was the first published exposition of Hegelian principles in Danish.

7. *Fædrelandet*, nr. 890, 897, 29th May 1842, 5th June 1842. The essay was also accorded an anonymous review in the *Corsair*, nr. 51, 22nd October, 1841.

8. *Fædrelandet*, nr. 904, 12th June 1842. Cf. *Samlede Værker*, XIII, 433-42. The tone of Kierkegaard's ironic reply to A. F. Beck effectively served to remove the essay from further public discussion.

9. Weltzer, 'Omkring Søren Kierkegaards Disputats,' in *Kierkehistoriske Samlinger*, sjette Række, sjette Bind, Copenhagen, G. E. C. Gads Forlag, 1948-50, pp. 284-311.

10. It is often asserted in Scandinavian Kierkegaard literature that Paul Martin Møller had let it be known that he wanted Kierkegaard to succeed him as Professor of Philosophy in the University of Copenhagen.

11. The brevity of Martensen's reply contrasts markedly with the detailed comments of the other academic readers, a fact which does not emerge sufficiently from the excerpts cited above.

12. These studies receive considerable impetus from the *Søren Kierkegaard Selskabet* in Copenhagen, which effectively provides a scholarly framework for stimulating and communicating the independent researches of students of Kierkegaard everywhere. The intimate relationship between Kierkegaard's individual writings and specific conceptual problems, historical contexts, and literary forms acquired new emphasis in the post-war era with F. J. Billeskov Jansen's editing of the texts in *Kierkegaards Værker i Udvalg*, 4 vols., 1950, and his informative *Søren Kierkegaards litterære Kunst*, 1951. This new historical orientation has been most successfully carried on by Niels Thulstrup, the indefatigable secretary of the Kierkegaard Society, with his excellent editions of Kierkegaard's *Breve og Aktstykker*, 1953-54, *Philosophiske Smuler*, 1955, *Søren Kierkegaards Bibliotek*, 1955, *Frygt og Bæven*, 1961, *Afsluttende uvidenskabelig Efterskriftet*, 1962, and his valuable notes to the Hegner Verlag edition of Kierkegaard's works in German, etc. Lars Bejerholm's Swedish dissertation, *Meddelelsens Dialektik*, 1962, is another substantial contribution to this orientation with respect to the historical-conceptual background for Kierkegaard's theory of communication. It is still to be hoped that one or more of the many scholars contributing to this detailed historical research will soon make available a volume, suitable for translation into the major languages, bringing together the relevant historical information necessary to view Kierkegaard in his immediate, Danish cultural milieu. This remains a serious gap in Kierkegaard studies that only Danish scholarship can fill, and one which it may be said to owe not only its greatest thinker but the rest of us interested in learning from him.

13. J. L. Heiberg, *Samlede Prosaiske Skrifter*, 11 vols., Copenhagen, 1861. Cf. vol. 1, pp. 381-436. After identifying the present age as 'the place of crisis' and the younger generation as clearly 'Faustian,' Heiberg goes on to affirm that only philosophy (Hegelian) can order the present chaos. It is the function of representative men, poets, religious teachers, and philosophers 'to hold up a mirror in which humanity may see itself and become

conscious of itself as its own object' (p. 391). Here, then, is the significance of Hegel and Goethe: 'Goethe and Hegel are undeniably the two greatest men the modern age has produced. No one else deserves so much to be called the representatives of our age. In their work the entire intellectual life of our time is concentrated as the past and present, the future in unity with the past' (p. 417).

14. Cf. Carl Roos, *Kierkegaard og Goethe*, p. 75.

15. Cf. *Papirer, I C 83*, p. 236; *II A 163*.

16. I am indebted to Fru Kamma Brun Roos for kind permission to quote extensively from Professor Roos' penetrating analysis of Kierkegaard's relation to Goethe.

17. Moreover, the clarification of his personal relationships, the reconciliation with his father, his subsequent religious conversion, the painful years of repentance, the cognitive labours of reconstruction, and the attempt to realize the universal, etc., all follow immediately in the wake of this event and may be said to be a function of such an experience of total crisis. In Kierkegaard's mature thought it becomes the decisive category of 'the repulse.' Incidentally, such crises are encountered repeatedly during this period of cultural history among intellectuals of almost every persuasion.

18. Roos, *op. cit.*, p. 102.

19. The reduplication by Martensen of Kierkegaard's own conception of Faust appears less coincidental within a Danish context if one takes seriously, as did both Kierkegaard and Martensen, Heiberg's Goethean-Hegelian synthesis mentioned above. Nor is the claim altogether without substance. In his first major work, *The Phenomenology of Mind*, pp. 135-6 (II, 71), Hegel describes the consummated scepticism of the dialectical method from the point of view of natural consciousness as the negative way, 'the doubt unto despair.' What this coincidence does argue, it seems to me, is that Kierkegaard was into Hegel's *Phenomenology* much earlier than is ordinarily believed (Hirsch, Thulstrup, etc.), a fact which is sufficiently warranted by the Gillileie Journal with its conscious allusions and literary echoes. Cf. *Papirer, I A 72*, pp. 46, 47, *et passim*.

20. The possibility of direct influence ('plagiarism' is too strong an expression since neither had published anything on the subject yet) is also discussed by Professor Roos, *op. cit.*, pp. 124-5. Technically, it was possible for Faust as 'the personified doubt' to have entered their free discussions in the spring of 1834, especially in connection with the problems of predestination and grace (the earliest theme in Kierkegaard's Journal and one he underscores in the folk book when Faust discusses it with the devil). Faust was, after all, paradigmatic for an individuality on the 'way to perdition' for both these theological students. The possibility remains technically open that Kierkegaard might have got the idea from Martensen as well.

21. *Papirer, II B 1-21*.

22. It is the nature of such an 'incipient subjectivity,' according to Hegel, that it: '. . . turns away from the existence which confronts it with passionate indignation, or more subtle wit and more frosty bitterness, and either is wroth with or scorns a world which gives the lie direct to its abstract notions of virtue and truth . . . retaining with discontent the existing discord between the writer's own state of mind and its abstract principles and the empirical reality which mocks them.' (*Philosophy of Fine Art*, vol. II, p. 276).

23. This passage derives from the unpublished but completed draft of a polemical answer to Hans Christian Andersen's play 'En Comoedie i det Grønne,' performed in Copenhagen on 13th May and 8th November and published on 26th October 1840. The situation was as follows. Kierkegaard's first small book, *From the Papers of One Still Living* (1838), in the course of an examination of recent trends in Danish literature, makes a devastating attack on H. C. Andersen as a novelist. The work discloses a thorough grasp of Hegelian principles personally appropriated, but oriented critically against Hegel's followers. The syntax is so labyrinthian, however, that local wits had it that only Andersen and Kierkegaard had read it cover to cover. Two years later Andersen wrote the above comedy wherein an affected character cast as an Hegelian, a barber, is given whole passages from Kierkegaard's book to recite from the stage of the Royal Theatre with the young Kierkegaard in attendance. Some time between 26th and 31st October Kierkegaard composed an answer to Andersen in the form of a newspaper article entitled: 'Just a Moment, Hr. Andersen' (*Papirer, III B 1*, pp. 105-10). Stylistically, the piece is as perfect an example of satirical irony and calculated insult as Kierkegaard ever penned, but as Andersen left Copenhagen on 31st October, it remained unpublished. Cf. also *Papirer, III B 192*, p. 231, 232.

THE CONCEPT OF IRONY

Part 1: The standpoint of Socrates conceived as irony

Introduction (pages 47-50)

1. The words 'progress,' 'appearance,' and 'manner' are all translations of the single Danish noun *Fremtræden*. The essay begins with a rhetorical question which must be rendered in English as a conditional sentence. To make the sentence properly suggestive I have deemed it best to render this word with its several distinct meanings.

2. Throughout the present translation 'genial' is used in its now almost archaic sense as an adjective for the noun genius.

3. *fœminini generis*, of the feminine gender. While I have ordinarily

eliminated such obvious Latin phrases from the translation, it was deemed unsuitable in the present case because the use of Latin in his opening paragraphs is a recognizable feature of Kierkegaard's literary style, cf. *Philosophical Fragments*, *Postscript*, etc. Niels Thulstrup once made the point that Kierkegaard's initial paragraphs resemble musical overtures orchestrated with a strong brass section and a brisk tempo.

4. The only surviving draft of any part of the essay is a fragment corresponding to these first two sentences. Although the imagery is somewhat expanded, it contains no significant differences in meaning. Cf. *Papirer*, *III B 12*.

5. See Howard Hong's helpful discussion of the terms *Tilblivelse* and *blive til* in his preface to *Philosophical Fragments*, 2nd edition, Princeton University Press, 1962, pp. xii-xiv. Cf. also *Papirer*, *II A 305, 528*.

6. Cf. the last sentence of the 'Introduction' to Hegel's *Phenomenology of Mind*, p. 145 (II, 80).

7. There is an ambiguity in the original which does not come through in English: the word *forklarede* means 'transfigured' but more often 'explained.' Hegel, too, made full use of this ambiguity with its theological overtones.

8. Kierkegaard means Socrates' own age, the several conceptions of Socrates at the hands of his own contemporaries.

9. Cf. Appendix, thesis x.

10. In this translation 'other' signifies a quasi technical term which Kierkegaard took over from Hegel (through Heiberg). Apart from the section of Hegel's logic dealing with *Etwas* as a moment in the explication of finitude, and certain parts of the Doctrine of Essence, the term ideally occurs in Hegel, as in Kierkegaard, without calling attention to itself. It has seemed best to apprise the English reader of its Hegelian associations by means of half-quotes whenever such associations are either important to the full meaning of the text or where its presence otherwise detracts from a more natural locution.

11. The word *Mellemværende* literally means a 'being between,' an issue or affair concerning the internal relationship between two persons, unsettled business of economic or other sort, a reckoning or accounting, an unresolved point of dispute, or a common concern shared by two parties. As early as 1838 it appears to be a term pregnant with subjective meaning for Kierkegaard (cf. the letter to Emil Boesen in *Breve og Aktstykker*, edited by Niels Thulstrup, vol. I, p. 41). In the present context it signifies the objective issue between two personified disciplines. Throughout the essay on irony it appears to gain in significance when related to another noun coined by Kierkegaard to sound almost like it, viz., *Mellemhverandre*. The latter literally means 'between each other,' but, being original with Kierkegaard, its meaning is best derived by observing its several contexts. *Mellem-*

værende occurs in this translation on pp. 48, 73, 139; while *Mellemhverandre* occurs on pp. 176n., 205n., 308. That the latter term is also pregnant with subjective meaning for Kierkegaard may be seen from the fact that the work we now know as *Fear and Trembling* was entitled in an early draft simply *Mellemhverandre*, and a marginal note explained the meaning of the title as 'movements and postures,' cf. *Papirer, IV B 78, II A 799, III A 94, 96.* The first occurrence of the term in the present essay (p. 176n.) throws considerable light on some of its internal associations. It appears in a passage contrasting the consolidating movement of personality with the dispersing effect of sophistry, a passage contrasting the isolation of the ironist Socrates with an infinite company of Sophists, more specifically, to describe the infinite series of movements and postures traversed in a humming and buzzing confusion of a swarm of phantastical insects (it is similarly used in a passage from Kierkegaard's first published book: *From the Papers of One Still Living,* S. V. xiii, 68, 69n.). Both terms, in other words, enter Kierkegaard's subjective terminology about the same time, just as in the present essay the one is like the echo of the other. The unity of both, taken literally, is therefore a 'being between each other.' The two terms appear to be the conceptual rendering of two juxtaposed aspects of Kierkegaard's early formulation of the problem of indirect communication.

12. This is an obvious innuendo at Hegel's logic which represents itself as beginning without any presupposition, with pure Being. Cf. *Science of Logic,* vol. i, p. 79*ff.* (iv, 69*ff.*).

13. *prius,* prior, the first of two (parts). Kierkegaard has the term, philosophically, from Hegel, cf. *Science of Logic,* vol. i, p. 80 (iv, 70) *et passim.*

14. 'This statement of the relation between philosophy and history formally derives from the influence of Karl Daub. Cf. E. Hirsch, *Kierkegaardstudien,* vol. ii (1933), p. 539*ff.*' (H). Daub, of course, was a leading right-wing Hegelian.

15. Cf. Vergil, *Aeneid,* vi, 703*ff.*

16. *Hebrews* 4 : 12.

17. As Plato had defined knowledge as an identity of the knower and the known, and Kant as the conjunction of concepts and precepts, so the same general conception may be expressed in Hegelian terminology (but now radically extended to a knowledge of the historical past) as the unity of the concept with the phenomenon. The wry humour of Kierkegaard's opening paragraph is to be seen in the fact that in representing such a presumed organic unity by the image of the medieval knight and his lady, wherein the philosophical knight is first congratulated and then cajoled into behaving himself, something of Kierkegaard's own reservations towards Hegel's historical method may be suspected. As the essay progresses the initial humour will increasingly be seen to be part of an ironic

parody on the entire conception, as already in the next sentence the ground is being laid for one of Kierkegaard's constant gripes throughout the essay, viz., that Hegel (*sic*) has 'failed to conceive the concept' of irony, for in becoming 'infatuated' with the phenomenon nearest him, i.e., romantic irony, he has wholly neglected the original phenomenon of Socratic irony. See above pp. 282-3.

18. Cf. Hegel, *Science of Logic*, vol. II, pp. 241, 242 (v, 45); Heiberg, *Prosaiske Skrifter*, vol. II, p. 38.

19. The point that the sum total of natural existence constitutes an imperfect medium producing not satisfaction but longing is taken over by Kierkegaard from J. L. Heiberg's poem 'Gudstjeneste. En Foraars-Phantasie,' one of the four Hegelianizing poems in Heiberg's *Nye Digte*. Heiberg, in turn, is Hegelianizing the Pauline thesis that all nature longs for redemption. I am indebted to Billeskov Jansen for calling my attention to the more concrete source behind Kierkegaard's discussion and pointing out that the word for longing here is *Forlængsel*, the older poetic form, i.e. Heiberg's poem. All this is apparently in Kierkegaard's mind, for he ends the passage with a most abstruse bit of syntax which only becomes meaningful when construed as a polemical barb directed at H. L. Martensen, who explicated Heiberg's *Nye Digte* for the Danish public. (See below note 20.)

20. The phrase here translated as 'face over against face' is in Danish *Ansigt til og mod Ansigt*. The linguistic problem is the following. Ordinarily, the Danish preposition *til* translates as 'to,' while *mod* translates as 'against' except when indicating direction, in which case it is also 'to.' To say 'face to face' in Danish one ordinarily says *Ansigt mod Ansigt* (except in some Bible translations where *Aasyn til Aasyn* is used). The question is what did Kierkegaard have in mind when he put both prepositions together to construct such an awkward phrase? Obviously, the phrase is deliberately meant to echo I *Corinthians* 13 : 12: 'For now we see through a glass, darkly; but then face to (*pros*) face: now I know in part; but then shall I know even as also I am known.' The conjunction of both prepositions in the above phrase would appear, therefore, to be a concern to render the Greek *pros*, but in such a way as simultaneously to assert a theological orientation, one sceptical towards the possibility of speculative or theological knowledge insofar as such a knowledge represents itself *now* with a knowledge of the perfect *then*. (Cf. *Papirer, I A 214*.) The latter, which approximates the position of H. L. Martensen, is everywhere viewed by Kierkegaard as utterly 'theocentric,' as 'impatience,' as an 'attempt to have the perfect before its time.' The issue between Kierkegaard and Martensen is here an epistemological one. In the latter's dissertation for the *Licentiate* in 1837, the cognitive standpoint of Franz von Baader, with certain modifications, was disclosed as the basis upon which Martensen, as already

promised in 1836, proposed to 'go beyond Hegel.' He calls his theory of knowledge a theory of light, and quotes with satisfaction the words of Eckhart: 'Das Auge darin ich Gott sehe, ist dasselbe darin er mich siehet.' All knowing (*Viden/scientia*) is a knowing-with God (*Samviden/conscientia*), which is then immediately determined as conscience (*Samvittighed/conscientia*), an experience which elevates the knower above the standpoint of doubt (*cogitor ergo cogito*). The epistemological disagreement between Kierkegaard and Martensen, focusing as it does on the cognitive significance of doubt and the possibility of overcoming it in experience, together with the intimate connection between doubt and irony in the present essay, motivates to some extent the undercurrent of polemic directed at Martensen which one occasionally senses in this work. In this connection, Kierkegaard, who as a theological student had filled books of *New Testament* translations, was well aware of the dogmatic sensitivity of *New Testament* prepositions. For example, in his notes from Martensen's lectures on Speculative Theology in 1837-8, wherein the latter proposed to set forth a theological phenomenology and began by rehearsing the history of modern philosophy out of Hegel commencing with Descartes and the principle of doubt, he writes apropos the lecture on Kant (*Papirer, II C 20*, p. 322): 'The great significance of the categories (an ode by Martensen: the worst drivel he has presented thus far, a forced cleverness). The categories are the necessary bonds of all thinking; the atmosphere of thought, etc. From this follows the significance of languages, the possibility of translation from one language to another; *the meaning of prepositions in the New Testament* . . .' To return to the text, I have translated this problematic Danish phrase 'face over against face' as being most sympathetic to the radical distinction, the repulse, which it seems to me that Kierkegaard here intends. It is derived from the use of *pros* in another well-known *New Testament* passage, John 1 : 1. Cf. *Moffatt New Testament Commentary, The Gospel of John*, p. 4: ' "The Logos was with (*pros*) God": "towards God," "not absorbed in Him, but standing *over against* Him as a distinct person." (E. F. Scott.) The word with (*pros*), while emphasizing the communion of the Logos with God, yet safeguards the idea of his individual personality.' For a critical discussion of Martensen's dissertation, cf. Skat Arildsen, *H. L. Martensen*, Copenhagen, 1932, pp. 119-141. For a recent examination of the relation between Kierkegaard and Martensen, cf. Arild Christensen, 'Efterskriftens Opgør med Martensen,' in *Kierkegaardiana*, IV, pp. 45-62.

21. 'To come to oneself' is the translation of *at besinde sig* (*paa sig selv*). As the Danish root is *Sind* or mind, the emphasis is on the intellectual moment. Hence 'to come to oneself' means to reflect upon oneself, to come to one's senses, to mind oneself. An interesting set of associations is called up when subsequently Kierkegaard, following Schleiermacher (see above,

p. 91), translates the traditional Greek virtue sophrosynē (temperance, prudence, self-control, self-possession, self-mastery) as *Besindighed* (German: *Besonnenheit*), a set of associations which develops throughout the essay and culminates in the section 'Irony as a *Mastered* Moment.' (Cf. *Papirer*, *III B 10*.)

22. An ironic barb directed at Hegel, and possibly his Danish imitators J. L. Heiberg and H. L. Martensen.

23. This sentence clearly exhibits the continuity between the essay on irony and the work immediately following, *Either/Or*. Cf. the first sentence of Victor Eremita's preface: 'Dear Reader: I wonder if you may not sometimes have felt inclined to doubt a little the correctness of the familiar philosophic [Hegelian] maxim that the external is the internal, the internal the external.' Cf. *Either*, p. 3 (I, vii).

24. Socrates' existence is only available to a later age as it was mediated through the conceptions of his contemporaries, i.e., through reflection, through a refracted angle.

25. This is the first of several references to the method by which Kierkegaard attempts to elicit the phenomenological existence of Socrates from the three contemporary accounts by Xenophon, Plato, and Aristophanes. From his teacher in ancient philosophy, Paul Møller, Kierkegaard had heard the following on the problem of extracting the Socratic from Xenophon and Plato (*Samlede Skrifter*, vol. II, pp. 364-5). 'The plasticity with which Socrates entered the intellectual spheres of others also enabled him to direct his conversation to the various needs of their individualities, and from this fact it is possible to explain how various persons conceived his world view in such different ways. This is apparently the reason Xenophon always praises him as a man who had high regard for the useful insight into practical affairs, whereas Plato represents him as a master in the subtlest dialectic and most metaphysical investigations. Undoubtedly, Socrates accommodated himself to the interests of the individual and perceived that Xenophon was made more for the practical life than for speculative thought. It was therefore fundamental to Socrates' whole nature to appear as a Proteus under many different shapes, whence it is so difficult to reproduce his philosophy in its essential features. The main source is clearly Plato, but the latter did not represent the Socratic philosophy with historical fidelity: Plato was himself a more speculative thinker than Socrates, and allows the latter to appear in his dialogues in a glorified form. Xenophon is surely more faithful as a reporter, but undoubtedly his lack of philosophic talent often caused him to misunderstand Socrates. Both Xenophon and Plato must in some way correct each other, and what is common to them both must belong to the historical Socrates.' Møller goes on to propose that Aristotle's account of Socrates be used to mediate (*et Tredie*) between Xenophon and Plato. While Kierkegaard seems to have made

some of Møller's insights into the personality of Socrates his own, he got real methodological assistance from Hegel and his school. He employs the Hegelian dialectic in allowing the three contemporary conceptions of Socrates to negate and determine each other reciprocally in an ordered succession, all the while eliciting their common agreement in an emerging higher unity everywhere present as presupposition and result. Kierkegaard appears to have come to clarity about how to proceed with the application of the dialectic to his problem from studying J. E. Erdmann's *Vorlesungen über Glauben und Wissen* towards the end of 1837. An illuminating methodological passage is the following (p. 105): 'Thus the proof that a certain point is actually the centre of a sphere is carried out when one demonstrates that the perpendiculars drawn to various tangents all pass through it.' This, in effect, is what Kierkegaard attempts to show through his 'new integral calculus.'

26. 'The contradiction rendered in Hegelian terminology consists in the fact that irony is negative, whereas the substantial aspect is affirmative' (H). Another way of expressing the disparity is to note that substantial moments in the dialectic are immediate (either the lower or the higher), while irony is mediate or reflection.

27. By 'negative concepts' Kierkegaard appears to mean concepts of the nature of Hegel's categories of Essence. He held that the attempt to express them directly, that is, apart from their proper locus in the individual human being and other organic structures, is 'self-consuming.' An example from the early Journal is the following (*Papirer, I A 294*): 'When I consider the matter abstractedly, I must quite consistently arrive at the result that the romantic resolves itself in classicism (the romantic striving is self-consuming, and I cannot render it eternal, since I would then acquire an eternity consisting of an infinite aggregate of moments—yet all this *in abstracto*); whereas every attempt to show the classical age in time is naturally of a mythological sort, and only forthcoming because of a human weakness which can never maintain a concept in its whole infinite disappearance . . . since every attempt to say: now it is finished, is an attempt to transform it into mythology.' (November, 1836). An illuminating comment from the late Journal is the following (*Papirer, X² A 354*): 'It is a fundamental error to suppose that there are no negative concepts. The highest principles of all thinking or the proofs of them are, after all, negative. Human reason has limits; there lie the negative concepts. The border warfare is negative, designed merely to repulse the invader. But people have an infantile and conceited idea of human reason, especially in our age, since they never speak of a thinker, a reasoning man, but of pure reason and such like, which do not even exist, inasmuch as probably no one, be he Professor or what have you, is pure reason. Pure reason is a fantasy and a phantastical lack of boundaries that finds itself at home

where, in the absence of negative concepts, one conceives of everything like the witch who ended by devouring her own stomach' (1850).

28. A reference to the *Tarnkappe* or cloak of invisibility in Nordic mythology.

Chapter I. The conception made possible (pages 51-3)

1. Baur's essay appeared in *Tübinger Zeitschrift für Theologie*, 1837, *drittes Heft*; it was reprinted in *Drei Abhandlungen zur Geschichte der alten Philosophie und ihres Verhältnisses zum Christentum*, by F. C. Baur, edited by Eduard Zeller, Leipzig, 1876, p. 228*ff*. The references cited above are to the original source.

2. *Memorabilia*, III, 14, 2*ff*.: 'He observed on one occasion that one of the company at dinner had ceased to take bread, and ate the meat by itself. Now the talk was of names and the actions to which they are properly applied.

' "Can we say, my friends," said Socrates, "what is the nature of the action for which a man is called greedy? For all, I presume, eat meat with their bread when they get the chance: but I don't think there is so far any reason for calling them greedy?"

' "No, certainly not," said one of the company.

' "Well, suppose he eats the meat alone, without the bread, not because he's in training, but to tickle his palate, does he seem a greedy fellow or not?"

'Here another of the company queried, "And he who eats a scrap of bread with a large helping of meat?"

' "He too seems to me to deserve the epithet," said Socrates. "Aye, and when others pray for a good wheat harvest, he, presumably, would pray for a good meat supply."

' The young man, guessing that these remarks of Socrates applied to him, did not stop eating his meat, but took some bread with it. When Socrates observed this, he cried: "Watch the fellow, you who are near him, and see whether he treats the bread as his meat or the meat as his bread." '

3. See above p. 206n.

4. *John* 14 : 6. In this and the following New Testament passage Kierkegaard cites the Greek.

5. *Luke* 10 : 24; *Matt.* 13 : 17.

6. *loquere ut videam te*, speak that I may see you. Hirsch suggests that the phrase appears to be from a Latin comic poet, but Drachmann, a competent classicist, offers not a clue as to its source. One wonders whether it may not be a Latin translation of Hamann's line from *Aesthetica in Nuce*: 'Rede dass ich dich sehe,' and one wonders still more when subsequently

reading in *Aesthetica in Nuce*: 'All Reden ist Übersetzung.' For Hamann nature, history, and revelation were words which God utters and which all refer back to their divine author. Kierkegaard appears to want to apply the thesis to Socratic discourse, and subsequently (p. 262) he applies the line to the representation of negative standpoints. In his correspondence with Emil Boesen during the thirties, Kierkegaard alludes to this line in the same self-conscious fashion. Cf. *Breve og Aktstykker*, pp. 41, 42, 55, 200. What appears to be at issue is a species of appropriation and communication. For both Hamann and Kierkegaard *Job* 42 : 5, 6 may be relevant.

7. Cf. Appendix, thesis 1.

Xenophon (pages 53-64)

1. *ubique et nusquam*, everywhere and nowhere.

2. *John* 5 : 2-4.

3. Cf. *Solgers nachgelassene Schriften*, vol. 1, p. 538, and Hegel's review of same in xx, 154. Tieck writes to Solger (24th March 1817) the following: 'It was with Jacobi that I was first able to enter into a species of dialogue where we stood shores apart and conversed over an abyss, and where we heard more the echo than our words.' Kierkegaard appears to be attributing the same quality to the Socratic conversation or dialectic.

4. Plutarch, *The Parallel Lives*, 'Aristeides,' ch. 7.

5. Literally, *The People's News*, a liberal publication by the 'Society for Freedom of the Press' printed in Copenhagen from 1835 to 1848 (D).

6. Per Degn (Peter Parish Clerk) is the stock comic character for a parish clerk in Holberg's comedy *Erasmus Montanus*. In act I, scene 4, Per Degn boasts that he has taken the 'faith' from ten other parish clerks, by which he means that in a contest to see who can sing a well-known hymn loudest and longest where the climax falls on the word 'faith,' Per Degn won over ten other contestants. This is the origin of Kierkegaard's frequently* mentioned *Degneskrig* (the *tenuto* of Per Degn).

7. I *Corinthians* 3 : 9.

8. I have here departed from the correlations listed in the Glossary and translated the Danish *Anskuelse* as intuition.

9. Kierkegaard's Journal contains numerous passages developing this Goethean-Hegelian imagery contrasting an organic with an inorganic view. For example *I A 313*: 'The polygon (square) is the parody of the circle, whereas the petrefacts of life resolve themselves in crystallized forms that never become a sphere . . .' Cf. *III B 14*: 'It requires a trained eye to see what is round because it cannot be seen all at once, and the inner sense must exercise diligent control over the external eye's hasty, inquisitive, and desultory observations so that one does not get a polygon instead of a

circle. The same is true when considering the sphere of history: the manifold observations must not dilute the impression of continuity. The thesis "all is new" is the angle of refraction, that "nothing is new" the bond of unity; but these must be in and with each other and only in this lies their truth.'

10. This refers to Hegel's conception of the 'true infinity' (*Reflexion in sich*) in contrast to the 'spurious or bad infinity' (*unendliche Progression*), a theme pervasive in Hegel's writings. Cf. *The Logic of Hegel* (Wallace), p. 174*ff.* (VIII, 222-7); *Science of Logic*, vol. I, pp. 150-63 (IV, 157-75).

11. It was generally known that Socrates had compared the thirty tyrants to negligent cowherds because under their protection the number of cattle (citizens) decreased. The reply of Charicles, one of the thirty tyrants, is therefore a scarcely veiled threat directed at Socrates.

12. *Mem.* IV, 7: §2 concerns geometry, §4 astronomy, and §6 the warning against Anaxagoras (D).

13. *Zum Gebrauch* . . . for everyone's use, for everyday use.

14. *Phædrus* 249 A.

15. *Platonis quae extant opera* . . . rec. Frederic Astius, Lipsiæ, 1819*ff.* (D).

16. *Republic* 527 D, E.

17. Hirsch holds that Kierkegaard has severely misunderstood Xenophon on this point (*Mem.* III, 11), that the passage is thoroughly ambiguous and hence ironic: 'Thus understood it belongs to those passages where one feels it likely that we have a genuine recollection of Socrates by Xenophon.' I rather suspect that Kierkegaard is here imitating Xenophon's own style, and that the expression of indignation is mock seriousness. Kierkegaard, after all, is contrasting Xenophon to Plato, and the emphasis is on the words: 'when *in Xenophon* we hear Socrates,' the inference being that we would surely not be disgusted were we to read it in Plato.

18. *Symposium* 223 C, D.

19. *quantum satis*, a sufficient amount, a due portion. Cf. *Mem.* I, 3, 15.

20. Cf. Xenophon's *Apology* §4 where it is related that Socrates' daimon had forbidden him to prepare a defence.

21. Christiansfeldt was a small Danish town in which the pietist Moravian Brethren (Herrnhuterrn) had established schools to which members of the sect sent their children to be educated. Kierkegaard's father, prior to his attachment to Bishop Mynster, was for some years active in the movement, and Kierkegaard's single, life-long friendship with Emil Boesen dates from the period when their two families were associated together in the movement in Copenhagen. Several of Emil Boesen's sisters were sent to school in Christiansfeldt.

22. Chladni figures are the symmetrical patterns which emerge in the sand or iron filings on a glass plate in response to the vibration induced by the stroking of a bow. The Danish word *Klangfigur* is most descriptive.

H. C. Ørsted, Kierkegaard's physics teacher and noted for his harmonious nature, had published his scientific researches on the phenomenon in the form of a dialogue in 1807 ('Om Grunden til den Fornøjelse, Tonerne Frembringer'). The same Ørsted was also Rektor of the University when Kierkegaard submitted the essay on irony. In his Journal Kierkegaard had compared Ørsted's face to a *Klangfigur* (*I A 72*, p. 49), while the painter Ecksberg had done a portrait of him with a glass plate in his hand. Cf. Vilhelm Andersen, *Tider og Typer*, Første Række: Humanisme, Anden Del: Goethe, vol. II, pp. 111, 112.

23. The phrase is subsequently acknowledged by Kierkegaard as deriving from Hegel. Cf. *Philosophy of Fine Art*, vol. I, pp. 93*ff.*, 217*ff.* (XII, 105*ff.*, 221*ff.*). 'The first of these two references asserts that the "infinite absolute negativity" is an integral moment in the dialectic of the Idea, the Idea which negates itself and through this negation emerges as the true affirmation. The second reference is to one of the famous polemical passages in which Hegel pronounces judgment on romantic irony because it incorrectly transforms a valid moment in the dialectic of the Idea into a universal *Vernichtigungskunst* disruptive of every excellence whereby it becomes characterless and void of content' (H).

24. This account of Orpheus' descent into the underworld, which differs from that of the myth, derives from Plato's *Symposium* 179 D (D).

25. A drama by J. L. Heiberg. Cf. *Poetiske Skrifter*, vol. II, p. 22*ff.*

26. I have again departed from the Glossary and translated *Anskuelse*, which appears twice on this page, as 'intuitive view.' As employed in this sentence it appears to be sarcastic.

27. *James* 1 : 17.

28. Kierkegaard means Callicles.

29. *Gorgias* 490 E.

Plato. Introductory Remarks (pages 65-78)

1. *eminus et quasi . . .*, at a distance and as if through a screen.

2. The Danish is here *Recensent*, a term ordinarily meaning reviewer or critic. In the present case the reviewers are essentially Kierkegaard's academic readers of the essay.

3. Abraham a Sancta Clara, *Sämmtliche Werke*, Passau, 1835, vol. VIII, p. 14. Kierkegaard has adapted the example to suit his own purposes (D).

4. Of the scarcely six and one-half pages of notes which the Danish editors of the *Papirer* are able to determine with certainty as pertaining to the essay on irony and composed before the book was printed, there occurs the following comment concerning a foreword, which, one feels, must refer to this lyrical prelude to the section on Plato (*III B 2*).

'Foreword

'Its significance: it is, to be sure, irrelevant to the essay but a necessary moment in personality.' There follows a reference (which the editors have reproduced) to what is now printed as *II A* 432.

'Whether this foreword will be long or short I do not at this moment know. Only one thought fills my soul: a longing and a thirst to lose myself in the lyrical undergrowth of the foreword, to cast myself into it. Just as the poet now feels moved lyrically, now drawn to the epic, so as a prose writer I feel at this moment an indescribable satisfaction in abandoning all objective thought in order to vent myself in hopes and desires, in a secretive whispering with the reader, in an Horatian *susurratio* at eventide. A foreword should always be conceived in the illumination of twilight as this is undeniably the most beautiful. It fills one therefore with wonder to read that our Lord used to walk in the cool of the day (*Genesis*) at eventide, when the bustle of objective thought resounds solemnly in the distance like the lee of the reaper.'

5. As used here the word 'sympathy' suggests its seventeenth-century connotations. Cf., for example, Milton's *Paradise Lost*:

> 'whatever draws me on,
> Or sympathy, or some connatural force
> Powerful at greatest distance to unite
> With secret amity things of like kind
> By secretest conveyance.'

Bk. x, 245-49

By the time Kierkegaard wrote, however, the word 'sympathy' had inevitably been drawn into the wake of those satellite terms and associations revolving around the central category of 'romanticism.' Cf., for example, Goethe's *The Sufferings of Young Werther*, edited by H. Steinhauer, Bantam, 1962, pp. 131, 251, *et passim*.

6. This and the following Latin terms are designations from Kierkegaard's Hebrew grammar signifying that a word stands alone or is conjoined with other words (D).

7. Approach [*Tilløb*] in the sense of a preliminary run.

8. *John* 20 : 22.

9. *Matt.* 9 : 5.

10. *aliud in lingua* . . ., to have one thought locked in the breast, another ready on the tongue. Cf. Sallust, *Catilina*, ch. 10.

11. 'A relationship which initiates a new epoch in time in the history of the receiving individual' (H).

12. *John* 4 : 14.

13. Cf. *Theatetus* 149 A, where Socrates compares his own art of conversing with that of a midwife.

14. The other conception referred to must be what Kierkegaard takes

to be Socrates' own conception of his activity, a conception which Kierke-gaard here aligns with the negative analogy: the individual is 'begotten and engendered by silence' through the Socratic dialectic—not the Platonic nor even the Hegelian dialectic (both of which would be an attempt to simulate 'the word that creates the individual'). It may help to clarify Kierkegaard's distinction between the negative and the positive analogies, between 'silence' and the 'word,' between indirect and direct communication, by recalling the familiar distinction within 'expressionistic æsthetics' between *impression* and *expression*, two interrelated aspects of the artistic process or two necessary conditions of the science of linguistics. The fruitful assimilation of the Socratic, the negative, has eventuated in the Platonic representation exhibiting both aspects and is a complete expression. As for the truth inherent in the negative side of this analogy, Hegel appears to have put his finger on the principle involved when he wrote (xx, 153): 'Here we see the old doctrine, first articulated by Socrates (and Plato), that what is to serve man as true and good must be original with the mind or spirit as such.' The earliest roots of the problem of indirect versus direct communication are therefore already at issue in Kierkegaard's attempt to delineate the Socratic from the Platonic in Plato's dialogues. It is to be observed that the same distinction recurs in Kierkegaard's sub-sequent discussion of romantic irony when he is at pains to differentiate between formalism and realism by contrasting the consequences of 'poeti-cally to produce oneself and poetically to let oneself be produced' (see above p. 297).

15. Cf. *Meno* 81 D; *Phædo* 75 E.

16. Diogenes Laertius, III, 50.

17. See above p. 51.

18. The foregoing discussion may seem unnecessarily confused to those readers who are accustomed to call 'dramatic' the dialogues termed 'narrative' by Diogenes, Baur, and Kierkegaard. For the average reader, at least, the dramatic dialogues contain the most drama, even though their true form is that of a narrated drama of ideas.

19. Hegel's pupils are often clearer expositors of the system than Hegel. J. L. Heiberg, whose writings provided Danish students like Kierkegaard with their introduction to Hegel, sums up the principle of trichotomy in §13 of his *Guidelines to Lectures on the Philosophy of Philosophy, or The Speculative Logic* (for students of the Royal Military Academy) as follows: 'The method of philosophy cannot be determined outside philosophy itself. Only as a result of having philosophized can it be historically set forth in advance (to come to the aid of the understanding) that just as the whole of philosophy consists of three parts, so the same trichotomy repeats itself in every subor-dinate division. But this trichotomy is conditioned by the method which consists in developing each concept through three phases so that through

the last it returns to the first, but with the essential difference that it has now completed its immanent movement. The first of these moments is the immediate, a given unexplicated unity without multiplicity as its presupposition. The second is the negation of the first, a difference is explicated between itself and the foregoing. The third is the negation of the negation or the positive, but no longer immediate as in the first; on the contrary, it is a result of the foregoing, a developed and explicated unity of the preceding difference. The first is the abstract wherein thought moves as understanding . . . The second is the dialectical or negative reason, for in this sphere the finite determinations of the understanding are abrogated and pass over into their opposites. The third is the speculative or positive reason, for in this sphere reason conceives the resulting unity as the positive contained in the foregoing, internally opposed determinations as reciprocally abrogated.' *Prosaiske Skrifter*, vol. I, pp. 120-121. Cf. Hegel, *Science of Logic*, vol. II, pp. 478-479 (V, 344, 345).

20. See above pp. 132-3, 136-8.

21. However Hegelian such passages may appear at first glance, it still remains to be determined in what respects Kierkegaard's theory and practice of dialectic was identical with Hegel's.

22. Cf. *Gorgias* 448 A, 471 D.

23. *versus inopes rerum* . . ., verses void of thought, and sonorous trifles. Cf. Horace, *Ars Poetica*, 322.

24. Cf. *Protagoras* 338 A, where Hippias describes Protagoras' long speeches these words, except that Kierkegaard has changed 'ocean of words' to 'ocean of truth.'

25. Relevant to Kierkegaard's discussion of method in Plato's dialogues is the controversy between Hegel and the German romantics concerning the significance of the principle of philosophic dialogue. Kierkegaard appears to have assimilated the arguments of both sides, and attempts to accommodate both claims in what might be construed as a third alternative. Hegel had held that 'the plastic form' of the Platonic dialogue, which had dialectic as its soul and where all content resided in the question as such, was transformed by Solger into mere 'Sophistic conversation.' The romantic insistence that the philosophic dialogue yielded a 'representation unifying reason and understanding with a certain elevation of feeling and disposition' was termed by Hegel 'that hypochondriac method' reminiscent of Tieck, whereas the true solution, the dialectical method, is called a philosophic 'Rechenschaft.' It is here that Kierkegaard's terms *Mellemværende* and *Mellemhverandre* find their widest application. He ultimately recombines the several features in question into a solution of the 'Socratic problem' that posits a development in Plato allowing for two species of irony and two species of dialectic, a Socratic and a Platonic, with certain illegitimacies in both the romantic and Hegelian

positions falling to the lot of the Sophists. Cf. Hegel's remarks on Solger in xx, 190-99 together with Solger's defence of his principle in *Nachgelassene Schriften und Briefwechsel*, vol. II, pp. 189-99.

26. Cf. Hegel, *Science of Logic*, vol. I, p. 66 (IV, 53): 'That by means of which the concept forges ahead is the above mentioned Negative which it carries within itself; it is this that constitutes the genuine dialectical procedure.' For Hegel the essential merit of Kant's transcendental logic was to have reinstated dialectic as a necessary feature of reason; and as employed by Kant it vindicated the necessity of contradiction as pertaining to the very nature of thought determinations. 'This result, grasped in its positive side, is nothing other than the inherent Negativity of these thought determinations, their self-moving soul' (p. 67).

27. Lessing, 'Eine Duplik,' in *Gesammelte Werke*, Berlin (Aufbau-Verlag), 1956, vol. VIII, pp. 24-107. Cf. pp. 26, 38, 106.

28. *Den g jenopstandne Uglespil*, Copenhagen, p. 63 (D).

29. Horace, *Odes*, I, 4, 7.

30. 'In Hegel's *Philosophy of Religion* the moment of higher unity is the Christian Idea of the God-Man, the lower is that of naïve paganism not yet permeated with reflection'(H).

31. A reciprocally retroactive pronoun (D).

32. Dependent cases (includes all cases except the nominative) (D).

33. The words 'I beg of you, Polus', are Kierkegaard's own interpolation.

34. In Homer Oceanus is represented as encircling the earth (D).

35. *Apology* 23 B.

36. *Apology* 36 D, E.

37. *Apology* 39 E 42 A.

38. Diogenes Laertius, II, 40.

39. *tentamen rigorosum*, strenuous examination.

40. *Judges* 16 : 29, 30.

Symposium (pages 78-89)

1. *Symposium* 201 D.

2. *Symposium* 212 B.

3. *Symposium* 215 A.

4. See above pp. 69-70.

5. *Symposium* 187 A.

6. *prius*, the first of two (parts).

7. Hirsch points out that Kierkegaard's criticism of the discourse of Eryximachus is an elaboration of Hegel's criticism of the same in defence of the Heraclitean principle of the unity of opposites. Cf. Hegel, *Lectures on the History of Philosophy*, vol. I, p. 285 (XVII, 252).

8. *Symposium* 191 D.

9. The word here translated as 'jargon' is *Kragemaal*, literally crow-jargon, hence twaddle, gibberish. Hirsch attempts to read the reference as a barb directed at Grundtvig but without evidence. It seems more plausible to regard it as a barb directed at H. L. Martensen whom Kierkegaard never tires of satirizing for mouthing Hegel, Baader, etc., especially when corroborated with an entry from the Journal belonging to those sardonic fragments which Carl Roos has identified as Kierkegaard's despairing reaction to the publication of Martensen's essay on the Idea of Faust in 1837.

10. Cf. Hegel, *Philosophy of Fine Art*, vol. II, p. 337*ff.* (XIII, 178), where the precise expression does not appear.

11. 'Abstract in the ontological sense is for Kierkegaard, as for Hegel in the *Logik*, the concept of pure Being. Abstract in the sense of being without content Kierkegaard calls the subjectivity which, through the infinite negation of irony, estranges itself from the actual' (H).

12. The priests of Cybele who in the worship of her cult brought themselves to a condition of ecstasy by loud music (D).

13. *Odyssey*, XII.

14. *Odyssey*, IV.

15. *Maximes*, 271. La Rochefoucauld is speaking of youth.

16. 'A theological expression in Lutheran doctrine specifying that Christ in his earthly existence made continual use of his divine attributes, but always in a concealed manner.' (Peter P. Rohde, editor of *Samlede Værker*, 3rd edition, Copenhagen, 1952*ff.*, vol. I, p. 348).

17. The words 'with sensual desire' are Kierkegaard's interpolation (D).

18. 'With respect to the dialectical content of the concept of nature Kierkegaard is here dependent on what Hegel says of the "other" (τὸ ἕτερον) of Plato in connection with Nature as the "other" of *Geist* and the negativity of such a determination' (H). Cf. Hegel, *Science of Logic*, vol. I, p. 130*ff.* (IV, 134*ff.*).

19. Cf. Baur, *op. cit.*, p. 108. Baur, however, is quoting David Friedrich Strauss, *Leben Jesu*, vol. II, p. 276. It is Strauss who explicitly points out the unity of the comic and tragic in Socrates' person at the end of the *Symposium*, although it is implicitly present in Hegel, XVIII, 55, 56.

20. *Symposium* 174 D, 220 C.

Protagoras (pages 89-98)

1. Cf. Schleiermacher, *Platons Werke*, second edition, Berlin, 1817, vol. II, p. 45*ff.* 'Kierkegaard refers to the general introduction to Schleiermacher's translation of Plato, where, after an initial distinction between the spurious and authentic Platonic works, he divides the dialogues into three (not two) groups. The third group is designated the instructive

or constructive dialogues and includes, as Kierkegaard reports, the *Republic*, *Timæus*, and *Critias*. The first group is termed the elementary dialogues and contains the earliest dialogues (*Phædrus*, *Protagoras*, and *Parmenides*). Between both groups falls the remainder of the dialogues whose character, according to Schleiermacher and others, is the artfulness of their construction together with the prominence of antithetical elements. It is not altogether clear from Kierkegaard's account, however, that Schleiermacher's criteria for dividing the dialogues have to do with content, nor that he has provided a systematic plan for the whole Platonic authorship' (H).

2. *Gorgias* 518 B *ff.*

3. Kierkegaard has interpolated 'at our questions' for the Greek 'at what we say.'

4. *nomen appellativum*, a class name.

5. *Republic* 392 C *ff.*

6. *Platons Werke*, vol. II, p. 8.

7. *Op. cit.*, p. 7.

8. *Op. cit.*, p. 228*ff.*

9. Destouches, *Le dissipateur*, act V, scene 9. The expression may be translated perhaps as 'left high and dry'.

10. Kierkegaard is here touching on the nerve of the Hegelian dialectic, namely, that the negations in the dialectical evolution are not empty negations, not pure nothingness, but negations of something, of a determinate content. It is in this way that the first moment may be said to be 'contained in' or 'preserved by' the second, that the true negation becomes an affirmation, and a unity of opposites is effected. Cf., for example, Hegel's discussion of two kinds of scepticism in the introduction to *Phenomenology of Mind*, p. 136*ff.* (II, 71*ff.*); *The Logic of Hegel*, p. 151 (VIII, 194); *Science of Logic*, vol. II, p. 476*ff.* (V, 340*ff.*), *et passim*.

11. The anecdote derives from Hebel's *Schatzkästlein* (H).

12. In this anecdote Kierkegaard displays a sound grasp of the organic character of Hegel's dialectic, its propensity to constitute experience. By contrast, the infinite correlation exhibited in this example undergoes no progression but exhausts itself in mutually conditioning each side, disperses itself in a vacuous reciprocity. Beyond this the anecdote furnishes another instance of Kierkegaard's ability to clothe utter abstract conceptions in the most concrete forms.

13. *habitus*, internal constitution or nature.

14. Those readers who can follow the Danish might enjoy the adverbial phrase qualifying 'ironic smile' (at any rate, I confess my translation is here almost a paraphrase): 'og enhver nogenlunde sympathetiske Læser vil vist ikke kunne undlade at forestille sig *det med ironisk Alvor stridende og derudaf sig tvetydigt udkjæmpende ironiske Smiil* . . .' (XIII, 163).

15. *meta*, the conical columns set in the ground at each end of the Roman circus, the goal or turning point in a contest of speed; by extension, critical points, limits.

16. *opposita juxta se . . .*, opposites become clearer when placed beside each other.

17. Schleiermacher, *Der christliche Glaube*, second edition, Berlin, 1830, vol. I, p. 334*ff.* (D).

18. A character in Tieck's drama *Der gestiefelte Kater, ein Kindermärchen*.

19. *e concessis*, by way of concession.

20. Cf. *Papirer, III A 117*.

Phædo (pages 98-115)

1. Schleiermacher, *Platons Werke*, Part Two, vol. II, p. 370*ff.* The reference is to the introduction accompanying Schleiermacher's translation of the *Phædo*.

2. J. Heise, *Udvalgte Dialoger af Platon*, Copenhagen, 1830-38, vol. II, p. 224*ff.* Occasionally, Kierkegaard cites Plato from this Danish translation instead of the Greek text edited by Ast.

3. *Platonis dialogos selectos* rec. G. Stallbaum, Gothæ et Erfordiæ, 1827, vol. I, sect. 2 (D).

4. Hirsch points out that the conception of death as a metamorphosis is a recurrent theme in Kierkegaard's subsequent writings; cf. 'At a Grave', in *Thoughts On Crucial Situations in Human Life* (V, 261*ff.*).

5. *Phædo* 70 C.

6. 'The influence of the idealistic representation of an eternal life through continual activity, production, and development as communicated in J. G. Fichte's *The Vocation of Man*, is apparent throughout the present discussion' (H).

7. *Phædo* 61 E-62 C.

8. I *Corinthians* 3 : 9.

9. Hirsch calls attention to the fact that Kierkegaard's first edifying discourse in 1843 concludes with almost the same words as this sentence. Cf. III, 41, 42.

10. 'This sentence contains the first trace of the characteristically Kierkegaardian thesis that the distinction between immediate contemporaneity and mediated information about the life of a past individual makes no essential difference for a knowledge and appropriation of the historical' (H).

11. *Phædo* 60 A.

12. *Phædo* 60 B, C.

13. *Phædo* 117 B. The following quotation is from the same source.

14. 'This is the basic proposition from which is derived the protest of Kierkegaard's Christian individualistic philosophy against Idealistic

377

speculation: the latter depersonalizes the knower and transforms him into an empty abstraction' (H).

15. 'This is the first proof for the immortality of the soul (*Phædo* 69 E-72 E). If opposites arise through the constant passing over of each into its other, then the living arise from the dead and the dead from the living. Death is therefore understood as the transition to another life. Kierkegaard's account of this first proof merely reproduces that of Baur' (H).

16. 'This is the second proof for the immortality of the soul (*Phædo* 72 E-77 B). The fact that the soul bears the Ideas as an innate possession from birth, and that knowledge of the Ideas can only be understood as a recollection of this innate possession, proves the pre-existence of the soul as well as a continuity extending through both birth and death' (H).

17. 'Kierkegaard displays himself in this judgment as a fastidious dialectician. If one firmly apprehends the concept of a coming into being out of opposites as contained in the first proof, then it cannot be denied that what arose from its opposite cannot have existed previously. The coming into being involved in affirming the pre-existence of the soul, therefore, would have reference to the new animated body arising from one already dead. The unhistorical character of this irrefutable comprehension of the concept involved in combining both arguments is that Plato, of course, did not take coming into being in the narrow sense but coming into being and passing away, transition and recurrence, as moments of one and the same existent entity' (H).

18. *in Mente*, in mind. 'The expression "*in mente*" was part of the pedagogical language of arithmetic in Kierkegaard's day, and signified that an integer was to be "carried over" or added to the next column in calculating a compound sum. The expression occasionally occurs in Kierkegaard (but is now capitalized) to designate a thought which functions in a dialectical context as the understood or constant presupposition throughout a dialectical calculation' (H).

19. *Phædo* 75 E.

20. 'To illumine Kierkegaard's argument one must recall the difficulty experienced by the incipient philosophy of romantic individualism when confronted with Kant's synthetic unity of apperception and Fichte's pure Ego. These elaborate constructs of Kant and Fichte appeared to the youthful romantics as pure universal *geistige* form. Just as the concrete universal ego, each particular human being, must be understood as the consolidation through birth of this universal *geistige* form towards a particular individual life, so with the representation of the eternity of *Geist* there arises within me the terrifying thought that I experience through a thousandfold birth this consolidation of myself towards this concrete individual ego, and through a thousandfold death the dissolution of this individual ego into universal *geistige* form; that is, I am eternal only as an

arbitrary discontinuous chain of such endless individualizations. Heinrich von Kleist has characterized this thought to his bride as the terrifying despair into which Kant's philosophy plunged him, while the same thought was dazzlingly portrayed by Clemens Brentano in *Nachtwachens des Bonaventura* as the zenith of the perception of nothingness. Kierkegaard, who was familiar with the philosophy of romantic individualism through the influence of Schleiermacher, Steffens, and Jacobi, here asserts the very same thought as Kleist and Brentano against the intellectual epistemological basis for immortality in Plato's *Phædo*. A pure pre-existence of the soul based on the eternity of the universal and ideal realm is for the soul immersed in concrete life a nothingness, a night. Here we have arrived once again at the root of the criticism which Kierkegaard subsequently directs against the speculation of Hegel as a denial of individual existence. What is characteristic of Kierkegaard's undeniably unhistorical interpretation of the *Phædo* is that the nihilism he attempts to display in the Platonic argument for the idea of immortality is not asserted as an externally derived criticism of the Platonic Socrates, but understood as the disclosure of the innermost intention and thought of the great ironist Socrates as he approaches death. Socrates sought to drive each man from every resting place into a sense of heightened finitude, and thereby to release in him that infinite movement which is the negative condition for the development of *Geist*' (H).

21. *John* 3 : 2.

22. Cf. Karl Rosenkrantz's review of Schleiermacher's *Dogmatik* in *Jahrbüchern für wissenschaftliche Kritik*, 1831, column 949 (D).

23. *Odyssey*, XI, 487*ff*.

24. *Colossians* 2 : 19; II *Peter* 3 : 18; II *Timothy* 3 : 17.

25. 'The Church of the early Christians made a practice of celebrating the day of a martyr's death as his day of birth. Cf. *Martyrium Polycarpi*, 18; and Tertullian, *De corona*, 3' (D).

26. *Phædo* 64 A.

27. Wessel applied the epitaph to himself. Cf. *Samtlige Skrifter*, Copenhagen, 1817, vol. II, p. 149 (D).

28. I have again departed from the Glossary and translated *Anskuelse* as 'intuition.'

29. *Genesis* 1 : 3*ff*.

30. *sin post mortem* . . ., but if after death all consciousness and even the soul are extinguished. This is Stallbaum's paraphrase of the Greek.

Apology (*pages* 115-28)

1. Cf. Ast, *Platons Leben und Schriften*, p. 474*ff*.

2. Ast does not give preference to Xenophon's *Apology* but regards it as

spurious; on the other hand, he emphasizes that the representation of Xenophon in the *Memorabilia* is superior to Plato's *Apology*. Cf. Ast, *op. cit.*, p. 482 (D).

3. *aut-aut*, either/or. It is probably significant that the first appearance in Kierkegaard's published works of the phrase 'either/or' occurs in Latin; for it is as the Latin *aut-aut* that Bishop Mynster uses the phrase in the logical debate with J. L. Heiberg and H. L. Martensen on the principle of contradiction in 1839.

4. Kierkegaard is no doubt thinking of the conclusion to his discussion of the *Symposium* as presented above on p. 89; otherwise the reference should be to the *Phædo* (see above p. 104n).

5. *Apology* 28 E.

6. *Apology* 41 A. King Minos and his brother Rhadamanthus from Crete, together with Aeacus, son of Zeus, from Aegina (D).

7. See above p. 76.

8. 'This footnote is naturally to be understood ironically, something like The Soul's interest in the poets in Heiberg's "A Soul After Death. An Apocalyptical Comedy," inasmuch as infinite progress and eternal inquiry are there expressions for "the bad infinity." ' (Peter P. Rohde, editor, *Samlede Værker*, 3rd edition, Copenhagen, 1962*ff.*, vol. I, p. 352.)

9. Some of the older texts read 'three' instead of 'thirty.'

10. *Apology* 23 B. Ast, of course, cites the Greek, which may be part of the fun.

11. Cf. Ast, *op. cit.*, p. 477*ff.*

12. It may, perhaps, come as something of a surprise to the reader to learn of Ast's own position concerning irony in the *Apology*, especially as Ast's own words are here being utilized in this rather elaborate construction to provoke an awareness of irony in the reader. *What* is being said is commensurate with *how* it is said, as Kierkegaard here divides his page and breaks out in dialogue: two voices on two simultaneous levels. Something of Kierkegaard's complex attitude towards his material may be seen in this example, an attitude which is to be borne in mind when judging of the Hegelianism and the romanticism of the present essay. In the treatment of romantic irony in Part Two, for example, one suspects the same deliberate arbitrariness in the manipulation of his material. That he should have chosen to deal with Schlegel's irony by confining himself to a discussion of *Lucinde*, that in his discussion of Tieck not so much as a single word by the poet finds its way into the text, and that the pedantic discussion of Solger curiously omits all reference to his major philosophic dialogue *Erwin*—all this discloses either an exceptional callousness or calculation on Kierkegaard's part.

13. The Danish editor calls attention to the fact that Kierkegaard has changed the *var* [was] in Heise's translation to *blev*. Although there is

no significant difference in this for a translation, the change in Danish amounts to the substitution of an historical past for an indeterminate past tense.

14. Kierkegaard apparently thinks of himself over against his academic readers as in a similar situation, for he obviously had this passage from the *Gorgias* in mind when he wrote *Papirer, III B 2* (cited in the translator's introduction). The passage is clearly the source for his reiterated barb at H. L. Martensen about his new 'recipe' of the new wisdom.

15. This description of the polemical situation is reminiscent of a passage from 'The Discipline of Pure Reason in Respect of its Polemical Employment' in Kant's *Critique of Pure Reason* (English translation by N. K. Smith, p. 604): 'There is, therefore, properly speaking, no polemic in the field of pure reason. Both parties beat the air, and wrestle with their own shadows, since they go beyond the limits of nature, where there is nothing that they can seize and hold with their dogmatic grasp. Fight as they may, the shadows which they cleave asunder grow together again forthwith, like the heroes in Valhalla, to disport themselves anew in the bloodless contests.'

16. Cf. Baggesen, 'Kallundborgs Krønike' in *Danske Værker*, Copenhagen, 1845, vol. I, p. 184 (D).

17. *Gorgias* 473 E-474 A.

18. *Apology* 36 A.

19. The gist of the verse may be rendered as follows:

> 'No child of man is gainfully said
> To slay a man already dead;
> For though the thief gives up the ghost,
> More profit has than e'er his host.'

20. *Apology* 39 E.

21. *Apology* 25 C-26 A.

22. The reference is obviously to Raphael's Madonna in the Vatican Museum (D).

23. The Danish editor thinks the footnote belongs here instead of above. Kierkegaard has changed Ast's 'sich selbst zu verherrlichen' to 'sich selbst zu erheben' (D).

24. Kierkegaard has changed Ast's 'er' to 'ich' (D).

25. Kierkegaard has changed Ast's 'aber alle anderen noch mehr' to 'aber alle andere erniedrigt' (D).

26. Kierkegaard has changed Ast's 'affectirt um die Ruhmredigkeit zu verbergen' simply to 'affectirt' (D).

27. Kierkegaard has changed 'verwandelt' to 'gewendet' (D).

28. *Asmus omnia secum portans*, Asmus, who bears everything with him. 'This phrase is a variant on the title of the collected works of Matthias Claudius: "*Asmus omnia sua Secum portans oder Sämmtliche Werke des Wands-*

becker Boten" ' (D). 'Kierkegaard has omitted the word *sua* ("what is his") after *omnia* ("everything") as inappropriate to Socrates for whom "everything" is nothingness' (H).

29. *Apology* 21 A, 30 C.

30. *Apology* 20 E; cf. 17 C, 27 B, 30 C.

31. *Apology* 31 E.

The Mythical in the Early Dialogues (*pages* 128-40)

1. In *Gorgias* 461 B Polus says that Gorgias made the admission demanded by Socrates because he was 'ashamed' to deny that the rhetoricians knew the just, honourable, and good; while in *Gorgias* 482 C Callicles upbraids Polus because he made the admission to Socrates out of 'modesty' that to do injustice is more disgraceful than to suffer injustice.

2. *Gorgias* 523 A*ff.*

3. *Phædo* 107 D-114 D; *Gorgias* 523 A-527 A; *Republic* 614 B-621 B.

4. *Republic* 427 B.

5. ἐποπτεία, seeing face to face; the highest grade of initiation in the Eleusinian mysteries.

6. *Republic* 376 E*ff.*

7. *Republic* 598 D*ff.*

8. 'In *Lectures on the Philosophy of Religion* Hegel says in connection with Plato that the mythical is the external phenomenon (*äusserliche Erscheinung*) of an eternal, a *Geistigen*. Cf. XV, 157*ff.*' (H). As Kierkegaard had not yet read Hegel's *Philosophy of Religion*, he could of course have got this from Erdmann or another Hegelian source.

9. *Phædrus* 246 A-D.

10. 'The sentence contains, in slightly poetized form, the Hegelian doctrine of Idea, space, and time' (H).

11. The expression 'pantheism of the imagination' occurs in Hegel's *Philosophy of History* (rev. edition), p. 141 (XI, 193*ff.*); cf. also *Philosophy of Fine Art*, vol. II, pp. 89, 106 (XII, 485, 502) for the related expressions 'pantheism of art' and 'phantasy of pantheism' respectively.

12. Kierkegaard's distinction between the mythical and the poetical based on the difference between the indicative and subjunctive moods first appears in the Journal in 1836. The idea undergoes some development under the impetus of teaching Latin in 1837-8. Cf. *Papirer, I A 241, 300*; *II A 155-161*. The idea appears in his published works in *Stages On Life's Way*, p. 195*ff.* (VI, 217*ff.*).

13. This vivid description of the departure of myth echoes a sentence from Hegel's *Philosophy of History*, p. 140 (XI, 193) describing the æsthetic quality exhibited, for example, in the painting of the dying Mary by Schoreel.

14. *Phædo* 114 D.

15. This, of course, is how an Hegelian, or someone using Hegelian perspectives and terminology, would be inclined to view the matter.

16. *John* 3 : 8.

17. Steffens, *Karrikaturen des Heiligsten*, 2 vols., Leipzig, 1819-21.

18. 'Kierkegaard, who at this time regards Plato as a kind of forerunner of Hegel, criticizes the Platonic dialectic in comparison with the Hegelian, inasmuch as he attempts to show that while the Socratic dialogue is an attempt to induce thought to appear in its objectivity, as required by Hegel, still, he is unsuccessful in actualizing the Hegelian dialectic with its three phases as expressed by the relation between questioner and answerer. The third moment, the synthesis, is lacking, and hence "movement" is not introduced into logic. Moreover, the negative obviously does not function as a necessary moment which is able to drive the process of thought forward, but remains something accidental and subjective. Thus the Platonic dialectic remains merely negative, i.e., ironic, and never actually speculative (in the Hegelian sense), and is therefore to be regarded as unripened fruit in the development of speculation. Accordingly, we read on page 134 that "Plato's element is not thought but representation." ' (Peter P. Rohde, editor *Samlede Værker*, 3rd edition, Copenhagen, 1962*ff.*, vol. 1, pp. 355-6.) I think it would be a mistake to regard the statements of Kierkegaard in the essay comparing the Platonic to the Hegelian dialectic as providing in any way a sanction for the latter. There is in the early Journal, for example, a passage comparing the ripening of speculation to the process of fermentation where the end product is ambiguously represented both as maturation and putrefaction. In dealing with Kierkegaard's statements on this head one simply cannot do without the possibility of irony.

19. 'It may here be seen that for the young Kierkegaard faith is as rigorously determined as a cognitive act whose object is determined as a non-mythical reality' (H).

20. *Symposium* 201 D.

21. Cf. Hegel, *Science of Logic*, vol. 1, p. 36 (IV, 17, 53, 54): 'Mind is the negative, it is that which constitutes the quality of dialectical reason'; 'This movement of mind . . . is the absolute method'; p. 66: 'That by means of which the concept forges ahead is the above mentioned negative which it carried within itself'; p. 67: 'This result, grasped in its positive side, is nothing other than the inherent negativity of these conceptual determinations, their moving soul, the principle of all physical and intellectual life.'

22. Cf. Hegel, *Philosophy of History*, p. 163 (XI, 222).

23. 'The following remarks show Kierkegaard to have been aware of Kant's conflicting usages of the term *Ding an sich* as pointed out by Jacobi and Fichte' (H).

24. Cf. Kant, *Reason Within the Limits of Reason Alone*, translated by T. M. Greene and H. H. Hudson, Harpers (TB 67), p. 15*ff.*

25. Ast, *op. cit.*, p. 312.

26. Baur, *op. cit.*, p. 96n.

27. *Gorgias* 523 A, 524A, 526 D.

Republic, Book I (pages 141-9)

1. *Schleiermacher's Introductions to the Dialogues of Plato*, translated by William Dobson, Cambridge: Deighton, 1836, p. 356.

2. Kierkegaard is misled in regarding the *Republic* as one of Plato's latest compositions; but the observation of Schleiermacher, to which he subscribes, that the first book of the *Republic* exhibits a style much earlier than the other books is generally borne out even in Lutoslawski's definitve work on the chronology of the Platonic writings. Lutoslawski holds that the first book of the *Republic* was written before the *Phœdo*, although the latter is no longer regarded as an early dialogue. Cf. *The Origin and Growth of Plato's Logic*, London, 1897, p. 92. Kierkegaard is more fortunate in his intuition when on p. 153 above he breaks with Schleiermacher and regards the *Parmenides* (along with *Theaetetus*, *Sophist*, and *Statesman*) as belonging to the last period of Platonic writings.

3. *Republic* 336 B; cf. *Gorgias* 461 B, 481 B.

4. *Gorgias* 473 D.

5. *Schattenspiel an der Wand*, a play of shadows on the wall. A parlour game of the period.

6. A festival in honour of the Thracian goddess recently introduced into Athens (D).

7. *Republic* 331 E.

8. Schleiermacher, *Platons Werke*, Part One, vol. I, p. 228*ff.*

9. *Republic* 346 A-347 A.

A Confirming Retrospect (pages 150-6)

1. Ast, *Platons Leben und Schriften*, p. 53.

2. Ast, *op. cit.*, p. 157*ff.*

3. *confinium*, a limit, a common boundary.

4. Schleiermacher, 'Über den Werth des Sokrates als Philosophen,' in *Abh. d. kgl. Akademie d. Wiss.*, 1814-15, p. 63*ff.*

5. *On Sophistical Refutations*, 183b.

6. See above p. 66.

7. Kierkegaard here picks up Martensen's fateful phrase (from his review in 1836 of J. L. Heiberg's 'Introductory Lecture to a Course in

Speculative Logic') to the effect that he (Martensen) had 'gone beyond' Hegel.

Aristophanes (*pages* 158-84)

1. This is a recurrent theme in Kierkegaard's Journal during the thirties. Cf., for example, I A 285: 'Every development is in my opinion only complete with its own parody'; and I A 288: 'Parody (the last stage in a development) exhibits itself even in the way childhood repeats itself in old age: "a second childhood." '

2. One wonders whether Kierkegaard, being aware of Hegel's recent rehabilitation of the Aristophanic Socrates and of Hegel's insight that Aristophanes' comic characters are distinctive in being conscious of themselves as comic, is not here writing with tongue in cheek. At least to argue, as he does in thesis VII, that Aristophanes has come extremely close to the truth about Socrates is to follow Hegel with a seriousness bent on parody, just as to utilize the Hegelian method of historical conception 'in the strict sense' to the point of characterizing it as baldly as he does on p. 183n, is tantamount to developing its vagaries to an absurd lucidity.

3. Most of the reasons set forth here were already advanced in antiquity; cf. Zeller, *Die Philosophie der Griechen*, Part One, vol. II, p. 202*ff*. (D).

4. Aelian, *Var. hist.*, II, 13.

5. *Op. cit.*, ch. 7, p. 43*ff*.

6. Aristophanes attacks Cleon, a demagogue, in the *Knights*, Euripides in *Thesmophoriazusœ* and *Frogs*, and Socrates in the *Clouds*.

7. Cf. Rötscher, *op. cit.*, chap. 19, p. 272*ff*. where the history of previous interpretations of the *Clouds* is discussed, and chap. 22, p. 319*ff*. where he sets forth his own conception (D).

8. The work was published in Leipzig, 1803 (D).

9. Cf. Hegel, *Philosophy of Fine Art*, vol. IV, p. 315 (XIV, 545): 'In modern times, considerable discussion has been raised over the significance of the Greek chorus. . . . In this view we have to this extent the fact rightly conceived that the chorus is, in truth, there as a substantive and more enlightened intelligence, which warns us from irrelevant oppositions, and reflects upon the genuine issue. But, granting this to be so, it is by no means a wholly disinterested person, at leisure to entertain such thoughts and ethical judgments as it likes as are the spectators. . . . The chorus is the actual substance of the heroic life and action itself.'

10. Kierkegaard cites all passages from the *Clouds* in Greek. His text is that edited and translated by Friedrich August Wolf, Berlin, 1811. I have cited the *Clouds* in the English translation of Benjamin Bickley Rogers.

11. *Clouds*, 265*ff*.

12. *Clouds*, 340-346.

13. *Clouds*, 379. Hirsch explains that Kierkegaard derived his analogy between the negative dialectic and the whirlwind from Wolf, the editor of the Greek text. Wolf had remarked that here Aristophanes alludes to the 'ethereal vortex' of Anaxagoras.

14. In Kierkegaard's draft of a satirical comedy directed at the Danish Hegelians entitled: 'The Conflict Between the Old and the New Soap Cellar,' the image of nebulosity (clouds of smoke) is used analogously to the present explanation of Aristophanes' use of clouds as the symbol of the chorus. Cf. *Papirer, II B 10*, p. 289.

15. *Clouds*, 218ff.

16. A statement such as this appears to me to be ironic in Kierkegaard's own sense of the term, for it is nothing so much as a self-conscious statement of his polemical strategy. As Aristophanes' comic characters (according to Hegel) are themselves aware of being comic, and as the chorus (according to the Hegelian Rötscher) is itself conscious of having arrayed itself in a symbol, so, too, the essay on irony is aware of itself in its total design and intention as embodying an 'ironic negative result.'

17. *Clouds*, 856ff.; cf. 497ff.

18. According to the well-known fable of Aesop.

19. One is reminded here of the controversy then being argued in Copenhagen intellectual circles over the status of the 'principle of contradiction' between Bishop Mynster, on the one hand, and J. L. Heiberg and H. L. Martensen on the other. Cf. 'Modsigelsens Grundsætning' by V. Kuhr in *Kierkegaard Studier*, Part Two, Copenhagen, 1915.

20. See above p. 169n.

21. *vita ante acta*, previous life.

22. Cf. Rötscher, *op. cit.*, p. 285 n. 3.

23. Kant, *Critique of Pure Reason*, transl. by N. K. Smith, p. 505: 'A hundred real thalers do not contain the least coin more than a hundred possible thalers.' Cf. Hegel, *Science of Logic*, vol. I, pp. 98ff. (IV, 93ff.).

24. *Aristophanis Nubes* cum scholiis . . . rec. G. Hermannus, Lipsiæ, 1799, p. 32 (D).

25. Hirsch has contributed his own ingenious interpretation of this much discussed passage. Cf. *Über den Begriff der Ironie*, p. 351 (note 174).

26. In defending the relative validity of the Aristophanic Socrates, Kierkegaard is consciously following Hegel. See above pp. 246, 247. The originality of the discussion lies in the rigorous way he applies Hegel's insight, even allowing it to culminate in itself as a unified view of Socrates. The irony lies in the fact that such a rigorous application of Hegelian method and perspectives brings him everywhere into collision with the Hegelians, in this case Rötscher, against whom he will argue that the

standpoint here described is not that of a full-blown subjectivity but irony, the mere beginning of subjectivity.

27. *Op. cit.*, pp. 276*ff.* and 312ff. (in agreement with Süvern) (D).

28. See above p. 84*ff.*

29. *Phædo* 97 C-98 B.

30. *Apology* 33 A.

31. For the significance of the term *Mellemhverandre* see above p. 361, note 11.

32. Cf. *S.V.* XIII, 68.

33. Cf. Xenophon's *Symposium*, chap. 5 (where nothing is said of Socrates' large feet but instead his broad, pug nose, his large mouth, and his protruding eyes) (D).

34. *Op. cit.*, p. 319*ff.*

35. *Clouds*, 889*ff.*

36. *Clouds*, 483*ff.*

37. Implicit in Kierkegaard's easy apology for Aristophanes' treatment of the Socratic dialectic as a 'forthright comic parody' is his own theory of epos or 'the right use of words' developed as early as 1838 in his first publication *From the Papers of One Still Living*, in which he set forth his views on the nature of the philosophical novel in the course of a bristling attack on Hans Christian Andersen as a novelist. In this critique Kierkegaard argues that Andersen has 'leaped over his epos,' by which he means the 'serious involvement with a given actuality,' the *conditio sine qua non* of which is the possession of a developed view of life (*Livs-Anskuelse*). Cf. *S.V.* XIII, 66, 67, 73-81.

38. Cf. Holberg's *Erasmus Montanus*, act I, scene 2; act III, scene 3.

39. *Clouds*, 423*ff.*

40. *Irische Elfenmärchen*, Leipzig, 1826, xxxvii.

41. These words are traditionally ascribed to Archimedes in his pride over his discoveries in the science of mechanics. As predicated of an intellectual standpoint they occur frequently in Hamann. Here in a single play on words Kierkegaard has allowed us to *see* the standpoint which he has been developing through the reciprocal determination of these three contemporary conceptions of Socrates. Between the all too mundane conception of Xenophon and the all too idealistic conception of Plato, we have Aristophanes' unforgettable image of Socrates suspended in a basket between heaven and earth. The actuality of irony is therefore to be a *confinium* between the empirical and the ideal self.

42. *Op. cit.*, p. 247*ff.*

43. Cf. *Memorabilia* I, 2, 6*ff.*

44. See above p. 169n.

45. Drachmann calls attention to the fact that this sentence is meant to echo *Job* 1 : 21.

46. Rötscher, *op. cit.*, p. 20 (it is related of Aristophanes' comedies generally and not just the *Clouds*) (D).

47. It is impossible to render this phrase in English with the ambiguity of the original. The best I can do is to discuss its several meanings separately. The Danish phrase: *jeg har søgt at være selv Tredie mod Een*, literally means: 'I have sought to be myself (the) third against one.' In the first place, the Danish *Tredie* is a straightforward translation of Hegel's quasi technical term *der Dritte*, 'the third' or mediating moment in any dialectical development. One must not be misled because there are here four moments (the conceptions of Xenophon, Plato, Aristophanes, and Kierkegaard), whereas there are ordinarily three terms in Hegel's dialectical progressions. The essential thing for Hegel is that there is only one mediating activity throughout any series of terms, the dialectical element immanent in the material, the movement throughout any extended succession whereby the implicit rationality or interrelatedness of the material is made explicit, the work of reason mastering or informing its content. For Hegel the division of successive determinations or negations into triads is actually the work of the understanding, while for reason there is only a movement to be traversed, a network of relations to be explicated, a content to be assimilated. Kierkegaard is therefore saying that given a content (the three contemporary conceptions of Socrates), his discussion is itself the dialectical agency by which its rational transformation is effected and the substantive result into which the relative truths are assimilated. That the discussion should itself become aware of this movement is also thoroughly Hegelian; in Kierkegaard's terms it is 'the transubstantiation of the given content' whereby the consciousness of an object is transcended in a new unified consciousness constituting itself as experience. This is the essential meaning of the phrase, and the others are merely verbal accessories. For example, the phrase also bears the meaning: 'I have sought to be myself three to one,' pretty fair odds if one is going to play at Hegel. The phrase also plays on an old idiomatic expression which Hirsch dwells on: the combination '*selv Tredie*' sounds to the ear like the compound noun '*Selvtredie*' (German: *Selbstdritter*) employed in such idiomatic expressions as when one 'makes himself a third' in accompanying two companions on a walk (discussion). By extension, to be the third (party) between two disputants is to be the mediator, but the latter connotation is already contained in the Hegelian term *der Dritte*. Finally, the phrase also admits of a satirical allusion to Kierkegaard's relation to H. L. Martensen as enacted in the present essay.

48. For Hegel's dialectic of whole and part, cf. *Science of Logic*, vol. II, pp. 143-148 (IV, 641-648).

49. That Kierkegaard has been concerned with the order of knowing or the problem of communication throughout the foregoing discussion

suddenly appears from the present reference to a 'moment of contemplation' on the part of the reader, for the sake of which this long first chapter has assumed its present structure. The assumption is that *what* is being said is not independent of *how* it is said. Here we have one of the overlapping concerns of the German romantics, Hegel, and Kierkegaard, and although at such crucial points of coincidence Kierkegaard's terminology may incline towards the romantics, his appreciation of the issue appears to be conditioned by an enviable grasp of Hegel. What Kierkegaard here calls 'contemplation,' for example, resembles what Hegel called 'verification and proof.' Cf. *The Logic of Hegel*, translated from the *Encyclopädie* by William Wallace, p. 285, 286 (VIII, 351, 352): 'When, as now, the Concept is called the truth of Being and Essence, we must expect to be asked, why we do not begin with the Concept? The answer is that, where knowledge by thought is our aim, we cannot begin with the truth, because the truth, when it forms the beginning, must rest on mere assertion. The truth when it is thought must as such verify itself to thought. If the Concept were put at the head of Logic, and defined, quite correctly in point of content, as the unity of Being and Essence, the following question would come up: What are we to think under the terms "Being" and "Essence," and how do they come to be embraced in the unity of the Concept? But if we answered these questions, then our beginning with the Concept would be merely nominal. The real start would be made with Being, as we have done: with this difference, that the characteristics of Being as well as those of Essence would have to be accepted uncritically from figurative conception, whereas we have observed Being and Essence in their own dialectical development and learned how they lose themselves in the unity of the Concept.' The point on which all three seem to be agreed is the need for some form of *via negationis*.

Chapter II. The conception made actual (pages 185-221)

1. *crux philologorum*, a cross or plague for the philologist.

2. H. Oehlenschläger, 'Skattegraveren,' in *Digteværker*, Copenhagen, 1846, vol. XVII, p. 24.

3. *Xenophon Sokratiske Merkværdigheder*, translated by J. Block, Copenhagen, 1792, p. 35ff.

4. 'Kierkegaard is thinking of the Hebrew name for God in the *Old Testament* which is written only with consonants since it may not be pronounced. Instead of the correct vowels those from the substitute word "The Lord" are used' (H).

5. T. Heinsius, *Sokrates nach dem Grade seiner Schuld*, zum Schutz gegen neuere Verunglimpfungen, Leipzig, 1839, p. 19n. (2) (D).

6. *Platons Leben und Schriften*, p. 484ff.

7. *Apology* 31 C-32 A.

8. *De genio Socratis*, chap. 10-12.

9. *De divinatione*, I, 54, 122.

10. *Apology* 31 C.

11. *Apology* 27 B-E.

12. 'Kierkegaard is here in agreement with the speculative theism of I. H. Fichte' (H).

13. *Matt.* 23 : 24.

14. Hegel, VII, 385.

15. Hegel, XI, 350, 351.

16. The text of Hegel's *Vorlesungen über die Geschichte der Philosophie* used by Kierkegaard is reproduced in *Jubiläumsausgabe* (XVII-XIX) and is quite different from the second amended edition by Michelet (1840). The latter edition was made the basis of the English translation by E. S. Haldane, *Hegel's Lectures on the History of Philosophy*, vols. I-III, London, 1955. I have therefore had no other choice but to follow the text used by Kierkegaard even though this has occasionally meant translating from the *Jubiläumsausgabe*. Most often, however, there is a passage to be found in Michelet (Haldane) corresponding either in part or in whole to the original edition. In the body of the translation will be found the German reference to the *Jubiläumsausgabe*, while in my notes I refer the English reader to the corresponding passage in Haldane's translation where one exists. Cf. *Lectures on the History of Philosophy*, vol. I, pp. 421*ff.*, 431*ff.*

17. *Ibid*, pp. 422, 423.

18. *Ibid*, p. 423.

19. Hegel, *Lectures on the History of Philosophy*, vol. I, p. 422.

20. *Ibid*, p. 425.

21. *Ibid*, p. 422.

22. *Ibid*.

23. *Ibid*, p. 425.

24. *Ibid*, pp. 424, 425.

25. Plutarch, 'Cæsar,' chap. 38 ('thou carryest Cæsar and Cæsar's fortune in thy boat').

26. Hegel, *Lectures on the History of Philosophy*, vol. I, p. 424.

27. Hegel, XVIII, 96 (Haldane, vol. I, p. 423).

28. II *Corinthians* 10 : 5.

29. *idem per idem*, the same for the sake of the same.

30. Cf. XVIII, 53: 'Seine Philosophie, als die das Wesen in das Bewusstseyn als ein Allgemeines setzte, ist als *seinem individuellen Leben* angehörig anzusehen; sie ist nicht eigentliche spekulative Philosophie, sondern *ein individuelles Thun* geblieben. Und ebenso ist ihr Inhalt die Wahrheit des *individuellen Thuns* selbst; das Wesen, der Zweck seiner Philosophie ist,

das individuelle Thun des Einzelnen als *ein allgemeingültiges Thun* einzurichten.'

31. I have here departed from the correlations listed in the Glossary and translated *afrunde* as 'round off' instead of 'culminate.'

32. *sine ira atque studio*, without anger and partisan feeling. Cf. Tacitus, *Annals* I, I.

33. Besides Hegel (XVIII, 120ff.), Kierkegaard is undoubtedly thinking of P. W. Forchhammer, *Die Athener und Sokrates*, Die Gesetztlichen und der Revolutionär, Berlin, 1837 (D).

34. Diogenes Laertius II, 40: 'This indictment and affidavit is sworn by Meletus, the son of Meletus of Pitthos, against Socrates, the son of Sophroniscus of Alopece: Socrates is guilty of refusing to recognize the gods recognized by the state, and of introducing other new divinities. He is also guilty of corrupting the youth. The penalty demanded is death.' The Metroön was a sanctuary in Athens in which were housed the archives.

35. Anaxagoras, Protagoras, Diagoras of Melos, among others (D).

36. *Phædo* 97 C-98 B; *Apology* 26 D.

37. *Republic* 531 D-533 C.

38. *Symposium* 210 A-212 A.

39. *Apology* 20 B, C.

40. The full title is *Abhandlungen der philosophischen Klasse der Königlich-Preussischen Akademie der Wissenschaft* aus den Jahren 1814-15, Berlin, 1818, p. 50ff.

41. Hirsch translates this as 'nicht Weisheit zu sein,' but Kierkegaard appears to mean what he says: 'not to be as such.' The point of this Socratic ignorance, here designated human wisdom, is that man comes to see himself as he is as such, i.e., in his autonomy apart from a relationship to creative personality, i.e., the negative presupposition for every subsequent change or transformation. As in the cognitive sphere much positivity accrues to this 'human wisdom' that has come to see itself as 'ignorance,' so in the metaphysical sphere there remains a possibility that the experience of non-being, the confrontation with nothingness, may function constructively or creatively for some.

42. *John* 3 : 17.

43. *Apology* 23 B.

44. *Matt.* 5 : 26.

45. Cf. *Lectures on the History of Philosophy*, vol. II, p. 4.

46. *beata culpa*, fortunate sin. Cf. Augustine, *De diligendo Deo*, ch. 6: 'felix culpa' (D).

47. Cf. *Lectures on the History of Philosophy*, vol. I, p. 399.

48. *Timæus* 29 E.

49. Presumably, Kierkegaard is here distinguishing the negativity residing in the Socratic ignorance from the negativity inherent in the Hegelian

dialectic. Negations for the latter are not empty negations but negations of a determinate content, and hence results which may function as points of departure for deeper speculation. While both dialectics concern the way, only the Hegelian posits itself both as the way and the truth.

50. *Der christliche Glaube*, second edition, vol. 1, p. 183*ff*. (D).

51. 'The expression "a much more concrete development" is Kierke-gaard's way of distinguishing the age of Schleiermacher from the age of Socrates. That the modern is a more concrete age than antiquity is a perspective taken over directly from Hegel's philosophy of history' (H).

52. 'To relate to God as object rather than as infinite spirit is, according to Hegel, to have a finite relationship to the deity' (H).

53. See above p. 57n.

54. *Alcibiades II* 138 B, C. The citation below is from 143 A. Kierke-gaard is also well aware that this dialogue is spurious.

55. One of the apophthegms inscribed on the temple of Apollo at Delphi.

56. The term 'scientificity' (*Videnskabelighed*) has a negative connotation for Kierkegaard and refers to the Hegelian systematicians. Hegel discusses the significance of 'know thyself' at least once in each of his works. Cf., for example, the following from the *Encyclopädie* (x, 9*ff*.): 'A knowledge of mind is the most concrete, highest, and most difficult of all. The absolute demand: "know thyself" does not mean—either in itself or as it appeared historically—a self-knowledge of the particular capacities, character, drives, and weaknesses of the individual, but meant a knowledge of the truth about man as this is in and for itself, the essence of mind itself . . . The requirement that went out to the Greeks from the Delphic Apollo concerning self-knowledge does not bear the sense of a law deriving from an external power addressed to human mind; on the contrary, the god who urges self-knowledge is none other than the laws of absolute mind itself. All activity of mind is but an apprehension of itself; the goal of all true science is only that mind know itself in everything in the earth and under the heavens.' As the expression applies to Socrates, Hegel writes (XVIII, 107): 'Socrates it was who carried out the command of the god of knowledge, "know thyself," and made it the motto of the Greeks, calling it the law of the mind and not interpreting it as meaning a mere acquaint-ance with the particular nature of man. Thus Socrates is the hero who established in the place of the Delphic oracle the principle that man must look within himself to know what is truth.' (Haldane, vol. 1, p. 435.)

57. Kierkegaard's expression: *adskil dig selv fra Andet* contains the quasi technical Hegelian term the 'other' (*Andet*). As it appears without quali-fication, so it signifies a negation of the widest possible extension. Here I would interpret it as meaning 'everything else,' while on the following page he adds to it the specific connotation 'the state.'

58. The distinction implied in this sentence between the speculative and the practical adequately characterizes the different orientations of Kierkegaard and Martensen at this time.

59. *Apology* 28 E.

60. *Apology* 32 B; cf. Xenophon's *Mem.* I, I, 18.

61. It was impossible to handle the ambiguities of this sentence without the help of brackets. The parenthesis is here, as elsewhere, Kierkegaard's.

62. *Apology* 23 B; 31 C-32 A.

63. *Mem.* I, p. 8; see above p. 186n.

64. *Op. cit.*, 6, 15.

65. 'Kierkegaard means that a concrete speculative mode of thought like that of Hegel or Daub is assurance against an enthusiasm which flees from actuality; Socrates, on the other hand, had only the abstract aspect of thought in his power' (H). This, of course, is one possible interpretation of what Kierkegaard means.

66. *Apology* 28 D.

67. *Tusculan disputations*, V, 10 (D).

68. See above p. 51.

69. 'Kierkegaard is thinking of the dogma of the liberal movement in his day that the question of the proper constitution is more urgent than questions concerning beneficial particular arrangements within the state' (H).

70. *Op. cit.*, p. 54*ff.*

71. 'Über den Werth des Sokrates als Philosophen,' p. 52.

72. Hegel, XVIII, 107*ff.* (Haldane, vol. I, p. 435*ff.*)

73. Cf. *Lectures on the History of Philosophy*, vol. I, p. 438.

74. *Apology* 19 D, 31 B, 33 A; *Euthyphro* 3 D; Xenophon's *Mem.* I, 2, 5-8; I, 2, 60; I, 6, 11.

75. *Clouds* 1146*ff.*; cf. also 668*ff.*

76. The continuity in Kierkegaard's development of the 'three great Ideas': Don Juan, Ahasuerus, Faust (*Papirer, I A 150*) is here seen to go through his initial work with Socrates in the present essay. After the 'three great Ideas' found their consolidation in a single project, the Idea of Faust, and after this was abandoned after the 'collision' with Martensen, the theme of the 'reflective seducer' breaks out again in his discussion of Socrates' relation to his disciples. It ultimately requires literary expression, and becomes the content of his novelle. See next 'Diary of a Seducer' in *Either/Or*.

77. *Symposium* 222 B. See above p. 86.

78. *Matt.* 5 : 28.

79. The image has reference to the process of refining silver, and recurs in *Stages On Life's Way*, p. 71 (VI, 71). It was probably derived originally from Goethe's *Wilhelm Meister's Apprenticeship*, Bk. I, ch. 15.

80. I *Corinthians* 15 : 52.

81. This would seem to be a literary allusion of sorts, yet neither Drachmann nor Hirsch have been able to locate the precise source. It might be that no 'precise' source was intended, however, and that it is a literary allusion, to be sure, but one now transformed in accordance with Goethe's theory of 'productive criticism,' to which Kierkegaard wholeheartedly subscribed and even elaborated. As such it has seemed to me to be an obvious allusion to and comment on Goethe's *Eclective Affinities*, chapter 28, naturally adapted to Kierkegaard's own purposes and reduplicated in highly compressed form, an instance of that kind of converse characteristic of original minds which a literary tradition makes possible. Otilie, in Goethe's novel, is in a situation similar to the confrontation between the Athenian youth and Socrates described by Kierkegaard in this section of the essay. That the parallel is intentional may be seen from the fact that Kierkegaard has borrowed more than one Goethean phrase from this pivotal chapter of the novel.

82. *Symposium* 180 c-185 c.

83. Hegel, *Philosophy of History*, p. 238 (xi, 314): 'This stamps the Greek character as that of individuality conditioned by beauty, which is produced by mind, transforming the merely natural into an expression of its own being. The activity of mind does not yet possess in itself the material and organ of expression, but needs the excitement of nature and the matter which nature supplies: it is not free, self-determining mentality, but mere naturalness formed to *Geistlichkeit*—spiritual individuality.'

84. Xenophon's *Symposium* ii, 10; cf. also Diogenes Lærtius ii, 37.

85. *Apology* 38 A, B.

86. *Apology* 36 A-37 D.

87. *Lectures on the History of Philosophy*, vol. i, p. 444.

88. An allusion to Hegel's theory of the 'qualitative leap'; cf. *Phenomenology of Mind*, p. 75 (ii, 18).

89. Some of the older editions read 'three' instead of 'thirty.'

90. Horace, *Odes*, iii, 24, 6.

91. Hirsch points out that by 'formation' Kierkegaard here means geological formation, that is, age, epoch, period.

92. This refers to romantic irony as discussed in Part Two of the essay.

Chapter III. The conception made necessary (pages 222-40)

1. In 1849 Kierkegaard applied this simile to himself during the intense reflective struggle with himself over the publication of his new religious production of 1848 (*Sickness unto Death*, *Training in Christianity*, *The Point of View*). *Papirer*, XI A 422: 'As the river Guadalquivir at one place plunges underground for a time only in order to emerge once more, so

must I now plunge into pseudonymity. But this time I have also understood where I will emerge again in my own name' (н). Cf. *XI A 510*, p. 329. Kierkegaard had already used this simile as early as 1839 to characterize 'the great parenthesis'—the preparations for his examination in theology. Cf. *Papirer, II A 497*.

2. The Danish is more descriptive: the word for a dash is *Tankestreg*, literally 'a thought mark'.

3. The term is taken over from Hegel's conception of universal history, cf. *Philosophy of Right*, pp. 216-220 (VII, 446ff.) and *Philosophy of History*, revised edition, pp. 25, 30, *et passim*.

4. *via negationis*, the way of negation; and *via eminentiæ*, the way of perfection or idealization. These are technical terms from scholastic philosophy for two methods of defining the attributes of God, and used 'particularly by orthodox Lutheran theologians of the seventeenth century. The first is done negatively by denying God all finite and imperfect qualities, the second positively by attributing to God all absolute and perfect qualities. Kierkegaard knew these two modes of approach through lectures in dogmatics covering standard material and most likely through Karl Hase, *Hutterus redivivus*, para. 59, where the argument is summarized.' (Thulstrup.) Cf. *Philosophical Fragments*, with an introduction and commentary by Niels Thulstrup, Princeton U. Press, 1962, p. 220.

5. Here we have a glimpse into an earlier organization of the material. What is now chapter III in an earlier draft belonged to Part Two, most likely to the section entitled: 'The World Historical Validity of Irony.'

6. Hegel, XVIII, 42 (Haldane, vol. I, p. 384).

7. *Ibid*, p. 42: 'Socrates . . . is not only a most important figure in the history of philosophy, perhaps the most interesting in the philosophy of antiquity, but is also a world-famed personage. For *an intellectual turning point* exhibited itself in him in the form of philosophic thought.'

8. Plato only says this in the *Apology*. Kierkegaard must mean several times within this single dialogue.

9. Hegel, XI, 207.

10. This an unmistakable barb directed at H. L. Martensen. For three consecutive semesters (1837-39) Martensen, as *Docent* in moral philosophy, had gone through the history of modern philosophy according to Hegel's broad perspectives beginning with Descartes and the principle of methodological doubt (*De omnibus dubitandum est*). Kierkegaard was so 'interested' in following Martensen over this ground that he attended these lectures the first two times through himself, and got hold of three other sets of notes (all in the same handwriting and more complete than his own), and so had in his possession five versions in all (*Papirer, II C 12-28*). It was in the fifth lecture on 29th November, 1837, that Kierkegaard heard

his own conception of Faust as the 'personified doubt' from the lectern which signalled the collapse of his own Faust project and triggered the series of satirical sketches and ironic barbs in his Journal at the Danish Hegelians from that time onwards. In the sketch for a satirical comedy 'The Conflict Between the Old and the New Soap Cellar' (*Papirer, II B 1-21*), for example, the philosopher *von Springgaasen* is an obvious parody of J. L. Heiberg, while his disciple *Phrase* ('I have gone beyond Hegel') is clearly H. L. Martensen. Both vie with each other in their eagerness to rehearse the history of modern philosophy beginning with Descartes and the principle of doubt, and between them they actually make eight starts within five pages periodically punctuated by *Phrase*'s ejaculation from 1836. This whole sequence of events was first set forth and convincingly documented in Prof. Carl Roos, *Kierkegaard og Goethe*, Copenhagen, 1955.

11. It is one of the peculiarities of Hegel's interpretation of Socrates that he makes the decline of fifth century Athens reflect itself in the fate of Socrates. Cf. *Lectures on the History of Philosophy*, vol. 1, p. 447: 'The principle of Socrates is hence not the transgression of one individual, for all were implicated. The crime was one that the spirit of a people committed against itself.' Cf. *Philosophy of History*, pp. 265-271 (XI, 345-352).

12. On the principle of unjustified subjectivity, cf. Hegel, *Philosophy of Right*, pp. 93-103 (VII, 204*ff*.).

13. *Mark* 5 : 9.

14. This is less true of the second revised edition prepared by Michelet.

15. Cf. *Philosophy of History*, p. 5 (XI, 30): 'A history which aspires to traverse long periods of time, or to be universal, must indeed forego the attempt to give individual representations of the past as it actually existed. It must foreshorten its pictures by abstractions; and this includes not merely the omission of events and deeds, but whatever is involved in the fact that thought is, after all, the most trenchant epitomist.'

16. *ein fliegendes Blatt*, a broadsheet, the form in which poetry was circulated in the sixteenth century. The expression is one of many characteristic phrases of Hamann taken over by Kierkegaard and adapted to his own use. On Kierkegaard's lips the phrase had by this time come to have a tone of satire directed at Martensen for the latter's not very independent assimilation of the thought of the German Catholic philosopher Franz von Baader, whom Martensen conferred with in Munich on his two-year travelling fellowship (1834-36), and whose influence on Martensen's development was decisive. This is the background, for example, behind the sardonic phrase in Kierkegaard's Journal '*ein fliegendes Blatt aus München*' (*Papirer, II A 8*). Kierkegaard's own indebtedness to Baader is apparent in his use of the term *Samviden* in his discussion of the intimate intellectual relationship between Plato and Socrates (see above p. 68). In

the present essay, it can scarcely be accidental that whenever Kierkegaard appears slavishly Hegelian, the satiric references to Martensen increase accordingly.

17. This appears to be another barb at Martensen whom Kierkegaard was fond of regarding as an itinerant scholastic. The term 'itinerant' has reference to Martensen's travelling fellowship, while the term 'scholastic' has reference to Martensen's attempt to reunite philosophy and theology in his lectures as a private *Docent* which began as follows (*Papirer, II C 12*): 'An earlier age, the Middle Ages, required that the theologian *qua* theologian should be a philosopher, the philosopher *qua* philosopher a theologian. Although they were subsequently separated, they have now been reunited again. Speculative dogmatics is Christian metaphysics.' Martensen subsequently published two well-known studies of the German mystics Meister Eckhart and Jakob Boehme. Carl Roos has called attention to one of the aphorisms of 'Diapsalmata' which also alludes to and develops the theme with the same overtones as here in the essay on irony. Cf. *Either/Or* (Anchor), pp. 24, 25.

18. *Protagoras* 318 D, E.

19. *Faust* 1868*ff.*

20. *Gorgias* 466 A, B.

21. Hegel, XI, 349, 350.

22. *Protagoras* 309 C-310 E.

23. *loci communes*, general arguments or positions.

24. It is, perhaps, worth mentioning that Kierkegaard's only experience with a tutor was in 1834 when he secured Martensen as his private tutor for purposes of discussion. From Martensen's point of view it can scarcely be construed as anything but a personal attack to read here that the Sophists resembled nothing so much as tutors. In his autobiography which he published in 1882-83 Martensen describes these sessions with the young Kierkegaard as follows: 'He had his own method of letting himself be tutored. Refusing any prescribed reading, he asked only that I should discourse for him and engage in conversation with him. I chose to lecture on the chief points in Schleiermacher's *Dogmatik* and to converse with him about it. I immediately perceived that here was no ordinary talent, but also one with an irresistible hankering after sophistry, a playing with overly subtle distinctions which exhibited itself on every occasion and frequently became tiresome. I am particularly minded of how it displayed itself when we discussed the doctrine of predestination where there is, so to speak, an open door to sophists.' (*Af mit Levnet*, part I, pp. 78, 79.) One of the discernible features in Martensen's autobiography is the wholly understandable yet undeniable strain of apology running through it, whereby Bishop Martensen is concerned to present his side of the narrative covering an unusually long and brilliant public career, and one which,

by the very nature of the offices he occupied, must inevitably have involved numerous conflicts, debates, and controversial decisions on important cultural issues of the day. The impartial reader will always be able to sympathize with Martensen in his confrontation with such a splenetic, polemical, and satiric genius as Kierkegaard. It was, after all, the fact that the young Kierkegaard regarded him as a peer and rival which attracted him to Martensen in the first place. Martensen's behaviour surely requires no defence: literary, philosophical, theological, and scientific controversies and rivalries are part of the intellectual scene and as old as the muses themselves. My concern in pointing this out is to try to illuminate, wherever possible, an ambiguous text, to try to understand what Kierkegaard is doing with language and saying in his books.

25. Similarly, the contemporary discussion of 'a methodological doubt' was for Kierkegaard an abortive doubt that effects little. As he everywhere aligns doubt with irony, however, and is concerned throughout the essay to endow irony with a life, a career, a history of its own; so as surely does he envisage a more intimate acquaintance with and a more concrete function for doubt than its reduction to an initial premise in a demonstration. A revitalized scepticism is one of the pervasive themes throughout his literary production. It seems necessary to add, however, that what Kierkegaard would term 'authentic doubt' is at certain points appropriately characterized as a 'pathological doubt.' Hence his frequent allusions throughout the essay to the 'precarious,' the 'unwarranted,' the 'danger' for the self posed by certain forms of irony.

26. Hegel was fond of using the term *raisonnements* as a synonym for the standpoint of the Greek Sophists. Cf. *The Logic of Hegel*, p. 228 (VIII, 286), *et passim*.

27. *Exodus* 1 : 14.

28. *Lectures on the History of Philosophy*, vol. I, p. 352.

29. πάντων χρημάτων . . . , man is the measure of all things.

30. Both Drachmann and Hirsch find unnecessary difficulties with Kierkegaard's interpretation of Hegel on this point. Cf. *Lectures on the History of Philosophy*, vol. I, pp. 373, 374 (XVIII, 30, 31): 'The main point of his (Protagoras') system of knowledge he expressed thus: "Man is the *measure* of all things; of that which is, that it is; of that which is not, that it is not." . . . Now Protagoras' assertion has a certain *ambiguity*: as man is the undetermined, either he may in his individual particularity, as this contingent man, be the measure, or else self-conscious reason in man, man in his rational nature and universality is the absolute measure. . . . Thus here the great proposition is enunciated on which, from this time forward, everything turns, since the further progress of philosophy only explains it further: it signifies that reason is the *end* of all things.'

31. *Maal*, measure, end, goal. As Hegel was not translated into Danish,

the reference to the ambiguity of the word *Maal* (there is no such linguistic ambiguity in German) has immediate reference to Martensen's second lecture which capitalizes on the above mentioned ambiguity (*Papirer, II C 14*).

32. Kierkegaard's own period of serious doubts can be documented as early as 1833, and by 1835 he had abandoned the serious study of theology. He resumed the academic study of theology after a conversion experience and his father's death in 1838.

33. *Meno* 95 C.

34. The three theses of Gorgias are the following. (1) Nothing is; (2) If something is, it cannot be known; (3) If something can be known, it cannot be expressed. Cf. Zeller, *Die Philosophie der Griechen*, vol.12, p. 1101*ff*. (D).

35. *Lectures on the History of Philosophy*, vol. I, p. 384.

36. It is not clear where Kierkegaard gets this phrase from. On page 143 above he referred twice to the insolence of the Sophists but did not use the exact phrase. It does not occur as such in the *Gorgias*, although it leaps to mind with Socrates' ironic reply to Callicles (487 D): 'And of the frankness of your nature and freedom from diffidence I am assured by yourself, and the assurance is confirmed by your last speech.' It may be a phrase which remained with him from his extensive reading of the Platonic literature then available.

37. This thesis, together with the one immediately following, is advanced by Callicles, cf. *Gorgias* 483 D and 483 A respectively.

38. It is statements such as this which warn the reader that he may not simply identify the position of Kierkegaard with the conceptual determinations used to delineate the figure of Socrates.

39. ' "Hero" is a *terminus technicus* in Hegel's philosophy of history for historically momentous, epoch-positing personalities, particularly when their work consummates itself through their own apparent dissolution. The concept was popularized by Carlyle' (H).

40. *Matt.* 11 : 15; *Mark* 8 : 18.

41. 'The expression derives from a particular orientation within Lutheran christology and has reference to the presence of divinity in Christ. The theologically trained reader will perceive in this sentence an implicit comparison of Socrates with John the Baptist. Cf. *John* 1 : 20*ff*. and 3 : 28*ff*.' (H).

42. *Apology* 30 E.

43. Zopyrus, after a physiognomic investigation of Socrates, maintained that Socrates had numerous bad features. Cf. Cicero, *Tusculan disputations* IV, 80 (D).

44. The word in Danish is *forklarede* and means both 'explained' and 'transfigured'.

45. The term designating the calm state of mind which the Sceptics endeavoured to attain by suspending judgment (ἐποχή) on every question. Hirsch has pointed out the relevance for Kierkegaard's discussion of Hegel's analysis of sceptical self-consciousness in *Phenomenology of Mind*, p. 248 (II, 164): 'Sceptical self-consciousness thus discovers, in the flux and alternation of all that would stand secure in its presence, its own freedom, as given by and received from its own self. It is aware of being this *ataraxy* of self-thinking thought, the unalterable and authentic certainty of self.'

46. *Zeitschrift für Philosophie und spekulative Theologie*, edited by Dr. I. H. Fichte (Neue Folge, 2 BD.).

47. As relevant as *Romans* is to this discussion, the more obvious reference is *Galatians* 3 : 23, 24.

48. It will no doubt seem rather strange to the contemporary reader to hear the term 'happy' regularly applied to Greece in the fifth century B.C., and must be put down to the inertia of classical scholarship dating at least from the Enlightenment. Over against this rather sentimental tendency the reader will have to bear in mind that much of what Kierkegaard reads into or out of the figure of Socrates via the concept of irony was for the nineteenth century the daemonic.

49. This must refer to the period between Kant and Hegel discussed in Part Two.

50. This must refer to the second 'phenomenological manifestation' of irony discussed in Part Two.

51. *Luke* 16 : 26.

52. 'Über den Werth des Sokrates als Philosophen.'

53. W. T. Krug, *Geschichte der Philosophie alter Zeit*, vornehmlich unter Griechen und Römern, Leipzig, 1815; cf. also *Allgemeines Handwörterbuch der Philosophen Wissenschaften*, Leipzig, 1827-29 (D).

54. Lactantius, *Institutiones* III, 19, 17.

55. *Rheinisches Museum für Jurisprudenz, Philologie, Geschichte und griechische Philosophie*, ersten Jahrganges, erstes und zweites Heft, Abtheilung für Philologie, Geschichte und Philosophie, pp. 118, 119 (D).

56. *Lectures on the History of Philosophy*, vol. I, p. 449.

57. *Lectures on the History of Philosophy*, vol. I, p. 452.

58. See above p. 175n.

59. *Lectures on the History of Philosophy*, vol. I, p. 449.

60. *Ibid*, pp. 452-53.

61. Part One of the essay has been concerned to establish the standpoint of Socrates as irony, by which is meant *infinite absolute negativity*, or what may be termed the 'reversal joint' of the Hegelian dialectic. It is appropriate that Kierkegaard finally acknowledge what the reader has only gradually become aware of, namely, that such irony entails infinite ambiguity. The section therefore concludes by having recourse to the tech-

niques of the sublime in a final attempt to conjure forth the spirit of this phenomenon in the image of the whirlwind that sweeps the particular subject, the Sophists, and ultimately Socrates himself out beyond the ancient world into the all encircling Oceanus stream wherein the Abstract Universal mysteriously determine themselves towards the infinitely concrete.

Supplement: Hegel's conception of Socrates (page 241-56)

1. 'In folk tales and fairy-tales, for example in *1001 Nights*, it often occurs that at every stage of the imaginary hero's journey he meets a watchman, etc., for whom he monotonously rehearses the course of his adventures up to that point.' (H). Another barb at Martensen.

2. Jacob Brucker, *Historia critica philosophiæ*, Leipzig, 1742, vol. I, p. 522ff. (D).

3. Tychsen, 'Über den Process des Sokrates,' in *Bibliothek der alten Litteratur und Kunst*, erstes Stück, Göttingen, 1786, pp. 153, zweites Stück, 1787, pp. 1-60 (D).

4. W. T. Krug, *op. cit.*, pp. 152-163; and vol. III, p. 711ff.

5. Schleiermacher, 'Über den Werth des Sokrates als Philosophen.' See above p. 196n.

6. This is undeniably the centre of gravity in Hegel's entire conception of Socrates as interpreted by Kierkegaard. Accordingly, the essay recurs to this insight on five separate occasions, cf. pp. 193, 241n, 243, 245, 247.

7. *Op. cit.*, p. 126.

8. *Phædrus* 265 D.

9. *principium exclusi* . . ., the principle that between two contradictories the middle term is excluded.

10. *Op. cit.*, p. 90ff.

11. Cf. Appendix, thesis I.

12. ἐποχή, suspension of judgment, withholding of assent. Kierkegaard has identified irony as a determination of personality, as the weakest possible suggestion of subjectivity, as the true beginning of authentic selfhood. With his theological assumptions, however, personality only acquires its fullness, subjectivity its content, selfhood its most complete instantiation in the concept of God as person, i.e., the incarnation. Accordingly, the recurrent comparison between Socrates and Christ, the relationship between Humanism and Christianity, underlies not only the present discussion but touches the basic presuppositions of his thought. He would hold that there is indeed a similarity between Socrates and Christ, a true analogy, deriving from the validity both have as personalities. The standpoint of irony as embodied in the person of Socrates is therefore *warranted* and *correct* as far as it goes. The ironist Socrates exhibits the true *form* of all personality,

and Kierkegaard unhesitatingly and unequivocally assigns 'a movement back into oneself' as its definitive characteristic. To illustrate this characteristic movement of personality, Kierkegaard here has recourse to a technical term derived from Greek Scepticism: *epochē*. Ordinarily, this term translates as listed above. But Kierkegaard subsequently translates it as 'retiring doubt,' cf. *Papirer, IV B 13*, p. 178 (*De omnibus dubitandum est*), where he refers to Diogenes Lærtius, IX, 70, 76, passages in which the standpoint of the Greek Sceptics is called *doubt* 'because of the state of mind which followed their inquiry, I mean, suspense of judgment.' There may be some uneasiness in following the translation here because the English reader most readily associates the quality of 'openness' with the term *epochē* or 'suspension of judgment.' The same is true in Danish, where *epochē* is ordinarily translated as *Tilbageholdenhed*. It is here that we must have recourse to etymology to discover Kierkegaard's full meaning. For his description of this characteristic movement of the form of personality ('turning back into oneself, seeking back into oneself, terminating in oneself, drawing back into oneself') clearly derives from the etymology of *Tilbageholdenhed*, a compound noun having as its root meaning 'holding back.' And yet in the crucial passage under discussion, Kierkegaard deliberately abandons *Tilbageholdenhed*, the obvious Danish translation of *epochē*, and inserts his own original translation of *epochē* as *Paaholdenhed*. Ordinarily, this word translates as 'closedness,' and suggests associations like 'close-fistedness.' The etymology indicates better what he must have in mind. The root meaning of *Paaholdenhed* is 'holding on to.' In other words, the two opposing attitudes most often associated with *epochē*, viz., *openness* vs. *closedness* (the latter may be seen in English by translating *epochē* as 'reservation of judgment' and developing what one means by 'reserved') have been abandoned in order to emphasize a different set of opposing attitudes derived from the etymologies of the Danish *Tilbageholdenhed* vs. *Paaholdenhed*, viz., *holding back* vs. *holding on to*. It is the latter, which is the positing of personal identity, that must be intended in this passage aligning irony with *epochē*, aligning the characteristic movement of the form of personality with the movement of retiring doubt, the pervasive negation of a world in affirmation of an incipient self. —It is more important, however, to observe that Kierkegaard is following Hegel's *Phenomenology of Mind* in making the position of Scepticism (Socratic irony) immediately precede and pass over into the position of 'the unhappy consciousness' (romantic irony), see above p. 235 and the note on 'ataraxy.' It is at such dialectical junctures as this that one comes to see an importance attaching to the last brief section of the essay ('Irony as a Mastered Moment') far in excess of its length.

13. *Colossians* 2 : 9.
14. *Ephesians* 5 : 30.

15. The statement is polemical against the Danish Hegelians. Part of the irony, however, is that Kierkegaard had thoroughly convinced his environment that he was himself a disciple of Hegel.

16. Hirsch makes the point that Socrates, unlike the *Ding an sich* of the Kantians, is not allowed to withdraw from cognition. For Kant the *Ding an sich* is a necessary condition for the cognition of objects.

17. According to Roman tradition Publius Claudius Pulcher, son of Appius Claudius, lost the battle of Drepana in 249 B.C. because he abused the warning of the augurs. The anecdote is from Livius (D).

18. *Meno*.

19. There is a polemical play on words here at the expense of Hegel's terminology. The Danish equivalent for Hegel's term *aufheben* (cancel, preserve) is *ophæve*, which I have consistently translated as 'abrogate.' In addition, there is in Danish the idiomatic expression: *at gjøre Ophævelser* meaning to find difficulties or to make a fuss or bother. Thus Kierkegaard manœuvres Hegel's technical expression to where it can be mocked by idiomatic language as here, for example, we have the bit of meaningful nonsense: Hegel is not at all fond of abrogations, i.e., fuss, difficulties, bother, etc. This satirical gambit occurs in the Journal as early as 1838 (*Papirer, II A 766*): 'The Hegelians devise many abrogations [*Ophævelser*] of the concept which it is not worth bothering [*gjøre Ophævelser over*] about.'

20. *Lectures on the History of Philosophy*, vol. I, p. 406.

21. *Ibid*, vol. II, p. 10.

22. *Ibid*, p. 13.

23. *Ibid*, p. 51.

24. *Ibid*, p. 52. The parenthesis is Kierkegaard's.

25. *Ibid*, p. 56.

26. *Ibid*, vol. I, pp. 384-448.

27. *Ibid*, p. 420.

28. *Ibid*.

29. *Ibid*, p. 422.

30. As true as this judgment is, it should be borne in mind that Hegel's *Vorlesungen über die Geschichte der Philosophie* were compiled, edited, and published by Hegel's students from mere lecture notes and unfinished drafts.

31. The puzzling thing about Kierkegaard's conception of Socrates is how it is possible for it to be so thoroughly dependent on Hegel's conception of Socrates in all its significant detail, and yet add up to such a wholly different totality: how it is possible for there to be such real dissimilarity within all this apparent similarity. It seems wholly fitting, for example, that Kierkegaard should here characterize his entire conception of Socrates as a mere 'modification' of the Hegelian Socrates. And yet the reader knows that it is just these little Socratic modifications which Kierkegaard is so fond of documenting in the dialogues (pp. 19n., 20n., 38, 39n., etc.) and upon

which everything ultimately turns—as when he quoted *Protagoras* 328 E: 'Yet I have one very small difficulty which I am sure Protagoras will explain,' and added with evident satisfaction: 'But it is precisely this "very small difficulty" on which everything depends.' In the discussion which follows, the 'modification' concerns whether or not there was a positivity in Socrates' negativity. At issue (*Mellemværende*) are two *toto cælo* different conceptions of man. The argumentation proceeds, however, by demonstrating that he and Hegel can agree (*Mellemhverandre*).

32. *Lectures on the History of Philosophy*, vol. I, p. 384.

33. *Ibid*, p. 430.

34. *Ibid*, pp. 394-96; 399. The second amended edition of *Geschichte der Philosophie*, the basis of Haldane's translation, twice affirms that Socrates had no system. However, this is only part of what the first edition was concerned to affirm. It is essential here to read the text used by Kierkegaard. Cf. XVIII, 52-56.

35. *Ibid*, pp. 396, 97.

36. *Ibid*, pp. 387-8 (XVIII, 46*ff.*).

37. Hegel discusses Morality in §§105-141, Ethical Life (second *Sittlichkeit*) in §§142-360.

38. *Philosophy of Right*, §§139, 140.

39. VII, 200.

40. *Lectures on the History of Philosophy*, vol. I, p. 412. Cf. Aristotle, *Magna Moralia* I, I (1182a 15*ff.*).

41. *Ibid*, p. 413.

42. *Ibid*, p. 394.

43. It is from statements such as this that Prof. Jens Himmelstrup has argued that Kierkegaard himself subscribed to the Hegelian ethic at the time he wrote the essay on irony. Cf. *Søren Kierkegaards Opfattelse af Sokrates*, Copenhagen, 1923, pp. 69, 80, 107, 172, 174.

44. *Lectures on the History of Philosophy*, vol. I, p. 414. Cf. Aristotle, *Nichomachean Ethics*, VI, 13(1144b 18*ff.*). The rest of this paragraph is a paraphrase of Hegel.

45. *Ibid*, p. 395.

46. 'This passage provides a convenient possibility of comparing the Kierkegaard of 1841 with the Kierkegaard of 1848. In *Sickness unto Death*, written in 1848 and published the next year, Kierkegaard again discusses rather extensively the Socratic thesis that sin is ignorance' (H). Cf. *Sickness unto Death*, Anchor, p. 218*ff.* (XI, 224*ff.*).

47. *Lectures on the History of Philosophy*, vol. I, p. 406.

48. *Ibid*, pp. 406, 407.

49. *Ibid*, p. 414 (XVIII, 79).

50. *Ibid*, p. 415 (XVIII, 81).

51. One wonders whether Kierkegaard would have urged this argument

against the very damaging objection that he nowhere takes account of the *Crito* in developing his conception of Socrates. As he had read this dialogue in Greek even before entering the University, one must assume the omission was deliberate.

52. *Lectures on the History of Philosophy*, vol. I, pp. 417, 418.

53. I am unable to find a reference in Haldane corresponding to this passage.

54. *Lectures on the History of Philosophy*, vol. I, p. 418.

55. In this transition from the indeterminate universal to the determinate universal wherein the subject himself appears as deciding, we have the abstract Hegelian paradigm, as it were, behind the several concrete individualizations of this movement in Kierkegaard's æsthetic works. It is, perhaps, most readily recalled by the formula from *Either/Or*: 'to choose oneself.' But already in the essay on irony there is a continuum formed by such expressions as: 'to come to oneself,' 'to become immersed in oneself,' 'to stare into oneself,' 'know thyself,' 'to take oneself,' 'to be transparent to oneself,' 'to decide oneself,' 'to possess oneself,' 'to enjoy oneself,' etc. —a positive continuum everywhere opposed to such expressions as: 'to lose oneself,' 'to be through with oneself,' 'to do away with oneself,' 'to forget oneself,' 'to remain obscure to oneself,' 'to give the arbitrary self free expression,' 'to lull oneself to sleep,' 'not to enjoy oneself,' etc. What is generally interesting about Kierkegaard's treatment of the problem of self-knowledge is not that he attempts to solve it by severing the individual off from a total system of actuality, but that he attempts to expand and enlarge the total actuality in which the individual finds himself involved and by which he feels himself engaged.

56. Cf. *Phenomenology of Mind*, pp. 629-641; *Philosophy of Right*, p. 102; *Philosophy of Fine Art*, vol. I, pp. 89-93; *Lectures on the History of Philosophy*, vol. III, p. 507.

57. It is likely that Kierkegaard had the germ of this argument from Paul Møller's lectures on ancient philosophy which he heard as a student. Møller had also had his Hegelian period. Cf. 'Udkast til Forelæsninger over den ældre Philosophies Historie,' in *P. M.'s Efterladte Skrifter*, vol. II, pp. 367-8: 'He (Socrates) endeavoured to assert the Idea of the good, as man's determination and task, in every way. . . . He desired that man by himself should know the good as a determination of being. . . . How does he secure the determinate content of the Idea of the good without which it cannot be realized in the actual world? He sometimes mentions the laws of the state, but in this he is inconsistent, since at other times his dialectic is designed to show the inadequacy of every finite maxim to function as absolute theses. In short, Socrates leaves this difficulty wholly unresolved. The stability which remains was Socrates' own noble and sane character. He was a living example to his associates of how the good could be worked

out in actual life.' The inconsistency which Møller attributes to Socrates himself Kierkegaard attributes to Hegel's conception of Socrates.

58. See above p. 196.

59. See above p. 152n.

60. *via negationis*, the negative way. See above p. 395, note 4.

61. Kierkegaard is undoubtedly thinking of Lucian, *Dialogues of the Dead*, 10. Cf. *Papirer, III C 1*, p. 242.

62. *Lectures on the History of Philosophy*, vol. i, pp. 397-406 (xviii, 58-70).

Part ii: The concept of irony

Introduction (pages 259-62)

1. 'Kierkegaard uses the word "contemplation" in the same sense as Karl Daub for whom it means the historical view [*Schau*] with respect to essential content (historical observation). To this extent contemplation finds its correlative in dialectic or speculation' (H).

2. The echoes here from the first paragraph of the essay are of course deliberate.

3. *John* 1 : 14.

4. Hegel writes of lyric poetry in *Philosophy of Fine Art*, vol. iv, p. 211 (xiv, 439): 'With the advent of a free self-consciousness is bound up the freedom of an assured art of its own. . . . A free art, however, is conscious of itself; it requires a knowing and willing of that which it produces.'

5. To avoid the implication of this judgment on romantic irony, Hirsch postulates a radical change in Kierkegaard's attitude towards it immediately upon completion of the essay. I confess I find no warrant for such a postulate.

6. A. W. Schlegel's famous *Vorlesungen über dramatische Kunst und Literatur* appeared in 1809-11. The review by Solger is in *Nachgelassene Schriften und Briefwechsel*, vol. ii, pp. 493-628 (H).

7. Hirsch has consolidated the most important passages in which Hegel discusses irony. With their corresponding English translations they are as follows. *Phenomenology of Mind*, p. 665*ff*.; *Philosophy of Right*, pp. 101*ff*., p. 258; *Hegel's Philosophy of Mind*, p. 179*ff*.; *Philosophy of Fine Art*, vol. i, pp. 90-94; vol. ii, p. 271*ff*.; *Lectures on the Philosophy of Religion*, vol. iii, pp. 183-185; *Lectures on the History of Philosophy*, vol. i, pp. 384-448 ('Socrates'); vol. iii, pp. 506-512 ('Important Followers of Fichte'). Cf. *Werke* ii, 566*ff*.; vii, 219*ff*.; x, 457; xii, 100-106, 221*ff*.; xiv, 388-390; xviii, 60*ff*.; xix, 642*ff*.; xx, 132-202.

8. *loquere ut videam te*, speak that I may see you. See above pp. 52, 367, note 6.

9. *Volsunga Saga*, Rafn, Copenhagen, 1822, p. 74*ff*. (D).

10. *Vorschule der Aesthetik*, in *Sämmtliche Werke*, Berlin, 1827, vol. 41, p. 199*ff*.

11. Kierkegaard probably has in mind Baader's *Vorlesungen über speculative Dogmatik*, in *Sämmtliche Werke*, Leipzig, 1855, vol. IX, p. 308*ff.* Kierkegaard owned an edition from 1828 (D).

12. It is possible that these judgments on Jean Paul and Franz Baader are ironical. To Sibbern, his teacher, Kierkegaard's own style most resembled Jean Paul whom Sibbern regarded very highly, and Kierkegaard's own indebtedness to Baader is well known. Moreover, Kierkegaard's Journal during this period is full of examples developing the exhibitive relationship between form and content mentioned here.

For orientation (pages 263-75)

1. The 'morsel of irony' in this passage is, of course, to be contrasted with the total irony of the essay. And in the phrase: 'and were not his golden age still a fresh memory for some,' one can hear an echo of the seventy-five-year-old Goethe in 1824 reading through his old correspondence with his friend Schiller with surprise and satisfaction, and remarking that he was aware that this correspondence marked the end of an epoch 'of which scarcely a memory remains.' Cf. Carl Roos, *Goethe*, Copenhagen, 1949, p. 115.

2. John 16 : 33. For what Kierkegaard understands by 'overcoming the world' during this period see *Papirer, III A 131*; *III A 238*; *III C 1*, pp. 248, 249.

3. *Ephesians* 2 : 19.

4. There is a mild play on words here which I am unable to reduplicate. In the original the words 'lofty' and 'loud' have the continuity of the word *høi*; one could say 'high' pathos, but 'high-voiced' pathos means shrill not loud.

5. One is forcefully reminded here of J. L. Heiberg's essay: 'On the Significance of Philosophy for the Present Age,' which appeared in 1833 as an advertisement for a course of public lectures on Hegel's philosophy. A single sentence will have to suffice. After characterizing the present generation as striving mightily towards a multitude of new directions without knowing where all these lead, Heiberg writes: 'Such a condition is properly no state at all, it is merely a transition from a past to a future; it is no true existence but only a becoming in which the old ends and the new begins; it is only the show of existence destined to make room for an actual condition. In other words, it is a *crisis.*' (*Prosaiske Skrifter*, vol. I, pp. 383, 384).

6. This is another satiric barb at Heiberg and Martensen and the principle of methodological or systematic doubt. In 'The Conflict Between the Old and the New Soap Cellar' from 1838, Kierkegaard had Heiberg's caricature *von Springgaasen* say: 'The popular is all well and good, but

my doubt is scarcely popular. It's not a doubt about one thing or another, not about this or that; no, my doubt is an infinite doubt. In fact, I'm even sometimes a little uneasy with a true systematic doubt about whether I've ever really doubted enough.' (*Papirer*, II B 16, p. 296). As for Martensen's 'unappropriated doubt' take, for example, the obvious allusion in *Fear and Trembling*, p. 119: 'But he (Faust) is a doubter, his doubt has annihilated actuality for him; for so ideal is my Faust that he does not belong to these systematic doubters who doubt one hour every semester in the professorial chair, but at other times are able to do everything else, as indeed they do this, without the support of mind or by the power of spirit.' (III, 174.) Incidentally, when Martensen got around to writing his autobiography almost thirty years after Kierkegaard's death, he is at great pains to describe the effect which the study of Hegel's philosophy had upon him during his travelling fellowship in 1834. Curiously enough, he calls this his period of 'doubting sickness.' Cf. *Af mit Levnet*, vol. I, pp. 98-106, 117, 146.

7. *Sophist* 263 E.

8. *semel emissum volat irrevocabile verbum*, the word once let slip flies beyond recall. Horace, *Epistles* I, XVIII, 71.

9. The Danish is *Fornemhed* (German: *Vornehmheit*), a predicate with which Hegel often chastizes Friedrich Schlegel and his circle. I have here translated it as 'exclusiveness' but elsewhere 'superiority.' See above p. 282.

10. The Danish is *ligefrem*, Kierkegaard's subsequent term for 'direct' communication (*ligefrem Meddelelse*).

11. *bon ton*, good breeding, manners.

12. I am unable to locate the source for this in Heine.

13. In this connection, it might be worth recalling the statement of A. F. Beck, a Danish disciple of Hegel who disputed with Kierkegaard at the oral defence of the essay, and who in his published review some months later had to write: 'It is regrettable that there are allusions and references in the work which obviously only the fewest understand, and in which the reviewer does not have the honour of following the author.' *Fædrelandet*, Nos. 890, 897, Copenhagen, 1842.

14. This is another of Hegel's frequent predicates for romantic irony.

15. In light of the dimension of irony which finds expression throughout the essay as personal satire, such remarks as this (to be followed with an elaboration of the techniques and strategy of irony viewed from the standpoint of 'those against whom its polemic is directed') endow the essay with an extraordinary quality of self-consciousness, one which suggests the quality of 'total irony' mentioned earlier in the discussion of Plato's earlier dialogues.

16. This is Kierkegaard's term for the kind of relation obtaining between

pairs of correlative terms or Hegel's categories of Essence or reflection. Such categories, e.g. positive and negative, inner and outer, etc., are always dual since they are what they are only in their unity with each other. Although in English we have the word 'correlation' (*Verhältnis*) to designate this relation (*Beziehung*), I have chosen to render *Modsætningsforhold* literally as 'relation of opposition' as facilitating a smoother translation in some contexts.

17. This may be the case with much of the obvious Hegelianism in the present essay.

18. The Danish for Chladni figure is *Klangfigur*, for which see above pp. 63, 369, note 22.

19. Kierkegaard writes *Arv*, Holberg's comic type for stupidity.

20. I *Corinthians* 1 : 27.

21. The reference is to a request of the parson when reading the banns corresponding to the phrase: 'let him speak now.'

22. Kierkegaard means Peder Ericksen, son of Erik Madsen, in Holberg's comedy *Den Stundesløse*, act II, scenes 7, 8.

23. The essay was written during the period coinciding with Kierkegaard's engagement to Regine Olsen.

24. 'Kierkegaard gebraucht unbefangen einen sehr groben Ausdruck des dänischen Volksmund für die kuppelwütige Vettel' (H). There is no way of being certain what Kierkegaard intends by this allusion, but it appears to be another sardonic allusion to Martensen, who in *Über Lenaus Faust* (1836) 'discovered' in Lenau the superior of Goethe as concerns the conception of Faust and wrote his critique in consultation with Lenau in Vienna, while in his review of Heiberg's *Nye Digte* (1840) he 'discovered' in Heiberg a Protestant Dante after discussing the project with its author on several occasions during its composition.

25. One is invariably reminded here of the situation surrounding the publication of Kierkegaard's early pseudonymous works which began to appear soon after completion of the essay on irony. Cf. also J. L. Heiberg, *Prosaiske Skrifter*, vol. II, p. 143n.

26. I *Thessalonians* 5 : 2. In his Journal Kierkegaard later (1845) consolidated the images of the merchant and the king into the following observation on the comic (VI A 22): 'If a king in order to remain unrecognized went dressed as a merchant, and if a merchant accidentally bore a deceptive resemblance to the king, one would laugh at them both but for different reasons: at the merchant because he was not the king, at the king because he was the merchant.

27. It might help to make Kierkegaard's point a little clearer to recall that he often uses the word 'beginning' in the sense of *arche* or principle.

28. 'During the Middle Ages certain French churches celebrated a

feast day with a procession and dramatic representation in which an ass played a role' (D). 'In the middle of the procession stood an ass covered with palm branches, a figure carved in wood (with or without an image of the mounted Christ) and carried along in the procession' (H).

29. 'The Feast of Fools was a residue of the ancient Saturnalias. In the twelfth century it was celebrated with the clergy performing parodies over certain church offices' (D). 'The Feast of Fools, a New Year's celebration, granted the liberty to parody the clergy' (H).

30. 'Easter Humour refers to the comic stories narrated from the pulpit during Easter week' (D). 'Easter Humour (*risus paschalis*), a late medieval practice, is the laughter provoked by a funny story related by the clergy from the pulpit in celebration of Easter Sunday. It was severely branded by Martin Luther' (H).

31. The statement suggests Hegel's definition of actuality (*Wirklichkeit*) as the unity of essence (*Wesen*) and existence (*Existenz*). He holds that actuality is the very content of philosophy, while thought is its form. Their unity warrants the normative assertion that 'what is rational is actual and what is actual is rational.' But Kierkegaard is speaking from the ordinary point of view, which knows, as Hegel also allows: 'that existence (*Dasein*) is in part mere appearance, and only in part actuality.' (*The Logic of Hegel*, p. 10.) As existence is not yet commensurate with actuality, so there remains a task for irony.

32. An allusion to romantic irony.

33. Talleyrand is reputed to have said this to a Spanish official (D).

34. *mundus vult . . .*, the world desires to be deceived, let it therefore be deceived. Hirsch remarks that the phrase is commonly attributed to Pope Paul IV, and that its oldest source is in S. Brant, *Narrenschiff*.

35. Implied in this transition from irony as a figure of speech to irony as a standpoint is Hegel's doctrine of the 'qualitative leap,' not as applied to the speculative sphere of world history, but actualized in the concrete history of a particular individual's consciousness.

36. As in 1838 he had maintained that it was by virtue of an appropriated total view that the writer creates in the particular, so Kierkegaard is now maintaining that it is by virtue of an appropriated total view that the ironist destroys in the particular. The first concerned the novel, the second concerns satire.

37. *sub specie ironiæ*, under the form or aspect of irony. A variation on Spinoza's *sub specie æternitatis*.

38. See above pp. 63, 370, note 23.

39. There follow five conceptual attitudes or positions, 'movements and postures,' ordinarily thought to resemble irony to a significant degree, two from the moral sphere and three from the contemplative sphere. In each comparison Kierkegaard finds a proximate similarity but an ultimate dis-

similarity; in none are the points of coincidence exhaustive enough to arrest its movement. In the end irony breaks entirely loose and stands mockingly over against the startled reader in the person of J. L. Heiberg. The section scarcely orients us as much as it disorients us. See below note 52.

40. Cf. Hegel's *Phenomenology of Mind*, pp. 629-641 (II, 471-484).

41. *Bergmaal* means speech or language of the mountains (echo), *Dvergmaal* means language of the dwarfs.

42. This statement is best clarified by another from the Journal (II A 102): 'Irony, to be sure, can bring about a certain repose (one which must correspond to the peace following the humorous development), but one which is far from being the Christian atonement. The latter is entailed in the expression "brothers in Christ," where every other difference is absolutely vanishing, a nothing in relation to that of being brothers in Christ. And yet, did not Christ make a distinction, did he not love John more than the others? (Paul Møller in a most interesting conversation the evening of June 30.) The repose induced through irony can bring about a certain love, the love whereby Socrates comprehended his disciples (Hamann calls it spiritual pederasty); but it is nevertheless egoistic because he stood for them as their deliverer expanding their anxious expressions and perspectives in his higher consciousness and comprehension [*Overblik*]. But the diameter of the ironist's movement is not as great as that of the humorist (heaven—hell—the Christian must have despised all things). The highest polemical movement of the ironist is *nil admirari*. Irony is egoistical, it combats Philistinism and yet it remains. It rises in the individual like a song bird, ascends into the air gradually casting off ballast until it runs the risk of ending in an "egoistical devil may care"—for irony has not yet killed itself by seeing itself, and this happens when the individual comes to see himself in the illumination of irony. Humour is lyrical (the deepest seriousness towards life, deep poesy which cannot fashion itself as such and therefore crystallizes itself under the most baroque forms. It is the golden *Aare non fluens*, the *molimina* of the higher life).

'The whole attitude in the Greek nature (harmony—the beautiful) made it necessary that even though the individual severed himself and the struggle commenced, it still bore the mark of having sprung from this harmonious view of life, hence it soon ceased without having described a great circle (Socrates). But now there appeared a view of life which taught that all nature was corrupted (the deepest polemic, the greatest wing expanse); but nature took revenge and now I have humour in the individual and irony in nature. They meet in the fact that humour wishes to be a fool in the world, and irony in the world actually took them to be such.

'One will say that irony and humour are at bottom but different degrees of the same thing. I will answer with Paul when he discusses the relation of Christianity to Judaism: All is new in Christ!

'The Christian humorist is like a plant whose root alone is visible, and whose blossom unfolds itself before a higher sun.' (6th July, 1837.)

43. περι εἰρωνείας, concerning irony. προσποίησις ἐπὶ . . ., the feigning of action and thought for the worse; *simulatio dissimulatioque* . . ., false and fraudulent dissembling and concealment. The edition of Ast was published in Leipzig, 1816.

44. 'The apparently curious comparison of irony to Jesuitism is derived from Hegel's *Philosophy of Right*, pp. 95-98 (VII, 208-212) wherein the chief thesis of the Jesuit ethic (the end justifies the means) and irony are treated as two stages in the same fallacious transition of morality into evil' (H).

45. The comparison of irony with hypocrisy derives from Hegel's *Philosophy of Right*, pp. 94, 95 (VII, 207) and *Phenomenology of Mind*, p. 669ff. (II, 506ff.). Hypocrisy is one of Hegel's constant predicates for irony.

46. There is an amusing bit of nonsense parodying the Hegelian dialectic in the Journal from 1839, which may clarify to some extent what Kierkegaard associates with the term 'the higher madness.' *Papirer, II A 808.*

Discursive *Raisonnements* and
Inconceivable Bulls-Eyes
concerning
The Category of The Higher Madness.

Preface

I believe I would be doing philosophy a great service were it to adopt a category discovered by myself and utilized with great profit and success to exhaust and dry up a multitude of relations and determinations which have so far been unwilling to resolve themselves:—it is the category of the higher madness. I only ask that it not be named after me, but that goes without saying, since in cases analogous to this we are not in the habit of naming something after the active party but after the passive one. Take, for example, our Shrovetide custom of awakening a person with a birch rod; we call 'The Shrove' not after the flogger but after the first person flogged.

It is, moreover, the most concrete of all categories and the fullest, since it is nearest to real life—not having its truth in a Beyond, a superterrestrial, but in a Below, a subterranean sphere. And if it were an hypothesis, the most grandiose confirmations from experience could be made as to its veracity.

It is this category by which a transition is formed from Abstract Fury to Concrete Madness. The formula for this category is already expressed on a page of Baggesen (cf. 'The Abracadabra of the Present Struggle,' vol. VII, p. 195) as follows:

412

'The Unity of Madness in the Duplicity of All.'
But expressed speculatively, of course, it becomes:
The All Mad in the Unity of Duplicity.
Now 'All' implies many, i.e. *Quodlibet* or the crazier the better. The 'Duplicity of Madness': unfortunately, we cannot be content with merely discrete and partial lunacies, but even here the concepts of genus and species must have their validity.

[In the margin]: 'This work is affectionately dedicated to all the inmates at Bellevue [*Bistrup*], and in general to all my worthy contemporaries who are so mad as to have understood me.'

(Papirer, II A 809)

47. As Kierkegaard has made it clear that he doesn't think much of Heiberg's and Martensen's appropriation of doubt as the first principle of modern philosophy, it might be interesting to include a passage from the Journal where he describes his own doubt. *Papirer, III A 103*: 'My doubt is terrifying—nothing can stop me—it has the hunger of a curse. I consume every *Raisonnement*, every comfort and assurance. I overtake every resistance with the speed of 10,000 miles per second.' The passage also calls to mind his well-known definition of faith as 'swimming above 70,000 fathoms.'

48. One may approach this comparison of irony to religious devotion (*Andagt*) expecting Kierkegaard to be discussing what both Goethe and Hegel manage under the rubric 'the beautiful soul,' the literary and philosophical representation of that form of piety, for example, associated with the Moravian Brethren.

49. See above pp. 243, 403, note 19.

50. *nisus formativus*, formative or creative impulse, effort, striving. Hirsch cites the following as background. Hegel, *Science of Logic*, vol. II, pp. 67, 68 (IV, 547): 'And similarly internal or self-movement, or impulse in general (the appetitive force or *nisus* of the monad, the entelechy of absolutely simple Essence), is nothing else than the fact that something is itself and is also deficiency or the negative of itself, in one and the same respect. Abstract self-identity has no life; but the fact that Positive in itself is negativity causes it to pass outside itself and to change. Something therefore has life only in so far as it contains Contradiction, and is that force which can both comprehend and endure Contradiction. But if an existent something cannot in its positive determination also encroach on its negative, cannot hold fast the one in the other and contain Contradiction within itself, then it is not living unity, or Ground, but perishes in Contradiction. —Speculative thought consists only in this, that thought holds fast Contradiction, and, in Contradiction, itself, and not in that it

allows itself to be dominated by it—as happens to imagination—or suffers its determinations to be resolved into others, or into Nothing.'

51. Positive statements concerning mysticism are rare in the Journal. The following is one of them (*Papirer, III A* 70): 'One hears a mystic like a certain cry of a bird only in the stillness of the night. Hence a mystic does not have as much significance for the clamorous age in which he lives as he does after the passing of time in the stillness of history for an individual of like mentality who is listening.'

52. The verb *spøger* means 'to haunt' as well as 'to jest.' The half-quotes around the ambiguity are mine. The use of *spøger* in this context has to my mind reference to the previously mentioned piece by Heiberg 'On the Significance of Philosophy for the Present Age,' in which Heiberg proceeds to sketch for his readers what is living and what is dead for the present generation. At one point, he writes: 'It is with a feeling of contradiction that the better among us have turned back to the rejected religion, but to no avail since it is impossible for them ever to recover the repose of a past age. . . . While they know that fundamentalism as well as heresy-hunting are ghosts [*Spøgelser*] from a bygone age without flesh or blood, they still fear them as one fears the jests of poltergeists [*Spøgelser*] which may, at least, tease the living by mixing into the affairs of life.' *Prosaiske Skrifter*, vol. I, pp. 395, 397. My point is that a polemicist like Kierkegaard would not have failed to take note of such a passage, while a satirist of his bent may well nigh have liked to spook Heiberg himself. (Ibsen, too, was a serious reader of Heiberg during the fifties.) That Heiberg subsequently got the point (my guess is after consultation with Martensen, who could not have failed to hear the ironic echoes in the essay directed at him) may be seen from a piece he published in 1843 entitled 'To Orient Oneself' in which he returns barb for barb against Kierkegaard. Cf. *Prosaiske Skrifter*, vol. IX, pp. 14, 19. With this much by way of explanation, I shall permit myself the following paraphrase: 'Finally, the ironic nothingness is that deathly stillness haunted by the ghoulish laughter of irony.'

The world historical validity of irony (pages 276-88)

1. 'The sentence contains a paraphrase of the words of Seneca, *Epistles*, 107: *Ducunt volentem fata, nolentem trahunt.* It goes without saying that the categories employed here and in the following are taken over from Hegel's *Philosophy of History*' (H).

2. A characteristically nineteenth-century generalization.

3. I suspect that the three categories delineated here of *prophet, hero,* and *ironist* were meant for local consumption and have reference to Heiberg, Martensen, and Kierkegaard respectively. See above p. 427, note 15.

4. *Acts* 5 : 9.

5. *John* 2 : 17.

6. These three Italian philosophers of the sixteenth century, Cardanus, Campanella, and Bruno, are discussed in Hegel's *Lectures on the History of Philosophy*, vol. III, pp. 115, 116 under the title: 'Eigenthümliche Bestrebung der Philosophie' (XIX, 219, 220). They are obviously selected solely because Hegel discusses them as he does.

7. There appears to be a shuffling with Hegel's logical categories here: *er til* is *Daseyn*, *er* is mere abstract *Sein*.

8. *Lectures on the History of Philosophy*, vol. I, p. 400.

9. This passage contains one of those effective images for a dialectical turning point in Kierkegaard and functions in some respects like the image of Dante's reversal on the knee of Lucifer in the *Inferno*. It first appears in the Journal in 1837 (*Papirer, II A* 595): 'As the sky appears just as deep in the sea as it is high above it, so Christ is at every moment as much God as man.'

10. *Exodus* 20 : 6; *Deuteronomy* 5 : 10; *John* 13 : 17.

11. Throughout this discussion Kierkegaard is speaking, as Hirsch reports, as a graduate in theology in conformity with the Lutheran catechism of the day. From an æsthetic point of view it may be remarked, however, that throughout the essay on irony Kierkegaard is working with the category and techniques of the sublime, of which the *locus classicus* remains certain books in the *Old Testament*. In fact, it may seem to some that his commitment to this æsthetic sphere ultimately dictates even his final theological bearings.

12. *Luke* 7 : 19.

13. *Luke* 17 : 33.

14. I understand this passage and others like it throughout the essay to signify the presence of the quality termed by Kierkegaard 'total irony.'

15. See above pp. 266, 267. So much for the obvious Hegelianism of the essay on irony. It is material for his pen and part of the polemical situation to which he addressed himself.

16. Another instantiation of 'total irony.'

17. Cf. Appendix, thesis VIII.

18. For 'substantiality' one may in this case read 'the objective ethical order assimilated into consciousness.'

19. In *Lectures on the History of Philosophy*, vol. I, pp. 401, 402 (XVIII, 64) Hegel says that the irony of Socrates has nothing to do with 'the irony of our times.'

20. The ironic bantering with Hegel in this passage is, of course, polemical. To say that Hegel has become 'infatuated' with the form of irony nearest him recalls the erotic imagery of the first paragraph of the essay as well as the caution that philosophy must not do this. It is, more-

over, an amusing irony which conceives the bitter quarrel between Hegel and Schlegel as a lover's quarrel and one not without insight. It is again polemical towards Hegel to say that his 'conception of the concept' is distorted and tantamount to accusing the philosopher Socratic fashion out of his own mouth.

21. A typical statement is the following from *The Philosophy of Fine Art*, vol. I, pp. 89, 90 (XII, 101-103): 'For every man during his life endeavours to realize himself and does realize himself. In relation to the beautiful and art this means that he lives the life of an artist, and shapes his life artistically. But according to the principle [of irony] now discussed, I live as artist when all my actions and expression whatever, insofar as it has to do with content, is for myself on the plane of mere semblance, and assumes a formal content which is wholly at my disposal. So I am not truly serious either about this content or, speaking generally, about its expression and realization. . . . No doubt for others my self-revealment, in which I appear to them, may be taken seriously . . . but therein they are deluded, poor, borné creatures, without the faculty or power to comprehend and attain to the height of my argument. . . . Whoever has reached such a standpoint of god-like geniality consequently looks down in his superior fashion on all other mortals. . . . This is the universal import of the genial god-like irony as this concentration of the Ego in itself, for which all bands are broken, and which can only live in the bliss of self-enjoyment. This irony was the discovery of Friedrich von Schlegel, and many have chattered about it after him, or it may be are giving us a fresh sample of such chatter.'

22. As applied to Hegel this statement is mildly ironic, for against the intuition and enthusiasm of the romantics Hegel had steadfastly maintained that philosophy must not seek or wish to be 'edifying.' Cf. *Phenomenology of Mind*, pp. 71-74 (II, 14-17). On this point the Journal contains the following explanatory entry dated 10th July, 1840: 'It is curious what a hate Hegel has for the edifying as is everywhere apparent. The edifying is not an opiate that lulls to sleep, however, it is the finite spirit's Amen and one side of knowledge that ought not to be overlooked.' (*Papirer, III A 6.*)

23. *Lectures on the History of Philosophy*, vol. I, pp. 397-406.

24. *Ibid*, p. 400.

25. A playful irony at Hegel's expense.

26. *Lectures on the History of Philosophy*, vol. I, p. 398.

27. *Ibid*.

28. *Ibid*, p. 400.

29. *Ibid*, p. 402.

30. *Ibid*, p. 404 (XVIII, 67).

31. Plato's *Parmenides* contains a dialectical inquiry into being and non-being, and is a late dialogue.

32. Hegel, xviii, 64: 'But his tragic irony is his opposition through subjective reflection to the established *Sittlichkeit*—not a self-consciousness that he stands above it, but the simple purpose of leading on to the good, the universal Idea.' Hirsch makes the point that the difference between Kierkegaard's and Hegel's conceptions of Socrates is most apparent in their respective interpretations of the nature of the tragedy of Socrates, and goes on to draw the consequences respecting the relationship between humanism (Socrates) and Christianity implied by each interpretation. 'For Hegel the Christian dimension is nothing but the depths of the human, and he can therefore allow the depths of the Christian experience of estrangement and reconciliation to illuminate and interpenetrate Socrates directly. Kierkegaard, on the other hand, at least at this time, must endeavour to validate a sharp internal limit between them, inasmuch as he distinguishes the essentially Christian experience off from Socrates' (H).

33. Hegel, xx, 132-202. 'Über *Solgers nachgelassene Schriften und Briefwechsel*,' edited by Ludwig Tieck and Friedrich Raumer, vols. I-II, Leipzig, 1826.

34. Hegel, xx, 184.

35. This is scarcely a trivial objection. At issue is the possibility of an ultimate positivity which is to emerge from the manipulation of proximate negations, and this applies as much to a theory of irony as it does to Hegel's theory of dialectic.

36. *ad libitum*, at will.

37. Another assertion of 'total irony.' It hardly needs to be said that throughout this discussion the Danish simply vibrates with ambiguity.

38. ditto.

Irony after Fichte (*pages* 289-302)

1. *Luke* 15 : 12.

2. Tithonos, the husband of Aurora (Dawn), was immortal yet vanishing until only his voice remained. The figure of the husband of Aurora occurs several times in the Journal, e.g. *Papirer*, *I A 302*: 'The whole Idealistic development in Fichte, for example, discovered an Ego, an immortality, to be sure, but without content, like the husband of Aurora who, although immortal, was without eternal youth and so ended by becoming a grasshopper. Similarly, Fichte dumped the empirical ballast overboard in despair and so capsized.'

3. In the well-known fable of Aesop.

4. The school of Paschasius Radbertus (831 A.D.), cf. F. C. Baur, *Die christliche Kirche des Mittelalters*, second edition, Leipzig, 1869, p. 59 (D).

5. Kierkegaard appears to be following Hegel in his presentation of Kant's *Ding an sich*.

6. 'As will appear at the end of the characterization of Fichte, Kierkegaard intends his discussion to apply only to the Fichte before the controversy over atheism, i.e., the Fichte of the Jena *Wissenschaftslehre*, *Naturrechts*, and *Sittenlehre*. All that Fichte wrote after *The Vocation of Man* is dismissed from consideration as being a partially edifying modification of his earlier standpoint. This is the common judgment passed on the Fichtian philosophy during Kierkegaard's day, a judgment inaugurated by Schelling and Hegel. As for the Fichte of the Jena period, Kierkegaard's discussion is written without any knowledge of the Jena writings. (During this period reference is made in the Journal only to the "popular" works, e.g., *Die Bestimmung des Menschen*, cf. *Papirer*, I A 68*). The discussion of Fichte by Kierkegaard concerns therefore a simplification and repetition of Hegel's conception worked up in literary fashion. Hegel's interpretation of Fichte is had most conveniently from the statements in the *Science of Logic*, vol. I, pp. 107*ff*., 155*ff*., 248*ff*. (IV, 104*ff*., 156*ff*., 282*ff*.)' (H).

7. In *Nachgelassene Werke*, vol. II. See below note 13.

8. *molimina*, exertions.

9. *nisus formativus*, formative or creative impulse.

10. *Colossians* 3 : 3.

11. Johann Tauler's *Nachfolgung des armen Lebens Christi*, Frankfurt a. M., 1821, p. 254: 'Doch diess Verlieren, diess Entschwinden/Ist eben erst das wahre ächte Finden.' It is now known that the work had nothing to do with Johann Tauler (D).

12. Kierkegaard has the term from *Colossians* 2 : 2 (D).

13. J. G. Fichte, *Nachgelassene Werke*, edited by I. H. Fichte, Bonn, 1834-35. On Fichte's relation to irony and his revised standpoint, cf. Hegel, *Lectures on the History of Philosophy*, vol. III, p. 505*ff*. (XIX, 640-42).

14. Young Germany was the name given to a group of writers during the 1830s who expressed their political resistance to the reactionism following the collapse of the July Revolution. It was called into existence by an infamous edict of the Federal Diet on 10th December, 1833, suppressing the past, present, and future writings of Heinrich Heine, Karl Gutzkow, Ludolf Wienbarg, Theodor Mundt, Heinrich Laube, and Ludwig Börne. Their sympathies embraced a mild Saint-Simonism and an æsthetic affirming the vital relationship between literature and contemporary social problems. Of the authors thus singled out for suppression some were already in exile, some fled Germany, and some were imprisoned. Their greatest influence was on German prose, criticism, and the social novel. Scholarship during the period between the revolutions was strongly infused with Hegelianism.

15. *Matt.* 16 : 19.

16. *vis inertiæ*, force of inertia.

17. A negative allusion to Goethe's literary autobiography *Poetry and Truth*.

18. Lessing, *Gesammelte Werke*, Leipzig, 1841, vol. III, p. 109*ff.* (D).

19. This and the following sentence contain unmistakable barbs directed at H. L. Martensen.

20. *Psalms* 104 : 26.

21. *Hebrews* 7 : 7.

22. *Philippians* 1 : 6.

23. 'This sentence already contains the germ of the basic proposition in the second volume of *Either/Or* that the ethical-religious Christian view of life is the true consummation and surpassing of the ideals of the æsthetic view of life' (H).

24. *für sich*, for itself; *an sich*, in itself.

25. Kierkegaard is no doubt thinking of J. Eichendorff's *Aus dem Leben eines Taugenichts* (D).

26. I *Corinthians* 3 : 18.

27. The Pythagoreans are ordinarily represented as believing in a transmigration of souls or metempsychosis.

28. Lucian, 'The Cock,' 19, 20.

29. *Psalms* 3 : 18.

30. Kierkegaard cites the rhyme in German. Cf. *Postscript*, p. 95 (VII, 92).

31. *sella curulis*, the chair set aside for the highest Roman official (D).

32. *Solgers nachgelassene Schriften und Briefwechsel*, vol. II, p. 514; see above p. 324n.

33. What Kierkegaard here says about 'becoming master over feeling' appears to be related to what he calls 'having experience' (*at gjøre Erfaring*) in the sketch for a sermon during 1840-1. The last paragraph is as follows (*Papirer, III C 13*): 'We see that neither the restless craving out into the world nor simply living in the world are sufficient to have experience. In one sense those who do this also have experience, but as there never develops in them the power of overcoming the whole, of surveying a whole, so they never learn from experience. For this there is requisite that act of will which wills to have an experience, which in the moment of sorrow will recollect to itself the joy it has experienced, and in the moment of joy will not forget the sorrow which threatens.'

34. 'This appellation was assigned to various mountains in Germany during the fourteenth century, especially in Swabia, and Venus was assumed to hold court inside the mountain. In this world of sensual dissipation Tannhäuser remained so long that his soul was no longer amenable to salvation after he came out.' (Billeskov Jansen in *Kierkegaard i Udvalg*, vol. IV, p. 22.)

35. Hegel, xx, 154*ff.*, in the review of *Solgers nachgelassene Schriften*.

36. 'Asa-Loke is characterized as follows in J. B. Møinichen's *Nordiske Folks Overtroe, Guder, Fabler og Helte*, Copenhagen, 1800 (Kierkegaard's Bibliotek, Nr. 1947). "Loke Laufeiason or Loptur, a most ambiguous person, accounted among the gods even though he was more devil or at least a consummate mixture of good and evil. He was always in the company of the gods and helped them out of many an embarrassment by his incomparable cunning . . . He was endowed by nature with every physical excellence: large, well formed, handsome, ingratiating, and eloquent; he was besides mean, light-minded, inconstant, malicious, and in every way mischievous." ' (Billeskov Jansen in *Kierkegaard i Udvalg*, vol. IV, p. 104).

Schlegel (pages 302-16)

1. *Rehabilitation des Fleisches*, rehabilitation of the material. 'The relationship of Young Germany to Schlegel's *Lucinde* stems from the fact that Karl Gutzkow, on the occasion of Schleiermacher's death in 1834, re-published Schleiermacher's *Vertraute Briefe über Schlegels Lucinde* (Confidential Letters Concerning Schlegel's *Lucinde*) in January of 1835 which raised a storm. The event occurred during Kierkegaard's student years, and as Danish literary life was closely involved with the German at that time, it was closely followed in Copenhagen. Kierkegaard's remark on p. 312 about one or another youthful ward of the Young Germany being imprisoned to save him from boredom probably refers to Karl Gutzkow, who was imprisoned in 1835 for his literary activity' (H).

2. Hegel, *Philosophy of Fine Art*, vol. II, p. 269 (XIII, 108): 'We have few traces of the wanton disregard of things that are sacred and of the highest excellence such as marks the period of Schlegel's *Lucinde*.' Cf. *Philosophy of Right*, p. 263 (VII, 245): 'Friedrich Schlegel in his *Lucinde*, and a follower of his in the *Briefe eines Ungenannten* [Schleiermacher, 1800] have put forward the view that the wedding ceremony is superfluous and a formality which might be discarded.'

3. Such passages tell more about the Copenhagen of Kierkegaard's day than whole essays.

4. This and the following citations from Schlegel's *Lucinde* are based on the incomplete English translation by P. B. Thomas printed in *German Classics of the 19th and 20th Centuries*, edited by Kuno Francke and W. G. Howard, vol. IV, pp. 124-174, New York, German Publication Society, 1913-15. The page references in the text are to the German edition used by Kierkegaard.

5. 'Kierkegaard undoubtedly has this from J. L. Heiberg's parody of B. S. Ingermann's tragedy *Blanca*. The hero and heroine's numerous "holy, sentimental, and Platonic children have neither muscles nor legs and their skin [*Skind*] is moonlight [*Maaneskin*]; they are merely the fruit

of our frequent public embraces." *Jullepøg og Nytaarsløier*, 1817.' (Billeskov Jansen in *Kierkegaard i Udvalg*, vol. IV, p. 104.)

6. 'In the old Lutheran marriage liturgy the text from *Genesis* 3 : 16*ff.* was read by the pastor before the exchange of wedding vows took place. —The reader will also recall that this section on Schlegel's *Lucinde* with its espousal of Christian marriage was written by Kierkegaard in the spring of 1841 during the crisis in his engagement' (H).

7. *Hoheslied*, I, 8 (H).

8. *peregrinationes sacras*, sacred pilgrimage; *profanus*, profane, secular (pilgrimage).

9. *en quatre*, in fours, 'quadrigamous.'

10. *Luke* 20 : 35; *Mark* 12 : 25.

11. *Luke* 14 : 20; *Matt.* 22 : 3.

12. *eureka*, I have found it. The expression is ordinarily attributed to Archimedes upon discovering the principle of buoyancy.

13. Kierkegaard writes 'strokes of the bow,' obviously thinking of the overture to Mozart's *Don Giovanni*.

14. Another reference to Mozart's opera.

15. See above p. 104n. and Hegel, XVIII, 54-6.

16. Hirsch calls attention to how much Kierkegaard learned from this portrait of Lisette. There are, he points out, numerous passages in the 'Diapsalmata' from *Either/Or* which draw upon it.

17. In his writings Caesar discusses himself in third person (D).

18. *vita ante acta*, previous life.

19. In the discussion which follows it appears that Kierkegaard is attempting to translate his æsthetic into an ethic. His views of the modern writer already developed by 1838 are here projected upon humanity at large.

20. The statement is polemical against Heiberg's claim: 'The system of Hegel is the same as Goethe's. . . . To characterize the Hegelian philosophy in a few words, one may say that it, like Goethe's poetry, reconciles the Ideal with actuality, our demands with what we possess, our wishes with what is attained.' *Prosaiske Skrifter*, vol. I, p. 430.

21. Kierkegaard is no doubt thinking of the Greek conception of nemesis. In the Journal he once relates irony to nemesis, cf. *Papirer*, I A 265.

22. It is interesting to consider this passage in light of the fact that Martensen reports that Kierkegaard came to him one night to read him this section of the essay on Schlegel's *Lucinde* (*Af mit Levnet*, II, 142). In every event, one will have to conclude that the essay on irony was written from the standpoint of 'mastered irony,' and that the incognito of the ironist in this case already concealed an ethicist.

Tieck (pages 316-22)

1. Short novels, stories.

2. The Danish here is *Hopsasa*, a popular expression for a waltz or dance in 3/4 time. That Kierkegaard associates the expression with the Hegelian triad may be surmised from the following entry in the Journal (*Papirer, II A 814*): '*Hopsasa* is the ecstatic—to sneeze. Our systematic discussions forbid it like a sentry with a rifle calling "halt." I shall nevertheless permit myself the use of it, just as also coughing and, in short, all *secernationes et quidem sensu metaphysico.*'

3. Hegel's most extensive discussion of Tieck is in his review of *Solgers nachgelassene Schriften*, cf. xx, 143-45, 152-160.

4. It was apparently this passage and Kierkegaard's defence of it that was rigorously opposed during the public defence of the essay. On 17th October, 1841 (after the oral defence) Kierkegaard noted in his own copy of the essay that in support of his own position (rejecting Hegel's grasp of romantic irony) he could use Hegel's entire discussion of the significance of satire in *The Philosophy of Fine Art*, vol. II, p. 273*ff.* (XIII, 113*ff.*). Cf. *Papirer, III B 29.*

5. H. G. Hotho was the editor of Hegel's *Vorlesungen über die Aesthetik*.

6. Heine, *Die romantische Schule*, Bk. I, in *Sämmtliche Werke*, Hamburg, 1874, vol. VI, p. 47.

7. *John* 4 : 14.

8. Cf. *Papirer, II A 580.*

9. The present-day Ny Østergade. (Billeskov Jansen in *Kierkegaard Udvalg*, vol. IV, p. 107).

10. 'In clarification of Kierkegaard's comparison the reader will recall that water from an artesian well rises higher the deeper the well is drilled' (H).

11. *unheimlich*, uncanny, uncomfortable, sinister.

12. The illustration is of a youth and a maid in medieval costume playing musical instruments (D).

13. Cf. *Papirer, II A 636*; *III B 2.*

14. Where Kierkegaard cites a line of children's nonsense poetry, I have inserted the first line of Lewis Carroll's 'Jabberwocky,' although it is far too literate to simulate the verse Kierkegaard refers to. It is included below in the version cited by Billeskov Jansen in *Kierkegaard i Udvalg*, vol. IV, p. 107.

> Ulen, dulen, doff
> Fingen, Fangen, Foff
> Foff for alle Mærkepande,
> E. B. ba, buff

Kaalvippen
Kaalvappen
Der slap En.

15. Cf. Hegel, *Philosophy of Fine Art*, vol. IV, p. 205 (XIV, 433): 'But, further, in so far as the individuality of self-conscious life is the true source of the lyric, the poet is justified in limiting his expression to his own moods and reflections without any further combination of them in a concrete situation that includes a truly objective character. It is in this direction that examples of what is little more than an empty fluting for fluting's sake, the song and trill simply on its own account, will yet give us genuine lyrical satisfaction.'

Solger (pages 323-35)

1. Hegel, XII, 105.
2. *schwerbegreifbarer* . . ., a philosophic clarity difficult to comprehend.
3. This statement with its metaphor of the inquiry that is a journey echoes the motto at the beginning of the essay. On the use of a motto Kierkegaard had written in 1838 (XIII, 90): 'Andersen, as everyone knows, usually divides his novels into chapters and gives each a motto. Now whether the reader will share my view that a motto (by means of the musical energy which it may well have without being verse) ought to function like a prelude and put the reader into a definite mood, into the rhythm in which the section is written . . .; or ought to relate in a piquant way to the entire section—not forming simply a witty word-play with a particular expression occurring in the chapter or a flat statement of what the chapter is about; still, he will have to agree with me that it takes a fair amount of taste and a good deal of inwardness with the subject and the caloric content of its mood to be able to choose a motto that is a little more than a vacuous exclamation point, or a mark like that which physicians set above their prescriptions.'
4. This was also the case with the last part of the section 'For Orientation', which attempted to navigate the transition from verbal irony to perspectival irony.
5. *Nachgelassene Schriften*, vol. I, p. 603 (Kierkegaard subsequently cites the passage, see above p. 328).
6. This refers to a witty verse by Wessel in which the cæsura plays havoc with the meaning. Wessel, *Samtlige Skrifter*, Copenhagen, 1817, vol. II, p. 119:

Jeg synger om en Kone. Hemistichen faldt,
Saa synes Læseren, en Smule splittergalt (D).

7. *Nachgelassene Schriften*, vol. I, p. 605.
8. 'The resurgent pietistical orthodoxy within Lutheranism operates on

two fronts during the nineteenth century. Against the "Pelagianism of the Enlightenment," on the one hand, it stresses the unconditioned miracle of rebirth through God's grace. Against the "pantheism of false speculation," on the other hand, it believed it only possible to rescue the freedom and personality both of God and man by strongly emphasizing man's liberty to avail himself of and co-operate with the working of grace. In this way it leaned both towards the monergism of grace and towards the synergism of Erasmus and Melanchthon, although not all who took up this view were as honest as Kierkegaard in unreservedly employing the word "synergism" ' (H).

9. *Genesis* 32 : 26.

10. There runs throughout Hegel's review of *Solgers nachgelassene Schriften* a relentless polemic against the romanticist's use of language. While Hegel clearly sees in Solger an ally with respect to rejecting the excesses of ironic formalism, still, Solger's commitment to philosophic dialogue as the proper method of philosophizing is obviously too close to the romantic position to get a hearing, and is rejected outright in the words (p. 190): '—*ein Missgriff, der ihn seine ganze Laufbahn hindurch verfolgte.*' In the discussion of the content of Solger's philosophizing Hegel's recurrent objection is that his abstract conceptions are constantly mixed together with concrete determinations, and that the major theses are therefore incommensurably joined to each other. It is in this connection that Kierkegaard's phrase 'the intermediate determinations are lacking' appears to be something of an explanation, if not yet an apology, for Solger's procedure; for in its way it points out how Solger's syllogisms got reduced to metaphors. Here the issue between the discursiveness of reason and the elliptical compressions of the imagination is clearly joined.

11. *Nachgelassene Schriften*, vol. I, p. 689 (cf. p. 652); vol. II, p. 515. Cf. Hegel, xx, 185 *ff.*

12. 'Kierkegaard often uses the word "art" (*Kunst*) in the restricted sense of the plastic arts, painting and sculpture, etc.' (H).

13. *Nachgelassene Schriften*, vol. I, p. 293 *ff.*, 350, 428.

14. I *John* 5 : 4.

15. *Vorlesungen über Aesthetik*, pp. 182-256.

16. See above p. 336 ('Irony as a Mastered Moment'). This apparently arbitrary decision to treat parts of Solger's æsthetic as belonging to 'a wholly different standpoint' means, of course, that there is a substantial area of agreement between Kierkegaard and Solger.

17. *Nachgelassene Schriften*, vol. II, p. 493 *ff.* Drachmann refers to the edition of A. W. Schlegel's lectures published in Heidelberg, 1809-11.

18. Cf. Hegel, *Philosophy of Right*, p. 102n. (vii, 217n.).

Irony as a mastered moment (*pages* 336-42)

1. *Vorlesungen über Aesthetik*, p. 199, 242*ff.*

2. For Solger 'objectivity' is synonymous with *Gleichgültigkeit* (which I refrain from translating as 'indifference,' since it tends to put the English reader on the wrong track). Cf. *Vorlesungen über Aesthetik*, pp. 199, 214, 244.

3. The chief source for this imagery, which treats contradictions as spirits to be mastered, is Goethe's *Wilhelm Meister's Apprenticeship*, Bk. III, ch. 9; Bk. IV, ch. 19; Bk. V, chs. 1, 2.

4. While this idea is pervasive throughout the æsthetics of the period (cf. for example, Hegel, XX, 172, and *Solgers nachgelassene Schriften*, vol. II, p. 112), Kierkegaard has it most immediately from J. L. Heiberg. In the frequently mentioned essay 'On the Significance of Philosophy for the Present Age,' Heiberg had diagnosed 'the crisis of the age' as 'a striving for philosophy,' and went on to invent a category which he designated 'speculative poets,' of whom he counted three (Dante, Calderón, and Goethe): 'The idealistic or speculative poets are themselves philosophers and present philosophy much as do philosophers except for the difference imposed by the accidental form of poetry itself.' *Prosaiske Skrifter*, vol. I, p. 419. In his positive appraisal of Shakespeare above, however, Kierkegaard is radically opposed to Heiberg (cf. *op. cit.*, p. 423).

5. Heiberg's characterization of Goethe is relevant here (*op. cit.*, pp. 427, 28): 'As regards Goethe, it remains to show how his poesy represents the philosophy the age seeks. . . . The speculative Idea runs through the composition of almost all his works. . . . Thus all his representations, both of characters as well as of events, are maintained as subordinate moments in unity, as finitudes which are only valid within their limits; and only when they are viewed in this way are they seen in their abrogation and their truth. . . . The impressive thing about Goethe is apparent in the love with which he loses himself in these finitudes, although he suddenly surprises us by standing above them and acknowledging them for what they are.'

6. Heiberg, *Poetiske Skrifter*, Copenhagen, 1833, vol. I, p. v *ff.*

7. In 'Irony as a Mastered Moment' we have the dialectical negation of negation or the truth of irony. Accordingly, as irony throughout the essay has been characterized as: the essence is *not* the phenomenon, the phenomenon *not* the essence; the internal is *not* the external, the external *not* the internal, etc., so here the incommensurability is cancelled and an equilibrium effected.

8. This theme becomes the first 'Diapsalmata' in *Either/Or*.

9. Kierkegaard writes 'science,' but it will appear from the discussion that he means Idealistic philosophy, specifically the Hegelian system.

Hirsch points out how in these lines Kierkegaard is consciously putting distance between his own views and concerns and those of Hegel and his followers.

10. *John* 14 : 6. See above p. 52n.

11. The reference is to the socialistic theories of Count Saint-Simon (1760-1825).

12. *Mark* 10 : 9.

13. Why this phrase should be in quotation marks I am not sure. It was used, however, once before on page 314 in the section on Schlegel. There is a long passage in the Journal explaining its philosophic meaning for Kierkegaard (*Papirer*, *III B 1*): 'The historical is the unity of the metaphysical and the accidental. . . . This unity of the metaphysical and the accidental already resides in self-consciousness. I am at once conscious of myself in my eternal validity, in my divine necessity, so to speak, and in my accidental finitude (that I am this particular being born in this land at this particular time under the manifold influence of all these varying circumstances). . . . The true life of the individual is the apotheosis of this latter aspect, which consists in . . . the divine coming to dwell in and accommodate itself to finitude.' (4th July 1840.)

14. *credo quia absurdum*, I believe by virtue of the absurd. The statement is commonly attributed to Tertullian. The relation between irony and humour is a pervasive theme in the early Journals. The following are some typical passages.

'Irony conceived in its conceptual determination is a moment of what the Greeks understood by sophrosynē (which shears away the salacious as insipid).' (III B 10.)

'Humour in its conceptual determination is a polemical moment in the Christian view of life.' (III B 11.)

'Irony is the birthpangs of objective mind (based on the disproportion between existence and the Idea of existence as discovered by the self). Humour is the birthpangs of absolute mind (based on the disproportion between the self and the Idea of the self as discovered by the self).' (III B 19.)

15. Heiberg's *Nye Digte* appeared on December 19th, 1840, and Martensen's review was published on three consecutive days in *Fædrelandet*, Copenhagen, 1841, Nos. 398-400, 10th-12th January. These poems form the centre of Heiberg's poetic production and their place is firmly established in Danish literature. Morten Borup wrote in his recent study of Heiberg: 'It is not through his prose essays that Heiberg lives in our time as an Hegelian but in the philosophic poems of *Nye Digte*, about which Martensen wrote in his review: "What philosophy has for so long whispered in the ears of its disciples, poetry now begins to preach from the house tops." ' (*Johan Ludvig Heiberg*, vol. II, p. 192). The most popular of these four poems was and still is 'A Soul After Death. An Apocalyptical Comedy.'

Here Heiberg wittily satirizes his contemporaries for their unresponsiveness to his teaching by locating Copenhagen with all its inhabitants in a part of Hell which turns out to be the Hegelian 'bad infinity.' Martensen's 'heroic' defence of Heiberg's 'vision' would fill twenty-five pages of print and is much too long to include here. I shall try to summarize only so much as seems necessary to indicate the irony of Kierkegaard's concluding paragraph. It appears from Martensen's semi-official exposition of 'A Soul After Death' that with this apocalyptical production Heiberg has finally joined the company of Dante and Goethe in what he himself had formerly termed 'the speculative poets.' Martensen defines this genre of poetry as one which 'gives us an insight into the next world in such a way that it reveals the present world risen to judgment.' Heiberg is called the Protestant Dante, and Martensen shows that the fate of a soul in such a Hell is not tragic but comic; the category on which the apocalypse dwells is not the evil but merely the bad, not the dialectical opposite of the Idea but only its 'immediate reflectionless contrast, the intellectual nadir,' namely, 'the kingdom of triviality.' Heiberg's vision is therefore a contribution to 'the metaphysics of the trivial.' Martensen expends considerable effort showing that 'the comic is a category that will have its validity even in heaven,' and as the content of this 'comic eternity' is the phenomenal world in its reflectivity, so Copenhagen with its trivial infinity will have 'phenomenal eternity.' The unity of the tragic and comic, for Martensen, is the exclusively Christian category of 'humour, not the negative but the positive comic, the speculative comic, which relates to irony as profundity relates to cleverness.'

The last paragraph of the essay on irony is thoroughly ambiguous. While everything in it undoubtedly has serious meaning in Kierkegaard's own terms, it is at the same time utterly polemical towards Martensen, consisting of an elaborate tissue of echoes, parallel and contrasting ideas, terms, phrases and even syntax drawn from Martensen's own writings, especially the review of *Nye Digte* and the *Licentiate* essay. Accordingly, Kierkegaard's term 'eternal validity' now acquires an ironic reference to what Martensen had called 'comic validity,' the kingdom of triviality. Agreeing with Martensen that this involves the category of humour, the rest of the paragraph is essentially a comparison of irony to humour, of 'cleverness' to 'profundity,' which proceeds by doubling Martensen's syntax through parallel construction. As for the scepticism of humour we have not sin but Martensen's term 'sinfulness,' and where Martensen's theological orientation would entail the often cited Anselmian thesis: *credam ut intelligam*, Kierkegaard inserts Tertullian's polemical: *credo quia absurdum*. As for the positivity inherent in humour Kierkegaard does not allow it to come to rest in humanistic determinations (Martensen's phrase: 'to make man into man'), but resorts to Martensen's favourite word 'theanthropic,' where, in addition to Kierkegaard's serious reference to the incarnation and his theory of true and false mythology developed in the early Journal, it comes to bear the ironic meaning of a systematic bird's eye view of universal history. And lest the contemporary reader fail to get the point, the essay ends by explicitly addressing this discussion to Martensen personally. Thus the essay ends as it began with ironic praise of modern speculation for its genial grasp on the phenomenal world—even securing for it a 'phenomenal eternity' by virtue of its validity as satire.

I may, perhaps, be allowed one final comment with which to try to assign this dimension of personal satire discernible throughout the essay, together with the documentation for it presented in these notes, its proper place. *Firstly,* it has long been recognized in Scandinavian Kierkegaard literature that this dimension of personal satire forms a running commentary on the Danish Hegelians and is a constant feature in the subsequent æsthetic and philosophic works. It has been construed as providing an unmistakable concrete index, a barometer for reading Kierkegaard's true atttiude towards the system. The significance of identifying it as already present in the essay on irony (it may even be discerned in his first book, *From the Papers of One Still Living,* 1838) is to dispose once and for all of the widely held view in historical studies that Kierkegaard, during his years at the university, was at one time himself an Hegelian. But it should now be clear that Kierkegaard was never an Hegelian, never had an Hegelian period *in this sense,* was ever an opponent of the system, although he appears to have understood Hegel in jest better than most who took him seriously. His study of Hegel is therefore an excellent example of what he understood by 'appropriation,' for to make something one's own is never to lose one's intellectual integrity, to master a content never to be mastered by it—and to this extent he may have been the truest 'Hegelian' of them all. *Secondly,* so much of Kierkegaard is problematic that nailing down this veiled element of personal allusion in the essay does help to eliminate some of the obscurity from the text, and if it shows us where not to look for profundity, it may also serve to introduce a little levity into the search. *Thirdly,* this material articulates an interesting literary situation within which Kierkegaard is seen engaging certain of his initially unsuspecting contemporaries in a private 'Socratic' dialogue extending all the way to his final confrontation with Martensen in 1854-55. That Kierkegaard intended to play the part of Socrates in this relationship is apparent from the academic essay, wherein the examined contrived to reverse roles and become himself the examiner. As the documentation of such a dialogue means not only immersing oneself in the Journal but familiarizing oneself with his local intellectual milieu as well, means plumbing the former to anticipate the question and invading the latter to reconstruct the answer, so it may often come to seem that what one is essentially grappling with is Kierkegaard's own formidable and enigmatical personality and nothing more. Aware of the similarity between my predicament and the psychologizing of great men condemned by Hegel as 'Thersitism,' I can only reply that every interpreter of Kierkegaard's Journal, whether he wants to or not, will inevitably come to see himself as playing *valet-de-chambre* to this literary phenomenon. And yet the most persuasive argument that the attempt to document this dimension of personal satire is not wholly idle and without meaning comes, curiously enough, from H. L. Martensen himself. In the above mentioned review of Heiberg's *New Poems* he steadfastly defends the right of the poet to descend to the level of personal satire with the following rebuttal. I trust that Kierkegaard subscribed wholeheartedly to Martensen's statement of the principle.

'There are some readers who will emphasize these local and personal allusions and innuendoes as the essential and substantial element, as if it had been the poet's chief concern. They would gladly pluck out all the satirical barbs as the gayest flowers in the garland, as the real amusement in the whole comedy. If they were to express themselves in German they would say: *das eben ist der Humor davon.* This conception is regrettable because it fails to perceive that the personal element is here merely an accidental and vanishing moment within that irony which has a wholly universal content. There are those, on the other hand, who will feel a moral disapproval at such satiric allusions. This is due to the fact that because of various subordinate concerns they fail to allow irony and the comic caprice their full freedom and abandonment. Nevertheless, it resides in the very nature of the comic to be reckless and wanton, while it pertains even to the Aristophanic wit to be local, not to allow its lightning flashes to play indeterminately through the air but to descend. *Vis eius integra si conversus fuerit in terram* applies even to wit. Accordingly, should one altogether reject every personal allusion, then one must reject the whole of Aristophanic comedy where not even a man such as Socrates can escape being thrown to the wolves.'

Appendix (*page* 345)

1. The Danish editor reports that Kierkegaard had inscribed the following page references opposite eight of his theses in the printed copy of the essay evidently used during the oral defence. I, 52n., 242n., 288; II, 53-64; III, 156-7; IV, 69-78; V, 115-28; VI, 221; VII, 181-2n.; XV, 338-9.

Glossary

In preparing this glossary I have been concerned to furnish the critical reader with enough information to decide for himself how Kierkegaard uses Hegelian terminology in the present work. Unlike English, there is no insurmountable difficulty in reduplicating Hegel's German terminology in Danish. The latter, being poorer in words, is happily or unhappily richer in ambiguity. I have made two translating conventions in the present work, and these I am concerned to account for here. The *first* convention involves certain key philosophic terms where it was felt that the ideal of consistency was both possible and highly desirable. —In the case of dialectical terminology a strict one-to-one correspondence obtains between the Danish and English terms—except one. The latter concerns the Danish verb *hæve*, and involves an incorrigible ambiguity at the heart of the dialectic and imagery of the book. As Hegel often explained, his term *aufheben* was ambiguous and carried the philosophic meanings 'to negate' and 'to preserve.' (The third meaning 'to elevate' often associated with the term is for Hegel not philosophic but imagery.) Similarly, Kierkegaard's word *hæve* (both as a transitive and reflexive verb) is ambiguous and bears the philosophic meanings 'to cancel' (negate) and 'to elevate.' Unfortunately, this ambiguity cannot be reproduced in English, and the reader will have to bear in mind that every instance of 'cancel' and 'elevate' is in the original the ambiguous *hæve*. Fortunately, there is no problem in deciding from the context which it must be in English. The reader can make up his own mind whether Kierkegaard's *ophæve* and *hæve* also carry the philosophic meaning 'to preserve' as does Hegel's *aufheben* and *heben* (ordinarily, the linguistic extension of the four verbs is the same). There is one difference between Kierkegaard's and Hegel's dialectical terminology obvious enough to warrant comment. Kierkegaard exhibits a tendency to refrain from using the readily available cognates for Hegel's terms *versöhnen*, *Versöhnung*, *vermitteln*, *Vermittlung*, and resorts instead to the terms *mediere* and *Mediation*. This, as Thulstrup has pointed out, is a deliberate attempt to restrict the Danish *forsone*, *Forsoning* to their theological associations 'to atone' and 'atonement.' I have also included words like 'suspend' (*suspendere*) and 'preserve' (*bevare*) under this convention for their possible dialectical overtones even though they seldom occur. The reader will also find that in Kierkegaard, as in Hegel, words

like 'destroy,' 'annihilate,' and 'perish' are not free from dialectical association with negation and nothingness, but as they are not exclusively
dialectical, they have not been included. When Kierkegaard reproduces
Hegel's constructions like *Ansichseyn, Fürsichseyn,* and *Anundfürsichseyn,* as
much dialectical as metaphysical terms, I have resorted to hyphenated
nouns in English. As listed in this glossary, the terms covered by the
first convention are indicated by italics.

The *second* convention mainly concerns metaphysical terms. Here the
problem is the unexpected abundance of Kierkegaard's Danish and the
relative flexibility of Hegel's German. I have chosen the most obvious
solution of putting the Danish in brackets. In the case of 'to become,' for
example, there is no satisfactory way of distinguishing in English when
Kierkegaard is using *blive* and when *vorde,* and with the noun it is worse
for now Kierkegaard has four terms: *Bliven, Blivelse, Vorden, Vordelse,*
besides *Blivende* and *Vordende* for 'that which becomes.' In the case of 'to
exist' there are three Danish terms which must be distinguished: (1) the
Latin derivatives *existere* and *Existents;* (2) the indigenous *være til* and
Tilværelse (Hegel's *Daseyn*); and (3) the use of *bestaae, Bestaaen, Bestaaende*
consonant with Hegel's use of *bestehen, Bestehen, Bestehendes.* To minimize
the use of brackets, however, I have begun by correlating 'to exist' with
existere, 'existence' with *Existents,* and 'to become' with *blive.* In every
other instance the specific Danish term accompanies the English in brackets,
and *blive* continues to be given when something appears to be gained by
it. I have also used brackets for a couple of terms, *Mellemværende* and
Mellemhverandre, which appear to have some special significance for Kierkegaard in this work, to indicate an occasional play on words, to render
excessively ambiguous passages, and where it makes for greater clarity.
As listed in this glossary, the terms covered by the second convention
are marked by asterisks.

This glossary also lists a number of sensitive terms, variously translated,
which I was unable to bring under either convention, since this information
might also be of interest. The English, Danish, and German correlations
and translations are listed below.

ENGLISH	DANISH	GERMAN
abrogate	*ophæve*	aufheben
abrogation	*Ophævelse*	Aufhebung
actual	virkelig	wirklich
actuality	Virkelighed	Wirklichkeit
affirmation	*Affirmation*	Affirmation

ENGLISH	DANISH	GERMAN
anxiety	Angest	Angst
appearance	Tilsyneladelse, Fremtræden	Schein, Auftreten
apprehend, conceive	opfatte	auffassen
appropriate (to)	tilegne sig	zueignen (sich)
arbitrary, wilful	vilkaarlig	willkürlich
*be	*være	sein
*being	*Væren	Sein
*being (determinate), −entity	*Værende	Seiendes
being-for-itself	Forsigværen	Fürsichsein
being-in-itself	Isigværen	Ansichsein
being-in-and-for-itself	Iogforsigværen	Anundfürsichsein
*become	blive, *vorde	werden
*becoming	*Bliven, *Blivelse, *Vorden, *Vordelse	Werden
cancel	hæve (sig)	aufheben, (sich) heben,
*come into existence	*blive til	—
*coming into −existence	*Tilblivelse	—
*conceive	*begribe	begreifen
concept	Begreb	Begriff
conception	Opfattelse	Auffassung
contradict	modsige	widersprechen
contradiction	Modsigelse	Widerspruch
culminate	afrunde sig	abrunden (sich)
determination, −vocation	Bestemmelse	Bestimmung
despair	Fortvivlesle	Verzweifelung
doubt	Tvivle	Zweifel
elevate	hæve (sig)	aufheben, erheben (sich) heben
*endure, *subsist, *exist	*bestaae	bestehen
essence	Væsen	Wesen
ethical	sædlig, ethiske	sittlich, ethische
*exist	existere, *være til	existieren, ist da
*existence	Existents, *Tilværelse	Existenz, Dasein
*existent, *established	*Bestaaen, *Bestaaende	Bestehen, bestehendes
hold fast, maintain	fastholde	festhalten
hover	svæve	schweben
Idea	Idee	Idee

ENGLISH	DANISH	GERMAN
idea, representation	Forestilling	Vorstellung
illustration	Anskueliggjørelse	Veranschaulichung
illustrate	anskueliggjøre	veranschaulichen
image	Billede	Bild, Bildliche
imagination	Phantasie, indbildningskraft	Einbildungskraft, Phantasie
in-and-for-itself	*iogforsig*	anundfürsich
intuition	Intuition	Intuition, Anschauung
light-minded	letsindig	leichtsinnig
mastered	behersket	beherrscht
maintain, hold fast	fastholde	festhalten
mediate	*mediere*	versöhnen, vermitteln
mediation	*Mediation*	Versöhnung, Vermittlung
melancholy	tungsindig	schwermutig
mind, spirit	Aand, Sind	Geist, Gesinnung
moral	moralsk	moralich, sittlich
morality	Moralitet	Moralität
negate	*negere*	negieren
negation	*Negation*	Negation
negative (the)	*Negative*	Negatives
negative	*negativ*	negativ
negativity	*Negativitet*	Negativität
nothing, nothingness	*Intet*	Nichts
oppose	*modsætte*	gegensetzen, etc.
opposite	*Modsatte*	Gegensatz, etc.
opposition	*Modsætning*	Gegensatz, etc.
opposition (relation of)	*Modsætningsforhold*	Verhältnis
'other' (an, the)	*Andet* (et, det)	Anderes
pass over into	*slaae over i*	umschlagen
phenomenon	Phenomen	Erscheinung
preserve	*bevare*	aufheben, bewahren
reality	Realitet	Realität
reason	Fornuft	Vernunft
recollection	Erindring	Erinnerung
representation, idea	Forestilling	Vorstellung
science, philosophy	Videnskab	Wissenschaft
scientific, systematic –scholarly	videnskabelig	wissenschaftlich
spirit, mind	Aand	Geist
suspend	*suspendere*	suspendieren
synthesis	*Synthese*	Einheit

433

GLOSSARY

ENGLISH	DANISH	GERMAN
third (the)	*Tredie*	Dritte
understanding	Forstand	Verstand
unity (*higher*)	*Eenhed*	Einheit
view	Anskuelse	Anschauung

Index

435

INDEX OF PLATONIC REFERENCES

INDEX OF XENOPHONTIC REFERENCES